SECOND EDITION

AT-RISK YOUTH:
A COMPREHENSIVE RESPONSE

FOR COUNSELORS, TEACHERS, PSYCHOLOGISTS, AND HUMAN SERVICE PROFESSIONALS

J. Jeffries McWhirter
Arizona State University

Benedict T. McWhirter
University of Oregon

Anna M. McWhirter
Arizona State University

Ellen Hawley McWhirter
University of Oregon

Brooks/Cole Publishing Company

I(T)P® An International Thomson Publishing Company

Pacific Grove • Albany, NY • Belmont, CA • Bonn • Boston • Cincinnati • Detroit • Johannesburg • London
Madrid • Melbourne • Mexico City • New York • Paris • Singapore • Tokyo • Toronto • Washington

Sponsoring Editor: *Eileen Murphy*
Marketing Team: *Jean Thompson,*
  Margaret Parks
Marketing Representative: *Holly Allen*
Editorial Assistant: *Susan Carlson*
Production Editor: *Kirk Bomont*
Manuscript Editor: *Kay Mikel*

Interior Design: *John Edeen*
Cover Photo: *Scott Barrow*
Art Editor and Interior Illustration: *Lisa Torri*
Digital Manipulation: *Robert J. Western*
Cover Design: *Laurie Albrecht*
Typesetting: *Carlisle Communications, Ltd.*
Printing and Binding: *Malloy Lithographing, Inc.*

COPYRIGHT © 1998 by Brooks/Cole Publishing Company
A division of International Thomson Publishing Inc.
I(T)P The ITP logo is a registered trademark under license.

For more information, contact:

BROOKS/COLE PUBLISHING COMPANY
511 Forest Lodge Road
Pacific Grove, CA 93950
USA

International Thomson Editores
Seneca 53
Col. Polanco
11560 México, D. F., México

International Thomson Publishing Europe
Berkshire House 168-173
High Holborn
London WC1V 7AA
England

International Thomson Publishing GmbH
Königswinterer Strasse 418
53227 Bonn
Germany

Thomas Nelson Australia
102 Dodds Street
South Melbourne, 3205
Victoria, Australia

International Thomson Publishing Asia
221 Henderson Road
#05-10 Henderson Building
Singapore 0315

Nelson Canada
1120 Birchmount Road
Scarborough, Ontario
Canada M1K 5G4

International Thomson Publishing Japan
Hirakawacho Kyowa Building, 3F
2-2-1 Hirakawacho
Chiyoda-ku, Tokyo 102
Japan

Printed in the United States of America

10 9 8 7 6 5 4 3 2 1

Library of Congress Cataloging-in-Publication Data
At-risk youth : a comprehensive response : for counselors, teachers,
   psychologists, and human service professionals / J. Jeffries
   McWhirter . . . [et al.].—2nd ed.
      p. cm.
   Includes bibliographical references and index (p.   ).
   ISBN 0-534-34580-8
      1. Socially handicapped youth—United States.   2. Socially
handicapped youth—Counseling of—United States.   I. McWhirter, J.
Jeffries.
HV1421.A8   1998
362.74'0973—dc21   97-21569
                                                              CIP

While we were writing this book and revising this second edition, the McWhirter clan increased by seven: Mary Veronica McWhirter Pitner, Anna Cecilia McWhirter, Paul John McWhirter Pitner, Mark Thomas McWhirter Pitner, Luke Robert McWhirter Pitner, Monica Clare McWhirter Pitner, and Marielena Rose McWhirter were born.

This book is dedicated to Mary Veronica, Anna Cecilia, Paul John, Mark Thomas, Luke Robert, Monica Clare, and Marielena Rose, and their future siblings and cousins. May we find ways to prevent them and all children from being at risk. May we find ways to help them and all children grow and develop into healthy, happy adults with people to love and important work to do. Albert Camus wrote, "Without work, all life goes rotten, but when work is soulless, life stifles and dies." And without people to love, nothing much matters anyway.

Contents

CHAPTER **3**

FAMILY PROBLEMS OF AT-RISK CHILDREN AND YOUTH   38

CHAPTER **4**

**SCHOOL ISSUES THAT RELATE TO
AT-RISK CHILDREN AND YOUTH**   60

CHAPTER 5

INDIVIDUAL CHARACTERISTICS OF HIGH-RISK
AND LOW-RISK CHILDREN AND YOUTH   78

PART 2

AT-RISK CATEGORIES   93

CHAPTER 6

SCHOOL DROPOUTS   95

C H A P T E R 7

C H A P T E R 8

CHAPTER **9**

CHAPTER **10**

PART **3**

CHAPTER **11**

CHAPTER **12**

CHAPTER **13**

CHAPTER **14**

CHAPTER **15**

CHAPTER **16**

PREFACE

Since 1983, when the National Commission on Excellence in Education issued its report *A Nation at Risk*, educators and counselors have used the term *at risk* to identify specific social-psychological problems. George Bush in his War on Drugs, local school districts in discussion of youth suicide and school dropouts, the correctional system in addressing concerns about juvenile delinquency, and the health system in expressing dismay about teen pregnancy, child abuse, and AIDS all use the term *at risk*. It is a useful rubric to denote the many young people whose potential for becoming responsible and productive adults is limited by problems at home, in school, or in their communities.

The goals of this second edition remain the same as the first edition. First, we provide up-to-date information and research on at-risk categories. All chapters have been completely revised to reflect the most current information and statistics. Second, we embed the at-risk categories in a unified and consistent conceptual framework. Finally, we present educational, psychological, and counseling interventions for prevention and treatment. For this edition, we have expanded this to reflect new trends and approaches, and we have been particularly diligent in adding strategies for elementary age and younger children.

We focus on various aspects of at-risk behavior for a broad population of helping professionals, but especially for counselors, psychologists and teachers. We direct our work primarily to students and professionals in school and agency counseling, regular and special education, applied psychology, and other human service disciplines at both the pre- and in-service levels. Teachers-in-training and other undergraduate students in psychology, social work, and human service fields may also profit from this text. Many of the intervention and prevention methods, for example, can be used by classroom teachers—some directly and some with modification.

This book is intended as a textbook for counseling courses in education, psychology, social work, special education, and other areas of human services. It is appropriate for developmental counseling courses, such as principles of counseling, school guidance, and counseling program development and management. This book particularly applies to courses related to counseling of students with special needs, maladjusted children, and, of course, at-risk children and adolescents. Both school and agency counselors should find this book useful.

This volume is also planned as a textbook for teacher education courses. Students in courses such as problems in education, strategies in teaching, and the teacher as counselor can profit from the material we have included here. Because of their extensive contact with at-risk students, special education teachers, in particular, should find this work useful.

Educators can use the entire text in the standard semester (or quarter) university course, or they can use parts of it as the basis for modular units elected by social science and human service students and teachers-in-training. One of our own universities, for example, is currently offering several modules on a variety of topics within an upper-division educational psychology course taught by graduate assistants. Eight such modules can be based on this text. In this second edition, we have supplemented many of the chapters with prevention and treatment interventions: refusal and resistance training; an Adlerian/Dreikurs model; William Glasser's reality therapy; crisis intervention; a parent training model; and peer influencing programs (cooperative learning, peer support networks, cross-age peer tutoring, and conflict resolution and peer mediation strategies).

Based on feedback from instructors and students, we have added several features to this edition that we hope will be useful. At the end of each chapter, we have included suggestions for further reading to supplement the information in the text. For this edition, we have added two new appendixes. Appendix A provides an extensive list with addresses and phone numbers of national organizations, agencies, and clearinghouses that provide information, technical assistance, and other resources on the problems that face high-risk children, adolescents, and families. Appendix B is a compilation of practical, concrete resources that counselors, teachers, psychologists, and other human service workers can use with the populations of interest.

Students in other areas of mental health and human services will find this book useful. Courses in child and youth care, case management, and the behavioral and emotional problems of children and adolescents in such disciplines as social work, justice studies, nursing, and community psychology can all profit from the information we present here. Finally, practitioners—counselors, teachers, social workers, health educators, nurses, caseworkers, physicians, psychologists, and program administrators—will find the information on prevention and treatment interventions especially useful in their work.

The book is divided into three major sections. In Part 1 we provide important information on the factors that contribute to school dropout, substance use, teen pregnancy, delinquency and violence, and youth suicide. We discuss environmental and societal, family, school, and individual characteristics that increase the risk that these problems will develop. Part 2 presents data about the five at-risk categories introduced in Part 1. We also discuss treatment and some prevention approaches for children and adolescents in each problem area. Part 3 incorporates more prevention strategies that focus on the family, the school, and the individual. We also examine legal concerns important to human service professionals.

Throughout the book we have used case studies to highlight, apply, and personalize the information in the text. In the first four chapters we introduce the Andrews family, the Baker family, the Carter family, and the Diaz family. These families represent various ethnic groups with diverse socioeconomic statuses, educational levels, and individual attitudes and behaviors. Each of the children in these families presents some risk of problem behavior. The background and circumstances of each family are described, and each family highlights and illustrates environmental, family, and school concerns and problems. The children introduced in these case studies reappear throughout the book to illustrate specific issues. Throughout the book, readers will also find vignettes that help to personalize and exemplify the issues being discussed.

If we do not confront the problems facing our young people, our society will lose nearly a quarter of its youth to at-risk categories—young people who might otherwise become productive, successful, and happy adults. We hope that this text serves to increase awareness of the problems and contributes to their solution.

About the Authors

This book is the latest of many McWhirter family projects that always seem to begin quite innocuously around the kitchen table but often take us far from home as they unfold. Such kitchen conversations led us to spend an intensive and exhilarating year in Turkey and another in Australia, both years as a Fulbright family. In Australia we developed a traveling road show with puppets and poems, music, and skits on learning disabilities and family enrichment. This book has not taken us nearly so far geographically, but it has been a richly rewarding process for each of us.

Any book with four same-name authors is bound to arouse curiosity, so perhaps we'd better explain who we are. Jeff is the father of Ben and Anna, and Ellen and Ben are married.

J. Jeffries McWhirter holds a diploma in counseling psychology from the American Board of Professional Psychology (ABPP) and is a fellow of the American Psychological Association (Division 17, 48, and 49), the American Psychological Society, the Academy of Counseling Psychology, and the Association for Specialists in Group Work. He is a professor in the Division of Psychology in Education, Arizona State University. A former teacher and school counselor, he has maintained a small private practice for nearly 30 years and consults regularly with schools and agencies that deal with at-risk individuals. He has published more than 100 chapters and articles in refereed journals, 12 training manuals, and 6 books or monographs. He has been a Fulbright-Hays Senior Scholar in Turkey (1977–78), a Fulbright Senior Scholar in Australia (1984–85), and has taught summer sessions or short courses at 20 other universities in the United States and internationally. In 1989 he received the Arizona State University Distinguished Teacher Award. He is the principal investigator of several externally funded projects including a large Safe and Drug Free School and Community grant and a violence reduction grant for an alternative high school. His other areas of interest include group counseling, family counseling, learning disabilities, international aspects of counseling psychology, and grandchildren—not necessarily in the order listed.

Benedict T. McWhirter received his Ph.D. in counseling psychology from Arizona State University. He is an assistant professor of counseling psychology at the University of Oregon. From 1993 to 1997 he was an assistant professor in the Counseling Psychology Program at the University of Nebraska–Lincoln. He is a licensed psychologist. He has taught seventh and eighth grades in Peru and academic survival skills and educational psychology courses at ASU. He has also counseled students with disabilities through the Arizona State University Disability Resources program. His current teaching focuses on counseling practica, supervision, counseling skills, and techniques of school counseling and guidance. He has published more than 30 articles and book chapters and has presented more than 40 papers at professional conferences in the areas of loneliness, depression, at-risk youth, and counseling intervention approaches. He has directed a collaborative teaching, research, and consultation project at an innovative alternative high school in Lincoln, Nebraska, in which he has implemented cognitive-behavioral group approaches for youth at risk. He is continuing this integrative and collaborative work at the University of Oregon.

Anna M. McWhirter is a Ph.D. candidate in the Reading Program in the Division of Curriculum and Instruction, College of Education, Arizona State University. She has had early teaching experiences in Peru and in Australia, has taught in elementary and middle schools in the United States, and currently is teaching a university survival skills course at ASU. She has published a number of book chapters and articles and presented papers on learning disabilities, reading strategies, and teaching techniques at professional conventions. She and her husband, John Pitner, a school music teacher, are co-directors of music at St. Benedict Parish in Chandler, Arizona.

Ellen Hawley McWhirter has a Ph.D. in counseling psychology from Arizona State University. As a graduate student, she was awarded a fellowship to complete her dissertation study by the American Association of University Women. She is currently an assistant professor of counseling psychology at the University of Oregon. From 1993 to 1997 she was an assistant professor at the University of Nebraska–Lincoln and is a licensed psychologist. Her teaching experience includes the Head Start program and university academic survival skills, and she has taught and counseled Spanish-speaking children and parents. She has published more than 20 articles, chapters, and poems and has presented more than 30 papers at national conventions on minority issues, career counseling, empowerment, and socioeconomic factors related to mental health. Her dissertation study tested a model of the career development of Mexican American teenage girls. She is the author of the book *Counseling for Empowerment*, published by ACA Press. She has been involved in evaluating school-based career exploration courses that include a school-to-work component.

Another son/sibling, Robert J. McWhirter, contributed Chapter 16, on legal issues related to at-risk populations. He is a practicing attorney with the Federal Public Defender's Office in Phoenix, Arizona. A faculty member for the Advanced Seminar for Criminal Justice, he lectures throughout the United States on immigration law and on litigation procedures. He has published several important articles in the *Georgetown Immigration Law Review* and *Criminal Law Practice Reports*. In addition to his legal writing, he has published articles and book chapters on learning disabilities and legal· issues of concern to mental health practitioners.

Acknowledgments

We five are the most visible in this family project, but other members of the clan contributed in many ways. Mark McWhirter and Paula McWhirter helped with library research, photocopying, typing, proofreading, editing, and many other tasks. Mark wrote one of the poems that introduce the chapters and was consistently interested in and supportive of this entire project. Paula, while a Fulbright Scholar in Chile working on her dissertation on adolescent substance abuse, and later while completing an internship at the Counseling Center at the University of Notre Dame, was a source of great ideas. Mary McWhirter (Jeff's wife and mother to us all) kept us working as a team, especially at particularly stressful and busy times. Both Mary and John Pitner were very helpful in numerous ways, especially in keeping us sane (mostly) and in taking care of seven beautiful babies. Each of the babies arrived during a different stage of this project. How can one adequately express gratitude for life itself?

We are also grateful to our colleagues at Arizona State University and at the University of Nebraska–Lincoln. Personnel at the university libraries were especially helpful. Sherrie Schmidt, Dean of ASU University Libraries, is to be commended for maintaining a professional, efficient, consistently friendly and helpful library staff. James O'Hanlon, Dean of the Teachers College at the University of Nebraska–Lincoln, was especially supportive.

Ruth Knibbs in the Division of Psychology in Education at ASU helped with typing chores. Our friend Reba Wilson pulled us out of a tight spot in the final stages of both the first and second editions and graciously volunteered much of her own time to help type and format the manuscript. Several students were also helpful. We are grateful to Carlos Alatorre for his help with the graphs and figures. Pam Lane and D. Scott Herrmann in particular helped with suggestions and library research, as did Junko Kozu, Michael Gottfried, and Jennifer Strang from ASU's Counseling Psychology program and Yassi (Phoebe) Kuo-Jackson and Benjamin Kuo from UNL's Counseling Psychology program. Jennifer Strang was particularly helpful in organizing, formating, and typing this second edition. Our thanks to all of you.

We appreciate the useful suggestions and comments offered by all those persons who reviewed the book in the first place: Mary Deck of Western Carolina University, Robert J. Drummond of the University of North Florida, Larry Golden of the University of Texas at San Antonio, Jack Sutton of the University of Southern Maine, and to the reviewers for the second edition: Marjorie A. Rust, University of Phoenix; and Adelaida Santana, Northern Arizona University. In addition, a number of colleagues who have adopted this book for classes have been generous in both their praise and their constructive feedback. They are Judy Daniels and Michael D'Andrea, University of Hawaii at Manoa; William E. Miller, University of Maine–Orono; Gary Ross-Reynolds, Nicholls State University; John Romano, University of Minnesota; Joanne Curran, Oneonta State University (SUNY); and Adelaida Santana, Southern Oregon State College and Northern Arizona University. To them all: Thank you again. You have helped to make a good book better. The Brooks/Cole staff, as usual, has been very helpful throughout this process. We are especially pleased to work with our new editor, Eileen Murphy.

J. Jeffries McWhirter
Benedict T. McWhirter
Anna M. McWhirter
Ellen Hawley McWhirter

At-Risk Children and Youth: The Ecology of Problems

■ Part 1 consists of five chapters. In Chapter 1 we discuss the term *at risk* and provide an overview of the book and a metaphor for unifying various aspects of at-risk concerns. The next four chapters provide an overview of the problems related to at-risk children and adolescents. We discuss environmental and societal issues; family, community, and school concerns; and high-risk/low-risk behaviors, attitudes, and skills that youngsters adopt. We also present four case studies that will be used throughout the book to illustrate specific problems and issues.

An Introduction to At-Risk Issues: The Tree

No matter what the environmentalists say, trees are a source of deadly pollution.

Ronald Reagan, 1980

Rather than the hasty tinkering of the mechanic, nurturing life requires the patience of the gardener. The fast technological rush of society leads us to be mechanics. We must preserve the long patience of the gardener.

J. J. McWhirter

Chapter Outline

Our society depends on our ability to prepare well-adjusted, responsible, well-educated young people to step forward as the older generation passes. Our nation's continuing strength and stability depend on our ability to ensure that our youth are prepared to fill the courtrooms and boardrooms, the classrooms and operating rooms, the high-tech factories and industries of tomorrow. If youngsters are to be prepared to meet the demands of the future, schools, families, and communities must be involved in the project.

Schools must deliver appropriate and well-designed curricula in an environment that maximizes learning. Families must provide sustenance, nurturance, support, and intimacy. Young people need positive relationships and role models to develop responsible attitudes and mutual interdependence. And finally, communities must confront the social problems that restrict our youth by creating political support groups, providing child care, education programs, and alternative work opportunities, and encouraging young people to work for the welfare of others.

In this chapter we highlight the problems that threaten children and youth and consequently our society. We present statistics that illuminate the severity and even epidemic proportions of some of these problems. We then personalize these statistics by describing one family. Next, we provide an overview of the entire at-risk arena, using the metaphor of a tree as an organizational and pedagogical device. This metaphor illustrates and encourages an examination of our society from an ecological perspective, which can broaden our notion of effective intervention.

The Scope of the Problems

Unfortunately, too many of our young people are not doing well. In fact, so many are falling by the wayside—so many are at risk—that our society itself is at risk. The scope of the problems is enormous. The statistics we list here (see Annie E. Casey Foundation,

1994, 1995; Carnegie Corporation of New York, 1994, 1995; Children's Defense Fund, [CDF], 1994, 1995; Donmoyer & Kos, 1993; Dryfoos, 1990; Mishel & Bernstein, 1995) will be discussed in detail in later chapters. For now, they provide a concrete reminder of the myriad problems that confront young people, their families, and their schools. Teachers, counselors, social workers, psychologists, and other human service workers who deal with young people and their families know these problems and their pervasiveness. They reflect a society at risk.

Facts of an At-Risk Society

- By 1993, 15.7 million children lived in poverty, 6 million more than in 1973. One in four children under age 6 now lives below the poverty line.
- Minority children are disproportionately poor. In 1993, 33% of Asian American youth, 41% of all Hispanic children, and more than 46% of all African American children lived in poverty, compared to 14% of European American children.
- Of the 3 million reported cases of child abuse or neglect in 1993, more than 1 million were confirmed by authorities. On average, three children die from maltreatment each day.
- The divorce rate has quadrupled in the past 20 years, and 24% of American children are now being raised in mother-only families. Fifty-four percent of children living only with their mothers were poor, compared to 12% for children living with both parents.
- Eleven percent of U.S. young people drop out of high school before graduation. In many urban areas the dropout rate is considerably higher. Students with low-income, low-skill, low-education family backgrounds are about twice as likely to drop out of school as are students from affluent families.
- Minority students are especially vulnerable to dropping out of school with 14% of African American and 28% of Hispanic youths withdrawing without a diploma. Dropout rates for Native Americans are considerably higher.
- The U.S. Public Health Service reports that about two-thirds of all high school seniors have used illegal drugs; 90% of high school seniors have used alcohol.
- Seventy-seven percent of eighth graders report having used alcohol, and 13.5% of eighth graders and 27% of seniors had five or more drinks at least once within the previous two weeks.
- More adolescents are experimenting with drugs at younger ages, especially before age 15.
- Increasing numbers of children under age 15 are becoming sexually active. About 30% of young adolescents report having had sexual intercourse by age 15. Fully one-fourth of all adolescents will be infected with a sexually transmitted disease before they graduate from high school.
- Only 60% of young teenagers use contraceptives at first intercourse, and they are slow to practice contraception thereafter. Teenage girls typically will not use contraceptives until six to nine months after they have become sexually active, and by that time approximately half of them are already pregnant.
- Between 1940 and 1991, the percentage of births to adolescent girls rose from 14% to 69%. In 1992 the teen birth rate dropped 2.3% from the 1991 level and has held constant ever since. Unfortunately, the proportion of births to unmarried teens has reached the highest levels ever recorded.

- Unmarried 13- to 19-year-olds who give birth have few social resources, lower educational attainment, reduced potential earnings, and limited or nonexistent support by the baby's father. The children they bear tend to be underweight and less healthy than average as teen mothers are much less likely than older mothers to receive prenatal care.
- Children who have such a poor start in life tend to perform poorly in school. Each year spent in poverty reduces by 2 percentage points a child's chances of graduating from high school.
- The National Institute of Education concluded that nearly 3 million students and teachers are crime victims in U.S. secondary schools every month. Additionally, crimes involving handguns committed by urban high school students increased significantly in the 1980s and early 1990s.
- The National School Boards Association found that of 720 school districts surveyed in 1993, 82% reported an increase in school violence in the past five years.
- Youth violent death rates increased 6% between 1985 and 1992. In 1992 nearly 12,000 teens died a violent death.
- For African American teenagers, murder is the major cause of death.
- The U.S. Senate Committee on Delinquency estimated that school vandalism costs our nation more than $600 million each year.
- In the last decade and a half, the rate of completed suicide among children 10 to 14 years of age increased by 75%, and increased 34.5% among 15- to 19-year-olds. Each year 7,000 teenagers commit suicide. Suicide is the second leading cause of death for those 10 to 24 years of age.

This gloomy catalog of the problems facing American children and adolescents shows only moderate signs of improvement (Gardner, Green, & Marcus, 1994; Holmes, 1995) and includes millions of personal stories, some of which are reported under headlines that scream of abandoned infants, battered and sexually abused children, suicides, and drug overdoses. The catalog also continues to reflect millions of less newsworthy stories. Those of troubled, depressed, and anxious young people; children who suffer at home and at school; young people afraid, bored, or angry; youngsters bewildered by family conflict, divorce, or absentee parents; and young people afraid of violence while at play and at school.

Defining the Term *At Risk*

During the past decade the term *at risk* has appeared frequently in literature on education, psychology, medicine, social work, and economics as well as in the legislation of various states and in federal government reports. Its origins are obscure, and its use in various contexts indicates a lack of consensus regarding its meaning. Psychologists, social workers, and counselors use the term to denote individuals who suffer emotional and adjustment problems. Educators use it sometimes to refer to young people who are at risk of dropping out of the educational system, sometimes to denote youngsters who are not learning the skills necessary to succeed after graduation, and sometimes to indicate children whose current educational mastery makes their future school career problematic. Medical workers use the term to refer to individuals with health problems. Economists and the business community use it to refer to workers who do not have the requisite literacy and numeracy skills to obtain employment or to succeed at their jobs.

We use *at risk* to denote a set of presumed cause-and-effect dynamics that place the child or adolescent in danger of negative *future events*. Youngsters who use tobacco, for example, are at risk for alcohol use. Young people who use alcohol are at risk for illicit drug use. Children and adolescents who use illicit drugs are at risk for drug abuse. Thus, a specific behavior, attitude, or deficiency provides an initial marker of later problem behavior. Conduct disorders, aggression, and low achievement in elementary school become markers that predict later delinquent and antisocial behavior in adolescence. To us, then, *at risk* designates a situation that is not necessarily current (although we sometimes use the term in that sense too) but that can be anticipated in the absence of intervention.

Perhaps even more important, at-riskness must be viewed not as a discrete, unitary diagnostic category but as a series of steps along a continuum. Figure 1.1 illustrates this continuum from minimal and remote risk to personal behavior that anticipates imminent risk and finally to the activities associated with an at-risk category.

Minimal risk. Young people whose families are of high socioeconomic status, who are subjected to few psychosocial stressors, attend good schools, and have loving, caring relationships with their families and friends are assumed to be at minimal risk for future trouble. We cannot speak of "no risk," because no one altogether escapes problems. Young people in all circumstances must cope with death, divorce, incapacity, or bankruptcy in their families. Increasing numbers of families are losing their homes. Such stressors can appear at any time. Depending on the young person's age, developmental level, and personal characteristics, the environmental resources available, and a host of other factors, the consequences may or may not be negative in the long term. Further, neither favorable demographics nor "good" families and schools provide invulnerability (Mitchell, 1996). Like anyone else, affluent adolescents may reject positive adult values and norms. Neither money, social status, popularity, nor the "good life" guarantees meaning and purpose in life. Finally, sometimes "perfect" families harbor secrets—alcoholism, incest, depression—that stem from and perpetuate dysfunction.

Remote risk. The point on the continuum at which risk, though still remote, seems increasingly possible is reached when demographic, family, school, and social markers of future problems appear. The demographic characteristics of low socioeconomic status and membership in a minority ethnic group are associated with greater dropout rates, drug use, teen pregnancy, and the rest. Risk factors do not emerge *due* to ethnic minority status. But members of ethnic minority groups often experience oppression, economic marginalization, and racism, which can have a negative influence on children and adolescents. Negative family, school, and social interactions and increased psychosocial stressors (such as divorce or death in the immediate family or loss of family income) are also markers of potential problems. Of course, most poor African American, Hispanic, and Native American young people do survive such difficulties to function well. Although these background factors are important, they are only partially predictive of at-riskness for an individual child.

One other factor is important here: The combinations add up. A young person from an impoverished, dysfunctional, ethnic minority family who attends a poor school in a marginalized neighborhood is potentially farther along the at-risk continuum, especially if there are major psychosocial stressors in his or her life.

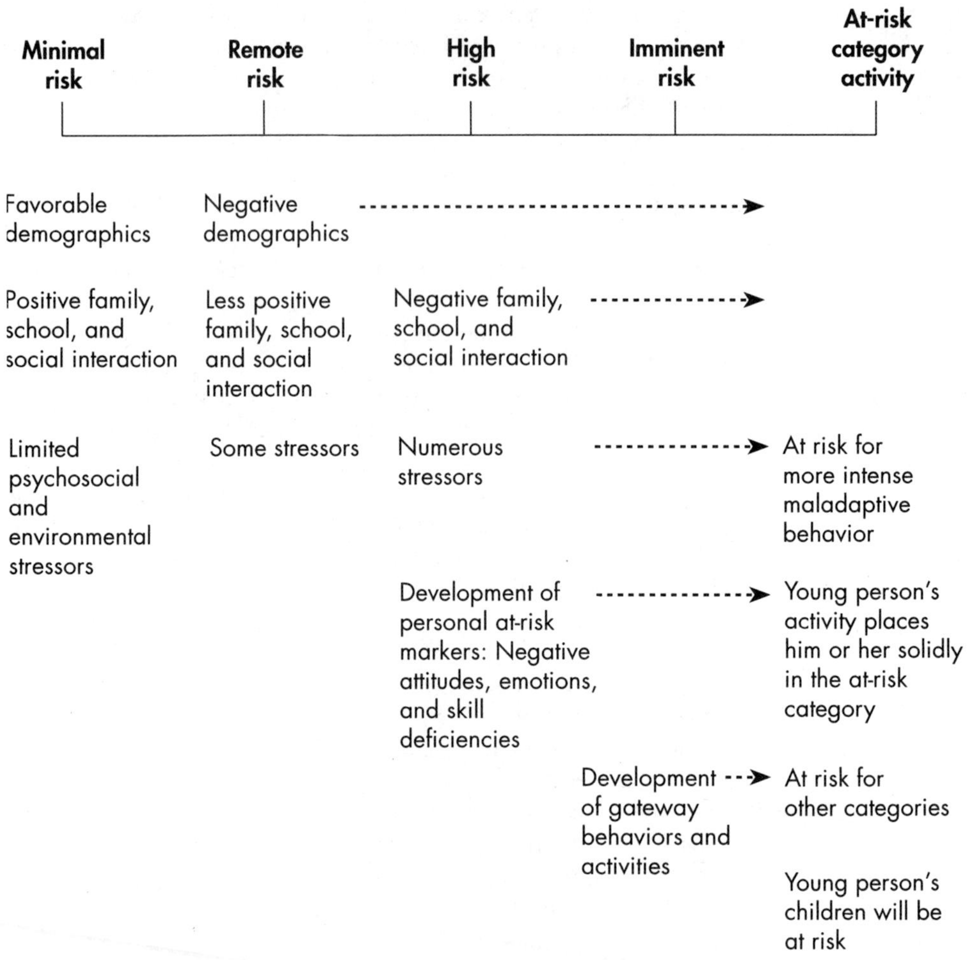

Minimal risk	Remote risk	High risk	Imminent risk	At-risk category activity

Favorable demographics | Negative demographics --------------------------------➤

Positive family, school, and social interaction | Less positive family, school, and social interaction | Negative family, school, and social interaction | --------------➤

Limited psychosocial and environmental stressors | Some stressors | Numerous stressors | --------------➤ | At risk for more intense maladaptive behavior

Development of personal at-risk markers: Negative attitudes, emotions, and skill deficiencies | --------------➤ | Young person's activity places him or her solidly in the at-risk category

Development of gateway behaviors and activities | --➤ | At risk for other categories

Young person's children will be at risk

FIGURE 1.1 The at-risk continuum

High-risk characteristics. Dysfunctional families, poor schools, negative social inter-actions, and numerous psychosocial stressors may nudge a young person toward at-riskness, but the final push is supplied by the person's own negative attitudes, emotions, and behaviors. High-risk characteristics include depression, anxiety, aggres-sion, and hopelessness, as well as deficits in social skills and coping behaviors. These characteristics are personal markers that often signal the internalization of problems and set the stage for participation in gateway behaviors, which are mildly or moderately distressing activities, frequently self-destructive, that can progress to increasingly deviant behaviors.

Imminent risk. Individual high-risk characteristics often find expression in gateway behaviors. A child's aggression toward other children and adults, for example, is a gateway to juvenile delinquency. Cigarettes may be a gateway to alcohol, which can be a gateway to marijuana, which can be a gateway to harder drugs. Although progression through each gate is neither certain nor predictable, evidence linking gateway behaviors with more serious activities is so strong that such behaviors must be recognized as placing young people at imminent risk.

At-risk category activity.   The final step in the continuum is reached when the young person participates in those activities that define the at-risk categories. Here we confront the conceptual problem with the term *at risk*. Although the literature in this area continues to refer to youngsters at this level as "at risk," these young people have passed beyond risk because they already exhibit maladaptive behavior. They have the problems that define the category.

The counterargument is, of course, that activity in an at-risk category can escalate. The young person who abuses drugs can become a drug addict. The delinquent can go on to commit violent crimes. Category activity by the adolescent can lead to lifelong involvement by the adult. In addition, individuals who participate in one category activity continue to be at risk for the other categories. The teen who drops out of school, for example, is at risk for drug abuse and delinquency and so forth. Consequently, we will apply the term *at risk* to behaviors and characteristics along the entire continuum, using the appropriate points along the way to anchor our discussion.

Blame Poverty and Racism, Not the Victim

The use of the term *at risk* has generated criticism and debate (Swadener & Lubeck, 1995; Tidwell & Corona Garrett, 1994). Viewing "at-riskness" as a continuum that denotes future possibilities resolves some of the objections to the term (B. T. McWhirter & J. J. McWhirter, 1995; J. J. McWhirter, B. T. McWhirter, A. M. McWhirter, & E. H. McWhirter, 1994, 1995).

Swadener and Lubeck (1995) argue that an emerging ideology of risk emphasizes a deficit model that locates problems and pathology in the victim. The electronic and print media, people in casual conversations, and even professional educators, counselors, and other caregivers often suggest that the problem is inherent in individual children, adolescents, and families. As will become abundantly clear (see especially Chapter 2), we place the blame for 14 million children living in poverty firmly in the public domain. Adequate parental leaves, affordable child care, more accessible housing, increased employment opportunities, full funding of Women, Infants, and Children (WIC) and Head Start initiatives, and accessible health care will go a long way toward eliminating at-risk problems in youth. Equally problematic is the fact that children labeled "at risk" are frequently children of color from low socioeconomic situations. Rearing children and adolescents in the context of economic disparities, political powerlessness, and a cultural and social milieu steeped in racism provides the soil for at-risk problems.

Behind each of the statistics we have cited are flesh-and-blood children, adolescents, and families. The case studies we provide are composites of individual children, adolescents, and families we know. We will return to these cases in later chapters to give life to the faceless statistics. In addition, the cases help clarify the effectiveness and applicability of educational, psychological, and counseling strategies. In the first case study we will introduce you to the Andrews family.

CASE STUDY

The Andrews family

The Andrews family consists of Burt, Alice, and two children from Mrs. Andrews's previous marriage. Mr. and Mrs. Andrews have been married for eight years, and this marriage is the second for both. They live in a modest and somewhat shabby house in a working-class neighborhood of a major city. They are European American.

Burt Andrews is a 46-year-old semiskilled laborer who was once employed as a technician in an electronics plant. About five years ago the plant was computerized, and the new technology reduced the labor force by 40%. Burt lost his job and now works occasionally pumping gas at a local service station. The family income, which was never very high, has fallen drastically. Burt is an angry, hostile man with limited insight and a blustering, aggressive style in his interactions with his family.

Burt was an only child. He alludes to a stormy relationship with his own father, who apparently was quite strict and harsh. Burt is especially critical of his mother, with whom he had a very poor relationship. When he was 13, his mother had a "nervous breakdown," and he lived with his aunt for about a year because "my mother didn't want me." He graduated from high school and served approximately 10 years in the army. He married during this time but divorced a few months later. He maintains no contact with his first wife. He met Alice about nine years ago, and after a brief courtship they married.

Alice is the third of four children. She lived with her parents until she was 6, when they divorced. Her mother could not support the children, so Alice spent the next two years with her grandparents. She then moved in with her father and his new wife. Alice dropped out of school after the ninth grade and never finished high school.

Alice went to work in a factory and married John Meadows at age 18. This marriage was difficult and stormy, beginning with Alice's almost immediate pregnancy with Allie. John had dropped out of school, was a heavy drinker as a young man, and continued to indulge in periodic drinking binges. The drinking escalated after Paul was born. John physically abused the children and Alice. When Alice discovered that he was also sexually abusing Allie, the tensions in the family reached the breaking point, and she divorced him. John was convicted of sexual abuse and served a prison sentence. Alice has had no contact with him since the trial, and neither have the children.

(continued)

The Andrews family *(continued)*

After divorcing John, Alice worked as a waitress in a coffee shop until she married Burt. She is now 34 years old and a homemaker. Alice appears to be shy, retiring, and somewhat depressed. She seems to be worried about the family interactions and often attempts to mediate family disputes and conflicts.

Mr. and Mrs. Andrews describe their marriage as an average one. They are somewhat hesitant to talk about their marital conflicts, but Burt has expressed his dissatisfaction with Alice's complaints about his "laziness." Alice says he is unwilling to work around the house, and she voices frustration about his limited income. They believe themselves to be fairly strict parents, and Alice sometimes fears they are too strict.

Allie Andrews, 16, is in her second year of high school. She is an attractive girl of average ability. About three years ago Allie went through what her mother refers to as a "sudden transformation," changing from an awkward tomboy into a physically mature young woman. At the age of 14, she expressed a desire to date. Her interest in boys was reciprocated, and she seemed to be popular among the older boys in high school. Her parents reluctantly gave in, but firmly stipulated the time she was to be home, the places she could go, the boys she could go out with, and so forth. During this time, her relationship with her parents became increasingly conflictual. Recently she has begun to violate her curfew and hang out with a "bad crowd." When she is punished by being grounded, she sometimes sneaks out to join her friends. Her school grades have been dropping, although she continues to pass all her courses. She became a cheerleader this year. Allie is currently dating three or four boys, one of them an African American student who is on the football team. She has been expressly forbidden to date African Americans, so she meets him away from home.

Allie is sullen around her stepfather. She believes that Burt has hurt her, and she hurts him in return by constantly defying him. Days go by without a word between them. Their mutual dislike is a consistent part of their interactions. Burt uses the same harsh, authoritarian child-rearing style that he resented in his own father. He is the unquestioned decision maker and controls the children primarily through shouting and grounding. The hub of the family,

(continued)

The Andrews family *(continued)*

however, is Alice. She wants Allie to have a good upbringing with the "right" relationships. Alice absorbs conflict between the other family members, attempting to mediate and keep everyone calm. As Allie has grown up, her parents, in particular her stepfather, have become increasingly suspicious and fearful. They suspect that she may be sexually active and fear she is not responsible enough to prevent pregnancy. They also suspect that her friends are drug users and fear that she will become addicted. Several times a week these issues erupt into loud arguments between Allie and Burt. In the end, Allie, faced with her parents' lack of faith in her, feels hurt and misjudged. When Burt insists on the rules he has set down, she sneaks out of the house. Her defiance invokes even more anger, and he tightens the restrictions. Lately she has threatened to run away if Burt doesn't let her choose her own friends, set her own timetable, and quit suspecting her of being a sexually promiscuous drug user.

The most recent confrontation occurred when Burt discovered Allie's dating relationship with her African American friend. This discovery has provoked a family crisis. Burt has threatened to "disown" Allie if she does not break off the relationship. Allie is sulking and threatening to run away. Alice is frustrated and depressed about the antagonism between the two people to whom she feels most closely connected. Allie feels deeply hurt and sees running away as a means to hurt back. Her stepfather, in his own way, feels deeply hurt that his once precious stepdaughter is now so unaccepting of his authority and protection. He expresses a strong dislike of his stepdaughter and is quite angry about her behavior.

Paul Andrews, 12, is a short, stocky eighth-grader with an air of bravado. Underneath the bravado, however, he appears to be a very anxious, depressed child. His parents' main concerns are Paul's dislike of school and his aggressive behavior. Paul says he feels very sad at times for no reason. His aggressive behavior is a problem in the classroom, and he is suspected of stealing other children's lunch money. His behavior at home is no better. Two months ago he set fire to one of Alice's dresses. He shows an intense interest in bloodshed, accidents, fires, and violent crimes. Underneath Paul's

(continued)

CASE STUDY

The Andrews family *(continued)*

facade, and perhaps behind his depression, he appears to have a great deal of anger. Between the incidents of aggression he seems overly controlled, and unless he gets help now, he may become increasingly violent or self-destructive as a teenager. He is also reaching the stage of development at which questions of personal and sexual identity are assuming some urgency for him. He seeks acceptance while at the same time rejecting pressures to conform. His relationship with both parents fluctuates from lukewarm to cold and back again several times a week.

AT-RISK PROBLEMS AND ISSUES

Who is at risk in the Andrews family? In many ways the family itself is at risk. But at risk for what? Perhaps it would be more accurate to say that the family's dysfunction is leading to at-risk behaviors that potentially could put the children within specific at-risk categories.

Cause or Effect?

One of the difficulties in trying to understand at-risk problems is the fragmentation of knowledge about them. School dropout, drug and alcohol abuse, teenage childbearing and unprotected sexual activity, juvenile delinquency and crime, youth suicide, and other major problem behaviors of children and adolescents are usually studied separately. In the real world, however, they interact and cluster together (Jessor, 1993; Jessor, Donovan, & Costa, 1991). Not only do problems cluster but so do the young people who have these problems; they tend to live in the same neighborhoods and communities and to be exposed to many of the same influences. The damage that begins in childhood becomes much more visible in adolescence. The problems reverberate within the community and frequently become an intergenerational cycle of social devastation.

Empirical research is a relatively recent development in the study of at-risk behavior. Much of this growing body of research is correlational, and the fact that two factors are correlated cannot be assumed to indicate that one is the cause of the other. When research suggests that depression in a parent is correlated with antisocial behavior in the child, for example, the direction of causality is unclear. Perhaps the child's negative behavior causes the parent's depression; or perhaps the underlying depression of the parent (that is, a depression based on factors other than the relationships with the child) results in inconsistent parenting that causes the child's predelinquent behavior; or perhaps both are the result of some other factor. More probably, a circular causality is operating—each contributes to the other. Our knowledge of families like the Andrewses suggests that at-risk families and at-risk young people "cause" and "affect" each other.

Vulnerable and Underserved

In addition to issues of cause and effect, particular attention needs to be directed to two groups of young people who are both vulnerable to risk and receive inadequate interventions. Several reports (Hechinger, 1992; Office of Technology Assessment, 1991) have suggested that the physical and mental health needs of children and adolescents in general are underserved, and certain subgroups are even more clearly underserved. Increasing numbers of ethnic minority children and adolescents are not receiving culturally sensitive, relevant, and acceptable interventions, and gay and lesbian youth are especially vulnerable and underserved because they are virtually invisible in our society.

Ethnic minority children and adolescents.   Demographics show increasing ethnic and racial diversity in the United States. In the last census, Hispanics reached 21 million people, a 44% increase since 1980. Asian Americans grew the fastest during the 1980s, up by 64%. American Indian populations continue to grow. African Americans continue to make up about 12% of the total population. Currently, 20% of young people under 18 years of age are from an ethnic minority group. By the year 2000, this figure is projected to be more than 30% for school-age children (Gibbs & Huang, 1991; B. F. Williams, 1992). One projection goes even further (Haveman & Wolfe, 1994). By the year 2000, more than one-third of all young adolescents will be members of ethnic or racial minorities: African American (16%); Hispanic (14%); Asian American (5%); and American Indian (1%).

The Asian American population is the fastest growing of any minority group, and it is also becoming increasingly diverse. As many as 32 different Asian American ethnic groups are now identified, with some subgroups growing faster than others. Soon the Filipino American population will be the largest Asian group, followed by Chinese, Korean, Vietnamese, Indian, and Japanese. Nearly 60% are foreign-born, often recently immigrated, and represent a very unique and serious challenge to educational systems and to mental health professionals (Cheng, 1996). Clearly, this nation is rapidly becoming a people of color, with significant growth in minority populations in virtually every region of the country.

For many young people, minority status is associated with fragmented families, poor living conditions, and low socioeconomic status. The historical mistreatment of ethnic minority populations and a continuing ethos of racism have contributed to the growth of large, high-risk ethnic minority groups that are considerably disadvantaged in the educational system. Thus, many of the conditions that predict negative outcomes place such youth at special risk. As we examine various frames of the at-risk picture, it is important to consider cultural, ethnic, and racial differences and to contemplate how we can make prevention, early intervention, and treatment approaches more culturally relevant and sensitive.

Gay and lesbian youth.   Although considerably fewer in number than ethnic minority children and adolescents, gay and lesbian youth are particularly vulnerable. J. D. Anderson (1994) and Savin-Williams (1995; Savin-Williams & Rodriguez, 1993) argue convincingly that gay and lesbian youth are ignored in most professional writing about children and adolescents. The increased visibility of homosexuality in our culture has not been paralleled by attention to the younger members of the lesbian and gay communities. This lack of attention is consequential, because these young people are disproportionately at risk for negative outcomes.

Most gay and lesbian youth experience stress in their lives because of their sexual orientation. On one hand, adverse responses of disapproval and rejection to an adolescent's homosexual orientation from family members, friends, and peers is common. On the other hand, inability or unwillingness to accept or acknowledge same-sex attraction leads to early feelings of confusion and alienation. These young people are vulnerable because of their fear of reaction from family and friends regarding their sexual orientation. However, not disclosing to family and friends may also be stressful, as it frequently entails living a lie, becoming emotionally isolated, and feeling terribly lonely.

Although lesbian and gay young people receive services from multiple systems, including education, mental health, child welfare, juvenile justice, and health, these service providers rarely identify or address the special needs of this population. Lesbian and gay young people are particularly vulnerable to alcohol and other drug abuse as they cope with the isolation, rejection, and stressors they experience. Homosexuals are probably the most frequent victims of hate violence, and because educators do little to support gay and lesbian adolescents, they frequently leave school before graduation. Finally, the suicide rate of homosexual youths is considerably higher than that of heterosexual youths. These issues will be considered in more detail in later chapters.

THE AT-RISK TREE: A METAPHOR

More than 15 years ago, cultural anthropologist E. Becker (1981) observed that information accumulated in the last half of this century has become "strewn all over the place, spoken in a thousand competitive voices. Its insignificant fragments are magnified out of all proportion while its major and world historical insights lie around begging for attention. There is no throbbing vital center" (p. 14). Becker's statement is still true today. Information about at-risk children and youth is indeed "strewn all over the place." What is cause and what is effect? How does one situation relate to another? What is the relationship between various aspects of a child's problem? What are the underlying connections? In efforts to solve the problem, intertwined and complex problems are divided into manageable parts. Programs to reduce school failure, for instance, are isolated from efforts to prevent juvenile delinquency. Strategies to ameliorate teen pregnancy ignore problems of substance abuse. Researchers and policy planners chip away at what remains unknown but often do not identify what is known. They attempt to determine the impact of narrowly defined interventions and strategies and ignore the powerful effects of a broad combination of strategies.

In this book we lay out a systematic framework to guide the reader toward an understanding of the scope and range of problems for which children and adolescents are at risk. We use a metaphor as a conceptual and organizing framework to pull together information and knowledge that is "strewn all over" and to focus on specific at-risk categories. This allows us to consider factors that precipitate category behavior and to emphasize certain aspects of at-risk youth that are often not considered.

We turn to horticulture for our metaphor. The analogy of a tree permits us to consider a range of issues that relate to at-risk children and youth. The soil of this tree is the individual's societal environment. The roots of family and school connect the tree to the soil (that is, the environment) to provide some support and nurturance. The trunk serves as the conduit of developing attitudes and behaviors that lead to specific at-risk categories, the branches of the tree.

We have written this book specifically for the gardeners, those who tend the weak and broken branches that produce the fruit—that is, specific children and youngsters at risk.

The soil.   Various aspects of the environment, such as socioeconomic status, political realities, economic climate, and cultural factors, must be considered if we are fully to understand at-risk issues. The environment/soil also includes the dramatic changes that are occurring in society. Urbanization, the feminization of poverty, and the fantastic changes in technology are part of the soil in which at-risk children and youth are nourished (or not nourished). These complex variables interact with and influence the individual and personal development of the child and adolescent. The Andrews family is embedded in the soil of its environment. The low socioeconomic status of the family, the limited access to mental health providers, the change of job status because of technological advances, and the racist attitudes expressed by Mr. Andrews all indicate environmental pressures that mold this family and affect its members.

The roots.   The at-risk tree has two primary roots: family and school. Just as the roots provide a network that anchors and nourishes life, so the family and the schools transmit culture and mediate young people's development. These primary social institutions provide the structure through which children assimilate their experiences.

The family is the taproot. In the Andrews family the conflict, friction, and vastly differing parenting styles contribute to Allie's and Paul's dysfunctions. Burt's anger and hostility and Alice's depression and placating behavior limit the nurturance and support the children receive. Multiproblem families such as the Andrewses present a challenge because of the variety of at-risk issues they represent.

The school system is another major root. Society looks to schools for help: to provide a secure environment for children, to foster appropriate learning experiences, and to attend to emotional problems. It has increasingly fallen to the schools to teach essential life skills that families and churches taught in the past. The role of the school in the future of the Andrews children is critical. How the school handles Allie's and Paul's situations will have both short- and long-term effects on their attitudes toward school, learning, and life.

The trunk.   The trunk is the support and brace for the tree's branches and the conduit from the soil and roots to the leaves, blossoms, and fruit. The trunk of the at-risk tree consists of specific behaviors, attitudes, and skills of individual youngsters. It represents young people's strengths and weaknesses, likes and dislikes, talents and disabilities. These personal characteristics spring from the soil of the environment and are transmitted through the roots of family and school. They are also a conduit to the branches, because specific characteristics such as inability to delay gratification, depression, anxiety, and low self-esteem lead directly to at-risk behaviors.

In the Andrews family, Allie's oppositional and self-defeating behavior and Paul's anxiety, depression, and aggressiveness are components of their trunks. These underlying emotions and behaviors indirectly lead to specific at-risk behaviors.

Box 1.1
Carrie

Several years ago one of us was asked to work with a distressed, disturbed young girl named Carrie. At the personal level, 13-year-old Carrie was self-defeating, angry, and fearful. She was obstinate and oppositional—a problem to her family, her school, and herself. Her behaviors and attitudes were more easily understood, however, when we analyzed the shifting ecology of her life.

Carrie had been raised in a rural community by a mother who worked part time as a waitress and received a modest monthly check for child support from her former husband. The mother was periodically anxious and depressed, and during these episodes Carrie assumed responsibility for herself, for her mother, and for their modest house. The living arrangements provided by both her mother and her other relatives (many of whom lived close by) could best be described as permissive and nonstructured, with a high tolerance for a wide range of behaviors.

Carrie attended the small local school and had known most of her classmates for years. Even though she gave evidence of a specific learning disability, Carrie's schoolwork was generally adequate, perhaps because the school's expectations were not high.

When her mother went through a particularly acute depressive episode, it was determined that Carrie should go to live with her father. Overnight she went from her small home in a peaceful, rural community to her father's huge house in a wealthy suburban neighborhood.

Carrie's father, a self-made millionaire, had become successful as the owner and chief executive officer of a chain of drugstores. He worked long hours, drove himself very hard, and had high expectations of everyone with whom he had contact—suppliers, tradespeople, employees, school personnel, and family members.

Carrie suddenly found herself in a household that included her father, his woman friend (who was shortly to become Carrie's stepmother), a housekeeper, and a live-in nanny hired to support, tutor, discipline, and provide companionship for her.

Carrie enrolled in the local public school. Because of the high socioeconomic status of the neighborhood, the academic expectations and achievement norms were high. Her classmates were the sons and daughters of university professors, physicians, and business executives. Most students in this school went on to graduate from college, a large proportion of them from the most prestigious universities in the country.

Considered from an ecological perspective, Carrie's deviant and pathological behaviors are a logical and obvious reaction to her environmental change. Carrie was like a fern that is transplanted from a shaded corner of the garden into the hot, glaring sun. The fern cannot thrive; neither could Carrie.

The branches.   The branches of the tree represent children's and youths' adaptation to society. Many young people are doing well; they are productive as workers, as parents, and as members of the community. Young people with this healthy adaptation contrast strikingly with those who isolate themselves from their cultural heritage, their families, and society through destructive attitudes and behaviors—those in specific at-risk categories.

The five branches that produce the most damaged fruit—that is, the five specific at-risk categories that seem most central to our concerns—are school dropout, substance abuse, risky sexual behaviors, delinquency, and suicide. Both Allie and Paul are approaching school dropout. Further, Allie is at risk for teen pregnancy and drug abuse; Paul is at risk for delinquency and violence, and possibly for suicide.

Foliage, fruit, and flowers.   The fruits of the tree are individual and specific youngsters, such as Allie and Paul Andrews. Some young people are whole and healthy; others are bruised and damaged; still others drop from the tree. Although broken branches sometimes produce good fruit and healthy branches sometimes produce damaged fruit, the fact remains that certain branches—the maladaptive behaviors in the five major at-risk categories—increase the probability that at-risk behavior will escalate. Perhaps even more tragic is the probability that at-risk youths will themselves be the seeds of future generations of at-risk trees.

The gardener.   Like all growing trees, the at-risk tree needs pruning, staking, and trimming; it needs adequate sun, water, and nurturing. This book is for the gardeners— the counselors and teachers, psychologists and social workers, health service providers, administrators, and policy makers—who nurture the Allies and Pauls of our society. Nurturing must be directed sometimes toward the soil, sometimes toward the roots; sometimes toward the trunk or the branches—but always the focus is on the fruit of the at-risk tree.

CONCLUSION

This chapter highlights the severity of the problems that American children and adolescents confront as they progress toward adulthood. The concept of an at-risk continuum can be most useful to teachers, counselors, psychologists, and human service professionals interested in identifying youngsters who are at greatest risk for specific problems. The Andrews family, whom we will meet again in later chapters, demonstrates the risks faced by some youngsters and the interrelationship of family, school, and social problems that young people frequently experience. This book is intended to clarify the problems of youth at risk and to provide multifaceted, comprehensive, practical, and ethical suggestions for prevention and treatment.

FURTHER READINGS

In addition to those books and articles cited in the reference section, the following books discuss general issues and themes related to at-risk children, adolescents, and families.

Capuzzi, D., & Gross, D. G. (Eds.). (1995). *Youth at risk* (2nd ed.). Alexandria, VA: American Counseling Association.

Carnegie Task Force on Meeting the Needs of Young Children. (1994). *Starting points: Meeting the needs of our youngest children.* New York: Carnegie Corporation of New York.

Hawley, W. D., & Jackson, A. W. (Eds.). (1995). *Toward a common destiny: Improving race and ethnic relations in America.* San Francisco: Jossey-Bass.

Holmes, G. R. (1995). *Helping teenagers into adulthood: A guide for the next generation.* Westport, CT: Praeger/Greenwood.

Swadener, B. B., & Lubeck, S. (Eds.). (1995). *Children and families "at promise": Deconstructing the discourse of risk.* Albany, NY: State University of New York Press.

CHAPTER 2

Environmental/Societal Factors That Contribute to Risk

If we put the same effort, worry, and bother into improving our society
That we do in propping up some fool over his people,
Or in selling cat food,
Or in putting pink stripes into toothpaste,
We would have solved many of our social problems long ago.

If we put the same effort, worry, and bother into societal reform
That we do in building bombs,
Or in advertising cigarettes and booze,
Or in putting white back into collars,
We would have solved most of our social problems long ago.

J. J. McWhirter

Chapter Outline

Heraclitus is credited with saying that "nothing is permanent except change." Perhaps at no time in history has this insight been clearer than it is today. Children and youth face the challenge of growing into mature, responsible, healthy adults amidst a maelstrom of economic, political, and social change. Technological advances are occurring more rapidly than ever before in history. The mobility of the population, the decline in the influence of the extended family, the disappearance of the small farm, the movement of industries from the Northeast to the Sunbelt or to Latin America or Asia, and increases in automation and technological development make this society one in which nothing seems certain. For the child and adolescent embarked on the hazardous journey to adulthood, these societal forces add roadblocks that can turn them from their chosen path or cut the journey short. Beyond these national issues, international instability and the pervasive awareness of the nuclear capabilities of several world powers affect individuals, families, schools, and local communities.

The evolution of society has virtually exploded in the last two decades. Social changes and new technologies have created new sets of influences and experiences for children and adolescents: marital transitions, changes in family composition, the presence and temptation of drugs, and an increasing number of celebrities who become media models of sexual permissiveness, irrational risk-taking, and resort to violence to cope with even the simplest of problems. For many young people, these changes are taking place in a context of difficult economic realities.

In this chapter we survey a variety of environmental influences that are associated with at-risk categories. We discuss economic policy trends, with particular attention to poverty and its hazardous effects on self-esteem, health, and mental health. The effects of socioeconomic status and ethnicity are surveyed as well as state and federal public policy issues.

The Changing Economy and Poverty

Changes in economic and political trends can be seen in many areas of society. Those trends most salient to at-risk young people include the increasing incidence of (a) job and income loss and the economic stagnation of the working poor, (b) poverty among young families, (c) single mothers, and (d) homeless families. These trends are devastating to at-risk children and adolescents. Each trend contributes to the growing impoverishment of young people. Poverty provides poor soil for the development of children and adolescents, and family and school roots are particularly affected.

Poverty is the risk factor most closely associated with the rise in family stress, and it is highly correlated with school failure and other problems. Of course, some children of poor families will succeed despite their disadvantages. Nevertheless, students whose families are poor are twice as likely to drop out of school than students whose families are economically advantaged (CDF, 1995). Further, the educational problems of poor youngsters often emerge at the very beginning of their school career. Many of these youngsters begin school developmentally unprepared to succeed in the classroom, and parental support for education often is limited.

What are we as a nation doing for the youth who must grow and develop in an impoverished societal environment? How are we tending to the soil of at-risk youth? To understand more clearly the changing environment of youth at risk, we must identify and explore the economic and political trends that shape this environment.

Job and Income Loss: Stagnation of the Working Poor

High rates of unemployment and job loss distinguish the 1980s and 1990s from the four preceding decades. Two factors have contributed to these problems. First, major manufacturing industries made decisions to alter production in response to foreign competition. Second, back-to-back recessions in the early 1980s resulted in an unemployment rate of more than 10%, the highest unemployment rate since the Great Depression of the 1930s. The economic upswing in the latter half of the decade only partially ameliorated these problems, and the deep, two-year recession in the early 1990s restored them. Reemployment lessened but has not reversed the decline because wages were not restored to their previous level. Generally, workers who lost their jobs and then were reemployed earned 20% less than they had earlier (CDF, 1995; Mishel & Bernstein, 1994).

Economic loss influences a child's development through the changes it produces in parental attitude, disposition, and behavior. Parents who suffered job and financial loss became more tense, irritable, and explosive, and became increasingly arbitrary and punitive in the discipline of their children (Schliebner and Peregoy, 1994). Further, there is solid evidence that mental health and physical well-being are affected by economic decline (McLloyd, 1989). Unemployed parents are more dissatisfied with themselves and with their lives, feel victimized, and are more anxious, depressed, and hostile than employed parents. The incidence of neurosis, psychosis, and suicide is higher among unemployed parents; they have more sleeping, eating, and somatic problems; and they consume more alcohol. These changes in attitude, disposition, and behavior strain family relationships and increase family stress. The net effect is not good for children's development and has an impact on their success at school as well.

In Chapter 1 we introduced Burt Andrews and his family. (The case study may also be found in the Appendix.) Recall that due to technological changes Burt lost his technician's job in electronics and that he now works part time in a service station. This change in his employment status and income level undoubtedly accounts in large part for his angry, hostile, aggressive feelings. These feelings cause him to be less nurturing with his stepchildren and more punitive and arbitrary toward them.

Allie Andrews's sullenness and defiance reflect her heightened stress and lowered self-esteem. Her sexual acting out (if indeed her parents' suspicions are correct) can be at least partially explained as a reaction to her stepfather's harsh and abrasive behavior. Similarly, Paul's anxiety, depression, and low self-esteem are exacerbated by his stepfather's situation. Paul's destructive behavior and poor school adjustment are among the consequences.

The Andrews family also serves to illustrate another economic class of Americans: the working poor. Stagnation of the working poor is a major economic trend that affects at-risk young people. The working poor are not an isolated few. Most poor children, (more than 60%) live in families where at least one person works. Nearly one in four poor children live in a family where parents worked full time throughout the year (CDF, 1995). For a variety of reasons, they continue to have insufficient earnings. The working poor are trapped by the inaccessibility of child care, the inadequacy of the minimum wage, even with its 1997 increase, and a lack of skills and education that would facilitate advancement. In the case of the Andrews, child care is not a problem because Alice does not work outside the home; however, the low minimum wage and especially Burt's limited education and lack of salable skills are important factors in this family's problems. We will return to these issues later in this chapter.

Vulnerable and underserved: Ethnic minority families. Ethnic minority families have experienced a disproportionate share of income and job loss, primarily because of structural changes in the economy. The steady transition of downtown areas from centers of production to centers of administration has generated some increases in white-collar employment but decreases in blue-collar jobs. In the last two decades, one in every four manufacturing jobs was eliminated (Jones, 1996). This phenomenon has been exacerbated by the shift of manufacturing employment from the cities to outlying areas, including outsourcing to other countries. Because African American and other minority groups reside in inner city areas in disproportionate numbers and are overrepresented in the blue-collar jobs that have been disappearing, they are disproportionately affected by displacement and unemployment. The problem is likely to be prolonged as this country continues its transformation from a goods-producing economy to a service economy (Interagency Council on the Homeless, 1994).

Ethnic minorities are disproportionately represented in the lower income brackets. Poverty rates among African Americans are consistently three times higher than among European Americans; for Hispanic Americans they are two and one-half times higher. Female headed households with children, which we will discuss later, are particularly vulnerable to poverty; more than 48% of those living in such households were poor in 1992. This figure rises to about 60% for Hispanic American and African American children. Nearly half of all African American children and 22% of all children lived below the poverty line in 1992 (U.S. Department of Commerce, 1993). These percentages translate into an increase of 5 million poor people between the mid-1980s and the mid-1990s. Also during this period, the very poor, with incomes less than 50% of the poverty threshold, increased by 3 million. Native Americans are generally unaffected by national economic cycles because they consistently suffer high unemployment. It hovers at about 30% on most reservations, and some Plains reservations report unemployment rates of more than 70% (La Fromboise, 1988).

Rural families.   Poverty is not restricted to urban areas (R. D. Conger & Elder, 1994; Sherman, 1992). Many rural families face a bleak economic landscape. Earnings from rural jobs are lower than in metropolitan areas, and unemployment levels are now higher. The very worst concentration of child poverty in this country occurs in rural areas. Twenty-eight counties in the United States—all rural—have child poverty rates that exceed 50%. These counties are clustered in four places, and their populations represent all ethnic groups. Two Appalachian mining counties in Kentucky have a 98% European American population. Two Texas counties along the Mexican border have a mostly Hispanic population, one with 98%. Three South Dakota Sioux Indian reservation counties are among the most poor. Finally, the Mississippi Delta area, with 21 counties in Arkansas, Louisiana, and Mississippi, have mostly African American families. Not surprisingly, in all 28 counties low education levels are a common factor. In most of these counties, fewer than half of the adults have finished high school (Sherman, 1995).

Young Families

The rising level of poverty among young families is another economic trend that contributes to at-risk problems. The sharply declining economic portrait of America's youngest families with children, those headed by someone younger than 30 years of age, fueled much of the continuing growth in child poverty. Two incomes are clearly better than one, but the poor tend to be poor before, during, and after they marry. The two-parent household is the fastest growing poverty group in the United States. The majority of the poor live in households with young workers who are employed full year and full time. Of course, working full time at minimum wage today leaves a three-person family $2,300 below the poverty line (Mulroy, 1995). The average income of families headed by someone younger than age 25 declined at an annual rate of 2.5% during the 1980s. The median family income for this age group is lower today than it was in 1967. This trend continued and even increased into the 1990s with an income decline of more than 5% early in 1990. Families headed by someone between the ages of 25 and 34 years of age have fared only slightly better. Because many families in these age groups are likely to be bringing up young children, their income problems represent economic hardship for the nation's children. The deterioration of income from these young families is one of the most significant income developments over the last two decades. Rising poverty rates have affected all young families, whether the parents are single or married, African American, Hispanic, or European American. No part of the country has been exempt from this trend.

If Allie Andrews continues her presumed sexual behavior, becomes pregnant (as is probable), and marries the father (as is less probable), and if she keeps her baby (also probable), the best she can hope for is a typical young marriage with a limited income and a heavy workload. She will assume most of the care for her baby and most of the household chores. She will probably also work outside the home.

Increasing numbers of married mothers are members of the workforce out of necessity rather than a desire for a career. Because of the decline in real family income from the mid-1970s to the mid-1990s, in many families both parents must work to maintain their standard of living. In some families both parents must work simply to keep the family out of poverty. Nearly 62% of married women with children younger than 6 participate in the labor force (Bureau of Labor Statistics, 1995). Most mothers in two-parent families work more hours than the fathers. Rexroat and Shehan (1987) found that in childless families wives worked an average of five to nine hours a week more than their husbands in combined housework and employment. They also found that in families with young children mothers worked 16 to 24 hours more per week than fathers, and when the children were under 3, the total hours per week worked by the mothers was approximately 90. Other researchers have found that when both parents are employed and the children are not yet of school age, the fathers do not spend significantly more time on household chores or child care than fathers in single-earner families (Nock & Kingston, 1991). This trend continues.

In the Andrews family we see the effects of the first two trends we have discussed: job and income loss leading to economic stagnation, and young families. The Andrews family structure, however, has less bearing on two other areas of concern: single mothers and homeless families. The Baker family—described in the Case Study beginning on the following page—knows these problems all too well.

Single Mothers

Although young married couples and their children have also lost income since the early 1980s, they have avoided severe loss by maintaining dual incomes. Few single mothers can depend on anyone's earnings but their own, and young female-headed families are at the greatest risk of poverty. Fifty-four percent of children living in mother-only homes are poor compared to 12% living with both married parents (CDF, 1995).

The growing proportion of young families headed by single women may be attributed in part to the earning losses suffered by young workers. In the last two decades the marriage rate of young men has declined along with their income. Falling marriage rates have coincided with the increased proportion of young female-headed families.

Families headed by one parent (usually the mother) are an increasingly common phenomenon with one of three marriages ending in divorce (Arendell, 1995). Out-of-wedlock births continue to increase. In the early 1990s, the portion of teen births to unmarried girls reached the highest level ever recorded (Alan Guttmacher Institute, 1994). Dryfoos (1990) suggests that throughout the 1990s approximately 60% of the nation's children will spend part of their childhood in single-parent families. The children and adolescents living in single-parent families are at greatest risk for poverty and all its problems (Dickerson, 1995; Mulroy, 1995).

The economic plight of young families headed by single mothers has steadily worsened in the past 15 years. Because of health factors, low skills, and the cost of child care, many of these mothers cannot work, but even if they can, they are still at risk. Whatever their employment status, single mothers are more likely to experience health problems, depression, and anxiety (Mulroy, 1995; Sklar, 1995). As we mentioned earlier, their financial resources are so limited that the risk of falling into poverty is great. Indeed, most single mothers—unmarried, widowed, or divorced—must work to avoid

CASE STUDY

The Baker family

Sally Baker is a tall, slender, 28-year-old African American woman. She is still legally married to the father of her 9-year-old son, Todd, and her 7-year-old daughter, Denise, although she has not lived with him for five years. Her 3-year-old son, Jerome, was fathered by a boyfriend whom she has not seen for over a year. During most of her nine years of motherhood, Sally's primary means of support has been Aid to Families with Dependent Children (AFDC). For several months she and her children have been residing at the Andre House, a shelter for homeless families.

Sally was born in rural Alabama. She never knew her father but thought that his last name was Johnson. When she was 8, her mother moved to Dallas with Sally and her younger brother. Sally remembers that her mother was not working and that "she couldn't afford to keep me and couldn't afford to send me back." As their situation became increasingly strained, her mother's frustration spilled over into abuse. After several years of intermittent abuse, Sally finally refused to take any more of it and at 14 left home. After living for several weeks in a local park, she was arrested for being out after curfew and was sent to a detention facility for status offenders. From there she went to the first of several foster homes. She reports being sexually abused in this home before she fled it. This became the pattern of her life over the next few years. She lived on the streets for several weeks or months until the police picked her up again and sent her to a detention facility, which placed her in another foster home. From then on, it was in and out of foster homes and girls' homes and detention facilities until she finally met and married George.

Sally's marriage to George was not particularly happy. After several years of conflict, George availed himself of a "poor people's divorce": He walked out and did not return.

In the year before their arrival at Andre House, the Baker family's lifestyle mirrored Sally's earlier life—a chronic pattern of lurching from crisis to crisis. Sally had been living on AFDC in a Housing Authority complex in a small city. Because her unit was subsidized by the Housing Authority, she was paying hundreds of dollars less than she would have had to pay for a private unit, but she had to contend with drug dealers, gang activity, and considerable neighborhood violence. When Todd started to wear the "colors" of one of the local gangs, Sally decided to move in with her

(continued)

CASE STUDY

The Baker family *(continued)*

sister-in-law in a neighboring town. The safety of this new living arrangement was offset by the crowded conditions; there were now two adults and seven children in a two-bedroom apartment. Sally was able to stay for three months and saved some money, but not enough to get a place of her own.

Sally and her children moved back to Dallas to live with another sister, who also had a two-bedroom apartment. The sister and her boyfriend slept in one bedroom, the sister's three children slept in the other, and Sally and her three children slept on the living-room floor. Again there were problems. Her sister's boyfriend used and sold crack cocaine. Sally contributed a share of the monthly rent, but a few months later both families were evicted because the boyfriend was not paying the rent.

Sally and her children moved in with a friend, but once again drugs were a problem—this time because friends of the friend were using her apartment to make their deals. The police frequently came to the house because of the drug activity and finally threatened to take Sally's children away from her unless she got them out of the house.

Bit by bit Sally had been saving money from her AFDC checks, but the $100 she had managed to put aside was still too little to pay the first and last months' rent on a place of her own plus a security deposit. In any case, the fruit of her prudence and foresight disappeared when the apartment was robbed by the drug-dealing friends of the woman with whom she was staying. She was beaten, her life was threatened, and even her children were threatened. The elderly couple next door called the paramedics, who took her to a clinic. After all the threats to her life, she was too frightened to let anyone call the police. The counselor at the clinic found a shelter that had room for them and gave her money for the bus. And so the Baker family found themselves at Andre House.

Sally's children reflect the type of chaotic life she has led. Todd especially seems to have been negatively affected by his experiences. His behavior is highly impulsive. His attention shifts rapidly from one object or activity to the next. At school he is an "attention-starved" child. He must be first in line, the one to sit next to the teacher, the first to play with a new toy. At times he hurts other children and is destructive. Sometimes conflict with his mother erupts into aggressive outbursts and he lashes out at his 3-year-old brother.

(continued)

CASE STUDY

The Baker family (continued)

Denise, by contrast, has a good relationship with her family. She and Sally talk frequently, and Denise is able to ask for what she wants and needs. Her calm, sweet disposition endears her to adults and apparently helps her with both of her brothers, even Todd. She is especially helpful in caring for Jerome. Even though this task is sometimes frustrating to her, she is quite responsible and affectionate with him.

Jerome is a shy, passive, sickly child who is fearful of strangers. He prefers to be left alone and makes few demands. He is apathetic and disinterested and when left alone mostly watches television. He seems indifferent to Todd's temper outbursts, even when they are directed at him. He tends to cling to Denise, though, and follows her closely about.

poverty. The problems of young female-headed families have increased with the deterioration in basic income support. Nationally, 46% of all female-headed families with children under age 18 were below the official 1993 poverty line, as were 23% of single-father families with children. In other words, single-father families have very high rates of poverty, but single-mother families have even higher rates (Sklar, 1995).

Not only are these young women at risk but so are their children. Consider their access to essential health care. The proportion of teens receiving prenatal care remains extremely low. In 1992, one in ten received no prenatal care or obtained it only in the last trimester. Only three in five received prenatal care during the first trimester (National Center for Health Statistics, 1992). Lack of prenatal care influences the child's future health, well-being, and learning ability. The consequences of impoverishment will be borne by our school systems as well as by our physical and mental health systems. Sally Baker and her children tragically illustrate these problems.

Homeless Families

The Baker family also illustrates the chaotic stress of homeless families. Nowhere is the soil more fertile for at-risk problems than among those families that are homeless. Families represent at least a third of the total number of homeless people, and families with children are the fastest growing segment of the homeless population (Milburn & D'Ercole, 1991). In a recent survey (U.S. Conference of Mayors, 1995), families with children accounted for 39% of the homeless in the 30 cities surveyed. One in every four homeless persons was a child younger than 18.

At the same time that the number of low-income households in the nation is rising the supply of low-cost housing is dwindling. Rapidly rising rents, gentrification, and urban renewal significantly decrease the number of affordable low-income housing units. By the early 1990s more than 8 million low-income families were competing for about 3 million low-cost housing units—that is, nearly 5 million houses and apartments fewer than the country needed (Dolbeare, 1991; Interagency Council on the Homeless, 1994). Because 90% of low-income households are families, we are seeing increasing numbers of homeless children and adolescents, all of whom are at risk (Quint, 1994).

Like poverty, homelessness is often explained at the individual, personal level. Sally Baker must be lazy or imprudent or unlucky. She didn't want to work. She should have put her savings in the bank. Well, yes, she should, but these arguments hardly explain her situation and don't come close to explaining away the systemic realities. Homelessness, at the aggregate level, is caused by a lack of low-cost housing. Whenever the number of low-cost housing units available is smaller than the number of poor households seeking them, some families are going to be squeezed out. In these circumstances, poor people do one of three things. Some pay more for their housing if they are able. Those unable to pay more move in with friends or family members (Interagency Council on the Homeless, 1994; Shinn, Knickman, & Weitzman, 1991). The remainder become homeless. When low-income housing units are far fewer than the poor households that need them, homelessness is inevitable. Basic arithmetic demonstrates that the Sally Bakers of this country have few, if any, choices. Instead, Sally and her children are caught in a bizarre game reminiscent of musical chairs. When the music stops, where do they sleep at night? She is not alone. Single mothers with children constitute 80% of homeless families (Lindblom, 1991).

The potential at-risk problems of homeless children and adolescents are growing, and researchers have found that mothers of homeless families are disproportionately of ethnic minority status. They are young, are more likely to have been abused as children and battered as adults, and have limited social support networks (Burt & Cohen, 1993; Massey & Denton, 1993). Life in shelters for the homeless has been linked to depression, anxiety, behavioral disturbances, and an assortment of educational problems among children and adolescents (Quint, 1994; Rafferty & Shinn, 1991). Researchers for Advocates for Children of New York found, as might be expected, that children of homeless families performed poorly in school and had more erratic attendance records than children with homes (Landers, 1989), a fact that continues into the 1990s (Interagency Council on the Homeless, 1994; Quint, 1994).

Here again the Baker family exemplifies the problems of homelessness. The early physical and sexual abuse, the chaotic and stressful living arrangements, and the lack of purpose and hope place Sally and her children at risk.

SOCIOECONOMIC STATUS

The social and economic environment in which children grow is the most important predictor of their overall well-being. Almost all available data support the conclusion that children's education, later employment, future earnings, and health greatly depend on the socioeconomic status (SES) of their families. Membership in the lowest SES group is clearly linked to a wide variety of problems among children and adolescents (Belle, 1990; Haveman & Wolfe, 1994).

■ ■ ■ Box 2.1

Decade of Greed, Decade of Decline

The environmental factors that place families at risk are obvious to teachers, counselors, and other human service workers. They are obvious to social science researchers. Perhaps they are becoming obvious to some politicians as well. As Senator Mark O. Hatfield (R., Oregon) reported in the *Congressional Record*:

> As good as the 1980s were for the military, what has happened to the children of this country? Many of the key measures of children's well-being dramatically indicate that the 1980s were a terrible decade. Child poverty, violent deaths among teenagers and births to unmarried teens all increased substantially.
>
> One American child in five now lives with a single parent. By the year 2000, both numbers will be one in four if current trends continue. . . . Every day, 135,000 children take a gun to school. Every 32 seconds, a 15- to 19-year-old woman becomes pregnant. Every 55 seconds, a child is born to a mother who does not even hold a high school diploma. And, finally, every 14 hours, a child the age of 5 or younger is murdered.

SES and Health Problems

Children and adolescents from impoverished families have an increased risk of health problems. In contrast to middle-SES children, they are more likely to have suffered neonatal damage, to have been underweight at birth and malnourished, to have had problems with vision and hearing that were unidentified and uncorrected, and to have experienced untreated childhood illnesses. Low-SES children usually grow up in environments characterized by high degrees of continuous stress. They live in disorganized and impoverished neighborhoods. Often they are socially isolated with very young mothers, without fathers, and with minimal support from other family members (Hamburg, 1994). Further, low SES is associated with problems of mental health, with impaired parent-child relationships, and with a high incidence of child abuse and neglect.

Parent-Child Relations and SES

The trickle-down model of economics extends to the family unit. Economic deprivation affects young people's image of their parents, which may affect their behavior toward adults in general. In the relationship of economic deprivation, child rearing, and psychological well-being, children are generally unaware of or unsympathetic to the difficulties associated with economic pressure (G. H. Elder, Conger, Foster, & Ardelt, 1992). Adolescents are likely to blame unemployment on internal rather than uncontrollable external factors. Thus economic deprivation gives them a distorted perception of their parents, which may lead in turn to acting out and other problem behaviors, including juvenile delinquency.

SES and At-Risk Categories

Low SES coupled with membership in a minority group is the strongest predictor of school dropout (Entwisle & Alexander, 1992; Mayer, 1990). Low SES is related to juvenile delinquency (Straus, 1994) and is the strongest predictor of teenage pregnancy (Alan Guttmacher Institute, 1994; Musick, 1993). We will examine the relationship between SES and each category behavior in later chapters.

AND THE RICH GET RICHER

What is most vicious and mean-spirited in the current assaultive rhetoric about the working poor, single mothers, and young and homeless families is that wealth is being redistributed *upward*. Most workers are finding it more and more difficult to meet their financial needs, and they are also losing ground to the wealthy. The income gap in Manhattan, New York, is worse than that in Guatemala (Roberts, 1994). The combined wealth of the top 1% of American families is nearly the same as that of the entire bottom 95% (Sklar, 1995).

Average family income in the United States has shifted dramatically among income groups in the last decade. The income for families in the middle and lower brackets has decreased as the income for the wealthiest families has increased. Families in the top 1% saw their incomes rise almost 50%, an average of more than $134,000. Those in the top 10% bracket saw their incomes rise 16.5%. The middle 50% bracket dropped 6.3%, and the average income for families in the lowest 10% income bracket dropped nearly 15% (Jones, 1996; Mishel & Bernstein, 1995; Sklar, 1995). As K. Phillips (1990) points out, "the 1980s were the triumph of upper America—an ostentatious celebration of wealth, the political ascendency of the richest third of the population, and a glorification of capitalism, free markets and finance. . . . *No parallel upsurge of riches had been seen since the late 19th century, the era of the Vanderbilts, Morgans and Rockefellers*" (p. 10; italics in original). Phillips, a conservative political analyst, goes on to point out that this increased concentration of income among the wealthy came largely as a consequence of federal policies adopted in the last decade (K. Phillips, 1990). These income increases have been accompanied by a lower standard of living for most workers and an increase in the number of poor. Much of this redistribution of wealth upward is based on income-producing assets—bonds, trusts, and business equity—so this trend will likely continue through the 1990s and into the next millennium. And it will continue to have a negative effect on children, adolescents, and families at risk.

ENNUI AND PURPOSE   *Onwe*

We have described in detail the declining economic conditions of a portion of our population because poverty exacerbates at-risk problems for children and adolescents. It would be a mistake, however, to conclude that only poverty creates at-risk categories. Many young people from affluent backgrounds are also at risk. Hewlett (1991) concluded that affluent children spent the largest amount of time on their own, apparently because their parents' careers were so time-consuming. Further, more than 80% of parents who participated in a National Commission on Children (1991) survey believed that parents and children no longer spend enough time together.

Changes in our society have contributed to ennui among our young people. Ennui is defined as boredom, but the meaning is broader than simple boredom, encompassing an emotional state of noninvolvement characterized by a lack of connection and a lack of purpose. Ennui can occur in children from all types of families: rich and poor, blue collar and white collar, working class and professional class. It is both cause and effect for many young people who are aimless, alienated, and directionless.

Changes in two areas have greatly affected our children and youth: parenting networks and training for life. We consider these two concepts more fully in Chapter 3, which focuses on family problems, and Chapter 4, which deals with school issues, but because they are part of the "soil" for at-risk youth, we briefly introduce them here.

Parenting Networks

In earlier generations the majority of children were raised through the collective efforts of a network of in-laws, friends, and relatives who interacted with them throughout childhood and adolescence. Today children have fewer adults to help them develop responsibility, judgment, and self-discipline, even though the task requires more understanding, care, and awareness than ever before. Most young people do not have an extended family network of grandparents, in-laws, aunts, and uncles to support them and their parents on their journey through childhood and adolescence. For example, only about 5% of American children see a grandparent regularly (Hamburg, 1995). Today a typical American youngster experiences parenting as a part-time occupation by inexperienced parents.

Television has taken the place of those adult role models in many homes. Children become acquainted with the adult world through television programs that portray casual sex, drinking, gratuitous acts of violence, and self-centered aggrandizement as routine behavior. Through commercials, television also frequently provides negative messages about sacrifice, self-discipline, and patience. Many young people lack the elements that promote a sense of bonding—a commitment and an emotional attachment between young people and the larger social institutions of society—and don't feel that they are part of this society, this culture, their schools, or sometimes even their families.

Training for Life

Our young people have no significant role in society. In school they are often told to "stay out of trouble," "be quiet," and "do what we tell you." They no longer serve as tutors and teacher aides as they did in one-room schools. They no longer take part in the family's economic activities.

One of the greatest human needs is to be needed. Too often our society fails to let young people affirm their worth to themselves and to others. By doing too much for our children, we destroy their self-confidence and foster low self-esteem. Not infrequently, adults provide their children with an environment that demands nothing of them and teaches them nothing. Then the adults criticize these children for appreciating neither the lifestyle nor the parents who provided it.

Young people have been progressively denied the opportunity to engage in work that is important to others and therefore denied the rewards that such work produces. Children and adolescents who tutor their peers or younger children, who assist disabled people, who help care for young children, who visit with the elderly, and who participate in other programs to help their families, schools, and communities are filling the void that our age of technology and specialization has created in their lives. They are responding to real needs of their society, and they are assuming meaningful roles. In so doing, they are satisfying their own need to be needed.

MODEST PROPOSALS AND SUGGESTIONS: FAMILY/SCHOOL/COMMUNITY LINK

What can be done? In later chapters we provide some of the answers. Here we suggest several measures that may help to nurture the soil. These measures focus on child care, deficits in skills, and comprehensive preschool programs.

Child Care

Child care is an issue that affects all families, and the joint efforts of families, schools, and communities are needed to provide healthy choices that are beneficial for children and their parents. The number of children who are cared for by people other than their parents during work hours is rising and will continue to rise. Access to adequate child care enables parents to work without undue stress and concern for the welfare of their children. Adequate child care prevents parents from missing days of work because arrangements have fallen through, because quality care is not available, or because a child is ill. When both parents work, some of the socioeconomic limitations of their children's environment are likely to be overcome. The benefits of adequate child care are obvious both in the absence of the neglect, abuse, poor nutrition, and poor health that are likely in poorly run facilities and in the presence of stable, consistent child-care workers who act in the child's best interest.

Many beliefs about the effects of child care on mother-infant attachment, social interaction, and cognitive development are based on fantasy rather than research findings. Studies cited in support of the negative effects of child care often fail to account for variations in the type of care provided (from in-house caretakers to centers that care for more than 100 children), the family/home environment (from abusive to highly supportive), and the quality of care (from minimal attention by untrained caretakers to programmatic enrichment by child-care professionals). "In sum, there is near consensus among developmental psychologists and early childhood experts that child care per se does not constitute a risk factor in children's lives, rather, poor quality care and poor family environments can conspire to produce poor developmental outcomes" (Scarr, Phillips, & McCartney, 1990, p. 30).

The quality of child care is determined by the ratio of children to caregivers, the number of children cared for in the setting, the caring and responsiveness of caregivers, the stability of caregivers and settings, and the training and experience of caregivers (Gormley, 1995). The low pay and lack of benefits received by the majority of child-care workers make for a high turnover rate in this occupation; perhaps it is time to ask legislators why the people who care for our most precious national resource are so poorly compensated that many of them cannot survive on the income the jobs provide.

This country needs a national policy to shape and direct child-care services (Clarke-Stewart, Gruber, & Fitzgerald, 1994). We also need a commitment from workplaces throughout the nation to reevaluate personnel policies that inevitably create difficulty for employees with families. The absence of opportunities for parental leave, inflexible work hours, and restrictions on leaving the work site to attend to the problems and opportunities that arise in a child's life create stress for working parents. The resulting frustration and tension is often directed at children and spouses instead of at the workplace. The social values that prevail in this country require families to adjust to the demands of the workplace rather than expecting workplaces to modify policies to meet the realistic demands of families.

Teachers and counselors can be effective advocates of parents by informing them of procedures for reaching their legislators. In recent years the number of child-care proposals put before state legislatures has increased (Gormley, 1995). Such efforts should be supported. In addition, teachers and counselors might devise ways to facilitate exchanges of information on child care and to link parents interested in sharing child-care arrangements.

The lack of adequate day care is a persistent problem in particular for the poor. Workers with children are often prevented from securing full-time or even part-time employment because affordable day care is unavailable. Mishel and Bernstein (1995) suggest that mothers out of work due to child-care problems were disproportionately poorly educated, lowering their potential to earn a wage that might have allowed them to purchase the very child care they needed to go out and work. Thus, they are stuck in a vicious cycle. Although the federal government subsidizes some day care through the child-care tax credit, Head Start, and Social Service Block Grant programs, the majority of poor people do not benefit from them. If low-cost, adequate day care were more readily available, the work efforts of parents might enable them and their children to escape the cycle of poverty. Unfortunately, the child-care tax credit primarily benefits middle- and upper-income families, and day-care facilities are available to only a minority of impoverished parents.

The cost of child care is a particularly serious problem for poor and single parents. In the early 1990s, the typical cost of a year of child care for one child was about $3,300, which makes child care the fourth largest household expense behind shelter, food, and taxes (Gormley, 1995). Families with incomes under $15,000 spend nearly 25% of their annual income on child care (Mishel & Bernstein, 1995). In addition, current economic policies that affect the quantity and quality of day care are inadequate. The dependent-care tax credit, for example, is the major federal support for child care. A family may deduct a portion of annual child-care expenses from their federal income tax, up to a maximum of $2,400 for one child, but the credit cannot be greater than the family's tax liability. The very poor do not pay any income tax, so the tax credit does not benefit those who need it most—the poor and single mothers.

Reviews of child-care literature (Clarke-Stewart, 1989; Scarr, Phillips, & McCartney, 1990) suggest that high-quality child care has no detrimental effects on children's language or cognitive development. In fact, high-quality child care promotes social and cognitive development and has been shown to compensate for a poor family environment (Gormley, 1995). Thus child care per se does not constitute a risk factor in children's lives. The problem is that nearly 70% of mothers with young children and infants will be employed by the mid-1990s (Bureau of Labor Statistics, 1995), yet affordable, high-quality child care is still scarce.

Deficits in Skills

Although the general level of education has risen in the United States, a large number of Americans lack basic skills, and these deficits impede gainful employment. About one in four Americans lacks a high school diploma and one in eight is illiterate. Basic competence is essential in today's labor market, even in most entry-level jobs. Employers require workers who can read, write, and do basic math. Low proficiency in these skills is correlated with low educational attainment and low earnings. It is people with low skills who end up with minimum-wage jobs.

Through most of the 1960s and 1970s, a full-time worker earning the minimum wage was able to support a family of three above the poverty threshold. In the 1990s the earnings of a full-time, year-round minimum-wage worker with two dependents is nearly 25% below the poverty level (Mulroy, 1995), and by 1995 the actual purchasing power of the minimum wage was at its lowest level in more than three decades. Contrary to the popular notion that most minimum-wage workers are teenagers in their first jobs, nearly half of minimum-wage earners are 25 years old or older and 21% are 20 to 24 years old; 28% are heads of households and 28% are spouses. Only 31% of all minimum-wage earners are teenagers (Sklar, 1995). It is no surprise that the number of working poor has risen in direct proportion to the decline in the purchasing power of the minimum wage since 1978.

More important for children and youth, the difficulties of the unskilled worker are often transferred to the next generation. The proportion of young people from households with low skills and low incomes who do not complete high school is twice that of youths from more affluent families (Hamburg, 1994). Thus children of the unskilled and poor are more likely than children from affluent families to be poorly prepared when they enter the workforce. Their chances of escaping the cycle of poverty are not good.

Current trends suggest that people without adequate education and job skills will have increasing difficulty gaining employment. And the likelihood of getting a well-compensated job is not very promising. Most of the occupations with the largest job growth projected between 1988 and 2000 are ones that provide limited benefits and relatively low wages, such as waiters and waitresses, janitors, office clerks, retail salespersons, truck drivers, and nurses aides (Berliner & Biddler, 1995). There is growing global competitive pressure for a highly skilled workforce. The United States is facing a tremendous mismatch between the jobs available and the ability of Americans to perform them. An undereducated and unskilled workforce will continue to lose jobs to international labor that meets the knowledge and skill levels employers require.

Comprehensive Preschool Programs

Another way to link family, school, and community is to provide comprehensive preschool programs for children who are identified as at risk. Evidence suggests that overcoming deficits in skills needs to begin early. Preschool is extremely important. Consultation with the state's economic security or human service agency as well as familiarity with the local human services directory will provide counselors and teachers with ample resources and referrals for the families with whom they are in contact. Head Start, a nationwide, federally funded program for economically disadvantaged prekindergarten children, is one comprehensive preschool program (Zigler, 1995). Head Start programs vary from locale to locale, but each provides a classroom-based, multicultural learning experience for 4-year-olds. Through Head Start, children with little structured home stimulation and lack of exposure to the resources of the middle class are given a "head start" on kindergarten. They have a year to become familiar with school-related vocabulary in a nonpressured environment. These children are assessed for a variety of developmental problems and may have access to speech therapists, psychologists, and other professionals as the need arises.

Head Start provides enrichment for the rest of the family as well (Zigler, 1995). By actively participating in the daily events of the classroom and by receiving specific training in parenting, life skills, and health and employment issues, parents become engaged in an empowering process that extends beyond the nine months of the school year. Head Start programs have helped disadvantaged students to persevere, cope, and eventually graduate from high school (Zigler & Muenchow, 1992). Preschool programs generally have had a positive impact on children's cognitive and social development (Barnett, 1992). And compensatory education programs such as the Perry preschool program have demonstrated impressive results over an extended period of time. Child-care assistance and comprehensive preschool programs have also enabled welfare-to-work programs to succeed (Gueron & Pauly, 1991).

The combination of inadequate child care and pervasive deficits in skills contribute to the stagnation of the poor and leave their children at risk. If Sally Baker has adequate child care for her youngsters, a reasonable wage, and support to improve her skills, she and her children might escape from their predicament. Unfortunately, the safety net our society provides for Sally and others like her is badly in need of repair.

CONCLUSION

Providing training for life and developing childraising networks are only two ways to enhance the potential of youth at risk. Ultimately, preventing and assisting youth at risk may require us all to be active in securing the type of public policy that affects everyone, especially those families most economically distraught and socially marginalized. In this chapter we have discussed the problems of job loss and the stagnation of the working poor, the struggles of young families, pervasive racial and ethnic problems, and SES as contributors to the risk that young people face. A determination to develop social policies that focus on providing child care and better opportunities for both youth and adults to acquire skills is the necessary first step in confronting these environmental problems.

FURTHER READINGS

In addition to those books and articles cited in the reference section, the following books provide more detailed information about societal/environmental problems of high-risk young people.

Bronfenbrenner, U., Wethington, E., McClelland, P. D., Ceci, S., & Moen, P. (1996). *The state of Americans: This generation and the next.* New York: The Free Press.
Chase-Lansdale, P. L., & Brooks-Gunn, J. (Eds.). (1995). *Escape from poverty: What makes a difference for children?* New York: Cambridge University Press.

Gormley, W. T. (1995). *Everybody's children: Child care as a public problem*. Washington, DC: Brookings Institution.

Haveman, R., & Wolfe, B. (1994). *Succeeding generations: On the effects of investment in children*. New York: Russell Sage Foundation.

New York Times. (1996). *The downsizing of America*. New York: Author.

Sklar, H. (1995). *Chaos or community? Seeking solutions, not scapegoats for bad economics*. Boston: South End Press.

Solow, R. M. (1994). *Wasting America's future: The Children's Defense Fund report on the costs of child poverty*. Washington, DC: Children's Defense Fund.

Two particularly useful resources that are published yearly are:

Annie E. Casey Foundation. (yearly). *Kids count data book*. Washington, DC: Author.

Children's Defense Fund. (yearly). *The state of America's children*. Washington, DC: Author.

CHAPTER 3

Family Problems of At-Risk Children and Youth

Why are some families like bubbling fountains, filling goblets full for the thirsty people living there, while other fountains fill cups with dark, bitter liquid, and yet other fountains are dead-dry—nothing flows and mugs remain empty? Too many children have either dusty-dry, empty vessels or bitter-brown, sewage-filled ones.

How do we turn on the fountains so that the cold, clear water flows?

J. J. McWhirter

Chapter Outline

Shifting economic, political, and policy trends have created a new and often disturbing environment that directly affects the roots of the problems young people face. Nowhere is this fact more evident than in the family. Because the family is a major influence on individual development and behavior, in this chapter we focus on family issues as they affect at-risk children and adolescents.

Societal Changes Affecting the Family

The American family has undergone major structural and functional changes in recent decades. Indeed, the American family has changed more during the past 30 years than at any other time in history. Striking family demographic transitions are apparent to all. Politicians, scholars, and even the popular press have made much of the so-called revolution in the family. In Chapter 2 we considered the impact of SES and poverty and noted the increasing numbers of single parents and mothers in paid employment. Here we highlight two related trends that influence modern family life: divorce and the decline of extended-family networks.

Divorce

The marked rise in the divorce rate that characterized the late 1960s and 1970s leveled off and (except for teens) actually declined during the 1980s and now remains stable.

Nevertheless, the divorce rate remains high and still affects enormous numbers of people. In 1990, 1,175,000 marriages ended in divorce. If this trend continues, three in five first marriages will be dissolved, and the divorce rate for second and more marriages is likely to be even higher, as it is now (U.S. Bureau of the Census, 1992). Because divorce is more likely in younger marriages, children are involved in approximately two-thirds of all divorces (Arendell, 1995). Twenty-four percent of American children are now being raised in mother-only families (Alan Guttmacher Institute, 1994), and nearly 55% of all African American children and about 33% of Hispanic youngsters live with a single parent (Duany & Pitmann, 1990). Some studies have estimated that the probability that a child will live with only one parent at some time before age 18 is between 40 and 60% (Bumpass, 1984; Norton & Glick, 1986), prompting Dryfoos (1990) to predict that during the 1990s 60% of U.S. children will spend a portion of their childhood in single-parent families. Divorce, in conjunction with out-of-wedlock births and declining marriage and birth rates, has significantly altered the composition of the typical family.

The Erosion of Extended-Family Networks

Not only is a mother or father likely to be absent from the home but aunts and uncles, cousins and grandparents are also less likely to be involved in family life. Grandparents in particular—once part of the family constellation—are no longer available to assist with child care. Now it is estimated that no more than 5% of grandparents see their grandchildren regularly (Hamburg, 1995). Years ago the extended family provided a variety of role models, opportunities to anticipate and vicariously experience problems related to the various stages of life, and individuals available to serve as resources. Today children and their parents have less access to the extended family as they face life crises. The family, once vibrant with life, is now stretched thin. Not infrequently, recreation, spiritual training, and education all take place outside the home. Although the family is not dying, it is certainly undergoing significant transformations.

Divorce and the decline of the extended family do not necessarily result in a reduction of social networks for children and young people. Indeed, the increased complexity of family patterns may actually increase the availability of people who can serve as resources. Consider Lisa, born in 1966. Her father has several children from a previous marriage with whom she interacts when they come for visits. When Lisa was 8 years old, her parents divorced. She lived with her mother but continued to see her father in the summer and on weekends. When Lisa was 13, her mother remarried. Lisa and her stepfather got along well and did many things together. Lisa continued to see her father, although less frequently, as he had now moved to another state and had married a woman with two children. Lisa graduated from high school and entered college. During two of her college years she lived with a man, and soon after graduation she married another man. She and her husband have a son. After several years, Lisa and her husband divorced and she was awarded custody of her son, who continues to see her ex-husband in the summer and on weekends. Three years later Lisa remarried. She and her second husband have two more children. During Lisa's life so far she has lived in nine families either part time or full time.

Lisa's situation is not typical but neither is it unusual. Although the relationships in some of Lisa's families may not have been ideal, in each case there were people she enjoyed doing things with, wanted to continue seeing, and loved. This situation represents a substantial change from the experience of people who grew up several decades ago, when one might have been part of two or three families at the most. Some of these family experiences have the potential of enriching children's lives by providing more adults to serve as role models and by providing a greater variety of experiences. Unfortunately, for many youngsters these changing patterns and variable family experiences produce alienation, a sense of rootlessness, and anomie. The stress and frustration of changing family circumstances can serve to place children and adolescents at risk.

CHANGES WITHIN THE FAMILY

Even in the absence of structural changes arising from evolving societal conditions, the family changes over time. Young people get married and have children; their children become adolescents, then young adults, and get married themselves. All of these changes necessitate shifts in the relationships of family members. At each stage the family has specific developmental tasks to accomplish, which lay the foundations for later stages.

The Family Life Cycle

The family life cycle is the name given to stages that a family goes through in its developmental history (Carter & McGoldrick, 1989). The family group begins with each newly married couple even though the couple continues to be part of two family groups established earlier: the wife's family of origin and the husband's. The fact that a new family cycle begins with each new marriage does not cut short the cycles of the families of origin.

Duvall and Miller (1985) proposed an eight-stage model of the traditional family life cycle that is appropriate for many families because most progress through certain predictable marker events or phases (such as marriage, the birth of the first child, the onset of adolescence, and so forth). Each stage is determined by the age of the oldest child, and each stage has its own set of tasks for the family to complete before it moves to the next stage. Carter and McGoldrick (1989) have outlined sets of developmental tasks for nontraditional blended families and single-parent families. They also add an initial stage—the unattached young adult—to the family life cycle. The inability of the family to negotiate developmental tasks at any of the stages contributes to and exacerbates the problems of many children and young people. Teachers, counselors, and psychologists need to be aware of the developmental tasks and help the family to develop the necessary skills to meet them. The following description of each of the stages draws upon the work of Duvall and Miller (1985), Carter and McGoldrick (1989), and Norton (1994):

Unattached young adult stage. The young adult must accomplish several developmental tasks. The young person must develop responsible habits and become established in a work environment. In addition, it is important that the young adult establish close peer relationships and begin to separate from the family of origin through an ongoing process of differentiation.

Establishment stage (married, no children). This stage begins with marriage. The young adult continues to break away from the family of origin. The major task for the couple at this stage is to establish their identity as a new unit. Making rules, defining roles within the marriage, and realigning relationships with friends and family are important components.

New parent stage (infant to 3 years). When the husband and wife become parents, their duties and roles change. Their relationship as a couple must shift to accommodate the infant.

Preschool stage (oldest child 3 to 6 years). Parents continue to develop their work and family roles. The major developmental task at this stage is learning and applying effective parenting skills to help the children learn how to interact positively with others.

School-age stage (oldest child 6 to 12 years). The family becomes more involved with community and school activities as the children grow and develop. Members of the family fulfill assigned roles and must learn to renegotiate boundaries to include the children's peer group.

Teenage stage (oldest child 13 to 20 years). The married couple is required to deal with individual, work, and marital issues along with the developmental tasks of their children and their own aging parents. Adolescents, who are going through the individual developmental task of establishing their own identities and independence, challenge the boundaries and rules of the family system.

Launching stage (departure of children). Children and parents must separate emotionally and physically from one another. The primary task of the family at this point is to let go. Other tasks are reestablishment of the marital system as a dyad and negotiation of adult relationships between the parents and the children. Many families must cope with the death of a grandparent.

Two final stages, the post parental middle years and the aging family, are equally important in the family life cycle, but they do not bear directly on our subject so we will not describe them here.

Cultural variations.   Cultural variations influence the nature of the tasks within each stage. In some cultural groups, for example, young people are expected to leave home at age 18 or soon thereafter, whereas other groups expect young adults to live with their parents until they marry. In any assessment of a family's passage through the stages and the completion of tasks, the cultural norms of the family must be explored.

Helping professionals should view cultural, ethnic, and unique aspects of families' backgrounds as resources and strengths that can be fostered and supported for the families' benefit. This appreciation of diversity is critical. Learning about cross-cultural practices is an essential, ongoing process synonymous with professionalism, whether the helper is a teacher, a counselor, or a psychologist (Sandau-Beckler, Salcido, & Ronnau, 1993).

Normal crises.   Families undergo such profound changes as they move from one stage to another that the transitions present all families with normal family developmental crises. Most families negotiate these transitions adequately, but some families have such difficulty with the transitions between stages that they compromise the well-being of their children. Such families are dysfunctional. To understand dysfunctional families, we have to view the family as a system.

The Family System

A system is a set of connected components that interact dynamically to maintain a balance or state of equilibrium. Each element is dependent on the state of functioning of each other element with which it has a relationship. The family is a natural system consisting of connected components (family members) who are organized around various interactional functions. Among those functions are giving and receiving affection, child rearing, and the division of labor.

As they live together from day to day, families develop systematic patterns of behavior that serve to maintain the system in a state of equilibrium. Each family member contributes to this equilibrium or homeostatic balance. Homeostasis is represented by a particular family's ongoing behaviors, habits, expectations, and communication patterns.

To see the family as a homeostatic system, consider a family in which the husband/father is an alcoholic. He serves as a scapegoat and maintains the system by receiving all the blame for the family's problems. Rather than accept the blame, he projects it onto his spouse. She internalizes the blame and tries to improve her own behavior and that of the children rather than confront the fact of his drinking. One child may try to keep the parents from fighting by diverting their attention to his or her own problems through drug use, pregnancy, or truancy. Another child may attempt to dissipate tension by being the family clown. These roles are not conscious attempts to keep the family in balance, however precarious it may be, but are patterns maintained at an unconscious level, in a manner that is sometimes blatantly obvious and sometimes extremely subtle. When the patterns of behavior that maintain homeostasis are rigid and unyielding, the family system is considered "closed."

A closed system is dysfunctional because it is isolated from the environment, is less receptive to external stimuli, and is unresponsive to change. Because of its impermeable boundaries and nonreceptiveness to change, a closed family system tends to move toward increasing disorder. Open systems, by contrast, interact with the environment and are capable of both adaptation and flexibility. Adaptation depends on maintaining enough stability to permit the family members to develop coherent, separate identities, as they make the necessary accommodations to environmental changes.

Closed system families contribute a disproportionate share of troubled children and youth to society. In other words, children and adolescents are at risk for problem behaviors when they live in a closed family system. Closed family systems typically demonstrate two major types of problems: detachment and enmeshment.

Detachment.   In a detached family individual members function separately and autonomously, with little family interdependence. When one family member faces a time of stress, the family hardly seems to notice or respond at all. Detached families tend to be unresponsive because each member is isolated within the system. In such families, the boundaries are so rigid that only a high level of individual stress will activate support from other family members. The family members cannot get their social and emotional needs met within the family, nor do they learn appropriate ways to meet the needs of others. It is relatively pointless for such a family to remain together, yet they often do so because they seem to have no alternatives. Unfortunately, detached families produce youngsters who form inadequate or dysfunctional relationships outside the family because they have not learned how to have good relationships within the family. Obviously, such people are at risk for a variety of problem behaviors.

Enmeshment.   Enmeshed families demonstrate such intensity and closeness in family interactions that the members are overinvolved and overconcerned with each other's lives. In enmeshed families, the children experience a distorted sense of involvement, attachment, and belonging within the family, and fail to develop a secure sense of individuality, separateness, and autonomy. When a member of an enmeshed family encounters a stressful situation, the family is likely to respond by rescuing rather than teaching constructive problem solving. Subsystem boundaries are weak, easily crossed, and poorly differentiated—children may act like parents, and parental control may be ineffective. The young person's distorted sense of belonging and attachment interferes with the capacity to negotiate developmental tasks successfully. For example, a child may remain isolated from classmates and repeatedly feign illness so as not to "threaten" the mother-child relationship.

The Carter family demonstrates the difficulties of negotiating a transition point in the family life cycle and gives us insight into one kind of dysfunctional family. As you read this case study, take a few minutes to reflect on the family life cycle, the family as a social system, and issues of detachment and enmeshment.

The Carter family is at the transition point leading to the teenage stage of the family life cycle. Jason's underlying problems are intensifying precisely because adolescents begin to challenge the rules and boundaries of the family system as they seek to establish their own identities. We may surmise that at the same time that the family is struggling to negotiate this transition, both Mr. and Mrs. Carter are attempting to cope with their own midlife crises.

The Carters illustrate not only the family life cycle but the family as a social system. The presenting problem—behavior difficulties at school—is an extension of Jason's role in his family. His "angelic" younger sister supports this role; his angry and depressed mother maintains it; and his isolated father covertly encourages it. Everyone in the family maintains the homeostasis. Even though each of them is in some pain, the sense of facing the unknown if Jason's position should change is more anxiety-provoking than the status quo. In other words, although Jason is the catalyst that prompts the Carters to seek an outside helper, the underlying causes of his behavior are inherent within the family's interaction. Each family member maintains equilibrium in the closed circle of the family because each is vulnerable.

Christie is vulnerable because she builds her self-esteem on being the model child. If things shift, she may become the bad one—the "devil" in the family. She appears to be enmeshed in the family system. Mrs. Carter is vulnerable because if she loses the reasons for her depression she may need to be more guilty and self-punitive to maintain her depression. Jason provides her with a scapegoat on which to vent her emotions. Without her depression, Lois would have to develop a new relationship with both Christie and her husband, and any change appears threatening. Doug Carter might have to confront directly his anger and resentment toward his wife. He might also have to redefine Christie's role and change his behavior toward Jason. Jason is vulnerable because if his role changes he might have to improve in school and he will have fewer excuses for acting out. These shifts in perception, roles, and behavior are inevitably threatening.

Each family member has a vested interest in maintaining his or her current functioning. This family is particularly disturbed. The system maintains itself by avoiding new communication and new role definitions despite family counseling.

CASE STUDY

The Carter family

The Carter family came to our attention after Jason, a thin, dark, and intense 13-year-old, got into a particularly vicious fight. The other family members were Jason's parents, Doug and Lois Carter, both of whom were European American, and his 10-year-old sister, Christie. Jason was referred by his teacher because of fighting and other behavioral difficulties. He frequently disrupted his classes by harassing and fighting other children and by talking back to teachers. **His short attention span and apparent inability to sit still were** the focus of a subsequent neurological examination, but no neurological impairment was discovered. Next Jason underwent an evaluation at school, consisting of a standard social history and an intake interview.

The findings suggested that poor family communication and ineffective discipline might be the sources of Jason's problem behavior. On the basis of this information, family therapy was strongly recommended. Referral to the neurological clinic, contact with school personnel, the social history, and the intake interview were all accomplished by a school social worker assigned to the case. She was also responsible for the family casework and referred Jason and his family to a mental health clinic that provided individual and family therapy.

Lois Carter, a chronically depressed woman, was torn by guilt over her perceived failure to rear a youngster who could function adequately in the neighborhood and in school. She also seemed to have considerable unspoken anger, which was frequently directed at Jason. Doug Carter, an engineer, was also a caldron of unexpressed anger. Emotionally locked out by his wife's depression, he seemed to resent Jason and continually put the child in a double bind by subtly sending the message that his acting out was just a case of "boys will be boys" and at the same time reprimanding him for his behavior. He seemed unwilling or unable to follow through with punishment. In part, this behavior was an acting out of his own angry feelings toward his wife.

Lois Carter was the second daughter in her family of origin. She described her parents, who lived close to the Carters, in ambivalent terms. Her father was a chronic drinker, and he physically and emotionally abused his wife and children. He suffered brain damage as a result of drinking and had mellowed considerably in recent years. Lois's mother was a

(continued)

The Carter family (continued)

passive-aggressive woman who turned to religion for comfort in her later years. Lois had an older sister who had twice married and divorced. After repeated attempts, the sister attained a college degree and now worked as an elementary school teacher. Lois's two brothers expressed the family dysfunction more obviously. The youngest brother had committed suicide several years earlier. The other brother continued to live with his parents. At 30 he was unemployed and unmarried and existed on a small payment for service-connected emotional disability.

Doug Carter was the older of two brothers. His father, a bookkeeper for a small manufacturing firm, was a harsh, critical, and sarcastic parent. His mother was a pleasant though ineffectual woman who "adored" Doug's younger brother. A paternal grandmother, now deceased, lived in the home while Doug was growing up, and she tended to favor him. Doug and his brother had been very competitive as children and now had little or no contact. Doug's parents resided in another state and contact with them was infrequent.

Both Jason and Christie Carter had been adopted as infants. Jason was considered the identified problem (patient), and Christie was regarded as a perfect little angel.

A counselor saw the family weekly for therapy that focused on their style of communication. During the first six sessions, the family discussed setting limits and the need for more direct communication. They reached an impasse, however, because the family members refused to listen to one another. Jason frequently pointed out, for instance, that his sister instigated many situations by teasing him. Doug and Lois refused to acknowledge that Christie could possibly do such a thing and reprimanded Jason for not listening to them and for trying to get his sister in trouble. Christie sat quietly and primly, in silent agreement with her parents. At the end of six sessions, the counselor felt that she was making little headway in helping the parents listen to Jason or to each other. Christie indicated little willingness to modify her secure position in the family structure. Jason continued to disrupt his classes and behave outrageously at school, in the neighborhood, and at home.

FAMILY PROBLEMS AND PROBLEM FAMILIES

A focus on societal change, stages and transitions in the family life cycle, and the family as a system helps us identify stressors that may contribute to problems for young people. Specific family problems also contribute to the development of at-risk behaviors. Let us examine some family situations that may place all family members, but especially the children, under moderate to extreme stress, and thus may put them at risk.

Stressed Families

As we saw in Chapter 2, single-parent and poor families experience considerable stress. Two other kinds of families that are subject to stress are blended families and latchkey families. All members of these families, especially the children, confront particularly stressful circumstances.

Blended families.   Blended families, sometimes called reconstituted families and historically known as stepparent families, are families in which one or both of the remarried partners bring children into the relationship. Because divorce and remarriage are increasingly common, blended families are becoming more and more numerous. Children in such families face an unfamiliar network of relationships, particularly with an adult with whom they have not fallen in love. They undoubtedly suffer some degree of discomfort. These children may have few resources to draw on in their attempts to cope with a new parent, new grandparents, possible new stepsiblings, and a new family lifestyle (Holmes, 1995). As the new couple shape and ritualize their lives, the young people face a whole new set of expectations, procedures, and interactions. Further, these children are struggling to adjust to their new conditions while the most significant people in their lives, their parents, are themselves adjusting to this new situation and are less available to them.

These stressors may be viewed in the context of the family life cycle. The newlyweds must negotiate the establishment stage—a complex task in itself—at the same time that they must adopt a satisfactory and consistent system of parenting and disciplining the children in their household. The needs and tasks of the children are unlikely to coincide with those of the parents. Obviously, this situation causes problems and stresses and may be a major factor in the fragility of second marriages, which are more likely than first marriages to end in divorce.

Latchkey families.   Latchkey families are those in which the parents are unavailable to the children before or after school and on school holidays. Because 65% of mothers of school-age children are currently in the work force, 2 to 7 million children are latchkey children (Long, 1988). According to one study (National Research Council, 1990), 25% of 11- to 13-year-olds and 5% of 5- to 7-year-olds take care of themselves. Although the latchkey experience can be positive—it can help children learn to be independent and responsible more quickly—many latchkey children suffer from fear, boredom, and loneliness. As Zigler and Lang (1991) explain, latchkey children pose risks to themselves and to their community. They may feel alienation and resentment as a result of their isolation. They are more susceptible to accidents and crime than are other children. They often adapt poorly in school and in society, and they may engage in acts of vandalism or delinquency because of lack of supervision.

Dysfunctional Families

All dysfunctional families subject children to stresses that may lead to at-risk behavior. Although there are many types of dysfunction within families, substance abuse by the adult caretaker, spousal violence, child abuse or neglect, and parental psychopathology are among those most likely to result in problems for youngsters. Most adults in such families were themselves abused as children or cared for by alcoholic or psychopathological parents. Now they perpetuate the same problems in their children.

Substance-abusing families.   Children of alcoholic (or drug-abusing) parents are at risk for neglect and abuse. But even without overt neglect or abuse, parental alcoholism inflicts emotional damage on the children. Such children may be predisposed to become alcoholic themselves or to enter into relationships with alcoholics. Children from these families are at high risk for emotional and social adjustment problems, including hyperactivity, relationship difficulties, aggression, depression, school absenteeism, and drug abuse (Watkins & Durant, 1996). The expanding literature on adult children of alcoholics documents the comprehensive, long-term impact that substance-abusing parents have on their children. The toll that these families exact on our society is enormous.

Violent families.   The degree of violence between spouses is strongly correlated with the severity of children's problems. Of course, violence signals general marital discord, which is also associated with problematic behavior in children. Even when the child is not a direct target of family violence, exposure to adults who verbally abuse each other, who break and throw things, and who are not in control of their explosive anger can have long-lasting repercussions (Fincham, 1994; Fincham, Grych, & Osborn, 1994; Fincham & Osborn, 1993). The psychological effect of family violence on the development of a child is wholly negative, whether the violence is experienced or only witnessed. It can destroy the child's self-esteem and confidence (Straus, 1994). Such children are more vulnerable to stress disorders and other psychological disturbances that impede development. Violence also begets more violence. As the level of violence in the family increases, so too increases the likelihood that the child will grow up to engage in violent and abusive behavior as well (American Psychological Association, 1996).

Child-abusing families.   Child abuse occurs in many forms: physical violence, verbal and emotional abuse, neglect, and sexual abuse. Physical violence is any physically harmful action against a child, from hair-pulling and slapping to beating. Verbal and emotional abuse occur when children are subjected to harsh criticism and ridicule, withholding of affection, irrational punishment, and inconsistent expectations. Neglect occurs when a parent fails to safeguard the health, well-being, and safety of the child. Children who are not fed and bathed regularly, who are left unattended, or who are consistently ignored by their caretakers are victims of neglect. Child sexual abuse is any form of sexual behavior with a child, and includes molestation, incest, and rape. Almost all children who grow up in such families find themselves at risk for future problems. For example, the positive correlation between various forms of child abuse and teenage pregnancy is well documented in clinical intervention programs for pregnant teenagers (Boyer & Fine, 1992). Two-thirds of the adolescent mothers surveyed by Boyer and Fine had been sexually molested or abused. The researchers suggested that the high rate of maltreatment inflicted by these young mothers on their own children was as likely to be associated with the stress of their abuse histories as it was with the immaturity associated with their young age (Boyer & Fine, 1992).

Parental psychopathology families.   Many children and adolescents are at risk because of parental psychopathology. Schizophrenia, bipolar disorders, and depression in adult caretakers seem to be particularly debilitating to young people (Goodman, Adamson, Riniti, & Cole, 1994; Radke-Yarrow, Nottelmann, Belmont, & Welsh, 1993). Usually the family is characterized by poor marital adjustment, a lack of warmth and support, and a low level of solidarity between the parents. The parent's mental illness contributes to a reciprocal pattern of disturbed parent-child interaction that leads to cognitive, emotional, and social development problems in the child. Interpersonal and school adjustment problems often emerge during middle childhood and adolescence. Teenagers in these families frequently have poor emotional and behavioral control. They may become easily upset, may disturb the class with unusual behavior, and may be discipline problems. These young people are at risk both for possible psychopathology themselves and for the types of at-risk behaviors we discuss in Part II of this book.

In reality, the various types of dysfunctional families often overlap. Battering, for example, is closely associated with alcohol abuse (60% of batterers have been found to be alcohol abusers) and drug abuse (32%); 22% of batterers have been found to abuse both alcohol and drugs (L. E. A. Walker, 1996). Violence between spouses is often accompanied by violence toward the children. Parental alcohol and drug use are often associated with the neglect or abuse of children (L. E. A. Walker, 1996). Individual psychopathology may be present in any of these situations. Alcoholic fathers are eight times more likely and alcoholic mothers three times more likely to abuse or neglect their children than parents who are nonalcoholic (American Psychological Association, 1996).

When a child or adolescent exhibits at-risk behavior, it is important to consider the family in which the individual is being raised. The behavior of concern may be a reasonable—even if disturbing or dangerous—response to the stress of living in a dysfunctional family. The problems of the parents are sad and distressing; their effects on the children are tragic. Parental problems of this nature inevitably affect the parents' child-rearing practices.

VULNERABLE AND UNDERSERVED FAMILIES

Ethnic Minority Families

Family life cycle and family system theory are useful constructs in understanding family dynamics. Unfortunately, they also reflect an inherent weakness that permeates many of the theories that guide our work; namely, they are most reflective of the values of the European American, dominant culture. These theories may be useful in understanding and helping ethnic minority families, but most of the time the framework must be adapted to cultural variations that are "normal" for a specific ethnic minority group. The helper's sensitivity to diversity is critical.

A specific example of this problem is the concept of enmeshment. What may well be enmeshment to a European American teacher or counselor adhering to dominant culture values of independence, competition, and individualism may be a reflection of collective sharing and interdependent loyalty to the ethnic minority family. We must be cautious in relying on stereotypes to guide us; the minority family often relies on a larger base of support than that portrayed by our typical nuclear family model. A brief review of a sample of minority groups illustrates the importance of other community and family members.

Professionals need to be aware of the negative stereotypes of the African American family and conduct their interaction with a particular family with a commitment to seeking information about its actual functioning and structure. Do not automatically assume that an African American child comes from a fatherless home. Equally important, many children who live in single-parent families belong to some variation of an extended family. Arnold (1995) reports that the majority of African American mothers in her study have a large and supportive social network of family and friends. The mean number of social contacts was 15.6 for single women and 18.1 for married women. Further, the church provides a rich network of support for many African American families. These relationships suggest family and community strengths and signal the presence of positive role models for children in these families.

Native American families often have an active kinship system that includes not only parents and children but uncles, aunts, cousins, and grandparents. This inclusion of multiple households within the kinship system often is broadened to incorporate unrelated individuals. Indeed, many American Indian groups have formal rituals to induct significant individuals into the family system.

Asian American families often have a close-knit hierarchical family structure with particular authority being vested in the father and elders. Asian American relatives are frequently available to participate in family life and in family decisions. Recent migrations from Southeast Asia continue to emphasize that community relationships are extremely important in many Asian American groups.

For traditional Hispanic families, the family structure is extended by formalized kinship relationships to the godparents. Loyalty to the family and to the extended family often takes priority over other social institutions.

We recognize that there are unique and important cultural considerations in European American subgroups as well and that there are large within-group differences for any ethnic minority population. We caution you to remember that the theories presented here represent only a "starting point" for understanding a particular family, child, or adolescent.

Families of Gay and Lesbian Youth

For many gay and lesbian youth, family life is not a very safe life. Violence against gay male and lesbian female adolescents is not uncommon in the home and is often perpetuated by family members. Significant numbers of lesbian and gay young people report that they have been verbally and physically assaulted (Rotheram-Borus, Rosario, & Koppman, 1991). After being discovered as gay or coming out to their families, many youth are mistreated and rejected and become the focus of the family's dysfunction. Relationships with fathers are particularly strained. D'Augelli (1991) found that youth feared retribution more from fathers than from mothers, and relations with the mother were significantly better than with the father (Boxer, Cook, & Herdt, 1991). Indeed, many intensely feared their fathers' reactions to their sexual identity, apparently with good reason. Boxer et al. (1991) discovered that nearly one out of ten gay and lesbian youth who disclosed their sexual orientation to their fathers were forced out of their homes.

This lack of support and acceptance at home leads to other problems. Many gay and lesbian youth run away from home to escape a family situation that is frequently chaotic and where they feel misunderstood, rejected, and unwanted. In one study, many of the young people seeking help from the Los Angeles gay and lesbian community services center were throw-aways (youth thrown out of their homes by parents) or runaways who had arguments and fights with their parents (Brownsworth, 1992). Obviously, young people on the streets are not attending school. Many are using alcohol and drugs. Many become prostitutes to survive, with the money helping them to become independent from their families. Half of them have been treated for at least one sexually transmitted disease, and almost all were at high risk for HIV infection (Savin-Williams, 1994).

CHILD-REARING PRACTICES

Family child-rearing practices inevitably influence young people. As we have seen, the parent-child relationship has great influence on the child's social and emotional development, the kind of discipline used, and the home atmosphere. An understanding of the variety of family patterns and child-rearing practices helps teachers, counselors, and other helping professionals to understand at-risk youngsters and may point them toward ways to help these children and adolescents.

In the last decades scientific knowledge about the effects of various combinations of parental behaviors on young people's behavior has progressed greatly—or minimally, depending on one's perspective. From the viewpoint of history, the increase in systematic knowledge has been substantial. From the viewpoint of teachers and counselors who address the complex and seemingly impossible problems of troubled youth on a daily basis, the gains seem trivial. Nevertheless, child-rearing practices and their effects are so important that they have become a prime issue in efforts to solve the problems of at-risk youth.

Three Dimensions of Child Rearing

Over the years, theorists and researchers have reached a rather remarkable degree of agreement on the existence of three basic dimensions of child rearing despite the diversity of instruments, methodologies, and samples brought to bear on the subject. Researchers examining the basic factors involved in child rearing have rather consistently found three fundamental bipolar dimensions, although the names assigned to them vary. Early work (W. C. Becker, 1964; Straus, 1964; Thomas, Gecas, Weigert, & Rooney, 1967) has found support in more recent research (Arnold, O'Leary, Wolff, & Acker, 1993; Baumrind, 1995; Carlson, Grossbart, & Stuenkel, 1992; Vickers, 1994), and these dimensions appear to provide an accurate description of parent-child interactions.

The permissiveness-restrictiveness dimension incorporates the constructs of control and power; permissiveness refers to low control and low power in the parents' behaviors, whereas restrictiveness refers to high control and high power. The hostility-warmth dimension ranges from low to high levels of affection. The anxious, emotional involvement-calm detachment continuum ranges from high anxiety to low anxiety and reflects the emotional engagement or connectedness of the parent. These three dimensions of child rearing appear to be relatively independent of each other and provide a key to understanding and helping children, adolescents, and families.

Figure 3.1 illustrates the three dimensions of child rearing in three-dimensional space. Note that the two end points of each dimension represent the extremes of parental behavior. The behavior of most parents tends to fall near the middle rather than at the extremes on most dimensions. That is, a father is not likely to be either completely hostile or overwhelmingly warm; most mothers neither permit nor restrict everything their children want to do. It is parents with either extreme or inconsistent behaviors that place their children at risk.

Parental Inconsistency

The at-risk child's family life is often characterized by parental inconsistency as well as by extreme behaviors. We know that consistent behavior by parents increases the child's ability to predict the environment and leads to more stable behavior patterns. Inconsistency has negative effects on children; however, we are not yet able to say precisely which types of parental inconsistency are most deleterious. Inconsistency may take various forms:

- Certain behaviors are permitted at one time but not at another, unpredictably: when father is present but not mother, or vice versa; because the parent's mood changes; because the parent is present, or because the parent is not present.
- What the child is told to do is inconsistent with what the child sees other family members doing, being rewarded for doing, or being punished for doing or for not doing.
- Patterns of rewards and punishments are inconsistent. The parent punishes a behavior at one time and does nothing the next time, rewards a behavior at one time and punishes it at another, threatens punishment and does not follow through, or promises a reward and does not give it.
- The nature of the consistency the parent does practice varies from parent to parent. One parent may be consistent in the overt goals set for the child but behave in ways that subvert them; another may be so rigidly and literally consistent that the result is ludicrous; another may gradually relax restrictive rules over time as the child approaches adolescence.

Research findings on the effects of parental inconsistency have been limited because of the variations in the forms of inconsistency observed and the difficulty of comparing the effects of inconsistency. Nevertheless, clear evidence of the deleterious effects of inconsistency emerges from the research literature on delinquency. Studies of delinquent behaviors have repeatedly demonstrated a strong connection between inconsistent and erratic discipline (both between parents and within an individual parent) and a youngster's antisocial behavior (Baumrind, 1990, 1995; Patterson, Reid, & Dishion, 1992). A related concern is the unstable home, or a home characterized by overstimulation and capricious discipline of the child. Children may be teased, taunted,

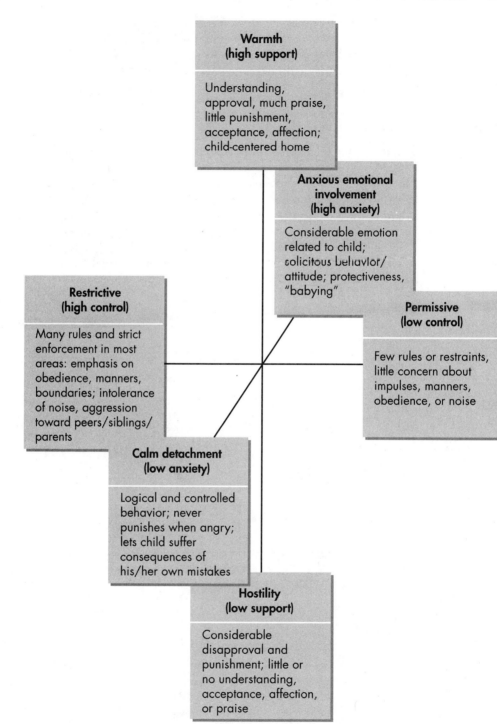

**Warmth
(high support)**

Understanding, approval, much praise, little punishment, acceptance, affection; child-centered home

**Anxious emotional involvement
(high anxiety)**

Considerable emotion related to child; solicitous behavior/ attitude; protectiveness, "babying"

**Restrictive
(high control)**

Many rules and strict enforcement in most areas: emphasis on obedience, manners, boundaries; intolerance of noise, aggression toward peers/siblings/ parents

**Permissive
(low control)**

Few rules or restraints, little concern about impulses, manners, obedience, or noise

**Calm detachment
(low anxiety)**

Logical and controlled behavior; never punishes when angry; lets child suffer consequences of his/her own mistakes

**Hostility
(low support)**

Considerable disapproval and punishment; little or no understanding, acceptance, affection, or praise

FIGURE 3.1   Dimensions of child-rearing practices

and encouraged to play rough, for instance, and then punished for their boisterous behavior. There is a positive relationship between such unstable families and children who lack social responsibility and display a low degree of conscientiousness. Inconsistent discipline apparently contributes to conflict, aggression, and maladjustment in the child (Patterson, De Baryshe, & Ramsey, 1989; Patterson, Reid, & Dishion, 1992).

Clusters of Child-Rearing Behaviors

To illustrate the interrelationships among the three dimensions of child rearing, we have transformed Figure 3.1 into a cubic model. Figure 3.2 depicts the resultant "parenting cube," which is made up of eight sections or clusters of parenting attitudes and behaviors. Sections 2, 4, 6, and 8, on the right, represent degrees of permissive parenting behavior, and sections 1, 3, 5, and 7, on the left, represent degrees of restrictive behavior. Sections 5 to 8, on the back half of the cube, represent anxious, emotional behavior, while the four in front, 1 to 4, represent calm detachment. The four cubes on the top, 1, 2, 5, and 6, reflect a highly supportive, warm parental behavior; the four on the bottom, 3, 4, 7, and 8, reflect hostility or low support.

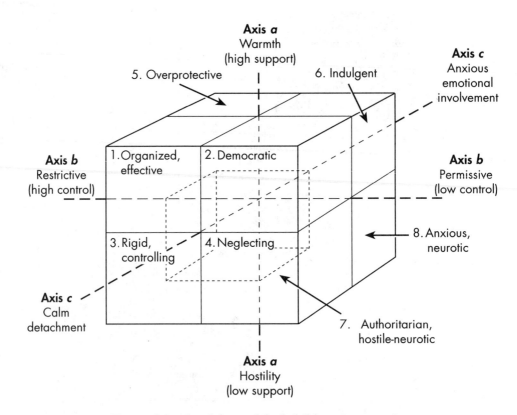

FIGURE 3.2   A cubic model of child-rearing practices

The parenting cube.   Each of the eight sections of the parenting cube represents a cluster of child-rearing practices that incorporate the three dimensions we discussed earlier. The eight sections have been labeled with descriptive phrases that provide a rough generalization of the parenting behavior within sections. Let us consider each one in turn.

Section 1. *Organized, effective behavior* (restrictiveness, warmth, calm detachment). Parents who occupy this extreme position tend to control, shape, and evaluate the behavior of the child according to a high standard of conduct. The parents are positively involved with the child and use rewards, praise, and encouragement to engage the child. They discuss issues, values, and behavior without emotional turmoil.

Section 2. *Democratic behavior* (permissiveness, warmth, calm detachment). Parents who occupy this section usually encourage or permit discussion of family rules and regulations and tolerate a fairly wide range of behavior. The home environment is generally positive; the parents logically discuss the reasons a behavior is unacceptable.

Section 3. *Rigid, controlling behavior* (restrictiveness, hostility, calm detachment). Parents in this category appear to be cruel in their interactions with their children. They generally have a large number of rules and regulations that they enforce in a cold, rigid, sometimes precise manner. The parents sometimes appear to relish punishing their children for misbehavior.

Section 4. *Neglecting behavior* (permissiveness, hostility, calm detachment). These parents allow their children to run free with few or no regulations. In extreme cases the child's basic needs are not met because the parent is so uninvolved or hostile that the child is rejected and neglected.

Section 5. *Overprotective behavior* (restrictiveness, warmth, anxious emotional involvement). Parents in this cell offer consistent support along with many rules and regulations, but they do so with inappropriate emotional involvement and high levels of anxiety. They are often described as a mother bear (or father bear) protecting the young against a hostile environment.

Section 6. *Indulgent behavior* (permissiveness, warmth, anxious emotional involvement). The parents occupying this area can be said to spoil their children. The children have few rules, break those that they do have with few consequences, and tend to control the emotions and behavior of the parents.

Section 7. *Authoritarian, hostile-neurotic behavior* (restrictiveness, hostility, anxious emotional involvement). These parents establish many rules and regulations and rigidly enforce them, not infrequently with much anger, shouting, and physical punishment. Extreme behaviors in this cell may constitute child abuse.

Section 8. *Anxious, neurotic behavior* (permissiveness, hostility, anxious emotional involvement). The parents in this category are also potential child batterers, and in most cases they exert little control over their children and exhibit little care for them. They tend to direct a lot of anger at their children (and others). These parents may do a great deal of ineffectual nagging and emotional battering with little expectation of modifying the child's behavior.

These eight parenting styles affect the development of children. Some styles are more likely to result in at-risk behaviors than others. All have consequences in children's and adolescents' behavior and are thus important to teachers, counselors, and psychologists because they provide insight into students and clients.

Consequences of parenting styles.   These eight clusters of child-rearing styles provide a reasonable model of the complex relationships between parents and their children. But the efficiency of the model is offset by a lack of comprehensiveness: Some patterns of parental behavior are not captured by these clusters. Many factors influence the consequences of these parenting styles in the behavior of children and adolescents. The age of the child, the personality and constitution of the youngster, and the degree and duration of the unhealthy (or healthy) relationship with the parents all influence the effects of parents' styles. Other factors include the child's perception of the interaction, the family setting, and the total life context. The life context includes alleviating conditions and subsequent experiences that may reinforce or correct early damage. A clear, direct causal relationship has not yet been established between dysfunctional family interactions and later psychopathology or antisocial behavior in the child. Likely responses to the various parenting styles, however, can be suggested:

Section 1. *Organized, effective parents = high-achieving conformers.* These youngsters tend to be highly socialized and conforming. Often model children and adolescents, they may experience some internal conflict and may be timid and withdrawn but are rarely a problem to society. Children in this category are high in compliance, dependency, responsibility, leadership, and conscience. They are rarely referred for counseling, although intrapersonal stress sometimes forces them to seek treatment.

Section 2. *Democratic parents = friendly, achieving bohemians.* These youngsters tend to be active, socially outgoing, and friendly. Often they take an aggressive stance on social issues and assume adult role-taking behavior quite early. They are often creative, independent individuals who achieve when and if they decide it is important to do so.

Section 3. *Rigidly controlling parents = delinquent runaways.* These children often exhibit considerable fear and rejection of authority figures. Outwardly conforming, they may develop a repertoire of manipulative behaviors that passively express their aggression. Ultimately the child may explode into highly delinquent behavior or escape by running away.

Section 4 *Neglecting parents = neglected children.* These children are poorly equipped to take on adult roles and may eventually reject society's standards. They may develop self-punitive and self-defeating behaviors, becoming isolated and socially withdrawn.

Section 5. *Overprotective parents = conforming, dependent children.* These youngsters are likely to show high compliance. They follow rules closely and with some anxiety. They may also be submissive, dependent, withdrawn, and timid. They frequently have a difficult time becoming independent.

Section 6. *Indulgent parents = spoiled children.* Children whose parents occupy this section tend to be pampered and spoiled. Often independent and creative, they can be disobedient, impudent, demanding, and "bratty." As they get older, they may develop antisocial, aggressive, or narcissistic behavior and then expect to be protected from the consequences.

Section 7. *Authoritarian, hostile-neurotic parents = abused/aggressive children.* Children in this category are fearful and angry and may eventually vent their rage against society. Often their rebellion takes the form of highly aggressive, delinquent, acting-out behavior. Some of these children run away.

Section 8. *Anxious-neurotic parents = emotionally disturbed children.* Children in this cell tend to be neurotic and disturbed. Often socially withdrawn, they may have poor peer-group attachment characterized by shyness and quarreling. They are likely to be unable to assume adult roles and to have poor self-esteem.

These profiles are based on professional observation, descriptive reports in the literature, and a review of research studies. Although much needs to be done to expand knowledge in this area, some common parenting patterns have been identified with enough certainty to enable us to characterize the parenting styles seen in families. These patterns are crucial to the family environment and to the overall personal development of children.

Parenting styles in the Andrews family.   Let us consider Allie Andrews, whom we met in Chapter 1 (or see Appendix). Recall that she and her stepfather were in open conflict regarding family rules and regulations and that their relationship had deteriorated.

While the Andrews case study does not provide a great deal of information about Burt and Alice's parenting styles, it does tell us enough to permit us to offer some tentative hypotheses about the family interaction and make a preliminary evaluation of the Andrews's parenting styles. This situation is not atypical. Indeed, one of the major problems for teachers and counselors is the difficulty of gaining access to the total picture. Helpers are called upon to teach and counsel, to make judgments and evaluations, to provide treatment plans, and to respond to conflict and pain in the youngster without knowing the full background and thus without completely under-standing the life situation of the individual. Effective and competent counselors, teachers, and others are always working with hunches and tentative hypotheses.

When we review Allie's situation, several issues stand out. First, we find descrip-tions of parental behavior that represent each one of the three dimensions of child-rearing practices. Burt appears to be highly controlling and restricting. He sets firm, perhaps harsh rules and upholds them with punishment. He also seems to provide little warmth and low support for Allie. His apparent dislike for Allie and his punishments reflect a hostile style of interaction. Finally, his emotional involvement is negative and extreme—he is hurt, angry, and fearful, as well as suspicious and mistrustful.

We find less information on the parenting behavior of Allie's mother. We do know that she has assumed the role of the family mediator, however, and that she occasionally has absorbed some of the conflict. Her parenting style appears to differ from her husband's in the area of emotional involvement. And so we come to the second issue: inconsistency. The mother's emotional response may have a calming and placating effect, but Allie may view it as encouragement to act out. This inconsistency may be a strong clue to the dysfunction within the family system.

The third issue that emerges from this case study is the intensity of the father's engagement in his parenting of Allie. On each of the three continuums, his behavior is extreme. That is, he is quite restrictive and provides Allie very low support. He is obviously very emotionally involved with her. This behavior places him in section 7: He is authoritarian and hostile-neurotic. Needless to say, Allie's stepfather is a major negative influence on her at this point. Figure 3.3 summarizes the behaviors that are involved in Allie's parenting.

The parenting issues raised in Allie's case suggest possible intervention strategies. The family system is already under considerable stress and might be amenable to intervention. It is obvious that Allie's stepfather is a major influence in her life. This observation leads to several questions that may eventually need to be addressed. Should

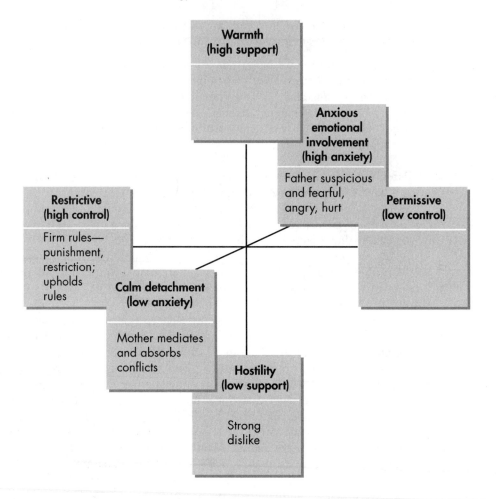

Comments: Allie's father, Burt, operates out of Section 7 of the parenting cube and has become more reactive and violent as Allie has reached adolescence. Mother's parenting style is different (calm detachment), but the case study does not provide enough data to locate her precisely in the cube.

Section 7: Authoritarian, hostile-neurotic parenting

FIGURE 3.3   Parenting behaviors (the case of Allie)

Burt be included in any treatment plans that are developed? Should Burt or the family as a whole be considered for intervention? Should school programs be arranged to provide Allie with a more reasonable limit-setting model? Possible answers to these questions will be provided in later chapters.

CONCLUSION

In this chapter we considered the social changes that affect today's families and the rapid changes that occur within families in response to them. Many families are characterized by detachment, enmeshment, or poor parenting practices, or are dysfunctional in other ways. The Carter family illustrates a fairly common family dysfunction. As families progress through developmental periods, or stages of the family life cycle, some of the interaction patterns that developed early, such as parenting styles, must adapt to the changing needs of the children. When they do not, young people are often at risk for engaging in maladaptive and self-defeating behaviors. The conceptual model of the three dimensions of child rearing is intended to clarify the continuums of parenting styles. The parenting cube can also help counselors, teachers, and health service professionals teach and encourage positive behaviors among children and, as much as possible, within the whole family. As the case studies suggest, ineffective and poor parenting and family interactions have to be identified before steps can be taken to promote effective and positive interactions.

FURTHER READINGS

Arendell, T. (1995). *Fathers and divorce*. Thousand Oaks, CA: Sage.

Clarke-Stewart, K. A., Gruber, C. P., & Fitzgerald, L. M. (1994). *Children at home and in day care*. Hillsdale, NJ: Erlbaum.

Cochran, M., Larner, M., Riley, D., Gunnarsson, L., & Henderson, C. R., Jr. (1990). *Extending families: The social networks of parents and their children*. New York: Cambridge University Press.

Combrinck-Graham, L. (Ed.). (1995). *Children in families at risk: Maintaining the connections*. New York: Guilford.

Dickerson, B. J. (1995). *African American single mothers: Understanding their lives and families*. Thousand Oaks, CA: Sage.

Newman, M. (1994). *Stepfamily realities: How to overcome difficulties and have a happy family*. Oakland, CA: New Harbinger Publications.

Singer, G. H. S., Powers, L. E., & Olson, A. L. (Eds.). (1996). *Redefining family support: Innovations in public-private partnerships*. Baltimore: Brookes.

Watchel, E. F. (1994). *Treating troubled children and their families*. New York: Guilford.

Westman, J. C. (1994). *Licensing parents: Can we prevent child abuse and neglect?* New York: Insight Books/Plenum Press.

School Issues That Relate to At-Risk Children and Youth

If families do not . . .
Then schools must

Provide roots for children . . .
So they stand firm and grow,

Provide wings for children . . .
So they can fly.

Broken roots and crippled wings
Destroy hope.

And hope sees the invisible,
feels the intangible,
and achieves the impossible.

J. J. McWhirter

CHAPTER OUTLINE

In education, the term *at risk* refers primarily to students who are at risk of school failure. Teachers and counselors ask themselves: "How do I keep this teenager in school?" "How do I help this student learn?" "How do I get this child to read?" As we know, *at risk* actually means much more than flunking reading or math, or even dropping out of school. "At risk" is a societal problem that needs society's attention. School problems in the form of school dropouts are linked to many other problems expressed by young people (Beauvais, Chavez, Oetting, Deffenbacher, & Cornell, 1996; Jessor, 1991, 1993). And yet, from an educator's perspective, educational concerns define at-risk issues. The strong correlations between school difficulties and other at-risk problems highlight the pivotal position of the school in efforts to confront and deal with other at-risk-problems. Thus it is critical to examine the educational environment.

THE VALUE OF EDUCATION

Just exactly what does our society think of the learning going on in our schools today? Countless news reports compare the scores of students in the United States and in other countries on tests in geography and spelling, math and science. These reports consistently favor students in other countries. They imply that the learning going on in U.S. schools is somehow not quite up to par. Unfortunately, these reports do not take into account the nature of these results. Does a student's ability to spell reflect his or her ability to think? Does recall of dates, locations, or facts indicate a student's problem-solving skills? Learning theorists tell us the answer to these questions is no. Learning is the act of acquiring knowledge or a skill through instruction or study, yet these comparisons suggest a view of learning that reduces this cognitive act to an isolated and mechanical process (Comer, 1996).

Another indication of the societal value of learning is reflected in some recent statistics. According to the Census Bureau (Information Please Almanac, 1991), the average family income in 1989 in the United States was $32,448, regardless of education level. Yet, according to the National Education Association (World Almanac, 1991), the average teacher's salary for the 1988–89 school year was $31,304. Our schoolteachers, many of whom hold master's degrees, are actually paid less than the national average family income, and they are poorly remunerated relative to other professionals. Teachers' salaries are generally lower than they should be, and low teacher salaries reflect the general value society places on education and learning.

Former Senator Dennis DeConcini (1988) quotes Albert Einstein: "A society that pays its teachers less than its plumbers will have neither good teachers nor good plumbers." He goes on to say:

> We will not attract the brightest and best people into the teaching field until we treat this profession as the priority we believe it to be. We will not attract and keep our teachers until we pay them truly professional salaries so that they can have the standard of living they should be able to earn with their skills and their abilities. (p. 115)

If U.S. schools are expected to combat the societal problems of at-risk students, we must accord the education of our children and youth our highest priority, not only verbally but financially as well.

School funding at the federal level provides further evidence regarding society's views on learning and education. In the final year of Jimmy Carter's administration, Congress created the Department of Education (DOE), elevating the subcabinet agency of the Office of Education to cabinet rank. During the 1980s, the Reagan and Bush administrations insisted that the DOE bring about educational reforms by "leadership and persuasion"—not by new programs or by allocating more funds to existing programs. In fact, during every year of Reagan's administration, educational funding was level or reduced for programs that provided aid for disadvantaged children, bilingual education, and work-incentive child-care initiatives (Carville, 1996). During the decade of the 1980s, educational funding fell from 2.3% to 1.7% of the total federal budget (Shearer, 1990). This decrease in funding has been accompanied by an increasing disparity between rich and poor schools. Kozol (1991) documents the conditions of some American schools and highlights the disparity in school funding. Both Kozol (1991) and Berliner and Biddle (1995) provide convincing evidence that some schools in the same city receive less per pupil and that these differences continue to increase.

It costs about $4200 a year to send a child to school. But it costs $4300 a year to support a family on welfare, and high school dropouts head more than half of those families. Taxpayers spend close to $14,000 a year to keep one prisoner in jail, and 62% of all prison inmates are high school dropouts (Perry, 1988). Any society that claims to be concerned with cost-effectiveness in its overall economy loses by producing nonproductive citizens. Educators know that if schools do not provide a safety net for children, their opportunities for health and happiness are reduced. Yet budgets continue to be cut, and programs are slashed. There is a constant onslaught about how teachers are not doing their jobs and how schools are inadequate and failing.

The most recent round of education bashing began with the publication of *A Nation at Risk* (National Commission on Excellence in Education, 1983), which Berliner and Biddle (1995) suggest was based on a political agenda rather than on evidence or data. The evidence they present to support this position is both thorough and

Box 4.1
New and Improved Education?

For some time American schools have been compared with businesses, and some public schools are actually operated as businesses. The teachers, the principals, and the school district have something to sell; parents and students are consumers. Minnesota currently participates in a system of parental choice (Perry, 1988). This educational voucher system allows parents to choose which school their child will attend. The chosen school then receives tax money to educate that child. Such a system rests on the assumption that schools will improve if they are forced to compete with each other financially. The parents' options may or may not be a positive influence on school reform. However, the attitude that knowledge is a good to be sold, that parents are first and foremost consumers, that educators are to deliver the goods, and that students are an end product—the result of a 12-year-long assembly line—seems to devalue the essence of learning itself. From this perspective, the education/business analogy cannot be carried very far.

Another problem with the Minnesota plan was revealed when a Minnesota school district sent a delegation to the 1990 Music Educators National Convention. The school district presented each person who attended its program with a package of professionally produced promotion material. Fine arts programs are typically the first to be cut when budgets are stretched tight, yet this district had enough funds to prepare and deliver what amounts to a high-cost advertising campaign. One wonders how much of the taxpayers' money will be diverted from educational programs—and from at-risk children and from learning—to advertisement and program promotion intended to attract new consumers.

sound. In *The Manufactured Crisis*, Berliner and Biddle (1995) point out that public schools in the United States have done a marvelous job of educating American children and that children actually know more than earlier generations, compare very favorably to students educated in other countries, and perform better than ever before. However, it is clear that educators are stressed, distressed, and perhaps depressed.

Most teachers work hard, are concerned about children, and try to do a good job of teaching. Teachers *know* that all children need support, care, and nurturing and that with the decline of economic stability, the pressures facing parents, and the fragmentation of neighborhoods and communities, the support and care children receive at school is even more critical. However, for education to succeed in general, and to help at-risk youth in particular, increased financial support is needed. Such expenditures will not be forthcoming unless our society as a whole, both at home and in the larger community, understands the value of learning (Comer, 1996). A more positive attitude about education and about teaching will lead to the development of more effective schools.

RESEARCH ON EFFECTIVE SCHOOLS

Variables in Research on School Effects

Researchers have identified several elements common to effective schools (Good & Brophy, 1994; Linney & Seidman, 1989; Wohlstetter & Smyer, 1994). These can be classified into the general categories of leadership behaviors, academic emphasis, teacher and staff factors, student involvement, community support, and social capital.

Leadership behaviors. Schools deemed effective tend to have autonomous management at the school site. That is, the school staff is able to make many decisions about programs and program implementation without the need to seek the school board's approval. Effective schools also place an emphasis on strong instructional leadership.

Academic emphasis. Effective schools provide a curriculum that emphasizes academics. They recognize academic achievement on a schoolwide basis, and they frequently monitor students' performance.

Teacher and staff factors. Effective schools are characterized by collegial relationships among the staff, encouragement of collaborative planning, and low turnover among the faculty. Further, staff development is provided on a schoolwide basis.

Student involvement. Students at effective schools tend to have a sense of community, a feeling of belongingness. They also are likely to have clear goals. Student discipline at effective schools is fair, clear, and consistent and is not oppressive or punitive.

Community support. The communities in which effective schools are located have high expectations of the schools and their students. Further, district support and supportive parental involvement are evident.

Social capital. Social capital is the network of relationships that surround an individual child and that are important for his or her development. Coleman and Hoffer (1987) contend that one of the major reasons some schools perform significantly better than others is that they are so rich in social capital. The nuclear and extended family, the neighborhood and church community, the social service agency, and community organizations form a supportive enclave of adults who are united around a system of similar beliefs and values about the nature and role of education. This network of relationships is extremely important to all children and to their education. Most school systems are severely constrained today because of the reduction of social capital in society in general.

Definitional Issues in Research on School Effects

Most studies on effective schools measure effectiveness by students' performance on standardized achievement tests, specifically reading and math scores. Unfortunately, this is an extremely narrow view of learning. Other cognitive criteria, such as decision making and critical thinking, are largely ignored (Adams & Hamm, 1994; Good & Brophy, 1994). Glasser (1990) states that "nothing of high quality, including schoolwork, can be measured by standardized, machine-scored tests" (p. 428). From this perspective, standardized tests may only provide a means of measuring low-quality work. Further, to judge school effectiveness by the narrow criterion of scores on standardized tests ignores and devalues high-quality work. Instruction is frequently test-driven, and learning for the sake of fostering and satisfying curiosity may be lost. A test-driven curriculum fails to meet the needs of at-risk youth and of society as a whole.

With regard to the at-risk population, results of research on school effects must be viewed with caution. For example, schools with higher dropout rates potentially have higher performance averages than do schools that retain their lower scoring students longer. Consequently, the school's effectiveness score rises. Alternative indices, such as students' involvement in the community, attendance rates, the incidence of vandalism and violence, and dropout rates are seldom used in school effects research (Aubrey, 1988), but these indices may be more relevant to the community. One aspect of education that is linked more to the success of the student than to the school is school culture (Grant, 1982). School culture focuses on aspects of education more directly relevant to at-risk youth. Before turning to this notion, let us consider another family whose young people are at risk, as presented in the Case Study on pages 66–68.

SCHOOL CULTURE

Every social organization has its unique culture, and schools are no exception. School culture is determined by student involvement, teacher factors, community support, curricular focus, and educational leadership—factors that also define effective schools. A culture provides its members with two things. First, it establishes a set of rules, expectations, and norms for members. Ramona's school, for example, stresses an expectation of high test scores. Carlos's teachers encourage an English-only norm. In Lidia's school, retaining students who do poorly is the rule. Essentially, school culture provides an informal understanding of the way things are done. Second, culture enhances self-esteem through shared values, beliefs, rituals, and ceremonies. Students, faculty, and staff who take pride in their school culture are likely to work more effectively than those who do not (Haberman, 1993). Thus Ramona's limited social contacts are the result of the fact that she does not share her peers' values; many of Carlos's teachers share negative views of bilingual education; Lidia's feelings of stupidity are due in part to her exclusion from her school's culture.

The culture of a school can be divided into two distinct portions: student climate and teacher/staff climate. The quality of the climate, or the psychosocial environment the students experience in the classroom, has been shown by B. J. Fraser (1994) to be a strong predictor of learning outcomes.

Student Climate

Several aspects of student climate relate directly to children and youth at risk. First, self-concept and self-esteem are critical for the at-risk student (Meggert, 1996; Mruk, 1995). Many students who are at risk for school failure know early that somehow they are different from—less acceptable and less accepted than—other students. Lidia Diaz is one such student. Consistent grouping of students by ability heightens such self-perceptions. Who of us did not know by the second grade which children were good readers and which children were not? More important, the expectations of students depend on the group they are in. Students who succeed in school have both high

The Diaz family

Enrique Diaz brought his wife, Alicia, and his three children to the United States two years ago. Enrique was forced to flee El Salvador when his membership in a small labor union was revealed to the government authorities. United States immigration regulations have caused the family considerable distress. A local church group that has joined the Sanctuary movement has provided them with legal support, however, and they have been allowed to remain in the United States. The threat of deportation continues to worry them, especially because Enrique believes that if the family returns to El Salvador their lives will be in danger.

The Sanctuary group was also helpful in finding employment for Enrique as a day laborer for a company that does maintenance work on swimming pools. Alicia works as a motel maid. Their joint income allows them to rent a small house, but their living standard is at best modest.

Both parents express concern about their children because family life is curtailed by the long hours the parents spend at work. They are especially concerned about their children's educational problems. Neither parent had much education, and they desperately want their children to have a better life. They view education as a necessary step toward that goal. Because their knowledge of English is rudimentary, however, communication with the school has been particularly difficult. For the last two years they have experienced insecurity and frustration with the school system.

Upon entering school, Ramona Diaz, the eldest child, was placed in an ESL (English as a second language) program in the local high school. Ramona was 16 when her family moved to the United States. Now, at 18, she is older than the majority of her classmates. Also, because she has been spending most of the school day in the ESL classroom learning to read, write, and speak English, she is behind most of her classmates in the other subjects she is currently taking. Ramona has been working at ABC Burgers for the past year. Although this job brings in some extra income for the family, it leaves her little time to catch up with her classmates academically. Ramona has little time to socialize, has few friends, and often feels left out of school activities. Her only real social group consists of other students in her ESL class. The other kids in the school tend to look on her and her ESL classmates as if they are stupid, and she often feels they are right.

(continued)

The Diaz family *(continued)*

This year is the first year that Ramona has not been exempted from the national standardized test, and the prospect has placed great stress on her. Not only will her performance be compared with that of native English speakers who are at least two years ahead of her in all subjects, but the scores of the test are made public. The high school principal believes that a competitive climate will encourage the students to do better on the test, so he has announced that when the results arrive all scores will be posted by homeroom class. Ramona's ESL teacher disapproves of such a practice. He doesn't believe a standardized test truly measures the knowledge his students have acquired. He also thinks this comparison with native English speakers will do more harm than good to a group of students who already have low self-esteem. The principal, however, maintains that his own school's scores will be compared with those of other district schools and that "we've got to give these kids some kind of incentive to do well on this test." One administrator even hinted to Ramona's teacher that encouraging the ESL students to stay at home on the day of the test might not be a bad idea.

Ramona's brother, Carlos, is in the seventh grade. An only son, he has had a solid relationship with his parents, particularly his father. Carlos, too, has had language enrichment at school. For the last two years he has been in a bilingual classroom. Carlos has generally done well in his schoolwork, but he is not a model student. He has often had trouble with his peers and at times gotten into fights on the playground. Since he has moved into junior high school, his social problems have decreased somewhat. He has several teachers now, and the classes are larger than those in the primary school. He has begun to make friends, although with so many classmates the task has been difficult.

Because of Ramona's job at ABC Burgers, Carlos has the responsibility of watching his little sister after school, and he has had difficulty completing school assignments. His after-school activities now include cleaning the house and helping to prepare dinner in addition to baby-sitting, so he has only a limited amount of time to complete the homework assigned by his five teachers. Some nights he works on every subject for at least a short time, but on other nights he is able to complete an assignment for only one of his classes. At the time they entered counseling, Carlos was behind in every class. Some of his teachers seem to think he is lazy, contrary, and

(continued)

CASE STUDY

The Diaz family *(continued)*

unresponsive. Many of them have little respect for the bilingual program. They seem to think Carlos should be able to function competently in English after two years in this country. When they look at the dwindling funds they are allotted for materials, when they consider their relatively meager paychecks, and when they see how Carlos has been encouraged to use his first language as a crutch in school, they may wonder if the money for such programs might be better spent.

Carlos's social studies teacher, Ms. Bassett, has taken a particular interest in him. At first, she found him inattentive in class and unresponsive to her questions, and she assumed this behavior was the result of the language barrier. After observing his verbal ability in the cafeteria, however, she changed her mind and spoke with Carlos's bilingual teacher. He suggested she give Carlos a more active role in his own education: find ways to give him the responsibility for learning, provide a means for Carlos to monitor his own progress, and generally encourage him to be more active in learning. The school counselor, too, was helpful. She suggested that cooperative learning groups might be especially beneficial to Carlos, not only academically but as a means to help Carlos develop better peer relationships. Ms. Bassett is currently struggling with ways to modify her teaching style in a school that bases evaluations of her teaching on direct instruction, a method that typically works well for social studies recitation classes but fails to allow students to take an active role in learning.

Lidia Diaz is in kindergarten this year. Last year she participated in Head Start, which greatly aided her language skills and helped prepare her for kindergarten. In spite of this advantage, she is progressing quite slowly. She is one of 30 kindergartners in the classroom. Many of her classmates attended private preschools and can already read. To deal with the large number of students in her class, Lidia's teacher groups the children according to their ability in reading and arithmetic. Lidia is in the lowest group in both subjects. Like her older sister, Lidia often feels stupid. Lidia's teacher believes that Lidia has the potential for school success and wishes she could spend more time with her. Lidia's elementary school has a retention policy for kindergarten students who do not make certain gains in achievement. In spite of her teacher's belief in her abilities, Lidia fits the criteria for the district retention policy, and if things do not improve, she will probably be kept back next year.

expectations of themselves and a strong, positive sense of belonging to the school community. Students who are at risk for school failure are often placed in the lowest ability groups and excluded from the academic success community. Exclusion from the school community limits the potentially positive effects of school culture on students at risk for failure.

Another aspect of student climate that bears upon at-risk youth is a student's ability to make healthy choices among alternatives (Charney & Clayton, 1994). Behaviors such as acting out in class, fighting or arguing with peers and adults, and neglecting to turn in homework all interfere with learning and are related to school failure (Knitzer, Steinberg, & Fleisch, 1990; Walker, Colvin, & Ramsey, 1995). Carlos's earlier playground fights demonstrate how poor decision making among students can hinder positive student climate. Some researchers have found that efforts to improve students' problem-solving and decision-making skills have a positive effect on the at-risk population (Beyth-Marom, Fischhoff, Jacobs, & Furby, 1989; and see Chapter 12). Some schools have reported a marked reduction in disruptive behaviors after students have been taught to mediate disputes on their own. Also, students who are given leadership opportunities exercise decision-making skills and learn the importance of self-control. The ability of students to solve their own problems and peacefully settle disputes directly and positively affects student climate. School mediation programs (discussed in Chapter 13) have been especially helpful in this regard (Lane & McWhirter, 1992, 1996).

Third, the student climate of a school is affected by students' ability to monitor their own behavior and progress (Shapiro & Cole, 1994). Most learning research focuses on methods and procedures that increase desired student behaviors, and current studies center on things teachers and other school personnel can do to enhance learning. Research that centers on what teachers can do to help young people learn, however, often ignores the ways teachers can help young people help themselves. At-risk youth are capable, thinking people who are able to see and monitor their own progress. They need to be taught how to do so.

A final aspect of school climate that relates to youth at risk is an attitude of shared responsibility for learning (Cobb, 1994; Driver, Asoko, Leach, Mortimer, & Scott, 1994; Good & Brophy, 1994). Students, along with their teachers, are responsible for learning. Fenstermacher (1986) addresses this issue in the context of what he terms "ontological dependence"; that is, the existence of one concept is dependent on the existence of another. If a person were to run around a track for a while, for example, one might say she was "running"; but if she were running around a track in the company of others who were trying to beat her, or trying to "win," then one would conclude that she was "racing." Regardless of whether she ever wins, without the notion of "winning" there can be no concept of "racing," and whatever it is people do on a track cannot be called "racing."

A similar relationship exists between learning and teaching. The concept of teaching is dependent on the concept of learning, but the reverse relationship is not true. That is, learning can take place without teaching (while one reads silently, for instance). In addition, although learning often occurs after teaching, that fact does not necessarily mean that learning is caused by teaching. "Those who argue for a causal relation between teaching and learning," Fenstermacher (1986) writes, "are, I believe, misled by the ontologically dependent relationship between the two" (p. 39). Fenstermacher goes on to propose a more balanced ontologically dependent relationship between the concept of teaching, things teachers do to facilitate and promote learning, and what he terms "studenting," things students do to facilitate and promote learning. Teachers and students are equally responsible for the outcome.

Students are responsible for their own learning, but how does an educator get them to take that responsibility? Some possible answers to this question are discussed in Chapter 15. One factor is student climate. The extent to which students take responsibility for their own learning, monitor their own progress, have positive self-esteem, solve problems, and make effective decisions are all aspects of student climate.

Teacher Climate

The working environment for teachers and other school employees is also part of school culture. Collegiality and collaboration among staff members, community support, autonomy, and strong leadership common to effective schools help to make up the faculty climate of a school.

Opinions differ concerning the goals of the teaching profession. Aksamit (1990) believes that a teacher's job is to keep students in school and prepare them for higher education or employment. Others see the ultimate goal of teaching as fostering skill in decision making, problem solving, and critical thinking (Adams & Hamm, 1994). Still others see the teacher as an adviser who should promote healthy social interaction and development of positive self-esteem (Comer, 1996). Regardless of the specific role played by teachers, teacher climate is important to the school's culture and ultimately to students' success.

Consistent and focused meetings with teachers and support staff (psychologists, counselors, social workers) encourage stability, development, collaboration, and collegiality among the staff. Unfortunately, school personnel usually meet for curative rather than preventive reasons—ultimately a costly and inefficient procedure (Comer, 1996)—largely because classroom teachers and support staff have a limited understanding of each other's work. Moreover, they generally have no training in a collaborative, collegial model of working together to prevent problems. If Carlos's teachers were able to work as a team, as middle school teachers do, they might gain a better understanding of his previous bilingual problems and devise potential solutions.

Professional language is another aspect of staff development that affects the teacher climate of a school. When we go to the doctor, we adapt to the technical language of the medical profession and welcome the use of professional, precise terminology. A technical language among teachers has developed only recently, but teachers are often discouraged from using it. Using a technical language in the education field is important for two reasons. First, it provides teachers with a medium through which to share their professional knowledge. Lidia's teacher believes Lidia can succeed in school, but she may be unable to communicate this belief in terms that others can accept as more than an intuition. In a society that asks for proof, intuition about a child's future is not enough. Second, a technical language helps to command an attitude of value and respect.

When teachers identify themselves and are identified by others as professionals, the effect on teacher climate is positive. The Education Summit in late 1989 was attended by the president of the United States and state governors, but no teachers. Would the same scenario be played out in any other profession? Would physicians be excluded from a national conference called to discuss problems and solutions in medicine?

Teachers have a base of professional knowledge and bring specific skills to their job. Yet teachers often must follow suggested lesson plans in prepared educational materials or the directions of others instead of relying on their own professional knowledge. As Giroux (1989) points out,

> teachers are increasingly reduced to the status of clerks carrying out the mandates of the state or merely implementing the management schemes of administrators who have graduated from schools of education that have supplied them with the newest schemes for testing and measuring knowledge, but rarely with any sense of understanding how school knowledge is produced, where it comes from, whose interest it serves, or how it might function to privilege some groups over others. (p. 176)

Teachers have this knowledge; acknowledging their professionalism can only enhance the education process.

Educational writers (S. M. Johnson & Boles, 1994; Smylie & Tuermer, 1992) describe the need for teacher empowerment in the workplace, particularly with regard to curriculum, and Shannon (1989) advocates that teachers' knowledge about lesson preparation should prevail over the prepared lesson plans found in teachers' manuals. Some educators talk about the need to see teachers as capable decision makers (Cambone, Weiss, & Wyeth, 1992). Others encourage involvement in school-based management (Johnson & Boles, 1994). Wohlstetter and Smyer (1994) describe a team-teaching situation in which teachers contribute to high-performance schools. Teachers in the teams receive immediate feedback from one another on their own behavior. The team provides teachers with a support group to help resolve judgment decisions. Consequently, teachers obtain higher performance in specific situations (V. Phillips, McCullough, Nelson, & Walker, 1992).

Providing teachers with a support group, giving them the power to make sound educational decisions, encouraging them to converse with one another in their professional language, and allowing for a collegial and collaborative preventive approach with support staff will enhance teacher climate; and a good teacher climate will in turn enhance the educational milieu for at-risk children.

EDUCATIONAL STRUCTURE: SCHOOLS AND CLASSROOMS

The structure of education can be manipulated at two levels: the school structure itself (type of building, grade configuration, curriculum) and the classroom (the teacher's philosophy and teaching style, the instructional method). We may need to reform both before we can identify and effectively assist students at risk.

School Structure

Grade configuration has been the primary organizing principle of our system. The rapid growth of high schools in the United States after the Civil War led some sections of the country to operate under an 8–5 schedule: eight years of elementary school, five years of high school. Other areas used a 6–6 plan: six years of elementary school, six years of high school. Toward the end of the century, the 8–4 pattern became popular. In 1909 the first junior high school was introduced. Since then, grades have been configured in a variety of patterns (6–3–3, 6–2–4, 7–2–3, 5–3–4, 4–4–4) in attempts to group students developmentally and meet their needs. Some schools have an optional before- and after-school supervised program (Dryfoos, 1994). Programs of this sort would help such at-risk students as Carlos and Lidia Diaz (see Chapter 6).

School philosophy. Perhaps more important than grade configuration is the philosophy of a school. Many junior high schools, for example, are just what the name implies: "junior" high schools. Because the philosophical concepts underlying high schools are less appropriate for students in early adolescence, the middle school concept was born. The conceptual differences between junior high school and middle school are discussed in Chapter 14.

Another factor that relates to school philosophy is school size. The school-within-a-school concept is one way of structuring the school so that smaller groups of students are clustered together (Cuban, 1989). For example, the school population of a specific secondary school is divided into four "houses." These houses become the major vehicles for social interaction, intramural athletics, school activities, discipline, and so forth. Thus the main reference group is reduced from some 2000 students in the comprehensive school to 500 students in the house. This increases the sense of community and personal identity for students.

Charter schools. The charter school movement is a recent trend in American education (Wohlstetter, 1994). Although charter schools are public schools that offer a free education for all their students, they differ from district-controlled schools in that they have a board of directors that is responsible for every aspect of the school's functioning. Charter schools share some basic features, but they embody many different visions of school improvement, unique to each community. Charter schools have the freedom to be innovative, and have the potential to become a source of good ideas throughout a school district.

Supporters view charter schools as a promising way to raise academic standards, empower educators, involve parents and communities, and expand choice and accountability in public education. Despite these innovations, however, charter schools are not yet advanced enough to provide definitive lessons regarding the improvement of information, knowledge, skills, and achievement of young people. Charter schools clearly have the potential to be an important educational innovation. It remains to be seen, however, whether transferring resources into the school will result in the improvement of school outcomes.

Classroom Structure

Classroom structure affects the self-esteem of at-risk students. Some writers discuss the need to help students feel a sense of empowerment (E. H. McWhirter, 1994). The structure of the class, as modeled by the teacher, can give at-risk students a feeling of control over their situation. An environment in which students are treated as unique individuals who have unique contributions to make to the group yields positive results (Elmore, Peterson, & McCarthey, 1996). Such an environment produces an acceptance and appreciation of differences, an increase in creativity, an enhancement of personal autonomy, and an improvement in mental health and the ultimate overall quality of learning. The caring relationship that can exist between teacher and student can help meet the needs of at-risk students.

Curricular and instructional practices also affect students who are at risk for school failure. Recent reviews of schooling conclude that much of the school day is spent learning facts and developing isolated skills (Good & Weinstein, 1986). Students have little enthusiasm for such a curriculum and over time become passive players in the schooling process, doing little but what they are required to do. Further, controversial and sometimes very interesting content areas are being omitted from the curriculum (Glasser, 1990). Educators agree that it is their responsibility, as well as the parents', to pass down the common values of society (Adams & Hamm, 1994; J. Q. Wilson, 1993). Yet anything associated with "values clarification," "values education," or "morals" sets off alarm bells in some segments of the community. Many districts tightly regulate classroom discussion of topics such as sexual behavior and pregnancy prevention in an effort to avoid controversy (see Box 4.2).

Curriculum issues.   A curriculum that hinders or ignores moral education, development of social skills, student dialogue, and critical thinking invites boredom and dependence, limits students' goals and decision-making capabilities, and does little to help at-risk students. The curriculum must be flexible enough to adapt to the needs of

---

■ ■ ■ Box 4.2
No Controversy, No Answers

In one very progressive school district, concepts related to acquired immunodeficiency syndrome (AIDS) are taught by the health teachers at a junior high school. An in-service session on the topic provides these teachers with the information they are allowed to disclose, along with cautions about potential community reaction. They role-play techniques on how to deal with situations and questions that may arise. All other teachers in the district have been given one specific instruction about handling students' questions about AIDS: Don't respond.

Teachers must refer any questions about AIDS to the student's parents and continue with the lesson at hand. Such a policy certainly minimizes controversy. It also limits the possibility that uninformed teachers will provide incorrect information and serves as a quality-control procedure for the dissemination of information on sex and AIDS—two very controversial topics. This policy does little, however, to promote safe sexual practices among the populations most at risk for AIDS and other sexually transmitted diseases because it encourages silence and secrecy.

students, and teachers must be free to discuss current issues pertinent to their students' lives, including sex, drug use, pregnancy prevention, and AIDS.

Measures to assess the curriculum need to be broadened as well. Ramona's ESL teacher knows that the standardized test his students must take will not reflect their achievement. Other factors that should be assessed include critical thinking, moral discourse, dialogue, and decision making (Cohen, McLaughlin, & Talbert, 1993).

Vocational education should be added to the curriculum and supported by the community. A study by the Department of Education found that approximately one-fifth of U.S. adults were "functionally incompetent"; 38% of those sampled were unable to match given personal characteristics to the job requirements specified in a series of newspaper help-wanted advertisements (Harris & Harris, 1986). Given Ramona's low self-esteem, she is unlikely to continue her education in an effort to improve her employment opportunities. Vocational education would provide her with some specific job and self-marketing skills that she is not now acquiring.

ESL and bilingual education programs should be supported. School dropouts are generally poor members of minority groups who lack skills in English and have less access to English instruction (Watt & Roessingh, 1994). This group includes a great many ESL/bilingual students. The Diaz children are members of a poor minority family and are behind their peers academically, yet all three of these children are able to converse in more than one language.

Class size.   Class size also affects at-risk students. Certainly Lidia's teacher would be able to meet Lidia's needs more effectively if she were responsible for fewer children. Indeed, academic achievement has been found to be related to class size (Berliner & Biddle, 1995; Ferguson, 1991). Because Lidia's class is large, students have been assigned to smaller groups based on ability levels. Lidia is in the lowest reading and arithmetic groups, and her self-expectations and self-esteem are low. Research on students grouped by ability indicates that while little advantage accrues to students assigned to the high groups, students assigned to the low groups suffer a great disadvantage in terms of time spent in the activity, interaction patterns, and affective and social factors (Slavin, 1993). Educational researchers now advocate smaller, heterogeneous groups that work cooperatively within the classroom in lieu of homogeneous ability groups (D. W. Johnson & Johnson, 1988, 1989; Sharan, 1994; Slavin, Karweit, & Wasik, 1994; Slavin & Madden, 1989). When teachers and students are encouraged to work collaboratively, there is a positive effect on the overall school environment (Reminger, Hidi, & Krapp, 1992). Students who are at risk for school failure are usually two grades behind their age mates; school structures that emphasize cooperation over competition among students meet the needs of these students better than competitive school structures (see Chapter 13).

PEER GROUP INFLUENCE

Children's experiences with their peers provide them with an opportunity to learn how to interact with others, develop age-relevant skills and interests, control their social behavior, and share their problems and feelings. As children get older, their peer group relationships increase in importance. The child's recognition that he or she belongs to a group is an important step in the development of identity. But belonging to a group has both benefits and costs in terms of the child's subsequent social development and behavior. Group membership is associated with attraction to in-group members and preferential treatment of them. The out-group is less valued.

As children grow older, the importance of parents decreases as a reference group and as a model for conformity. Interestingly, the degree of emotional closeness and values consensus between parents and youth has been directly related to problem behavior (Jessor, 1993). Although parental influence is more important for some young people than for others, peer influence becomes the dominant factor for many teenagers. Peer influence clearly can be part of the problem, but it also can be part of the solution. Peers not only influence each other negatively by coercion and manipulation but also positively by offering support, advice, and opportunities to discuss conflicting points of view. Thus, peer group pressure can be either a very powerful ally or a formidable antagonist, dissuading or encouraging problem behaviors.

Young people are very responsive to peer group comments as measures of self-worth and self-esteem. The peer group represents the transfer vehicle for transition from childhood to adulthood. It is within the peer group that the young person learns to relate to different roles and to experiment with interpersonal interactional skills that will eventually transfer to the world of adults.

The peer group exemplifies the world outside the home. Traits such as compliance, aggression, leadership, and need satisfaction are developed within peer group interaction. A teenager who is attracted to a peer group that values antisocial activity inevitably finds that resisting the encouragement of group members to engage in negative behaviors is an insurmountable task. In this situation the adolescent is faced with a decision—either abandon the relationships that provide social support or capitulate to the dictates of peer group pressure. Jessor, Van Den Bos, Vanderryn, Costa, and Turbin (1995) found that the most consistent risk factor for urban middle school students was having friends who modeled problem behavior. Interestingly, the most powerful protective factor was having an attitude that was intolerant of deviant behavior.

Peer cluster theory (Beauvais et al., 1996; Oetting & Beauvais, 1986) provides a way of operationalizing peer pressure, especially as it relates to problem behaviors. This theory suggests that antisocial behavior and school problems are a major factor in creating deviant peer clusters. Young people who engage in troublesome behavior have a tendency to find each other and to find other youths with problems. These individuals form peer cluster groups. These deviant peer cluster groups normalize, support, and encourage a wide range of deviant behaviors.

Peer cluster theory suggests that the dominant influences on an adolescent's drug use and other problem behaviors are the attitudes, beliefs, and behaviors of the young person's immediate peers (Beauvais et al., 1996; Oetting & Beauvais, 1987). According to this theory, social and environmental factors such as poverty, prejudice, family, community, and the presence of emotional stressors, as well as personality traits, values, and beliefs, provide a framework that makes adolescents susceptible to problem behaviors or resistant to pro-social ones. But these factors provide only a background. The peer cluster is *the* determining factor.

A peer group can be a large or small reference group; a peer cluster is a small subset of a peer group that influences the values, attitudes, and beliefs of each member. Peers within a particular cluster are likely, in the case of a substance-using adolescent, to use the same drugs, use them for the same reasons, and use them together. These characteristics are much more specific than those implied by the term *drug lifestyle*, which can refer to heavy and occasional drug users alike. Similarly, peer clusters influence sexual behavior, delinquency, gang membership, and school dropout. Early school leavers almost always are in close communication with other early leavers. *Peer pressure* implies the heavy influence of a group on an individual who usually has limited ability to resist it. Peer clusters are much more dynamic than the groups that apply pressure. Every member of the peer cluster is an active participant in developing the norms and behaviors of the cluster. The cluster is an interactive whole. Although some members will wield more influence than others (as in any group), the group as a whole determines the behavior, attitudes, and beliefs of the entire cluster (Oetting & Beauvais, 1987).

The dynamics of peer clusters may explain why many prevention and intervention treatments fail. Most adolescents return to their original environment and peer cluster after treatment. The norming influence of the peer cluster can diminish or eliminate the treatment effects. Treatment strategies must consider peer clusters and provide alternatives for adolescents who may be drawn back into a peer cluster that engages in unproductive, unhealthy, or antisocial behavior. In fact, removing young people from their peer cluster alone sometimes ameliorates their problem (Oetting & Beauvais, 1987). Another alternative is providing treatment for the whole cluster.

As we move into a discussion of specific categories of behavior that are so troublesome to at-risk children and adolescents, we will return again to a discussion of the influences of peer pressure in encouraging and maintaining deviant behavior. We will also consider the potential of peer cluster theory to explain peer influence on problem behavior and use it as a potential model for helping young people to overcome problems. In later chapters we highlight several prevention and intervention strategies that are designed to modify negative peer clusters or engage youngsters in identifying more closely with positive peer clusters. For example, in Chapter 13 we provide models for peer and cross-age tutoring, peer mediation programs, and other peer-assisted or peer-mediated interventions. In Chapter 15, we examine cooperative learning groups with a particular emphasis on peer support networks.

CONCLUSION

Educators can do little to modify the external environmental and social factors of at-risk students. However, educators do have control over some educational practices and policies that may improve the learning potential of at-risk students (Comer, 1996). First, adequate learning must be viewed as comprehensive. Practices that emphasize the entirety of students' learning and development rather than just isolated mechanical functions can be supported. Second, teachers and support staff must collaborate. Programs that encourage collegial support and collaborative decision making among adults who work with at-risk youth can improve school climate. Third, philosophies that encourage student empowerment can be promoted. Students need to approach their work, their interactions with others, and their lives with tolerance and democracy. They must see themselves as having the ability to take control. They must begin by looking at themselves as decision makers rather than as passive containers to be filled with knowledge. Finally, perhaps our educators should consider providing extended support for children and youth who are at risk. Before- and after-school supervision should be available to help students in their educational experiences. Compensatory education should begin at preschool. If at-risk children and youth are to receive an appropriate education, educators must be willing to face the problems and seek new solutions (Aksamit, 1990; Dryfoos, 1994).

FURTHER READINGS

In addition to those books and articles cited in the reference section, the following books may be useful to readers wishing to know more about school issues related to high-risk children and adolescents.

Benson, P. L. (1993). *Troubled journey: A portrait of 6th–12th grade youth.* Minneapolis, MN: Search Institute.

Berliner, D. C., & Biddle, B. J. (1995). *The manufactured crisis: Myths, fraud, and the attack on America's public schools.* Reading, MA: Addison-Wesley.

Donmoyer, R., & Kos, R. (1993). *At-risk students: Portraits, policies, programs, and practices.* Albany, NY: State University of New York Press.

Dryfoos, J. G. (1994). *Full-service schools: A revolution in health and social services for children, youth, and families.* San Francisco: Jossey-Bass.

Freire, P. (1970). *Pedagogy of the oppressed.* New York: Herder & Herder.

Freire, P. (1985). *The politics of education.* Granby, MA: Bergin & Garvey.

Goleman, D. (1995). *Emotional intelligence.* New York: Bantam Books.

Hawley, W. D., & Jackson, A. W. (Eds.) (1995). *Toward a common destiny: Improving race and ethnic relations in America.* San Francisco: Jossey-Bass.

Kozol, J. (1991). *Savage inequalities: Children in America's schools.* New York: Crown.

Quint, S. (1994). *Schooling homeless children: A working model for America's public schools.* New York: Teachers College Press.

Sherman, R., Shumsky, A., & Roundtree, Y. B. (1994). *Enlarging the therapeutic circle.* New York: Brunner/Mazel.

CHAPTER 5

INDIVIDUAL CHARACTERISTICS OF HIGH-RISK AND LOW-RISK CHILDREN AND YOUTH

What makes some young people resolute and sturdy enough to chip away at the ore, locate the diamond, and polish it . . . while others weakly and feebly patter in the soil, haphazardly searching for a gem, finding only dirt?

J. J. McWhirter

CHAPTER OUTLINE

Young people develop individual characteristics—likes and dislikes, talents and disabilities, strengths and weaknesses—that become ingrained in their personalities. These individual characteristics emerge from the societal environment and from the roots of family and school conditions. Most young people develop adequate knowledge, positive behaviors, pro-social attitudes, and other healthy characteristics. For them the risk of future problems is low. Others are less fortunate.

At-risk children and adolescents do not acquire the knowledge, behaviors, attitudes, and skills they need to become successful adults. They frequently exhibit interlocking dysfunctional patterns of behaviors, cognitions, and emotions early in life and especially in their early school years. If this pattern is not reversed, it may develop into a self-fulfilling prophecy, a downward spiral of multiple problems that could include school failure, drug use, teen pregnancy, delinquency, and suicide (Jessor, 1991, 1993).

Individual characteristics exhibited by children and adolescents form the trunk of the at-risk tree, which links the soil of environment and the roots of family and school to the branches of behaviors. These characteristics can nourish positive and healthful development or at-risk behavior. When studies of at-risk youth are reviewed, a "multiple-problem syndrome" appears. School dropout, drug abuse, delinquency, teen pregnancy, and youth suicide are all related to the same set of psychosocial variables and skill deficits in youngsters (Beauvais et al., 1996; Younge, Oetting, & Deffenbacher, in press).

Teachers, counselors, and psychologists realize that many young people exhibit maladaptive behaviors and attitudes. These at-risk youngsters have skill deficits in their physical, social, and psychological makeup. The term *skills* refers here not merely to mechanically performed actions but rather to proficiency in the behaviors, feelings, and thought patterns that are appropriate in recurrent circumstances or situations. Such broad use of the word *skills* may make some readers uncomfortable, because it groups together various patterns otherwise referred to as attitudes, habits, preferences, personality traits, and so forth. Yet it implies that proficiency in the response patterns under discussion may be increased by learning, and that counseling, psychotherapy, and some teaching approaches may promote psychologically healthy characteristics. All youth, including those defined as at risk, have the inherent capability of developing a more mature outlook, of having an interest in learning, and of functioning with more common sense.

Some young people manage to survive absolutely atrocious life circumstances. Somehow they rise above poverty, horrible family situations, poor school conditions—in short, those environmental conditions that we described in the first four chapters. These youngsters are considered to be at risk because their circumstances clearly suggest future problems. But something enables them to avoid falling into drug use, delinquency, and other at-risk behaviors. Can we learn something from them that will help us with other young people who are not so fortunate? We think so.

RESILIENCY AND INVULNERABILITY

Despite extremely debilitating environmental, familial, and personal experiences, many young people develop normally. They exhibit competence, autonomy, and effective strategies to cope with the world around them (Haggerty, Sherrod, Garmezy, & Rutter, 1994; Werner & Smith, 1992). Such youngsters have been called *invulnerable, stress-resistant, superkids,* and *invincible.* For consistency we will say that they exhibit *resiliency,* a capacity to cope effectively with the internal stresses of vulnerability concurrently with the external stresses imposed by the environment.

Garbarino (1994) contends that given sufficient exposure to miserable social, familial, and educational environments, all children and youth fail to do well. Each child has a "tipping point" between doing well (that is, having hope, positive attitudes about self, functional behaviors) and doing poorly (that is, feeling despair, having low self-esteem, dysfunctional behaviors). These researchers believe that the idea of a tipping point may be more useful than the concept of resiliency. A second criticism is that the justice system has used the term *resiliency* to help punish offenders—contending that a violent and abrasive upbringing provides no explanation for violent behavior because some youth who grow up in the same type of environment do not engage in violence (resilient youth). We acknowledge these criticisms and, in fact, agree with these concerns. However, we find the concept of resiliency to be a useful tool to distinguish between youngsters who do well and have hope and those who fail and feel despair.

Development of Resiliency Skills

The development of resiliency is a function of three related but distinct areas that provide protection to the child. First, the social environment can provide children with opportunities for development and support despite adverse conditions. External support systems at school, work, or church can reward the individual's competencies and determination and provide him or her with a sense of meaning and an internal locus of control, or a belief system by which to live. Second, the family milieu has both direct and indirect influences on a youth's development of resiliency. Affectional ties within the family provide emotional support at times of stress. Third, personality variables (cognitive skills, styles of communication, and other interactional skills) have positive influences on at-risk children and are correlated with the development of resiliency. Also important are dispositional attributes of the individual that may have a strong genetic base, such as activity level, sociability, and intelligence (Werner, 1995).

Social environment.   Resilient children derive support from the social environment—their school, their community, and their culture. The school environment is potentially a mediating milieu for children who experience severe family discord (Benard, 1991). When social support is low in one setting, other settings need to compensate for that lack or provide assistance in rebuilding the support in the weakened area (Coleman, 1991). Caring relationships increase resiliency in children. Supportive and encouraging teachers are particularly important. Counselors and psychologists can make a crucial difference as well. Resilient children often succeed in academic areas and may also achieve in art, music, drama, or sports (Werner, 1995). Contact with peers and adults in these extracurricular groups helps support at-risk youngsters.

The social support networks of the community also help to ameliorate the effects of stress on children. Resilient youth, more frequently than nonresilient youth, use community networks—ministers, older friends, and others. Resilient children often have a number of mentors outside the family throughout their development. These adults are models of resiliency for at-risk youth and provide emotional support for them. Resilient children also have one or more close friends and confidants among their peers. These networks provide at-risk children and adolescents with resources that enable them to develop the skills necessary for survival and success.

Minority children are often subjected to the stress of rejection and marginalization by the majority culture. Even though minority status is correlated with high risk, the way children learn to survive that stress makes a difference in their ability to maintain self-esteem and self-identity. Many young people of color develop specific survival skills that work in their setting. These skills provide them with mechanisms for coping with their environment, even though the environment is frequently destructive and violent (M. S. Arnold, 1995; Randolph, 1995). Unfortunately, many of these skills are functional and effective only within the subculture of the ghetto or barrio. Using such skills in other contexts is often seen as dysfunctional.

Carlos Diaz, whom we met in Chapter 4, is a potentially resilient youngster. His family background, particularly early in his life, and his relationship with his father have given his personality a secure foundation. His family responsibilities, although they interfere somewhat with schoolwork, have allowed him to develop important pro-social behaviors and improve his self-concept and self-esteem. Just as important is the special interest his social studies teacher has shown in him. Ms. Bassett's interest and support, coupled with reasonable expectations, provides a solid relationship with a caring adult. Further, her willingness to modify her classroom and teaching style encourages responsibility for learning and contributes to his resiliency. Carlos's bilingual teacher and counselor have also helped, perhaps enough to mitigate the bias and attitudes of other teachers.

Family milieu.   As we have seen, family environment is probably one of the most important influences on the psychosocial development of young people. The characteristics of a positive family and home environment include a lack of physical crowding, consistently enforced rules with strict but fair supervision, and well-balanced discipline (Rak & Patterson, 1996). The child who has a good relationship with even one caregiver demonstrates greater resiliency (Bushweller, 1995; Werner, 1995). These factors indicate adult support and involvement with the child and are useful in the development of the autonomy and self-direction that are central to resiliency.

Healthy communication patterns also prevail in the homes of resilient youth (McCubbin & McCubbin, 1988). The parents model such skills as attending, focusing, and sustaining task orientation. Focused, flexible, well-structured, and task-appropriate communication leads to academic and social competence in young people (Wolin & Wolin, 1993). The children in families that engage in "enabling" interactions—those that encourage and support the expression of independent thought and allow for give-and-take communication between parents and children—are more likely to exhibit psychosocial competence (Baumrind, 1995).

The family also contributes to resiliency indirectly, through its influence on the children's support networks. Some parents, for example, selectively expose their children to religious and church-related organizations or to such community organizations as the Girl Scouts and Boy Scouts or 4-H clubs. Adults in these organizations provide a useful support network that builds resiliency.

Christie Carter, whom we met in Chapter 3, may be resilient. She emerges from the case study as a prim, priggish, and slightly unpleasant little girl. Her role as the family's angel relegates Jason to the role of devil, but perhaps her adoption of this role is what will save her. She does receive a great deal of attention, support, and reinforcement from both her father and her mother. The security that this support provides may be enough to inoculate her against the dysfunction in the family and prevent her from developing characteristics that would place her at risk.

Personality characteristics. Resilient children appear to have certain personality characteristics or skills in common: better verbal communication and social skills, an internal locus of control, impulse control and reflectiveness, and high self-esteem and positive self-regard (Beardslee & Schwoeri, 1994; Canino & Spurlock, 1994). Resilient children also demonstrate a well-developed sense of humor, an ability to delay gratification, and an ability to maintain a future orientation. Presumably these skills receive reinforcement for development of further resiliency. They elicit positive reactions from family members as well as from strangers (Sayger, 1996; Werner, 1995).

Denise Baker, whom we met in Chapter 2, has a special relationship with her mother. She has developed good communication skills and has the ability to make her needs known. Her sweet, calm temperament elicits positive reactions from her mother and from others. At the same time, she has assumed the care of her younger brother. Although this responsibility sometimes frustrates her, it enhances her self-esteem. These personality factors contribute to her resiliency and may mitigate the effects of her environment.

Common Characteristics of Resilient Youth

Research (Haggerty et al., 1994; Rak & Patterson, 1996; Werner, 1995) points to several characteristics that resilient children exhibit:

- an active approach to life's problems, including a proactive problem-solving perspective, that enables the child to negotiate emotionally hazardous experiences
- an optimistic tendency to perceive pain, frustration, and other distressing experiences constructively
- the ability to gain positive attention from others, both in the family and elsewhere

- a strong faith that maintains a vision of a positive and meaningful life
- an ability to be alert and autonomous with a tendency to seek novel experience
- competence in social, school, and cognitive areas

These characteristics act as protective shields that allow the young person to avoid, regulate, or cope with aversive environmental or developmental conditions, modifying the impact of stressors and leading to less damaging results.

Resilient children and youth cope pro-socially with challenges by balancing short- and long-term needs of both themselves and others. This allows them to reap mostly favorable outcomes that bolster their self-definition and increases their future propensity for pro-social coping. These attitudes endear them to untroubled peers while alienating them from deviant peers.

Carlos Diaz, Christie Carter, and Denise Baker are potentially resilient youngsters. All of them have personal characteristics that reflect influences from their social environment and their family milieu that may inoculate them against the stress of their current situations and help them to avoid future difficulty. Interestingly, these characteristics of invulnerability or resiliency correspond to specific skills that distinguish low-risk from high-risk youngsters.

SKILLS THAT CHARACTERIZE HIGH-RISK VERSUS LOW-RISK YOUTH

As a result of our work in teaching and counseling at-risk children and adolescents, our discussions with other professionals, and an extensive review of research on at-risk children and youth, we have isolated five characteristics that mark the difference between low-risk and high-risk youth (J. J. McWhirter, B. T. McWhirter, A. M. McWhirter, & E. H. McWhirter, 1994). We call these characteristics the "five Cs of competency":

- critical school competencies
- concept of self and self-esteem
- communication with others
- coping ability
- control

These characteristics discriminate between youngsters who move through life with a high potential for success and those who are not doing well. Low-risk individuals exhibit proficiency, strength, or potential in the five Cs; high-risk individuals are deficient in one or more of these skills. The lack of these skills is closely related to the chronic dependency, aggressive behavior, or inability to cope with life that propels youngsters into the at-risk categories—school dropout, substance abuse, teen pregnancy, youth delinquency, and suicide.

Of course, these skills overlap. The critical school competencies, for example, may include skill in communication, coping, and control. Self-concept interacts in very important and powerful ways with the other characteristics. All the same, we can grasp their importance more firmly if we consider each in turn.

Critical School Competencies

Critical school competencies comprise those skills that are essential to success in school: basic academic skills and academic survival skills.

Basic academic skills.   In a high-tech industrial society, young people must learn the basic skills of reading, writing, and arithmetic to survive. If they are to thrive, they also need a fund of information about themselves and the world around them. The lack of such skills reduces the prospects for a useful, productive life.

One of the most obvious characteristics of at-risk students is academic under-achievement. Most often underachievement results from lack of basic numeracy and literacy skills. These academic deficits are an overwhelming cause of early school leaving and are often a contributing factor in many other at-risk problems. Mastery of academic skills encourages persistence in school. A lack of basic reading, writing, and arithmetic skills is often attributable to developmental delays, specific learning disabilities, a less than perfect grasp of English, or emotional disturbance. Other youngsters lack skills because of an inadequate educational structure, an uncaring and unresponsive school culture, limited instructional programs, or poor teaching.

Underachievers demonstrate a distinct pattern of dysfunctional social behavior that can be described in terms of two bipolar factors: anger/defiance versus cooperation/compliance and apathy/withdrawal versus interest/participation. Students at risk for academic underachievement may be withdrawn and apathetic or, conversely, disruptive and overly aggressive. A number of studies focusing on both elementary and secondary school students have found this fundamental pattern (Coie et al., 1993; Freeman, 1995).

Ramona Diaz is at risk. She has not learned the basic academic skills she needs to function in society. Her lack of proficiency in English, her disconnectedness from successful peers, an educational policy that mandates national standardized testing for all youngsters, and her growing disenchantment with learning all limit her potential for acquiring academic skills. She is likely to drop out of school. Ironically, because of her age, she may not even be counted as a dropout, although she is functionally illiterate.

Academic survival skills.   Morgan and Jensen (1988) argue that success in school requires students to master a variety of behaviors that technically cannot be classified as academic skills. They call them "work habits." These academic survival skills are prerequisites for academic success; they facilitate the acquisition of academic knowledge and make it possible for students eventually to achieve (B. T. McWhirter & J. J. McWhirter, 1990). Such behaviors as attending to the task, following directions, raising one's hand to ask or answer questions, and writing legibly are all important. Inability to demonstrate these skills affects acceptance by teachers and peers and negatively influences academic achievement.

A core of social-behavioral skills is necessary for student success. The lack of these essential competencies predisposes students to failure. Some research indicates that these skills are more important than academic achievement. Fad (1990), for example, provides evidence that some social-behavioral variables are more important for students' success than academic achievement and demographic characteristics. Work habits, coping skills, and peer relationships are three important domains. She identifies ten behaviors in each domain that are highly correlated with overall functioning. Strategies for mastering these behaviors may maximize students' chances for success.

Concept of Self and Self-Esteem

Many authors suggest that low self-esteem is a determinant of at-risk behavior. As children mature, their self-evaluations become more differentiated and less global and a strong relationship exists between young peoples' self-evaluations and their performance (Harter, 1990). Children and adolescents who have had few experiences of success may engage in antisocial, deviant behavior to increase their self-esteem.

Just as important is self-concept, or the way people perceive themselves to be. Assume that a student knows he is below average academically. That is his perception of himself, his self-concept. His self-esteem is the value he puts on that self-concept. The individual's feelings about being a below-average student may be influenced by his family background: Does he come from a family of scholars or from a family in which no one has graduated from high school? They may also be influenced by his peer group. We do not always have to excel at something to feel good about our performance and therefore about ourselves. Often our self-evaluation is dependent on the person or persons with whom we have chosen to compare ourselves. Self-esteem, then, is our perception of ourselves as competent and successful in relation to those with whom we compare ourselves. Therefore, we should not assume that all at-risk children have low self-esteem. Indeed, low self-esteem sometimes leads to a redefinition of self-concept, and this redefinition leads many at-risk young people to deviance. A marginalized adolescent who begins to take part in delinquent behavior and to identify with a gang, for instance, may actually find his self-esteem enhanced.

The path to deviance involves a negative learning process that results in a conditioned way of viewing oneself and one's relation to social institutions, such as the school. This negative learning process, which has been characterized as learned insecurity (Suarez, Mills, & Steward, 1987), leads to a spiral of negative attitudes (Jessor, 1991, 1993). A self-perpetuating cycle or self-fulfilling prophecy is started when young people encounter situations that reinforce their more insecure, negative perceptions. They perceive things negatively and lower their own expectations. Building on these attributions, they exhibit learning, discipline, and acting-out problems, or, alternatively, passivity and withdrawal. When adults react in an overly critical, judgmental, or punitive way or exhibit lack of caring and interest, the child is convinced that his or her subjective perceptions are valid. This confirmation of negative attitudes increases the cyclical nature of the self-confirming process and leads to increased alienation.

Thus one of the common denominators among high-risk youth consists of biased attributions (beliefs that they cannot learn, that they are not acceptable at school) that result in alienation. These young people interpret new experiences in the light of these beliefs. These learned expectations have been encoded in their personalities by earlier experiences. The biases result from their interpretation of an event's significance rather than from the event itself.

These attitudinal biases operate powerfully to influence the individual's perceptions. Young people who are aggressive and socially rejected, for example, negatively interpret their peers' intentions in ambiguous situations. They assume aggression in their peers when none is intended. Researchers have suggested that this attributional bias in children leads to future at-risk behaviors (Coie, Dodge, Terry, & Wright, 1991; Dodge, Price, Bachorowski, & Newman, 1990).

Obviously, attributional biases are important. Even when a peer's behavior is benign, a child who perceives the behavior as hostile is likely to respond aggressively.

Lochman (1987), for example, observed that aggressive boys underestimated their own aggressiveness when they described interactions with their peers; nonaggressive boys viewed themselves as more aggressive than they were. Such cognitive distortions can exacerbate at-risk problems. Further, when aggressive boys perceive a threat, their attributional biases increase (Dodge & Somberg, 1987). Cognitive distortions of this nature lead to unpredictable behavior and contribute to antisocial, deviant behavior. Unfortunately, young people mistakenly conclude that the meanings they give events are unbiased and are an accurate picture of what is going on.

Delinquents have been found to have lower self-esteem than nondelinquents (Oyserman & Markus, 1990), yet self-esteem does not predict delinquency when covariables are considered. As we have mentioned, some young people may shift their self-concept to incorporate their delinquent behavior and in that way increase their self-esteem. However, we (Herrmann, McWhirter, & Sipsas-Herrmann, 1997) found that young adolescents with lower self-concepts were significantly more involved in street gang activity than peers who possessed higher self-concepts. Conceptions of their own competence were particularly important. Those middle school students who were involved with gangs had less confidence in their ability to solve problems, obtain their goals, bring about desired outcomes, and function effectively within the environment.

Seligman (1995) demonstrates that it is not low self-esteem that causes low achievement at school, but the opposite: low achievement causes low self-esteem. Low self-esteem may reflect a realistic appraisal of negative life experiences. Undoubtedly, however, low self-esteem will continue to exacerbate the young person's problems. Attitudinal and self-concept deficiencies, especially when they are pessimistic, are critical determinants of school dropout. Interventions should directly aim at these psychological variables.

Allie Andrews, whom we first met in Chapter 1, is unable to feel good about herself and her behavior because of her negative relationship with her father. Her low self-esteem causes her to shift her concept of herself to include more and more deviant, antisocial behavior. She develops more biased, distorted attributions in regard to herself, to adults, and to nondeviant classmates. As she rejects her parents' (and other adults') beliefs and values, she becomes more closely aligned with and influenced by a negative peer cluster. In certain areas of her life, her self-esteem may actually increase. Unfortunately, her deviant behavior leads her down a path to potential disaster.

Communication with Others

Adequate social and interpersonal skills play an important role in psychological adjustment and psychosocial development. Basic interpersonal skills are necessary for competent, responsive, and mutually beneficial relationships and are perhaps the most important skills that an individual must learn. Unfortunately, many at-risk individuals do not sufficiently master these skills.

The level of a young person's interpersonal skills has been related to several areas of adjustment in later life. A high incidence of mental health problems, juvenile delinquency, dropping out of school, and other at-risk behaviors has been related to social deficiencies in children and adolescents. Good social functioning in childhood and adolescence, in contrast, has been related to superior academic achievement and adequate interpersonal adjustment later in life (Dodge & Price, 1994). Further, an individual's ability to achieve and maintain positive interpersonal relationships is a prerequisite to success in the most important areas of life: occupation and marriage.

Positive social interaction enhances social integration. Building and maintaining friendships is important not only for social reasons but also because of the interactive process involved in acceptable classroom performance and peer relationships (Richardson, Hammock, Smith, Gardner, & Signo, 1994). Children and adolescents who have positive peer relationships are more willing to engage in social interaction, and they provide positive social rewards for each other. They also use their abilities in achievement situations and behave appropriately in the classroom. The perspectives of many at-risk young people are so distorted that they have few positive social interactions with either peers or adults.

Perspective taking has been broadly defined as the ability to understand the perceptual view, cognitive reasoning, emotional feelings, and actions of others. Individuals must be able to distinguish the perceptions and reasoning of other people from their own. A young person's perspective-taking ability is related to his or her cognitive development, and some evidence suggests that it has clear implications for moral reasoning and empathy as well (Eisenberg, Fabes, Nyman, Bernzweig, & Pinuelas, 1994). At-risk young people sometimes perceive the world in a distorted way that leads to miscommunication in interpersonal relationships (Betancourt & Blair, 1992).

At-risk children not only have distorted perceptions but lack the core abilities that make for satisfying social relationships. Fad (1990) has identified several core skills: (a) developing and maintaining friendships, (b) sharing laughter and jokes with peers, (c) knowing how to join a group activity, (d) skillfully ending a conversation, and (e) interacting with a variety of peers and others. These skills allow for more effective interpersonal problem solving.

The ability to solve interpersonal problems is an important skill. Interpersonal problem-solving ability is related to interpersonal functioning in adults, adolescents, middle childhood, and children as young as 4 years old. Children usually develop this skill in the early grades (Shure, 1992a, 1992b, 1992c).

Jason Carter, whom we introduced in Chapter 3, has not developed adequate communication skills. He is at risk precisely because he cannot communicate his wants and needs without resorting to explosive, impulsive, and ultimately self-defeating behavior. His poor peer relationships, his lack of respect for adults, and his aggressive outbursts suggest serious deficiencies in communication skills. He has not learned those fundamental social skills that might help him deal more effectively with his dysfunctional parents, his competitive sister, his rejecting classmates, and his upset teacher.

Coping Ability

The ability to cope effectively with anxiety and stress is another skill that differentiates low-risk from high-risk young people. All individuals confront situations that cause conflict and stress. All young people sometimes feel disappointment, rejection, fear, and anger in their interactions with siblings and peers, teachers and parents. How they respond and how they cope with these emotions determines their adjustment.

Coping skills influence an individual's response to stress, which in turn affects the way that person deals with conflicts with other people. Some young people cope with humor and altruism, others by focusing their attention elsewhere. These methods result in a more relaxed and positive view of the situation. When young people are in a positive, relaxed state of mind, they are able to process information more objectively, exercise better judgment, and use common sense. They also demonstrate more effectiveness and competence in solving personal problems.

Some youngsters, unfortunately, cope poorly with stress and are thus at greater risk. They use evasive strategies such as compulsive acting out, withdrawal, and denial. Or they succumb to one of the twins of mental health problems: anxiety or depression. Anxiety interferes with the learning process, social judgment, and interpersonal relationships, and often leads to aggressive and destructive reactions. Depression has similar effects and can lead to suicide and other self-defeating behaviors (J. J. McWhirter & Kigin, 1988; B. T. McWhirter, J. J. McWhirter, & Gat, 1996).

Paul Andrews, Allie's brother, exhibits problems with stress. His bravado, aggressiveness, and destructiveness appear to mask considerable anxiety. His inability to modify his aggressive outbursts and his destructive hostility are a problem to him both at home and at school. His lack of skills in coping with the stress he feels foreshadows serious problems as he moves into adolescence.

Control

Lack of control—over decisions, over the future, over life—is a common characteristic of high-risk young people. Their inability to generate and follow through on competent decisions relates to failure to consider consequences, unwillingness to delay gratification, and an external locus of control. These problems influence the setting and achievement of goals. Many youngsters have an even more fundamental problem: Their sense of a purpose in life is limited, distorted, or lacking. Low-risk youngsters, by contrast, exert control in developmentally appropriate ways over their environment and their behavior.

Decision-making skills. Decision making is a goal-directed sequence of affective and cognitive operations that leads to adaptation of behavioral responses to external and internal challenges or demands. Deficits in decision-making skills are clearly linked to at-risk behavior.

Low-risk children and adolescents have access to relevant information on which to base decisions. They accurately perceive, comprehend, and store this information. They personalize the information by relating it to their own beliefs, values, and attitudes. They evaluate their solutions by considering the consequences. They demonstrate behavioral skills in their efforts to implement these decisions in social situations. They have feelings of mastery and a belief in their personal competency (Harris, 1995).

High-risk youngsters are deficient in the ability to make competent decisions (Cicchetti, Rogosch, Lynch, & Holt, 1993). Information on or knowledge of viable solutions is not the problem. The problem lies rather in the ability to set constructive and attainable goals (Compas, Banez, Malcarne, & Worshaw, 1991; Mash, 1989). Difficulty in this respect is significantly related to alcohol and drug use, delinquency, and low academic achievement. Further, high-risk youngsters are less likely to consider consequences fully (Bell & Bell, 1993). They also manifest an external rather than an internal locus of control. That is, they feel that the events in their lives and even their own behavior are controlled by forces outside of themselves and that they have no power to shape their own lives. Finally, many problems with decision making are related to an inability or an unwillingness to delay gratification.

Delay of gratification.   Individuals vary in their capacity to delay gratification. Enduring individual differences in self-control can be identified even in preschoolers. In later years, lack of self-control expresses itself in an inability to delay gratification. Low-risk individuals voluntarily postpone immediate gratification, maintain self-control, and persist in behavior directed toward a larger goal to be reached when the appropriate foundation has been laid. At-risk youngsters value immediate gratification and behave in ways calculated to attain it. This behavior often becomes self-defeating. Inability to delay gratification is related to depression, low social responsibility, conduct disorders, antisocial behavior, and a variety of addictive disorders (Weisz, Sweeney, Proffitt, & Carr, 1993).

Todd Baker, whom we introduced in Chapter 2, is one youngster who is unable to delay gratification. He is impulsive and lacks self-control. Because of the chaos in his home life, the lack of connectedness with his mother and siblings, and the absence of an adequate male role model, he simply has not developed skill in delaying gratification for the sake of a more important and more distant goal. His insistence on immediate gratification influences his decision-making ability and contributes to his high-risk potential.

Purpose in life.   A purpose gives life meaning. It is the positive end of a continuum whose negative end is meaningless or loneliness (B. T. McWhirter, 1990). Lack of a purpose in life, with its accompanying sense of boredom, futility, and pessimism, is an essential mediating factor in the relationship between self-derogation, depression, and thoughts of suicide (Harlow, Newcomb, & Bentler, 1986; Seligman, 1995). Further, lack of purpose in life is related to the subsequent use of alcohol and other drugs. When life has no purpose, why worry about school or friends or goals or even life itself? Why say *no?*

Low-risk youth have a purpose in life that is potentially attainable and that propels them forward. Their purpose in life orients them toward the future and often suggests short-term, realistic goals. One recent study (Drazen, 1994) explored factors that might predict student achievement. The most important characteristic was "student ambition and plans for the future." Students who had realistic and hopeful visions for themselves as successful in the future achieved well; those with weaker visions did not. This echoes the view of Clausen (1993) who identified "planful competence" as a strong influence on adjustment and overall success in adulthood.

Few high-risk youth give evidence of having a viable life purpose (see Box 5.1). If young people do not perceive themselves as having a viable future, "just say no" has no meaning. They need to discover what to say *yes* to. When young people feel that they have a limited future, they have little to lose by expecting little of themselves or by engaging in at-risk behaviors, including unsafe sexual behavior, delinquency, substance abuse, and suicide.

THINGS TO DO TO INCREASE THE FIVE CS

We have included specific behavioral strategies throughout the book that describe concrete and specific intervention skills to use with clients and students. Although these skills and activities are embedded in specific chapters, they usually have broader application beyond the particular problem area discussed. They also are related directly to one or more of the five Cs just discussed. Figure 5.1 is a "Things to Do" chart that indicates the location of various activities and approaches that can be used by helpers with at-risk children, adolescents, and their families. We have suggested the most

■ ■ ■ Box 5.1

One Week at a Time

Young men and women who have just left high school or are close to graduation frequently struggle with the reality of poverty. Manolo, who lives in Huascar, Peru, is one such young man. His face is alive with enthusiasm and excitement. His wide grin often gets him out of trouble, and it also covers up some of his problems.

When we spoke during his last year of high school, he said to me, "You know, Peru is a great country, but I don't think about the future too much; not more than a few days ahead, anyway."

"Why is that?"

"Because I have no idea what will happen to me after next week. There are no jobs, university costs too much, and when I'm at home, dry bread is sometimes the only thing we have to eat."

Then I asked him: "Are your high school studies going to help you later?"

"No," he replied with resignation. "School is taking up my time now, but what's the use? I'll never study in university. I'll probably work in a factory somewhere, if there's a job to be found."

Educational opportunities in the Peruvian barrios and in American inner cities are extremely limited. For many young people, a career is out of the question; even a job is unlikely. What happens then to purpose in life and control of environment and self?

appropriate age groups for the use of these skills and activities and indicated which of the five competency areas we believe to be most affected by the intervention. We hope the "Things to Do" chart will help you locate intervention and prevention activities that work.

CONCLUSION

This chapter has highlighted an important issue that we emphasize throughout this book: The problems faced by children and youth are mediated not only by their social, family, and school environments but also by the skills the children themselves possess and develop to overcome their difficulties. One way we can assist youngsters is by recognizing how some of them have developed resiliency and by teaching these skills to those who are at risk. Teachers, counselors, and other human service professionals who can recognize the characteristics of high-risk versus low-risk youth are in a position to identify the youngsters who are at greatest risk and to make well-focused interventions.

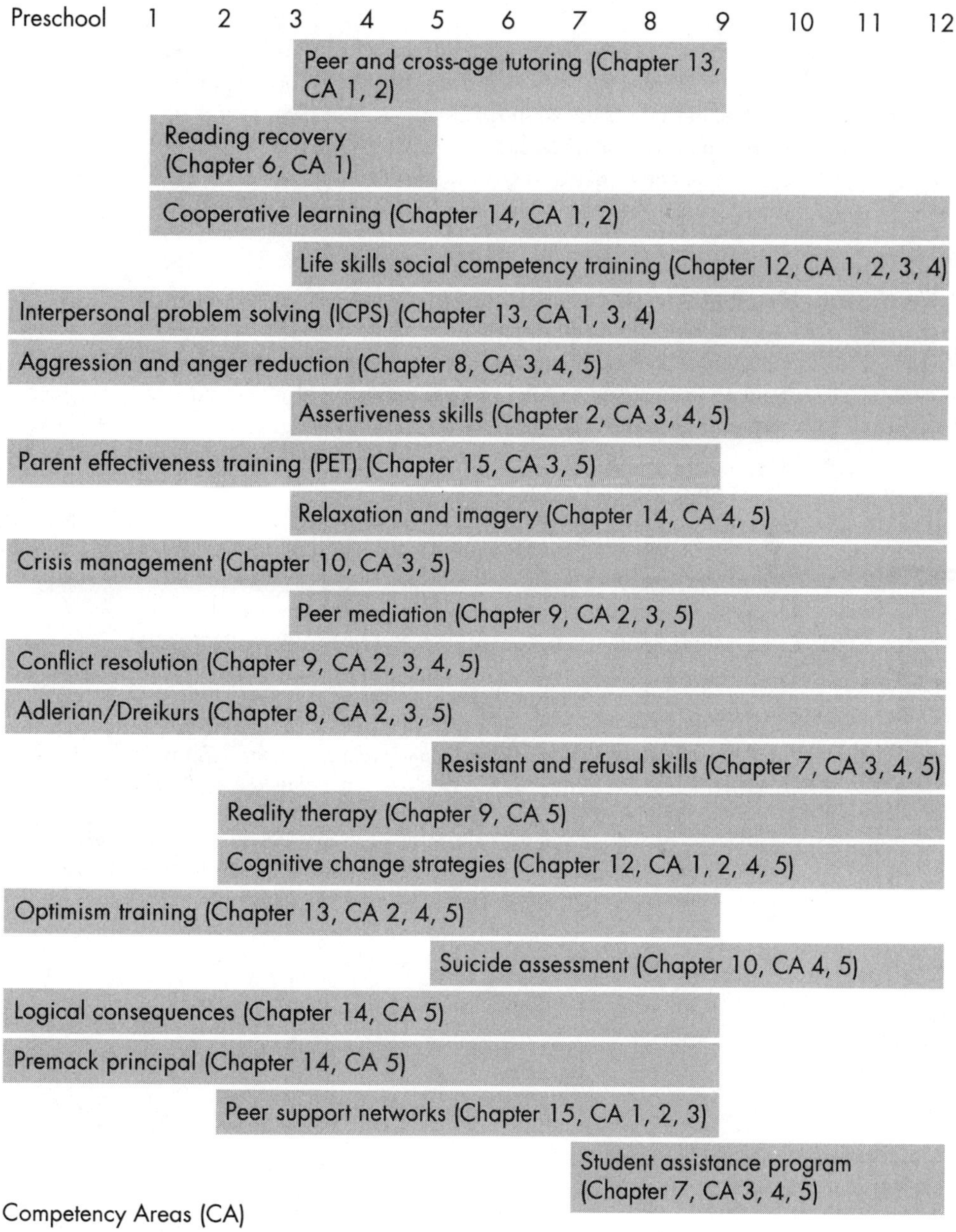

Preschool	1	2	3	4	5	6	7	8	9	10	11	12

Peer and cross-age tutoring (Chapter 13, CA 1, 2)

Reading recovery (Chapter 6, CA 1)

Cooperative learning (Chapter 14, CA 1, 2)

Life skills social competency training (Chapter 12, CA 1, 2, 3, 4)

Interpersonal problem solving (ICPS) (Chapter 13, CA 1, 3, 4)

Aggression and anger reduction (Chapter 8, CA 3, 4, 5)

Assertiveness skills (Chapter 2, CA 3, 4, 5)

Parent effectiveness training (PET) (Chapter 15, CA 3, 5)

Relaxation and imagery (Chapter 14, CA 4, 5)

Crisis management (Chapter 10, CA 3, 5)

Peer mediation (Chapter 9, CA 2, 3, 5)

Conflict resolution (Chapter 9, CA 2, 3, 4, 5)

Adlerian/Dreikurs (Chapter 8, CA 2, 3, 5)

Resistant and refusal skills (Chapter 7, CA 3, 4, 5)

Reality therapy (Chapter 9, CA 5)

Cognitive change strategies (Chapter 12, CA 1, 2, 4, 5)

Optimism training (Chapter 13, CA 2, 4, 5)

Suicide assessment (Chapter 10, CA 4, 5)

Logical consequences (Chapter 14, CA 5)

Premack principal (Chapter 14, CA 5)

Peer support networks (Chapter 15, CA 1, 2, 3)

Student assistance program (Chapter 7, CA 3, 4, 5)

Competency Areas (CA)
1 = Communication
2 = Concept of self (self-esteem)
3 = Control
4 = Coping
5 = Critical school competencies

FIGURE 5.1   "Things to Do" chart

They can reduce the risk to young people by helping them develop critical school competencies, boosting their concept of self and self-esteem, improving their ability to communicate with others, bolstering their coping ability, and helping them achieve control over their decision making and their desire for instant gratification. These five Cs of competency are attended to in greater detail in Part 2, where we describe problems in the at-risk categories and treatments for them, and in Part 3, where we suggest strategies for preventing them.

FURTHER READINGS

In addition to those books and articles cited in the reference section, the following books may be useful to readers wishing to know more about high- and low-risk characteristics, including resiliency.

Benson, P. L., & Roehlkepartain, E. C. (1993). *Youth in single-parent families: Risk and resiliency.* Minneapolis, MN: Search Institute.

Haggerty, R. J., Sherrod, L. R., Garmezy, N., & Rutter, M. (Eds.) (1994). *Stress, risk, and resilience in children and adolescents: Processes, mechanisms, and interventions.* New York: Cambridge University.

Jessor, R., Donovan, J. E., & Costa, F. M. (1991). *Beyond adolescence: Problem behavior and young adult development.* New York: Cambridge University Press.

Joseph, J. M. (1994). *The resilient child: Preparing today's youth for tomorrow's world.* New York: Insight Books/Plenum Press.

Marks, B. S., & Incorvaia, J. A. (Eds.) (1995). *The handbook of infant, child, and adolescent psychotherapy: A guide to diagnosis and treatment.* Northvale, NJ: Jason Aronson.

Werner, E. E., & Smith, R. S. (1992). *Overcoming the odds: High risk children from birth to adulthood.* Ithaca, NY: Cornell University Press.

Zeitlin, S., & Williamson, G. G. (1994). *Coping in young children: Early intervention practices to enhance adaptive behavior and resilience.* Baltimore: Paul H. Brookes.

AT-RISK CATEGORIES

In Part 2 we consider five specific at-risk categories: school dropout, substance use, teen pregnancy, juvenile delinquency, and youth suicide. In each chapter we provide (a) a working definition, (b) a discussion of the scope of the problem, (c) characteristics of the problem and strategies to identify and assess it, and (d) consequences of the problem. Finally, we examine major intervention and treatment strategies that address the specific problem described in each chapter. Although other kinds of problems may affect children, the five topics we discuss in Part 2 represent a substantial portion of child and adolescent problem areas. In addition, the treatment ideas provided here can be generalized to other concerns for at-risk youth.

SCHOOL DROPOUTS

I'm stupid.
At least, that's what they say
when they tell me my ideas aren't good,
or my hair is too long,
or I dress funny.
They tell me in so many ways
that I can't.
I can't because I won't.

Why couldn't they just encourage me?
Or help me?
Or understand that can't doesn't always mean won't, but can't.
Why couldn't they tell me
that I had something to offer?

Maybe if they had told me that,
I would have finished school.

M. J. McWhirter

CHAPTER OUTLINE

Fewer than 75% of students enrolled in the ninth grade go on to graduate from high school in four years (McMillen, Kaufman, & Whitener, 1996). Thus, the dropout rate in most states is greater than one in four, and this problem is magnified in some of our largest cities. Chicago authorities estimated in 1995 that over a third of its high school students dropped out before graduation. New York City's dropout rate is estimated to be 35%. In mid-sized cities such as Boston and Indianapolis, approximately 20 students drop out of school each week.

In this chapter we will concentrate on those young people who leave school before they can graduate. In the following pages we (a) evaluate changing literacy standards and discuss the definitions of the term *dropout*; (b) discuss the scope of the dropout problem; (c) outline some of the roots of the problem; (d) highlight the economic and moral consequences of the dropout problem; (e) present a checklist to help identify potential dropouts; and (f) describe some pragmatic, individual programs and second-chance interventions designed to lessen the negative consequences of dropping out.

DEFINITIONAL ISSUES OF THE DROPOUT PROBLEM

Literacy Standards

If we are to understand the decline in academic proficiency among today's students, we must be aware of the changes that have taken place in educational standards. In 1890 only 6.7% of the nation's 14- to 17-year-olds attended high school. By the late 1970s, more than 94% attended high school. In 1890, 3.5% of America's 17-year-olds graduated from high school. By 1970, 75.6% did so, and by the mid-1990s, 89% were graduated. In addition, the standards of functional literacy have changed. The Civilian Conservation Corps specified three or more years of schooling as a literacy standard in the 1930s. During World War II, the army established the fourth grade as the standard. In 1947 the Census Bureau considered people who had fewer than five years of schooling to be functionally illiterate. In 1952 the Bureau raised the criterion to the sixth grade. In 1960 the Office of Education set the eighth grade as the standard for functional literacy. In the late 1970s the criterion became completion of high school, and the level of literacy needed to function effectively in today's society continues to escalate. Over the years, skill levels and literacy standards have climbed, placing increasing demands on students. Today's high school dropouts are a major concern for educators and for society, but it's also true that in general the American educational system has been enormously successful (Berliner & Biddle, 1995).

Definition of *Dropout*

The U.S. Department of Education (McMillen, Kaufman, & Whitener, 1996) defines a *dropout* as a pupil who leaves school before his or her program of study is complete, before graduation, without transferring to another school. Students who die during their course of study are not considered to be dropouts, and their numbers are not reflected in dropout statistics. Before this definition of the term, there was no consistent criterion for counting dropouts. As late as 1986, educators, policy makers, and school district reports used various and often confounding criteria (Ekstrom, Goertz, Pollack, & Rock, 1986). Some districts counted anyone who left school as a dropout, and so included people who entered the armed forces, transferred to a different kind of school (for example, a school for the deaf or a business or vocational school), and even those who entered college early. The ambiguity of the term has left us with statistics that are less than precise.

Even statistics based on a common criterion rarely include students who dropped out before entering high school. Figures cited for Hispanic high school sophomores who drop out by their senior year may actually understate the dropout rate among Hispanics. For example, in one large secondary school district in Arizona, eighth grade students who do not register for high school are never counted in the high school census. These students don't graduate, don't even go, yet they are not counted in the dropout rate. It is believed that Hispanic students fit this profile in greater numbers than do African American or European American students.

SCOPE AND CHARACTERISTICS OF THE PROBLEM

Despite ongoing inconsistency in tallying dropouts, educators and researchers have made headway in their attempts to profile the student who drops out of school. Indeed, teachers know from their own experience that students who drop out are likely to be those who are unmotivated by their classwork; who have had problems with either the school authorities, the police, or both; who skip classes or are often absent; who are pregnant or married; who are poor and must work; who have family problems; who have drug or alcohol problems; who are members of a minority group; or who have fallen two or more years behind grade level (McMillen, Kaufman, & Whitener, 1996). The latter group includes many students who are learning English as a second language (ESL). In fact, students from non-English-speaking homes drop out in much higher numbers than do students from homes where English is the only language spoken.

Differences Between Stayers and Leavers

Over a decade ago, Ekstrom and her colleagues (1986) focused on a sample of high school sophomores over a two-year period. They found that those who stayed in school ("stayers") differed significantly from those who left ("dropouts") across a variety of dimensions: socioeconomic status, race/ethnicity, home support for education, family structure, school behaviors, and attitudes/abilities toward schoolwork. Students in the low socioeconomic group and members of racial or ethnic minority groups were disproportionately represented among the dropouts. In addition, dropouts were more likely to be older and male.

The students who left school before graduating tended to come from homes with fewer study aids and fewer opportunities for non-school-related learning than students who stayed in school. Dropouts were found to be less likely to have both birth parents living in the home, to be more likely to have employed mothers (who had less education and lower educational expectations for their children), and to have less parental monitoring of their in-school and out-of-school activities.

The students who dropped out of school also differed from the stayers in a variety of behaviors. They were less likely to be involved in extracurricular activities and had lower grades and lower test scores than the stayers. Interestingly, the gap between stayers' and dropouts' grades was greater than the gap between their scores on achievement tests. Dropouts did less homework: an average of 2.2 hours a week as opposed to the 3.4 hours reported by the stayers. The dropouts also had more discipline problems in school, were absent and late more often, cut more classes, got suspended from school more often, and had more trouble with the police.

Differences between dropouts and stayers also emerged in the affective domain. Many of the dropouts reported feelings of alienation from school. For many, classroom involvement was the only experience they had with the school. Most were not involved in clubs, sports, or student government. Not surprisingly, few dropouts reported feelings of satisfaction with their academic work. Dropouts did not feel popular with other students. They tended to choose friends who were also alienated from school and who also had low educational expectations. Finally, the dropouts were likely to have worked at jobs more hours during their high school years than the stayers. Their jobs were more enjoyable and more important to them than school.

Ekstrom and her colleagues (1986) also investigated what had happened to the students who had dropped out of school between their sophomore and senior years. They found that 47% of them were working either full or part time (more whites and males reported working for pay than did minorities and females), 29% were looking for work, 16% were homemakers, 10% were enrolled in job-training programs, and 3% were in military service. Of these dropouts, 58% hoped to finish high school eventually, and 17% reported that they had already enrolled in an educational institution. Fourteen percent had already obtained a General Educational Development (GED) high school equivalency certificate.

Exceptional Students

Ekstrom's study yields a general profile of the dropout, but many students who drop out do not fit it. Dropout statistics include students with disabilities as well. Approximately one in four students with disabilities drops out of school (Cohen & de Bettencourt, 1991) despite the school's legal obligation to provide these students with a free, appropriate education until they reach age 21 or receive a high school diploma, as mandated by the Individuals with Disabilities Education Act (IDEA) and the Americans with Disabilities Act (ADA).

Specific learning disabilities.   Students with specific learning disabilities who drop out of school feel more socially alienated toward classmates and teachers than do students with learning disabilities who completed school (Seidel & Vaughn, 1991). These young people also have far to go to reach the goals of adult adjustment. In one study, only 56% of learning disabled high school dropouts were employed full time, and most were working in service work or labor occupations (Sitlington & Frank, 1993). Results are similar for adolescents with attention deficit hyperactivity disorder (ADHD).

Gifted students.   Gifted students, who often demonstrate high ability and intelligence, high creativity, and a strong drive to initiate and complete a task, drop out of school more often than one would think. In fact, "instead of thriving in school, they drop out three to five times as often as their nongifted peers" (Sadker & Sadker, 1987, p. 512). These students must be kept in mind when we discuss the scope of the dropout problem.

Vulnerable and Underserved Students

Ethnic minority students.   Too often, students of color are not successful in our schools. Those children who don't do well are poor, of color, and many learn English as a second language. Two ethnic minority groups, Native Americans and Hispanics, have excessively high dropout rates. The estimated rate for Native American youth is 50% (Chavers, 1991), and the estimated rate for Hispanic youth is 40 to 50% (D. J. Carter & Wilson, 1991). Educators must understand the history, the cultural composition, and the basic needs of the population they attempt to serve to devise structures and methods for effective education. Schools must adapt to the communities they serve. Many of the students who do not graduate are the victims, at least partially, of school systems that failed to understand and respond to their legitimate educational and cultural needs. We might ask just who it is that has actually dropped out—the students or the schools? Schools cannot educate children without giving consideration to the economic, cultural, and familial contexts from which they come.

Gay and lesbian students.   Many of the school problems of gay and lesbian adolescents are related to the physical and verbal abuse these students receive from peers. Peer harassment contributes to poor school performance, truancy, and withdrawal from school. Educators need to understand that school is a dangerous and punishing place for many gay and lesbian students (Hunter & Schaecher, 1990; Price & Telljohann, 1991).

Unfortunately, educators do little or nothing to support and defend gay and lesbian teenagers in a world that reviles them and in a school environment that permits them to be called "dykes" and "faggots" (Anderson, 1994). Ironically, although educators will challenge and correct other personally derogatory terms, the words *dyke* and *faggot* often go unnoticed or at least unchallenged. Making school safe for gay and lesbian youth is the responsibility of all educators. (See Chapter 10 for a discussion of how gay and lesbian youth are very susceptible to feelings of depression and are at risk for suicide because of the internal turmoil and environmental harassment these adolescents experience.)

THE ROOTS OF THE DROPOUT PROBLEM

Although the profile developed by Ekstrom and her colleagues (1986) tells us some of the characteristics of young people who drop out of school, it does not tell us why they decide to leave. Over the past 30 years dropouts have consistently reported ("Dropout's Perspective," 1988) that their main reasons for leaving school before graduation were:

- a dislike for school because school was boring and not relevant to their needs
- low academic achievement and poor grades
- poverty, a desire to work full time, a need for money
- lack of belonging, a sense that nobody cared

All of these factors are closely linked to self-concept and self-esteem. They are highly interrelated and are probably related to indications of success as well.

Recall that Ramona Diaz (Chapter 4) gets poor grades and dislikes school. She does not think that school is meeting her needs, and she feels as though she does not belong there. Her family's economic situation is difficult, and Ramona feels strongly that she should work to help support her family. She also feels bad about herself and does not believe she has the ability to compete at school. Ramona has little social involvement with the school, partly because of the family's economic situation and partly because of her struggle with the English language. These factors make Ramona a prime candidate for dropping out.

A historical analysis of the nation's labor force provides another perspective on decisions to leave school early. A link can be seen between the dropout trend and changes in the youth labor market. At one time in our history, young people played an important economic role in American society. When most families lived on farms, the center of production was the household. Even in nonagricultural areas the family unit provided for most production, and the family unit expanded to include apprentices.

This pattern changed with the Industrial Revolution. The home and the workplace became separate institutions; production moved from households to factories. The young person's sense of belonging to a community broke down. The nature of labor itself changed dramatically. Much of the work available to young people was dangerous; factories were hazardous places. Still, young people continued to play an important economic role in society.

With the end of the 19th century came waves of immigrants, most of them unskilled and eager for jobs. As the supply of unskilled adult workers increased, the demand for young workers declined. The passage of child labor laws further diminished the role that young people played in society's economic structure. As the demand for young workers declined, enrollments in schools shot up (Sherraden, 1986). There are perhaps two reasons for this correlation. First, technological advances placed greater demands on the workforce and on the schools that prepared young people to do the work industries needed done. Second, because young people no longer played a significant role in the economy and because the family no longer supplied most of its own needs, society needed an institution that would occupy young people's time and control what they did with that time. The educational system took on the job of preparing students for jobs that required skills and assumed the socialization functions that earlier had been the responsibility of the family. Like the family and the labor market in earlier times, schools are now responsible for a child's transition to adulthood. Unfortunately, few schools have been able to fulfill all of these functions to our satisfaction. When we fail to maintain a sense of community within the schools and to foster students' understanding of the important role they play in society, we are failing our young people (Wehlage & White, 1995).

When we follow this line of thought, another aspect of the relationship between school, society, and dropping out becomes evident. A high school diploma no longer ensures gainful employment as it did in the past; and our economy needs large numbers of people to work at jobs that are not intellectually challenging. Unfortunately, most of these jobs do not pay well (Berliner & Biddle, 1995). Even college graduates are finding that their schooling does not ensure success in the hunt for a job (Rothstein, 1993). Many youths do not see employment opportunities as contingent on a high school diploma, so many working high school students see no need to finish their education. The perception of a lack of employment opportunities—often a realistic perception—accounts for the widespread belief among adolescents that school is irrelevant.

An understanding of students' reasons for dropping out must inform our efforts to alleviate the problem. The trend toward the perception of education as irrelevant can be reversed. Schools must help young people see the role they can play in society, and educators must encourage young people to participate in the wider community and to contribute to that community. Finally, members of the community, such as local business leaders, must actively demonstrate the relevance of education to a young person's life circumstances.

THE CONSEQUENCES OF DROPPING OUT

Dropping out of school has a significant impact on the life of the individual. However, the costs go far beyond individual consequences. The practice of dropping out of high school has serious economic and social repercussions for the larger society as well.

Economic Consequences

The individual who drops out of school is at an economic disadvantage. Unemployment and underemployment rates are high among high school dropouts. They earn significantly less ($100,000 to $250,000 less) over their lifetimes than high school graduates who do not attend college, and their unemployment rate is 50% higher (Rumberger, 1990, 1991).

The economic consequences of the dropout problem include loss of earnings and taxes, loss of Social Security, and lack of qualified workers. On the basis of attrition rates among people who had been ninth-graders in 1982–83, the loss in earnings and taxes is estimated to reach $17 billion (Gingras & Careaga, 1989). Not long ago, the Social Security checks of retirees were paid for by as many as 17 employed workers; people who retire in the next 20 years, however, will draw their Social Security from the wages of only three workers (Sklar, 1995), and one of those three workers will belong to a minority group. As discussed in Chapter 2, projections indicate that the percentages of minorities entering the labor force will continue to increase over the next 15 years. Schools, legislators, and minority group leaders must ensure that minority youngsters graduate in increasing numbers both to meet the needs of the national labor market and to provide equal representation of minorities in society's labor force.

Social Consequences

Students who leave school before completing their program of study are at a disadvantage in other ways as well. Dropping out of school often has an impact on an individual's psychological well-being. Most dropouts later regret their decision to leave school. Such dissatisfaction only intensifies the low self-esteem typical of potential dropouts. Dissatisfaction with self, with the environment, and with lack of opportunity is also associated with lower occupational aspirations among young people ("Dropout's Perspective," 1988).

When high school dropouts are unemployed or earn less money than their graduated peers, their children also experience negative consequences because they live in lower socioeconomic conditions. Proportionately few of these homes provide the study aids that children of graduates can expect to have. Parents who are poor are less likely to provide non-school-related activities for their children than parents of higher socioeconomic status. Further, low wages require parents who are dropouts to work such long hours that it is difficult for them to monitor their children's activities. As high school dropouts have lower occupational aspirations than their graduated peers, they also have lower educational expectations for their own children. The Andrews, Baker, and Diaz families (of Chapters 1, 2, and 4) are prime examples of this situation. In each of these families, at least one of the parents did not complete high school, and the children must face the consequences.

Dropping out of school truncates educational and vocational development in a manner that dramatically increases the probability of a downward spiral into greater physical, emotional, and economic problems. These problems create additional costs and losses to society to which some minority groups appear even more vulnerable.

The idea that dropouts beget dropouts conveys a hopelessness that does not have to exist. Not all dropouts have children who want to drop out, and not all students at risk for school failure today are children of dropouts. Nevertheless, a continuing cycle of early school leaving seems likely if schools do not take action. Schools can break the cycle in a variety of ways.

IDENTIFICATION AND WARNING SIGNS

Virtually all children, regardless of family background, social class, or other factors, enter first grade full of enthusiasm, self-confidence, and motivation. They fully expect to succeed in school. By the end of first grade many of these students have already begun to discover that school can be demeaning and punishing. Remediating learning problems later on is very difficult. Children who have experienced failure in school are likely to have poor self-concepts as learners, to be anxious about learning, to be unmotivated, and to hate reading and other school activities. Reform is needed at all levels of education, but no goal of reform is as important as seeing that all children start off their school careers with competence and success.

Effective implementation of any dropout-prevention program requires clear identification of those children for whom it is intended. To facilitate this task, we have prepared a checklist of warning signs that teachers, counselors, and psychologists may find useful in their daily work with students (see Table 6.1). Serious academic problems appear very early, so dropout prevention must begin in the earliest school years.

TABLE 6.1   Checklist for identifying dropouts

Family issues
❑ Student has one parent in the home.
❑ Student has relatives who dropped out.
❑ Student has little parental supervision.
❑ Parental expectations for student are low.
❑ Home has few study aids.
❑ Communication between home and school is poor.
❑ Student experiences financial distress.
❑ Student's home life is excessively stressful.
❑ Student's parents are migrant workers.
❑ English is not spoken at home.

School issues
❑ Student is frequently absent or tardy.
❑ Student has no definitive educational goals.
❑ Student feels alienated from school; lacks a sense of belonging.
❑ Student sees little or no relevance of education to life experiences.
❑ Student's ability and performance are discrepant.

Social issues
❑ Student's social group is outside of the school.
❑ Student participates little or not at all in extracurricular activities.
❑ Student socializes with drug users, delinquents, or persons who have attempted suicide.

❑ Student does not identify with his or her peer group.
❑ Student is two or more years older than classmates.

Personality issues
❑ Student cannot tolerate structured activities.
❑ Student relates poorly to authority figures.
❑ Student disrupts the classroom.
❑ Student's intelligence level is above or below average.
❑ Student experiences emotional trauma.
❑ Student is unhealthy.
❑ Student has low self-esteem.
❑ Student consistently seeks immediate gratification.
❑ Student works long hours at an outside job.

Success issues
❑ Student's proficiency in English is low.
❑ Student's grade level does not correspond to his or her reading level.
❑ Student has a history of poor grades.
❑ Student lacks basic skills.
❑ Student has difficulty learning math skills.
❑ Student has changed schools frequently.
❑ Student has been retained in one or more grades.

Source: Derived in part from Gingras and Careaga, 1989.

The checklist in Table 6.1 is provided to help counselors and educators identify potential dropouts early. Although none of the factors in isolation is an absolute predictor of early school leaving, students to whom many of these factors apply are at increased risk for dropping out. Let's take a closer look at each of these issue areas.

Family issues. To understand the family issues of the dropout identification checklist, one must acknowledge that schools are designed to meet the needs of children from European American middle-class families. Programs for subsidized meals (breakfasts and lunches) and requirements that teachers take courses in multicultural education are evidence of concern for students from other sorts of homes, but a great deal remains to be done. Children are still expected to be clean, alert, well-rested, and neatly dressed for school every morning. Despite the drastic changes that family life has undergone in the past several decades, schools still best serve those children whose families are akin to Beaver Cleaver's: mom is always at home with cookies and a smile, dad makes plenty of money, and everybody upholds the cultural and social values of the dominant-culture middle class. Most European American middle-class English-speaking children do well, but they are only a portion of the students served by our nation's schools.

Carlos Diaz, for example, spends his afternoons taking care of his sister. He is like countless other children who wear their latchkeys around their necks and stay home after school without supervision (Baker, 1990). The average latchkey child is left alone for approximately 2.5 hours a day (Sadker & Sadker, 1987), and evidence suggests that a direct relationship exists between the number of hours spent in after-school self-care and problem behaviors (Ross, Saavedra, Shur, Winters, & Felner, 1992). Many latchkey children are bored, lonely, and frightened. These experiences are even more intense for a youngster like Carlos Diaz, whose early childhood was colored by the violence of civil war in El Salvador. Although physical well-being is of utmost concern to their parents, nearly one-third of latchkey children are unable to reach either parent by phone. As many as one in four latchkey children may be extremely fearful—fearful enough to arm themselves with baseball bats as they watch television. For the latchkey child, television becomes the baby-sitter, anesthetist, and constant companion.

Given that parents must work and that the numbers of latchkey children will rise, widespread pre- and after-school programs that extend the number of hours children receive supervision are necessary. Many after-school programs function as "afternoon schools." Such programs may seem too academic after a full day in the classroom, especially for young children. By the time students reach the age of 18, however, they will have watched 15,000 hours of television and attended school for only 11,000 hours (Sadker & Sadker, 1987). Indeed, the benefits of extra schooling and afternoon supervision may outweigh the possible excess of academia. This is particularly the case when after-school activities include games, sports, assistance with homework, counseling groups, tutoring, and opportunities to explore music and art.

Zigler (cited in Dryfoos, 1994) argues convincingly that the community already owns the school buildings by virtue of having invested one to two *trillion* dollars in these properties. He would open the doors of the schools all day, every day, from 7 A.M. to 6 P.M. In the school, he would establish whole-day child care for 3- to 5-year olds, ensuring developmentally appropriate and high-quality services. He would also provide before- and after-school care to 6- to 12-year-olds that included enjoyable activities, recreation, and enrichment activities. These schools would also offer home visitors to all parents of newborns and organize and coordinate family day care for infants from birth to three years. The center would be run by early childhood educators trained to bridge the gap between home and school.

If schools with many latchkey children do not have the funds to offer pre- and after-school programs, they can still meet some of the needs of the students. For example, the school counselor or psychologist can conduct workshops to help children deal with the fears they encounter during their unsupervised hours. Children can be taught what to do in case of emergency or danger. They can learn their home address, their parents' business phone numbers, emergency numbers, and the phone number of a trusted neighbor. They can be taught to answer the phone by saying, "My parents can't come to the phone right now," and they can brainstorm other ways to conceal the fact that they are alone. Latchkey children can be helped to devise productive ways to fill the time until a parent returns home, such as completing specific chores, doing homework, and working on creative projects. Finally, schools can even educate children on nutritional snacks to eat when they are home alone.

School issues.   Dropouts rarely mention a lack of desire to learn as a reason for their decision to leave school before graduation. The teenager who speaks to us in Box 6.1 expresses concerns that are common to many high school dropouts: a lack of relevance between the school's curriculum and the circumstances of students' lives, and a lack of belongingness. This teenager, though, at least does have a goal: She is going to help her mother manage a restaurant. Clearly she is interested in learning, but the school she attends is not the place where most of her learning takes place.

One way to prevent this teenager from leaving school is to take a serious look at her school's curriculum. Because she seems to be so eager to learn about science, to read, and to use math skills, it is indeed a shame that she does not see the school curriculum in these areas as relevant to her life. At times teachers are restrained from discussing topics that are truly relevant to the lives of their students (see Box 6.2), but many excellent teachers are making the school day relevant to their students. Such teachers should be encouraged to provide in-service programs and workshops so that others might make the curriculum more relevant.

Most potential dropouts benefit greatly from a curriculum that encompasses goal-setting techniques. Identifying and writing down long-term goals, developing a plan to implement those goals, and periodically reviewing the actions taken to achieve the goals are useful skills. Todd Baker, for example, would benefit from such a curriculum. (We discuss goal-setting techniques in Chapter 12.)

Schools need to organize their efforts to bring truant students back to the classroom. For example, it is possible to assign truants to a study group that meets after school for an hour or two hours each day. Ideally, these after-school sessions allow students to work at their own pace and receive credit. Other efforts are made to stop truancy before students are assigned to the after-school classes, but these last-resort study sessions can prove to be a key element in a truant prevention program.

Social issues.   Social interaction—or lack of it—has a great effect on a person's decision to leave school. An opportunity to get involved with a social group and to work with the other members in a positive manner is beneficial to the potential dropout. Perhaps if 9-year-old Todd Baker could get involved in healthy social activities run by the

■ ■ ■ Box 6.1
Reflections of a Future Dropout

I wish I could leave school. It's so boring that I just daydream all day anyway. Why can't they just let me leave now, instead of waitin' till I'm 16?

When I leave I'm gonna help Mama in her restaurant. It's her own business and she runs it, but she also has to take care of my little sisters. We have it all worked out. I already help her every night when I get home from school. This week she let me work in the kitchen. I figured out a new way to make salad dressing, and it's really good. Mama says it's gonna be a house specialty. The first time we served it, I had to figure out how to make a batch for 100 people without messing it up.

Mama also lets me do the books. She don't have time for everything. If I didn't have to go to school, I could help her a lot more. Three weeks ago, we had a tax man in here checking through the books. He said he was impressed with the figures. We couldn't let him know I did them cuz I'm too young to work. Mama brings 'em home for me, and I do 'em at night. I'm usually right. I wish I could be like that in school. But man, those questions in my homework just get me all confused. I mean, once I was asked to figure out when two trains would meet if they was goin' toward each other and leavin' at different times and stuff like that. I mean, who cares? Someone's already got the train schedule all figured out so they don't run into each other, and I ain't never gonna be a train engineer, so why ask me? Usually, though, it don't make much difference cuz I'm so busy addin' up customers' bills that I don't have time to set down and figure out what some smart guy has already done. Mr. Larson is sorta gettin' used to me not turning in my homework. So is Mr. Poland. He says I

school, he would not be so susceptible to gang activities. School districts need to increase their spending on transportation so that economically disadvantaged students are able to participate in school sports, clubs, and activities. School arts programs provide valuable support and opportunities for achievement. At the Music Educators National Conference in April 1996, countless educators remarked on the numbers of students who would not be in school were it not for their participation in the school band or choir. Most school arts programs provide valuable outlets for young people and give them a sense of accomplishment. Yet fewer than half of our schools actively recruit potential dropouts for their arts programs (Barry, 1990). Moreover, when funding is tight, the benefits of school arts programs to the at-risk population are often ignored. Schools must acknowledge the importance of school arts programs and appropriate funds accordingly.

Some schools have addressed the social issues of future dropouts by lengthening the school day by 20 minutes for an activity and club period during school hours. These programs help students gain a sense of working together; they make friends in a

■ ■ ■ Box 6.1

(continued)

better start thinkin' about what I'm gonna do for the science fair or I'm gonna flunk his class. Well, excuse me, but I just don't have time to figure out how to make an atom bomb. I wish he'd just get off my case and stick to buggin' the smart kids.

If I didn't have to go to school, I could help Mama by takin' the kids to the library. They have story time, and my little sisters like to hear it sometimes. I just set and read the encyclopedias. The other day I was readin' that a kangaroo can have as many as three babies suckin' on her tits at once. There can be an embryo that attaches itself to the nipple, a newborn inside the pouch, and an older baby (they're called joeys, in case you weren't aware) that hops in for some chow. I really enjoy the library. Especially in summer cuz the air conditioner works real good. Some of those librarians are real nice to me. Mrs. Bishop is my favorite. She always asks me about the books I check out, if I liked 'em, and then she says what's another good one to read. One librarian there is kinda mean, but she's nothing like the one at the school library. Man, that lady won't even let you read the inside cover flaps cuz it'll mess up her nice clean shelf. She looks at me like I'm lookin' to take something all the time. Mama says she must have a board up her butt. I just hate goin' in there. Anyway, it doesn't matter much cuz we're only allowed to go to the library with our English class, and I never finish my work in that class. I just can't get into prepositions and garbage like that. I mean, who cares anyway? In Mama's restaurant, nobody says I'm not talkin' right, and I know I never heard anybody discussin' conjugatin' verbs while they was eatin' a French dip roast beef sandwich. I sure wish I could leave school so I could start learnin' something.

supervised setting and they relate to others with common interests. Because club meetings are held during the school day, all students can participate.

Peer and cross-age tutoring programs, too, can help young people at risk for dropping out of school. Such programs are popular because they blend learning with the development of social skills and a positive self-image. For example, schools can recruit college students to serve as mentors and tutors to potential dropouts. In Chapter 13 we provide an extensive discussion of the use of peer and cross-age tutoring programs to prevent school dropouts.

In addition, classroom techniques that provide students with the opportunity to communicate with each other in a positive manner help to address the social relationships that develop among students. Jason Carter and Ramona Diaz would benefit greatly from working together with other students in supportive groups. Some specific classroom practices are discussed in Chapter 15, including peer support networks and cooperative learning groups.

■ ■ ■ Box 6.2
The View from Suburbia

On January 15, 1991, the United States attacked Iraq to force its president to withdraw his occupying forces from Kuwait. For the first time in the lives of the students in one suburban middle school, the country was at war. Before students arrived at the school, the principal informed the teachers that they were not to take time away from the regular daily activities to discuss the situation in the Persian Gulf. The day was to proceed as usual.

Personal and success issues. Schools can also organize programs that directly address the personal and success issues of dropouts. Efforts to prevent pupils from leaving school should include methods to reduce antisocial behaviors, increase academic achievement, and encourage positive self-esteem.

One issue of importance to a potential dropout's perception of success is the practice of retention. Although retention provides slow children with the extra time they need to mature physically, emotionally, or academically, retention in grade does not help them achieve success in school (Roderick, 1994). In fact, retention at any time between kindergarten and eighth grade is associated with later poor academic, social, and personal outcomes regardless of the child's gender, socioeconomic status, or ethnicity (Meisels & Liaw, 1993). Moreover, students who were candidates for retention but not retained were better off on both academic and social-emotional measures.

Children who were retained after kindergarten did not differ much academically from children who were considered to be at risk but were not retained (Shepard & Smith, 1987). Their math scores were the same, and the retained group scored only one month ahead of the comparison group on reading measures at the end of the first grade. The biggest difference between the groups was found in their attitudes. The children who had been retained after kindergarten had more negative attitudes toward school than the children who had not been retained. Thus, retaining Lidia Diaz after her first year of schooling, for example, could be quite detrimental to her. Retention should be replaced by better teaching, counseling, and support strategies that help young people experience success.

One such approach would ensure that all children learn to read. Slavin (1994) argues forcefully that virtually every child can be successful in the early grades, and his Success for All program provides evidence that they can (Slavin, Karweit, & Wasik, 1994). He also argues that the most effective strategies by far for preventing early reading failure are those approaches that incorporate one-on-one tutoring of at-risk first graders. One of the best established of these programs is Reading Recovery.

Early reading issues. Children who do not learn to read early in their school careers are destined to struggle in school and are likely to drop out. Reading Recovery, developed by New Zealand educator Marie Clay (1985), is an early intervention program designed to reduce reading failure. It is a one-on-one tutoring pull-out program for first grade students who are experiencing difficulty learning to read. It is based on the idea that high-quality intensive intervention in the very early grades is an efficient and cost-effective strategy for preventing reading failure, a pattern of frustration and other long-term academic difficulties, and school dropout. This approach helps prevent children from developing ineffective reading strategies.

In this program, the Reading Recovery teacher first discovers what the children know. This serves as a basis for developing instructional approaches. After this initial period, each daily 30-minute session has a similar format. Problem words are worked on until they become fluent. Then, the youngster rereads two familiar books with an emphasis on fluency and on the teacher exploring strategies when the child experiences difficulty. A third book is used to create a running record of the child's accuracy in reading. After the session, the teacher goes back over the record with the student and asks questions: "How did you know that?" "Show me the hard part." "What did you do here?" Here, the teacher emphasizes the child's use of appropriate strategies in dealing with difficult sections. Next, the child dictates a sentence story to the teacher. This sentence is the basis for a writing activity and becomes part of the homework assignment. Then a fourth new book is introduced to the child. Upon conclusion of the session, the child is given a packet to bring home that includes a story to be read at home and a copy of the student-generated writing. When children begin to perform at the average reading level of their classroom, they are released from the program.

Reading Recovery has had substantial success in New Zealand (Glynn, Bethune, Crooks, & Ballard, 1992), Australia (Center, Wheldall, Freeman, & Outhred, 1995), and the United States (Pinnell, Lyons, DeFord, & Bryk, 1994). Unfortunately, the size and mobility of the United States population, along with an intensive year-long training to become a certified teacher, plus a year-long in-service staff development program, make this tutoring program difficult for some schools to adopt. In Chapter 13 we discuss alternative one-on-one programs of peer and cross-age tutoring that can be implemented more easily.

Issues of success and failure faced by most school dropouts are critical. The checklist in Table 6.1 focuses principally on a history of poor academic performance, which clearly is related to the failure of students when they are school dropouts. Professionals in the educational setting must address experiences of failure by providing ways for these young people to experience academic and personal success. In general, researchers focus on the differences between those who are successful in school and those who are not. Once the differences have been determined, instructional strategies can be devised to help poor students adopt the procedures that good students use. In Chapters 13 and 15 we outline several school and classroom interventions that provide potential dropouts with opportunities for academic success. Besides prevention and early intervention, accommodations have been made for students who are at imminent risk of early school withdrawal or who have already dropped out. In the next section we consider alternative education programs.

SECOND-CHANCE PROGRAMS: ALTERNATIVE EDUCATION

Some educational interventions are designed for students who have already dropped out of school. The state of Washington, for instance, provides educational clinics for economically disadvantaged high school students who have had to drop out of school because of financial need. These clinics focus on instruction in basic skills, employment orientation, motivational development, and support services. Instruction is conducted individually and in small groups. Students are then encouraged to return to school or to take the General Educational Development (GED) test to qualify for a high school equivalency certificate, and then continue their education or employment (Gingras & Careaga, 1989).

The Phoenix Union High School District in Arizona has several alternative education programs that provide a second chance for dropouts or potential dropouts: a technical vocational school, an alternative high school, a school for pregnant teens, two homebound programs, and two evening high schools.

Alternative education programs are designed for students who have trouble with conventional comprehensive school programs. We have been involved with two such alternative education programs in Arizona and in Nebraska: the Genesis Academy and the Bryan Community Alternative High School.

The Genesis Academy.   The Genesis Academy was established in 1991 and targets youth who meet the following criteria: 16 to 21 years of age, classified as over-aged and under-credited by their high school, school dropouts, youth who are unable to be served by traditional schools because of infractions of the law or school policies, adolescents involved or associated with gangs, and adjudicated individuals. The intent of the Genesis program is to move youth who have not made adequate progress in traditional public school settings into the educational mainstream. Most youth in this program aspire to post-secondary education, including a university education, and increasing numbers are being admitted upon graduation from the Genesis Academy to Maricopa County Community Colleges or to Arizona State University.

A unique component of the Genesis Academy is the Center for Counseling and Advisement (CCA), a joint venture between the Genesis Academy staff and the Counseling and Counseling Psychology programs in the Division of Psychology in Education at Arizona State University. The center provides individual and vocational exploration through group counseling, psychoeducational group interventions, and personal counseling for the young students. A particular problem that the CCA addresses is violence and aggression. Prevention and intervention psychoeducational groups are developed to serve as a comprehensive strategy to reduce violence and abuse. Young people participate in ongoing psychoeducational group experiences in (a) self-awareness and self-exploration, (b) anger reduction, (c) loss and grieving, (d) mediation training and violence reduction, and (e) other individual and group exercises that are effective in breaking the cycle of violence and abuse.

The Bryan Community.   The Bryan Community, an alternative high school in Lincoln, Nebraska, serves approximately 130 to 145 students each quarter. All students must apply for admission, stating their goals and the reasons they wish to attend. Most students at Bryan are "under-achievers" or have had "discipline problems," but some are B-average students whose social or academic needs were not met in the mainstream school environment. Bryan students complete credits that they apply toward graduation; a few continue on to four-year colleges, some to two-year colleges or trade schools, and others to GED completion. In many respects, the Bryan population is typical of the population of many alternative high schools nationally.

The school has an extremely receptive and committed principal, staff, and faculty who use innovative teaching strategies to meet diverse student needs. Courses, some co-taught, are scheduled in two-hour blocks, allowing personalized curriculum and creative planning. Courses are designed to teach basic academic, critical thinking, and job readiness skills. Applied and practical applications of the sciences, math, and English are emphasized. Courses in construction and use of computers are also offered. Teachers know the students personally, serve as their advisers, and provide a support network for them.

The receptiveness and philosophy of the Bryan staff and the flexibility of the school's schedule have led to establishing a psychoeducational skills program. As part of an advanced counseling practicum course, counselor trainees from the University of Nebraska–Lincoln co-lead psychoeducational skills groups with Bryan teachers. Content is determined through consultation, and groups focusing on anger control, goal setting, stress and coping, and respecting others have been conducted. Bryan students benefit from this program as do the counselors and teachers. Counseling students learn group leadership skills and gain experience working with adolescents. They also learn about an alternative educational environment and help to educate the teachers about counseling and psychoeducational interventions. Teachers receive helpful psychological consultation, learn counseling intervention skills, and help educate counseling students in how to work with high-risk adolescents. This project complements the efforts at Bryan Community to meet the needs of young people at risk for school dropout and other psychosocial concerns.

Continuation schools.   Continuation schools can be a successful alternative to traditional settings. These schools encourage students to follow their own interests through a learning process that provides continual experiences of success and is geared to maximize students' motivation. Students are given personalized instruction, occupational guidance, and counseling. Continuation schools provide many opportunities for parents, staff members, and students to interact with one another. They encourage character and moral development in their students. Continuation schools also accommodate the financial needs of working students by minimizing the length of the school day or by operating in shifts so that students can work either mornings or afternoons. Because such a school is generally established as a separate school, a satellite school, or a school within a school, classes are often smaller than those in traditional schools, and student participation is individualized. This helps students develop close relationships with their instructors, which fosters a sense of belonging and affiliation.

Opportunity programs.   Some children find school difficult and need more time to learn the concepts taught in elementary schools. Opportunity programs are designed for students who are academically behind their same-age peers. As in continuation schools, the classes in opportunity programs are quite small. Teachers in opportunity programs work with no more than ten students in several academic areas, including math, remedial reading, vocabulary development, writing, and study habits. Because the student-teacher ratio is low, teachers are able to individualize instruction to meet the needs of each student.

Independent study.   Some students who are at risk for dropping out of school but are capable of learning at home by themselves do best when given the chance to work independently. Contract independent study programs can address their needs. Here the student's course of study is based on a written contract signed by the student, the teacher, and the parent or guardian. Students receive two hours of personal instruction by a qualified teacher each week. They spend the remainder of their full-time program working on assignments on their own. Contract independent study is especially fruitful for students who work well alone, who are interested in learning, and who may benefit by removal from their peer group. Teenagers who drop out due to pregnancy, for example, may be able to complete their interrupted schooling in such independent study programs.

Occupational programs.   Links between the school district and local businesses can also provide effective help for at-risk students. Occupational programs provide students with quality vocational training. Schools that cannot add vocational courses to their curricula can use the facilities and training personnel of local businesses. Regional firms, offices, and factories, in turn, can increase their labor supply. Students receive valuable on-the-job training. Such occupational programs can supplement any vocational programs a school district may have. Recently initiated school-to-work programs funded by the federal government, often through block grants to states or to individual school districts, are good examples of this category.

Community schools.   Community schools are designed for students who have been involved in legal trouble. They have a smaller student-teacher ratio than continuation and opportunity school programs and allow students to continue their learning while they are incarcerated. Community schools are usually operated by the county in conjunction with the court system, probation office, and the district attorney's office. The programs help students obtain a high school diploma or GED; skills in basic reading, writing, and math; and marketable job skills. Moreover, community schools address a student's social disorientation and provide guidance in the development of more positive attitudes.

CONCLUSION

As literacy standards rise along with the demands of our increasingly technological society, we expect more from our young people than ever before. Unfortunately, these demands come at a time when economic resources are dwindling, and many communities and families are unable to meet young people's educational and motivational needs. When we recognize the family, school, social, and personality issues involved, as well as the effects of the experience of failure, we are in a better position to understand why youngsters drop out of school. We must attempt to effect changes in all of these areas if we are to make any headway against the dropout problem and the consequences it visits on the individual and on society.

   If at-risk children and adolescents do not stay in school, they move beyond the reach of effective prevention and treatment strategies that can be administered by and through the schools. And if young people do not develop the fundamental skills that schools can provide, they will continue to be dependent, unproductive, and discouraged members of society.

FURTHER READINGS

In addition to those books and articles cited in the reference section, the following books may be useful to readers wishing to know more about school dropout problems.

Carnegie Council on Adolescent Development (1995). *Great transitions: Preparing adolescents for a new century.* New York: Carnegie Corporation of New York.

Duttweiler, P. C. (1995). *Effective strategies for educating students in at-risk situations.* Clemson, SC: National Dropout Prevention Center.

Evans, I. M., Cicchelli, T., Cohen, M., & Shapiro, N. P. (1995). *Staying in school: Partnerships for educational change.* Baltimore: Paul H. Brooks.

Fibkins, W. L. (1996). *The empowering school: Getting everyone on board to help teenagers.* San Jose, CA: Resource Publications.

Holmes, G. R. (1995). *Helping teenagers into adulthood: A guide for the next generation.* Westport, CT: Praeger/Greenwood.

Ladson-Billings, G. (1994). *The dreamkeepers: Successful teachers of African American children.* San Francisco: Jossey-Bass.

Slavin, R. E., Karweit, N. L., & Wasik, B. A. (Eds.) (1994). *Preventing early school failure: Research, policy, and practice.* Boston: Allyn & Bacon.

SUBSTANCE USE AND ADDICTION

The smoke that leaves you breathless,
The booze that leaves you stressless,
The drug that leaves you careless,
Also leaves you
Jobless,
Friendless,
Homeless,
And, maybe, lifeless.

Unfortunately, immediate gratifications
Seldom provide immediate solutions.

J. J. McWHIRTER

CHAPTER OUTLINE

The consumption of tobacco, alcohol, and both legal and illegal drugs creates a tremendous burden for today's youth. In this chapter we accent the severity of substance use by children and adolescents, the problems associated with it, and potential solutions to these problems. This discussion is especially pertinent to the United States, which has the highest rate of alcohol and drug use and abuse by adolescents among industrialized nations (Johnston, O'Malley, & Bachman, 1995).

In this chapter we use the terms *substances* and *drugs* interchangeably. Although tobacco and alcohol are usually not thought of as "drugs," they are drugs, and their effects can be as devastating to children and teenagers as those of illegal substances—in some cases more so. In this chapter we (a) describe some of the definitional and assessment problems associated with substance abuse and propose a working definition of the term, (b) illustrate the scope of substance use among adolescents, (c) outline some of the personal attributes and social determinants that lead to drug use and addiction, (d) discuss the consequences (physiological, psychosocial, and legal) of alcohol and drug consumption, and (e) highlight treatment and prevention approaches found to be potentially effective in dealing with the interpersonal and intrapersonal issues of substance use.

DEFINITIONAL DIFFICULTIES AND ASSESSMENT

Substance abuse is difficult to define. The use of a chemical substance is not necessarily negative or abusive and must be considered in context, including the frequency and the purpose for which it is used. There is often a fine line between use and abuse. The causes of *substance use* are typically linked to social influences (for example, peers' use of drugs). *Substance abuse* may well be tied to internal processes; for example, using drugs as medication against emotional distress (E. F. Wagner, 1993). Yet most correlates of substance use are identical to those of abuse for teens and preteens. Consequently, these criteria cannot effectively define substance abuse.

Tobacco products and alcohol are accepted and legal, yet they may have severe negative personal and social consequences—even when they are used in relative moderation. Miller and Blincoe (1994) estimate the total dollars spent or lost for alcohol misuse in one year is $116.5 billion. Cigarette smoking is estimated to account for more than 400,000 premature deaths each year (McGinnis & Foege, 1993). Nevertheless, we do not define the occasional smoker or drinker as an abuser of substances.

Criteria have been established for identifying substance abuse and dependence in adult populations. The *Diagnostic and Statistical Manual of Mental Disorders*, fourth edition (DSM-IV) (American Psychiatric Association, 1994), distinguishes between substance dependence and substance abuse without making separate provisions for children and adolescents. Substance dependence is addiction. It involves the physiological responses of tolerance (increasingly larger doses of a particular drug are needed to maintain its effects) and withdrawal (painful consequences result when the drug is withheld from the body). Substance abuse is pathological use of a particular substance that causes impaired social, school, or occupational functioning. Each category is classified according to its current severity: "continuous," "episodic," "in remission," "unspecified." Substance abuse can be determined by (a) the frequency of use, (b) the quantity typically used, (c) the variety of substances used at the same time, (d) the social context in which drugs are used (Is the user being dared to try drugs? Does the user usually use drugs with friends, alone, or with strangers?), and (e) the emotional state of the abuser (Is the user typically depressed or feeling positive before engaging in drug use?). These criteria help clarify the nature and extent of substance use and abuse among children and teenagers.

THE SCOPE OF THE PROBLEM

The prevalence and incidence of substance use among young children have not been adequately documented, and systematic research on the incidence of substance use among teenagers is almost as rare (Newcomb & Bentler, 1989). The National Institute on Drug Abuse (NIDA), through its Monitoring the Future study, estimates drug use among 12- to 17-year-olds but rarely assesses drug use among younger children. The last Johnston, O'Malley, and Bachman (1995) survey of high school seniors suggests that 80 to 85% of high school students have used alcohol. (Those figures do not account for dropouts, who probably have higher rates of substance use.) More research is needed to establish the prevalence and incidence of alcohol and drug use among children and adolescents.

What we do know is startling. Experimentation with tobacco during adolescence is quite prevalent, and many children experiment with it as early as age 9 (Sussman, Dent, Burton, Stacy, & Flay, 1995). Similarly, substantial numbers of boys experiment with alcohol around age 12; girls begin to drink just a bit later. Trends suggest that the use of both tobacco and alcohol is beginning at increasingly early ages. Among high school students, alcohol and tobacco use remains very high. One study reported that 84% of high school seniors had used alcohol and about 52% of seniors had used tobacco (Kandel & Davies, 1996). Both tobacco and alcohol are considered "threshold" or "gateway" substances that precede use of illicit drugs. Although data are limited, the first consciousness-altering substances used by children are probably inhalants, perhaps because of their easy availability and relatively low cost.

Kandel and Davies (1996) reported that of the students in their sample less than one-third (32%) reported having ever used any illicit drug, and less than one-fifth (18%) reported having ever used an illicit drug other than marijuana. Marijuana was the most commonly used illicit drug (28%). Stimulants were next (11%), followed by cocaine (6%), inhalants (6%), psychedelics (5%), and crack cocaine (2%). Age of onset was important because earlier use of alcohol and tobacco and earlier use of marijuana signaled more intense poly-drug use as the person got older. For example, crack cocaine users initiated use of all classes of drugs at least two years earlier than any other group.

The Monitoring the Future study indicates a steady decline in the use of most drugs through the 1980s and into the early 1990s with the exception of cocaine use among young adults. Unfortunately, the study documents the fourth consecutive year of increases in drug use among eigth-graders and the third consecutive year of increases among tenth- and twelfth-graders. Equally distressing, two important determinants of drug use, peer disapproval of drug use and perceived harmfulness of drugs, are moving in the wrong direction. The norms against using illicit drugs have been softening in recent years, and the proportion of students who believe that drugs are dangerous continued to decline in 1995 (Johnston, O'Malley, & Bachman, 1995). These trends suggest that we are in a "relapse" phase in the long-term epidemic of child and adolescent drug use.

Vulnerable and Underserved Youth

Ethnic minority youth. The prevailing stereotype that minority youth abuse substances more than European American youth is not justified by the data. Wallace, Bachman, O'Malley, and Johnston (1995) suggest that the use of licit and illicit drugs is *not* higher among Hispanic and African American youth than among white youth. Rather, it is comparable to if not lower than that reported by white youth. This belief may stem from the disproportionate share of Hispanic and African American adults in alcohol and drug treatment, the health disparities between whites and people of color, and the relatively high number of arrests among African American and Hispanic young men. Although it is a disputed point, some authors (Oetting & Beauvais, 1990) suggest that a sizeable proportion of African American and to a lesser extent Hispanic youth may abstain from the use of most drugs. However, those youth who do use drugs may be using them in greater proportion and more heavily. That is, the prevailing socioeconomic and community stressors on youth of color may make a portion of them at very high risk for substance abuse.

Although the data are not terribly good, of all ethnic minority populations in this country, none seems to be more at risk than are Native American youth. Persistently high alcohol and other drug use remain the norm across most categories for young Native Americans, especially regarding inhalants, stimulants, and marijuana (Herring, 1994). Alcohol use by young Native American women is particularly critical. Fetal alcohol syndrome (FAS) and fetal alcohol effects (FAE) have risen in alarming numbers since the mid-1980s (Cahape & Howley, 1992; West, 1992). As ethnic minority youth become an increasingly larger portion of the nation's population, it is important to investigate, identify, and understand factors that influence their substance use.

Gay and lesbian youth.   The high incidence of substance abuse among gay and lesbian adults has been noted (K. Falco, 1991), but little information exists specifically related to gay youth. Shifrin and Solis (1992) report that the Hetrick-Martin Institute collected data on their gay and lesbian client population. The majority of clients presented a picture of poly-substance use, with marijuana and alcohol the two most frequently abused substances. Over a third had frequent and problematic use, suggesting a high incidence of substance abuse problems among these young people.

Gay and lesbian teenagers use drugs for some of the same reasons as straight youth, as well as reasons specific to their particular issues. Some probably use substances to medicate the anxiety and depression that often accompany initial development of a homosexual or gay identity. Others may use substances to fog an increasing awareness that they are gay; still others to escape the pain of ridicule, rejection, and exclusion from peer and family groups. Clearly, a better understanding of the reasons for substance abuse among lesbian and gay young people will improve prevention and treatment programs. However, even without further research, some actions can be taken now. Greater recognition that gay and lesbian adolescents exist and that homophobia can contribute to the development of substance abuse problems can lead to prevention and treatment programs relevant for these young people.

SOME DETERMINANTS OF SUBSTANCE USE AND COMMON CHARACTERISTICS OF USERS

Some environmental, behavioral, psychological, and social variables are so consistently associated with drug use that they can be considered true causal factors (Hawkins, Catalano, & Miller, 1992). Educators and counselors can use their knowledge of these risk factors to assess the likelihood of drug use among their students and to design and provide appropriate interventions. The most common determinants of substance use can be categorized as social variables, personal variables, and peer group variables.

Social Correlates of Substance Use

Adolescent drug use is often a function of positive reinforcement and behavioral modeling. For example, prior experience with drugs is the best predictor of future use. When children and adolescents use certain substances, they frequently experience physiological or social reinforcement. Drug use is physiologically reinforced by the drug's pleasant (often euphoric) effects and socially reinforced by peers, who bestow attention and status on the adolescent who talks about his or her experiences with various types of substances. Such reinforcement serves as a powerful force for continuing substance use or for experimenting with more potent drugs. Drug use may also be reinforced by the surrounding community. In many inner-city communities, for example, young people regard drugs as viable alternatives to facing the bleakness of the prevailing economic and social conditions (Hawkins, Catalano, & Associates, 1992). The lack of equal educational, employment, and economic opportunities often leads to despair, as we see in the children of the Andrews and Baker families (Chapters 1 and 2).

Drug use is also reinforced by the commercial media, which inundate us with images of substances as appropriate solutions to any physical complaint. Information garnered from media presentations should be considered suspect because the profit motive is implicit in their endeavors. Television and the movie industry are unashamedly straightforward in acknowledging their profit motive, and products are often glamorized to enhance their appeal to viewers, including young viewers.

Although society and community influences can be powerful, behavioral modeling by older siblings, parents, and peers is probably most highly correlated with drug use among children and adolescents. These role models play a significant part in many children's social environment and contribute substantially to a child's experimentation with drugs (Brook, Cohen, Whiteman, & Gordon, 1992; Weinberg, Dielman, Mandell, & Shope, 1994).

Drug use is also a function of negative physiological or social reinforcement (G. T. Smith, 1994). The physical pains of withdrawal, for instance, can be alleviated by the drug. Drug use provides negative social reinforcement when it provides the user with relief from social or environmental stress, anxiety from destructive family relationships, negative school or work experiences, and other upsetting problems. Not surprisingly, drug use is typically heavier among lower socioeconomic groups. Authoritarian, punitive approaches in the schools and in the family have not been helpful in inhibiting drug use. Teachers and parents who are punitive or rejecting usually exacerbate a drug-use problem, at least partly because these approaches do not help youngsters deal with the root problems that may have led to their substance use in the first place (see Box 7.1).

Teens whose family environments are disruptive or disorganized are more likely to use drugs. Adolescents whose families include an adult who uses drugs and who have no religious affiliation are at high risk for drug use. Parents who do not show their children love and care can inadvertently encourage drug use as an escape from the environment. Finally, poor parent-child communication puts adolescents at risk for multiple drug use and abuse (Tarter, Blackson, Martin, Loeber, & Moss, 1993). Thus the children in the Andrews, Baker, and Carter families are at serious risk. Jason Carter's situation—his dysfunctional family, his poor school adjustment, and his underlying emotional distress—is particularly fertile ground for the development of drug-use problems.

Personal Correlates of Substance Use

Children and adolescents who use drugs differ from their peers in a variety of ways. Some youngsters experiment briefly with drugs and never use them again, whereas others' experimentation leads to patterns of abuse and dependence. What is the difference between these two groups? Why do adolescents with relatively similar environmental stressors respond differently to chemical substances?

■ ■ ■ Box 7.1
Joe

One of us worked with a 13-year-old boy named Joe for two months after Joe's mother requested that he receive counseling. She and her husband, Joe's stepfather, were concerned about his poor school performance, his acting out, his group of "delinquent" friends, and his alternately hostile and completely withdrawn behavior at home.

Joe's stepfather was a machine operator who provided severe yet inconsistent discipline. Joe disliked his stepfather, and he reported that the dislike was mutual. He described his mother as "nicer" but complained that she did not permit him to do what he wanted. His mother was primarily a homemaker, but occasionally she did temporary office work. She frequently placated her husband so that he would not get angry with Joe. She felt Joe needed to change, however, and believed that counseling might "fix" him. Joe's parents refused to come in for counseling as a family because Joe was the problem.

Joe spent a great deal of time with his friends both during and after school. He reported smoking marijuana and cigarettes fairly regularly. Shortly after our first counseling session, he was arrested for possession of drug paraphernalia. His parents refused to let him see any of his friends after the arrest.

Joe's school performance was commensurate with his efforts: poor. Joe probably had a mild learning disability, but a recent psychoeducational evaluation had been inconclusive. Joe's primary problem at school was his acting out. Unfortunately, when Joe got into trouble with a teacher, he was inadvertently rewarded for his disruption. He could effectively avoid the schoolwork that he found so difficult and distasteful by sitting in the assistant principal's office "listening to stupid stories." Joe was doing so poorly at school and misbehaving with such frequency that

Two interacting factors often lead to chemical dependency: psychic pain and an inability to cope (Clark & Sayette, 1993; Simons, Whitbeck, Conger, & Melby, 1991). Youngsters' perceptions of stressful events contribute to drug use. Self-criticism and a chronic sense of failure, for example, often further lower their self-esteem. Such youths often believe that they are primarily responsible for all the problems they experience. Many youngsters internalize the difficulties they face and experience depression and anxiety as a result of the stressful events in their lives (B. T. McWhirter, J. J. McWhirter, & Gat, 1995). This kind of psychic pain can be overwhelming.

Some adolescents are unable to cope effectively with the pressures associated with normal development. At a certain point, many young people experience a threshold of emotional pain beyond which their coping skills no longer function. The interaction of emotional pain and an inability to cope with stressors can push youngsters to use drugs

■ ■ ■ Box 7.1

(continued)

his stepfather threatened to send him to a strict boarding school unless his behavior improved. Joe said that would be fine with him—he'd heard that the work was easier there. His stepfather's threat to cut his hair short was the only consequence he seemed concerned about.

Joe used drugs, primarily marijuana, with increasing frequency throughout the two months he was in counseling. We don't know whether Joe experimented with more powerful substances because he was so resistant to the counseling process. If he hadn't done so yet, it seemed likely that he would soon unless his circumstances changed, and that he would be at great risk for drug abuse. He was a frustrated and angry adolescent who resented his parents and received little direction or consistent structure from them. He was unsure of their expectations, hated school, felt isolated from his friends, and could see no solution to his problems. He directed his anxiety and poor self-esteem inward until he acted out by skipping school, talking back to his teachers, or roaming the streets with his friends.

Like many other young people, Joe faced difficult challenges in life and had few resources for coping with them. He had never learned to delay gratification, he did not know how to relate to others in a healthy and positive way, he received no consistent discipline and failed to develop a sense of responsibility for his actions, and he felt mistreated and betrayed by the school and by his parents. Drug use was simply a means for Joe to escape from the problems that troubled him so much.

Because Joe's parents were unable to accept the fact that his difficulties might be symptomatic of larger family problems, they refused to enter family therapy and eventually withdrew Joe from counseling.

for relief. Some youth merely experiment with drugs, but others experience drugs as a legitimate means to alleviate both their internal problems (frustration, stress, depression, feelings of low self-worth) and external problems (poor school performance, family discord, violence). Of course, a chemical solution is only temporary. More important, the drug use itself becomes part of a downward spiral and is ultimately self-defeating.

Jason Carter, of Chapter 3, is experiencing considerable psychological pain. His methods of coping are not working and, in fact, serve to exacerbate his distress. He is a prime candidate for potential drug dependency. Evidence exists (Cooper, 1994) that substance use to regulate negative emotions and "bad" feelings is strongly related to problem drinking and other substance abuse.

Substance use is often motivated by pleasure-seeking. Use of marijuana leads to a focus on the present moment and on internal sensations and decreases sensitivity to external events. Internal sensation-seeking is a consistent correlate of prolonged marijuana use among adolescents. The wish to increase internal sensations and to decrease external awareness may motivate prolonged use of other substances as well.

Rebelliousness, nontraditionalism, and tolerance for deviance are all associated with drug use and may predispose an adolescent to involvement in cults and gangs. Few of these subcultures provide support against drug use (Guy, Smith, & Bentler, 1994) and many support it. Deviant behavior, adventuresomeness, need for excitement, and risk-taking are also associated with increased substance use. Adolescents and children often use marijuana for the first time out of simple curiosity, but they become regular users to satisfy their need for excitement, adventure, and sensation-seeking (Newcomb & McGee, 1991).

Drug use is often associated with a desire for independence and autonomy. Many teenagers want to be free of their parents' influence. Adolescent drug users who do free themselves from their parents' influence, however, seldom escape that of their peers. Ironically, even though independence of parents is associated with adolescent drug use, the abuse of drugs by parents is related to increased drug use by youngsters. Many youngsters who fail to achieve the expected autonomy through substances increase their use of drugs.

Low interpersonal trust is also associated with substance use. An adolescent whose social environment is unrewarding or threatening may seek to withdraw from that environment by sustained drug use. Unfortunately, a child or adolescent who uses drugs in an effort to overcome feelings of inferiority and gain acceptance by the peer group will find drugs counterproductive. They mask feelings of inferiority instead of reducing or resolving them. If such a person develops skills for establishing and keeping positive and rewarding relationships, the perceived need for drugs is likely to disappear.

A common personality correlate of adolescent drug use is low impulse control with poor ability to delay gratification (Shedler & Block, 1990). Many adolescents place a high value on immediate gratification, as their decision-making processes attest. Impulsive behavior serves to relieve perceived internal needs, and although it is not always a precursor to drug use, it can lead to it. The almost immediate sensations provided by some substances reinforce impulsive and gratification-seeking behavior. Youngsters who behave impulsively are at risk for abusing substances once they experiment with drugs.

Drug interventions should focus on the problematic aspects of these personal risk factors. Some of these characteristics, such as high risk-taking behavior and adventuresomeness, are not in and of themselves a problem unless they coincide with other personal or environmental stressors. Youngsters need to be guided to become productive instead of self-destructive. Some prevention and treatment programs use adventurous activities as an alternative to drugs.

Finally, many substance users find it difficult to abstain from drug use, even when they want to. Two specific phenomena that make abstention difficult are cognitive dissonance and personal attribution. Cognitive dissonance is a result of conflicting internal messages. For example, the statements "I don't smoke anymore" and "After three months without a cigarette, I just smoked most of a pack" are inconsistent. They create dissonance, which brings on feelings of guilt, depression, and failure. These feelings are relieved when the internal messages are made harmonious: "I just smoked most of a pack" and "I'm a smoker." Personal attribution is the act of placing responsibility for a break from abstention on personal weaknesses and inadequacies. Despite situational factors that may greatly influence their behavior, such as unusually strong peer pressure, people blame themselves for using substances again after they have decided to quit. The feelings of loss of control, failure, and guilt that result from both of these cognitive processes can lead abstainers to turn again to substances in an effort to cope, to alleviate their negative feelings, and to engage in behaviors consistent and congruent with their self-concept (Towberman & McDonald, 1993).

Peer Influence on Substance Use

A third correlate of substance use is related to peer groups. Peer groups strongly influence a young person's decision to use drugs (J. G. Williams & Smith, 1993). Interventions that focus on the peer group may be the most effective means to prevent and treat substance use and the problems associated with it. Unfortunately, *peer group* and *peer pressure* have been used so loosely that their meanings are ambiguous. In one context peer group may refer to a group of friends, in another to an individual's ethnic group. Recently some clarity has emerged. As we discussed in Chapter 4, peer cluster theory (Beauvais et al., 1996; Oetting & Beauvais, 1986) provides a specific framework for understanding and explaining the influence of peers on a young person's decisions with regard to drugs. Peer cluster theory emphasizes that drug use is nearly always linked to peer relationships. Peers provide information about drugs and shape attitudes toward them, create a social context for their use, give rationales for using them, and make them available. This theory has been tested and supported by a series of research studies (Beauvais et al., 1996; Oetting & Beauvais, 1987; Swaim, Oetting, Edwards, & Beauvais, 1989) that highlight the importance of attending to peer clusters in both prevention and treatment.

CONSEQUENCES OF SUBSTANCE USE

Although data regarding the consequences of drug use continue to be collected, this is the least researched area of teenage substance use (Pagliaro & Pagliaro, 1996). Nevertheless, some of the physiological, psychosocial, and legal consequences of substance use have been determined.

Physiological Consequences

The physiological consequences of drug use vary with the drug. Most substances (alcohol, nicotine, marijuana, narcotics, hallucinogens) have relatively immediate physical effects. Alterations in one's sense of reality, judgment, and sensory perceptions are common. These effects are caused by interference with the normal functioning of the central nervous system and other body organs. The effects may be felt for hours (as with alcohol) or for days (as with marijuana).

Tragic events can often be traced directly to drug use. Drug overdoses and automobile accidents caused by drunk drivers are all too common (Pagliaro & Pagliaro, 1996). Both are consequences of physiological changes in the system. These consequences are so dramatic that society tends to focus on them to the exclusion of the long-term effects of substance use. Not all substances have severe and immediate consequences. Marijuana impairs perception and judgment, for example, but it is not physiologically addictive when used in moderation (although its ability to become psychosocially addictive is quite high). To focus exclusively on the short-term effects of marijuana is to miss an important point. Regular marijuana use has been associated with higher rates of lung cancer later in life (NIDA, 1987) and respiratory problems in young adulthood (Guy, Smith, & Bentler, 1993). Indeed, in the long run, this substance may be as dangerous as tobacco.

Although short-term effects are usually obvious, the long-term effects of many drugs are both less clear and in some cases more lethal. Nicotine is one example. As we emphasized earlier, cigarette smoking frequently creates extensive health risks for young users. Over a four-year period, cigarettes were found to have more negative health consequences and to account for higher health-care costs for the average adolescent than alcohol, cannabis, or hard drugs (McGinnis & Foege, 1993). Nevertheless, tobacco has only recently been considered for prevention or treatment because its short-term effects are gradual.

Addictive substances (cocaine, crack, heroin, other narcotics) used over a long time can cause severe impairment of the nervous system and internal organs. Addiction is typically defined as a physiological state in which the body needs increased amounts of a substance to maintain homeostasis (physiological balance). Users become tolerant of a drug and need increasing amounts of it to achieve the desired effect. Withdrawal is a painful physical experience that occurs when the drug is withheld from the system and the body reacts to the resulting lack of homeostasis. When the use of substances results in tolerance and withdrawal processes, treatment often includes in-patient detoxification.

Psychosocial Consequences

Drug use during childhood and adolescence leads to more serious problems in early adulthood. Early sexual involvement, early marriage, failure to pursue educational opportunities, and early entrance into the workforce or early unemployment are all associated with high levels of drug use during the teen years. Teens who use multiple drugs tend to miss the normal developmental milestones of adolescence. They are likely to assume roles for which they are unprepared, and the results are failed marriages and job instability (Newcomb & Bentler, 1988).

Moderate use of alcohol in the later teen years, without other drugs, tends to increase a sense of being integrated with others, positive feelings about oneself, and positive affect, while reducing loneliness and feelings of self-derogation in early adulthood (Shedler & Block, 1990). Heavy use of hard drugs during adolescence, however, increases loneliness, depression, and suicide ideation, and decreases social support in early adulthood (Newcomb & Bentler, 1988).

These data point to but a few of the potential negative consequences of substance use and demonstrate the dangers associated with prolonged and untreated use of drugs during adolescence. We must make young people aware of these consequences without attempting to scare them away from drugs; that approach has been found to be counterproductive.

Legal Consequences

The Controlled Substances Act of 1970 provides guidelines for judges to follow in setting penalties for the possession, manufacture, and distribution of drugs. This act expanded the role of community mental health centers and public health facilities in the treatment of drug abuse and encouraged distribution of educational materials on drugs to mental health and school personnel. It also established minimum and maximum penalties for drug offenses categorized in five schedules (Ray & Ksir, 1987). Counselors and teachers should become aware of these guidelines and of the potential consequences to adolescents who use or distribute drugs.

Laws vary from state to state. At a time when growing marijuana in the privacy of the home was legal in Alaska, it resulted in a two-year prison term and a $500 fine in Delaware. Parents and adolescents should be aware not only of their state's laws but of the rights of juveniles who are arrested. Currently, minors do not have a right to bail or to a jury trial. They do, however, have a right to a notice of the charges against them, a right to counsel, a right to cross-examine witnesses, privilege against self-incrimination, a right to a transcript of the legal proceedings, and a right to an appellate review (In re Gault, 1967). (We discuss legal issues and other concerns related to substance use more thoroughly in Chapter 16.)

INTERVENTION: PREVENTION AND TREATMENT STRATEGIES

The "war on drugs" that this country is supposedly fighting purports to attack the problems of the drug business. However, although politically correct, this "war" fails to attack the roots and the soil that nurture many drug problems (see Chapter 2). These problems include poverty, racial prejudice and violence, lack of educational and job opportunities, the dissolution of communities, and personal, interpersonal, and family issues with which youngsters must cope. It also fails to acknowledge or confront the inherent imbalance in the world's economic systems, which makes the drug trade both a viable and a profitable business (M. Falco, 1992). The war on drugs underscores the fact that we typically deal with drugs and their resultant problems through the criminal justice system. This system might deal effectively with criminal violence and other illegal drug activities, but it cannot address the reasons adolescents turn to drugs in the first place. Indeed, the punitive approach of the criminal justice system does not deal with the roots of racial or domestic violence, with hopelessness, or with critical family and personal issues. Nor does it deal with a lack of skills. Effective treatment, as well as effective federal funding for drug intervention, must address these fundamental issues before real change can occur.

Empirical knowledge about the prevention and treatment of substance use is limited. So is our knowledge about the incidence, contributing factors, and consequences of substance use among children and adolescents. Nevertheless, some prevention and treatment strategies have had some success (M. Falco, 1992; Gardner, Green, & Marcus, 1994; Ross, Quinn, Gardner, & Bass, 1993). Although we treat prevention and treatment separately here, some of the interventions can be applied in both contexts.

Prevention

Prevention programs are the most common form of intervention because many young people have not yet experimented with substances and because treatment for threshold drugs (tobacco, alcohol, and, according to some, marijuana) is at the same time prevention for abuse of these drugs and the use of so-called harder substances. Prevention, however, must focus on the very young (in the early grades at school) because children are experimenting with drugs increasingly early. (In Chapter 11, we provide a framework for prevention/intervention.)

School interventions.   Information-based intervention is probably the most common strategy and typically is administered by the schools. This approach attempts to increase young people's knowledge about drugs, foster healthy attitudes about them, and decrease the potential for drug use in the general population. Educators and counselors must provide accurate information about the effects and consequences of substance use. Young people's ability to make positive decisions about whether or not to use drugs is undermined if they perceive that the information they have been given is inaccurate, irrelevant, or phony.

Many drug education programs are like the television commercials that dramatically "demonstrate" the effects of drugs on the brain by cracking an egg into a sputtering skillet. Scare tactics neither provide information nor prevent drug use, and educational programs that rely on them are at best ineffective and may even perpetuate the use of drugs (Dielman, 1994). Relying on knowledge alone to change behavior concerning drugs is misguided (Dielman, 1994; Montagne & Scott, 1993), but providing inaccurate information may push youngsters to use drugs to satisfy their curiosity about substances and their effects.

The role of schools in prevention programs is extensive and varied (Botvin, Schinke, & Orlandi, 1995; Durlak, 1995; Sussman, Dent, Burton, Stacy, & Flay, 1995). Yet efforts to prevent drug use must go beyond factual information to provide the skills that young people need to resist the lure of drugs. Some school intervention programs provide alternative activities, such as adventurous recreational activities and service-related community and group projects. Other schools are beginning to restructure their environment to encourage awareness of drug education, increase teachers' awareness of drug use, provide better learning opportunities and more drug counseling, and support law enforcement efforts to limit the presence of drugs on the school campus. Some schools are enlisting the help of community organizations to educate parents about drugs. Although these comprehensive efforts are necessary and have been shown to be effective, they are still only beginning to gain popularity (and funding) (Hawkins, Catalano, & Associates, 1992).

Family interventions.   Because parental use of drugs and the family environment are key predictors of whether a youngster will use substances, prevention and treatment efforts should focus on the family. Families that expose children to physical and sexual abuse, alcoholism, and other drug-abuse problems put adolescents at risk for drug use. Single-parent families, blended families, and families that are inconsistent in setting limits and in other practices are also potential settings for drug use. Teenagers who use drugs report more misunderstandings, disagreements, and conflicts with their parents

(Lowe, Foxcroft, & Sibley, 1993; Tarter et al., 1993). Counselors, psychologists, and educators can work with families through parent education or family therapy. Many children and adolescents want parental direction and nurturance despite their expressed desire for autonomy. Parents who satisfy this need may well prevent or reduce a substance-use problem. Jason Carter's family could use some help along this line (see Chapter 3). The role Jason plays at home and at school makes him more likely to use and perhaps abuse drugs than he would be if his family cooperated with efforts to treat their dysfunction.

Community Treatment

If treatment programs are to be effective, they must distinguish between substance use and substance abuse. Unfortunately, some treatment facilities take advantage of the current national drug hysteria by assuring parents through their advertisements that adolescents who drink or smoke marijuana, even occasionally, need inpatient treatment for their "drug-abuse problem." This approach is irresponsible, not only because it places an unnecessary financial burden on families (and on society through increased health insurance costs) but because inpatient treatment is frequently unnecessary. Not every adolescent who uses drugs is addicted. The occasional use of alcohol or marijuana at a party is not automatically abuse. A person who has a drug-abuse problem (a) uses chemicals at inappropriate times; (b) has problems at school, with other people, or with the law because of drug use; (c) uses drugs frequently; or (d) uses a variety of drugs. Such people need treatment, and this treatment may be available in the community.

Unfortunately, very little work has been done to design treatment programs specifically for children and adolescents. Most juvenile programs are patterned on the traditional drug-free treatment models developed for adults in the 1960s. As more and more adolescents began to seek treatment in the 1980s, they were accepted into adult programs. Few of these programs are designed to take into account the family situations or the developmental problems faced by young users. Some programs for youngsters are available (Hawkins et al., 1992; Kaminer, 1994), although information regarding effective treatment for teenage substance abusers is limited at this time (S. A. Brown, Myers, Mott, & Vik, 1994).

Drug-free programs. The drug-free model relies on basic counseling strategies, without medication. These programs are administered by a wide range of organizations. Treatment is usually provided on an outpatient basis at a hospital, at a private office or clinic, or by a public nonprofit organization. Occasionally treatment is provided in a residential facility. Some programs maintain drop-in centers. Others are organized around activities, such as camping trips or challenge experiences. Still others range from highly intensive nightly group meetings to biweekly individual sessions. Therapy can be brief or long term.

Therapeutic communities. Some community-based residential programs are organized as "therapeutic communities" (M. Falco, 1988). Youngsters in this type of program have usually had previous treatment experiences and are likely to be referred to the program by the criminal justice system. The goal of a therapeutic community is to resocialize the drug abuser by creating a structured, isolated, mutual-help environment that relies on peer influence and group action to change behavior. Group therapy, counseling, and peer confrontation are employed to change the values and behavior that contributed to the drug abuse. The goal of therapeutic communities is to persuade adolescents to abandon their self-destructive behavior, to come to grips with their problems, and to pursue constructive alternatives to drug use.

Residential adolescent treatment programs.   Private residential treatment programs for adolescents operated by profit-making corporations have proliferated in the last two decades. Because these programs are not supported by federal and state funding agencies, little is known about them. Most have psychiatrically trained staffs and operate on a mental health residential rehabilitation model. Generally these programs attempt to help adolescents gain understanding of their problems and prepare them for long-term recovery. The time spent in the program gives the youngster an opportunity to develop personal recovery goals, to prepare for resocialization into the community, to learn skills needed to prevent a relapse, and to plan and rehearse an abstinent lifestyle. Many of these programs have 7-day, 14-day, and 21-day treatment regimes, yet little or no data are available as to which is best. Typically, insurance policies provide for either 7, 14, or 21 days of inpatient treatment. We suspect that this situation is driven primarily by economics rather than treatment outcomes.

Day-care programs.   Some young people attend day-care programs that also provide alternative schooling. They are less structured than residential communities but provide more comprehensive services than drug-free outpatient programs. Most provide academic instruction, counseling, and recreational and social activities for several hours daily. One of the benefits (and a potential weakness) of these programs is that they permit youngsters to attempt newly learned behaviors outside the structured, therapeutic setting on a daily basis.

Aftercare.   An aftercare program consists of those elements of treatment that are carried out after the young person has been discharged from treatment. Ongoing contact with the school counselor, social worker, or psychologist may become part of the aftercare program. Participation in Alcoholics Anonymous or Narcotics Anonymous is desirable. The aftercare program is based on the assumption that treatment does not end with discharge from a formal treatment program. Treatment is the beginning of a recovery that continues for the rest of the individual's life.

Unfortunately, the shortage of treatment programs for adolescents—especially residential programs—is a major problem in many communities. Just as troublesome is the fact that most of the programs that do exist for juveniles are private and expensive. Insurance may cover some of the costs, but if a family has no insurance or has exhausted its benefits, the only recourse may be intervention by school personnel.

School Treatment

If community referrals are not available or are unrealistic, students involved in the early stages of addiction or abuse need intervention by the school. The school counselor, social worker, or psychologist works with small groups of students referred for treatment after they have been caught using alcohol or drugs. Such treatment is useful for students who want to avoid administrative suspension. In-school treatment is designed for youngsters who have been referred by concerned parents, teachers, or peers. School treatment interventions typically include (a) confrontation, (b) accurate education, (c) assertiveness training, (d) decision-making strategies, and (e) peer cluster involvement.

Confrontation.   Confrontation of the individual about his or her behavior is the first step in a school intervention plan. This strategy is implemented initially by the teen's referral to a drug program. The referral step is an overt recognition that an alcohol or drug problem exists. The confrontation strategy is then employed in a group setting through discussions of the link between drug use and aberrant behavior. The teen must understand that what he or she has been doing—that is, using chemical substances—is not working anymore. Finally, the student is required to attend meetings of Alcoholics Anonymous or Narcotics Anonymous. These meetings deliver a clear message to the young person that the chemical problem is severe enough to warrant an association with self-admitted "alcoholics" or "drug abusers."

Confrontation continues throughout the youth's engagement in the treatment process and emphasizes taking responsibility and facing the consequences of one's behavior.

Accurate education.   Effective drug education should (a) provide accurate information about drugs; (b) teach skills for evaluating the social and personal costs of drug use so that young people can realistically assess the consequences of drugs and begin to develop a clear sense of the role of drugs in their lives; and (c) address the factors that have led to their use of substances, such as their peers' use of substances, family problems, poor interpersonal skills, and poor self-esteem. Educational approaches are not salient unless they address all of these fundamental issues. Fostering a sense of the effects of drug use on society is critical. Accurate education will help young people form more clearly thought-out moral decisions about drugs. It may also begin to form in children and adolescents a logical style of reasoning that allows them to develop a true sense of autonomy and independence.

Assertiveness training.   Nonassertive students who are trained in assertiveness generally have better assertiveness skills and are less willing to use tobacco, alcohol, and marijuana than students who do not receive training in these skills (Corbin, Jones, & Schulman, 1993; Herrmann & McWhirter, 1997). Teens who have learned assertiveness skills are often less willing to use drugs. This approach limits substance use among many teenagers who might normally succumb to peer pressure to try drugs. Assertiveness training (also called resistance training in this context) provides youngsters with the skills necessary to terminate drug use if they recognize the potential consequences yet are unable to change the way they deal with both the internal pressures to use drugs (a physiological craving, a perceived need to relieve stress) and external pressures from the peer cluster.

Allie Andrews might well profit from confrontation, accurate education, and assertiveness training. Her interaction with her stepfather suggests that she has few ways to respond to stress, and these are mostly acting-out responses. Her peer interaction hints that she may be turning to her friends for the acceptance she does not receive at home.

Thus her resistance to drug use may be quite low. Assertiveness and resistance training might help her develop the skills she needs to change her self-defeating patterns and prevent substance use.

Decision-making strategies.   It is particularly important to the decision-making process that the benefits and probable consequences of drug use be spelled out. Unfortunately, neither all the benefits nor all the consequences of drug use and abstinence are known. Nevertheless, decision-making strategies help users to (a) define the nature of their choice, (b) enlarge the number of alternatives under consideration, (c) identify all benefits and consequences of each alternative, and (d) implement their desired alternative. Because this strategy can be effective in efforts to cope with many of the root problems of substance use, it represents a valuable resource for at-risk youth.

Peer cluster involvement.   In view of the influence of peers on drug use, prevention and treatment efforts should focus not only on specific at-risk youth but also on their peer clusters. The relationship between adolescent drug use and the concurrent drug use of friends is the most reproducible and consistent predictive relationship in adolescent drug research (Dielman, Butchart, Shope, & Miller, 1990–1991; J. G. Williams & Smith, 1993). Peer-based programs represent a direct approach to the problems of substance use and can be used in conjunction with the information-based approaches discussed earlier. Peer interventions can be simplistic, such as the "Just say no" campaign, or more comprehensive, focusing on the development of assertive refusal and decision-making skills and dealing with the interactions of peers within the cluster. Peer programs that emphasize training in assertiveness and other social skills have the best success rate (Botvin, Baker, Dusenbury, Botvin, & Diaz, 1995; Herrmann & McWhirter, 1997; Sussman et al., 1995). If these skills are not taught to the whole peer cluster, or if adolescents return to the same peer cluster after receiving treatment away from their peers, they may regress to past patterns of use.

We advocate in-school approaches that make use of the peer cluster. First, schools can organize professionally led, weekly group counseling sessions for young people who use substances and for their peers. Also, schools can assign young people to a form of in-school suspension that requires them to spend one or more days each week together as a group, learning why they have been using drugs, learning the short- and long-term consequences of prolonged drug use, and developing the skills necessary to stop using drugs. Both strategies are designed to engage the peer cluster and modify norms and attitudes that support drug use. But be careful. The peer group may reinforce norms that adults are helpless to modify. If trained peer or cross-age counselors or facilitators are available, including them in the group can be very useful.

These approaches are less likely to be effective with extreme drug abusers. Children and adolescents who severely abuse multiple drugs usually respond less well to simple peer interventions because the social and peer influences supporting drug use are typically compounded by internal distress, unhappiness, loneliness, and limited opportunities for the future (S. A. Brown et al., 1994). These individuals may be best helped by student assistance programs (SAPs). Here again, modifying their peer clusters or developing new ones is still extremely important. Student assistance programs include some young people who have accepted responsibility for their own recovery, "straight" friends of the student, and trained peer group facilitators. These persons provide encouragement and support for a norm of abstinence from drugs.

Student assistance programs. Student assistance programs (SAPs) are particularly helpful in identifying young people who may have substance abuse problems and in providing recovery for those who are returning to school after treatment. SAPs provide a promising approach for intervening in and preventing alcohol and other drug problems among school-age young people. Modeled after the employee assistance programs developed in industry, the SAP focuses on performance and behavior at school and uses a referral process that includes screening for alcohol and other drug use. Student assistance programs also work with self-referred youth to address problems of substance use as well as problems that could lead to substance abuse. The program also assists students who are suffering from adverse effects from parental substance abuse and offers strategies for eliminating drug use both during and after school hours. The SAP gives school personnel a mechanism for helping young people with a wide range of problems that contribute to alcohol and other drug use.

SAPs are useful because they deal directly with two major problems. First, students are hesitant to seek counseling services when they are involved with alcohol and other illegal substances. Second, the illegal nature of substance use contributes to the reluctance of adolescents to seek assistance and accentuates the denial of problems associated with abuse itself. The typical SAP team includes representatives from key units in the school and a substance abuse specialist (D. D. Moore & Forster, 1993). The composition of this team includes administrators involved in student discipline, school counselors, and faculty representatives. SAPs have a structure and process for identifying substance abusing students, a network to community resources that provide preventive and recovery interventions, and a reentry program that includes case management and follow-up for students returning to school after treatment.

One particularly important component of follow-up is the school recovery support group. The type of support received when a young person leaves a treatment center and reenters the "real world" is extremely important in preventing relapse. Teens are faced with pressure to use drugs again within the first 20 minutes of returning to school (Hanson & Peterson, 1993). The recovery support group provides an opportunity for students to discuss emotional difficulties of being clean and sober and adjusting to school. Because they include students who are "working a program," they accentuate a pro-social peer cluster. In fact, it is detrimental to a school recovery support group to include students who are not actively engaged in their own recovery. Other types of group counseling should be available to the chemically dependent adolescent who chooses not to be committed to a drug-free lifestyle. Materials by Hanson and Peterson (1993), Fleming (1990), and G. L. Anderson (1987), cited in Appendix B, are quite useful.

A surprising number of young people turn to adults outside their families for help. It is possible to take advantage of this propensity to help youngsters relate to healthy adults, recognize and reinforce new personal skills, and identify healthier peer cluster norms as a means of changing a negative peer cluster and self-defeating behavior. The above interventions help accomplish that.

CONCLUSION

Both legal and illicit substances are widely used, and their abuse imposes great social, economic, and personal costs on individuals and communities. The best way to prevent problems is to provide youngsters with a future. The most effective prevention strategies involve schools and families. Treatment interventions are most effective when families, schools, and the community collaborate. Understanding and attending to the influence and attitudes of the peer cluster are critical for both deterring and treating the problems caused by drug use. Only when youngsters are taught to understand themselves, their motives, and their responsibility for their actions will the negative influences of drugs in our society be lessened.

FURTHER READINGS

In addition to those books and articles cited in the reference section, the following books may be useful to readers wishing to know more about teenage substance abuse problems.

Botvin, G. J., Schinke, S., & Orlandi, M. A. (Eds.) (1995). *Drug abuse prevention with multiethnic youth.* Thousand Oaks, CA: Sage.

Hawkins, J. D., Catalano, R. F., & Associates (1992). *Communities that care: Action for drug abuse.* San Francisco: Jossey-Bass.

Kaminer, Y. (1994). *Adolescent substance abuse: A comprehensive guide to theory and practice.* New York: Plenum Medical/Plenum.

Natasi, B. K., & DeZolt, D. M. (1994). *School interventions for children of alcoholics.* New York: Guilford.

Ottomanelli, G. (1995). *Children and addiction.* Westport, CT: Paeger/Greenwood.

Pagliaro, A. M., & Pagliaro, L. (1996). *Substance use among children and adolescents.* New York: Wiley.

Schinke, S. P., Botvin, G. J., & Orlandi, M. A. (1991). *Substance abuse in children and adolescents: Evaluation and intervention.* Newbury Park, CA: Sage.

Stimmel, B. (1996). *Drug abuse and social policy in America: The war that must be won.* Binghamton, NY: The Haworth Press.

Watkins, K. P., & Durant, L. (1996). *Working with children and families affected by substance abuse: A guide for early childhood education and human service staff.* West Nyack, NY: The Center for Applied Research.

CHAPTER 8

TEENAGE PREGNANCY AND RISKY SEXUAL BEHAVIOR

A young girl-woman, without education,
without resources, stressed and depressed,
rears her baby alone and
bends like the poplar.
Gentle summer rains nourish the soil . . . but
where do the poplars and the waters meet?

J. J. McWhirter

CHAPTER OUTLINE

Problems related to adolescent sexual activity are broad-ranging and complex. Issues related to teenage sexuality include pregnancy, abortion, sexually transmitted diseases (STDs), human immunodeficiency virus (HIV), acquired immunodeficiency syndrome (AIDS), childhood molestation and incest, and sex-related violence. No one chapter can fully attend to the interpersonal, psychological, and social issues related to these problems. We will focus on what we consider to be the two most critical problems related to a young person's sexuality, sexual development, and sexual activity: the problem of "babies having babies" and HIV/AIDS and other STDs.

In this chapter we discuss (a) the incidence and frequency of teenage sexual behavior and teenage pregnancy, (b) the causes of some of the problems related to teen sexuality and to sexual development, (c) the consequences of teen pregnancy, and (d) strategies for preventing teen pregnancy and treating girls who are at risk for pregnancy. We also discuss AIDS and the HIV epidemic among teens. Finally, we present several prevention and treatment strategies that can limit risky sexual activity and include a model to assist teenage fathers.

THE SCOPE OF THE PROBLEM

Approximately one million girls become pregnant each year in the United States, and half a million of them carry the pregnancy to term (CDF, 1995; Ventura, Martin, Taffel, Mathews, & Clarke, 1992). Almost all of these births were unintended (Moore, 1992). Data on births to teenage girls show that the birth rate in 1991 continued the rise that began during the 1980s. Between 1986 and 1991, the rate of births to adolescents rose 24%, from 50 to 62 births per 1000 females. This increase in the birth rate occurred among both younger and older teens and in nearly all states (Moore, 1994). Moore (1995) reports a slight decline in the birth rate among teenagers between 1991 and 1992. Nevertheless, overall levels remain 21% higher than they were in the mid-1980s. In the early 1990s, nearly one-third of all births were to unmarried women. Although childbirths among unmarried girls are higher among African Americans than European Americans (DaVanzo & Rahman, 1993), the overall increase in childbearing among unmarried women is primarily due to the steep rise in births among unmarried European American women (Ventura, Martin, Taffel, Matthews, & Clarke, 1992).

Levels of premarital sexual activity have risen steadily since the 1920s. The proportion of teenage females who report sexual intercourse was above 50% in the early 1990s (Centers for Disease Control, 1992), and 75 to 80% of adolescent males report having had sexual intercourse (Beymer, 1995). Increases in the levels of sexual activity were greater among younger teenagers than among older teenagers. This is particularly true for youngsters involved in other categories of at-risk behavior. For example, among adolescents involved in the juvenile justice system 87% reported having had intercourse by age 15, and 91.5% reported having had intercourse by age 17 (Melchert & Burnett, 1990). Regular use of alcohol, cigarettes, and marijuana by 14- and 15-year-olds is related to their sexual intercourse. That is, 87% of teenagers who regularly use marijuana have had intercourse, compared to 69% who regularly use cigarettes, and 66% who regularly use alcohol (Alan Guttmacher Institute [AGI], 1994). Interestingly, the youngest teenagers who are involved in sexual activity are especially vulnerable to coercive sex, with 60% of the girls who had sex before age 15 and 75% who had intercourse before age 14 reporting involuntary sexual encounters (AGI, 1994).

Because of limited knowledge of their own reproductive systems, lack of choice about intercourse, and sporadic, inappropriate, or nonexistent use of contraceptives, increasingly younger girls are becoming pregnant and bearing children (Melchert & Burnett, 1990). Although contraceptives can prevent sexually transmitted diseases and pregnancy, they can be complicated to use and difficult and expensive to obtain. They may also seem inappropriate to teenagers who have sex sporadically. Nevertheless, most sexually experienced adolescents do use contraceptives, and this trend has increased notably during the 1980s. Two-thirds of adolescents use some method of contraception, usually the male condom, the first time they have sexual intercourse (AGI, 1994). Nevertheless, at least a third of all sexually active teenagers are at risk for conceiving a baby during their first experience of sexual intercourse. In addition, they are at risk for contracting sexually transmitted diseases.

The response of adolescents to pregnancy is changing as well. Formal adoption has been chosen far less frequently over the last few decades, even though teens who give up their children suffer fewer negative consequences than those who keep them (Byrne,

Kelley, & Fisher, 1993). Most teens who carry the pregnancy to term keep their babies (90% of European American and 97% of African American teens) rather than give them up for adoption, even though they may not have adequate resources to care for them. Informal "adoption" by a member of the family is more common within the African American community. Children in Hispanic and Native American families are often parented by the clan. Current trends suggest that adolescent girls would rather have an abortion than carry an unwanted pregnancy to term and relinquish the baby for adoption.

Approximately a third of all adolescent pregnancies end in abortion; that's nearly 400,000 abortions a year (AGI, 1994). Many youngsters, perhaps because they are reluctant to acknowledge the pregnancy, do not seek medical attention before the end of the second trimester—long past the time for a safe legal abortion. Girls who choose abortion to escape an unintended pregnancy are most likely to be European American and in their early teens and cite their young age and low income as reasons for terminating their pregnancies.

Teenagers receive more than 25% of all the abortions performed in the United States, giving the United States the highest rate of teen abortion among developed, industrialized countries. Despite a marginally declining birth rate since 1970, adolescent pregnancy, abortion, and childbearing remain considerably higher in the United States than in most industrialized countries and continue to be a significant problem (Brown & Eisenberg, 1995).

The rise in adolescent sexual activity and subsequent pregnancies, abortions, and births can be traced to several factors: (a) a decline in the number of teenage marriages, (b) increasingly early onset of puberty (Dyk, 1993), (c) a change in the norms of sexual behavior in the direction of increased sexual activity, and (d) a change in youth culture (Holmes, 1995). Over the decades, the age of first menstruation has steadily fallen, although the mean age of marriage for women and men continues to rise. With the gap between physical maturity and marriage increasing, the need for responsible and early sex education has never been greater. Research on teenage sexual activity and the problems that stem from it is still somewhat limited. Few studies provide information related to such issues as demographic differences in adolescent sexual behavior, the consequences of early education for young boys regarding condom use (Kiselica, 1995), same-sex preferences and behaviors (Savin-Williams & Cohen, 1996), and fantasy and the meaning of eroticism in adolescents' lives. We hope to learn much more about these and other areas of adolescent sexuality in the coming years.

PRECURSORS OF TEEN PREGNANCY: COMMON BACKGROUND CHARACTERISTICS

Familial, psychological, and social issues as well as interpersonal characteristics contribute to teen pregnancy. The causes of teen pregnancy lie in (a) issues related to adolescent development; (b) antecedent characteristics that set the stage for pregnancy; (c) interpersonal influences, such as a youngster's peer relationships and family dynamics; and (d) the influence of the media.

Adolescent Development

In view of the normal challenges of adolescence, it is not surprising that many teens are involved in sexual activity or that pregnancy so frequently results. One of the primary ways in which adolescents attempt to negotiate the transition from childhood to adulthood is through sexual activity and fertility. Even though more than 80% of teenage parents never expected or wanted to conceive a child, many teens see sexual activity as a way to develop adult identity (Melchert & Burnett, 1990; Musick, 1993). Teens look to the opposite sex for validation and approval of the changes their bodies are undergoing. Sexual behavior also provides a means of challenging or confronting parents who seem to stand in the way of progress toward independence (Musick, 1993).

Preparation for career, marriage, and family life is part of this developmental period, and sexual activity serves as a way for adolescents to test these future roles. When an unwanted pregnancy occurs, the developmental process is accelerated. Adolescents must cope immediately with adult roles: parenthood, finding a job, dealing with social isolation and loneliness, and in many cases becoming dependent on public aid for survival. For many girls, pregnancy limits or precludes a great number of life options. However, if they already feel hopelessly restricted in their educational, occupational, and economic options, they may not perceive bearing and keeping a child as a barrier to the future. The nature of adolescence itself and the fact that many young people feel they have nothing to lose by having babies help to explain a great many teenage pregnancies.

Antecedent Characteristics

A variety of personal and demographic characteristics place teens at risk for premature pregnancy. Feelings of low self-worth, low self-esteem, difficulty with planning for the future, and frequent engagement in risk-taking activities are common (Robinson & Frank, 1994; Bell & Bell, 1993; Gardner & Herman, 1991). Teens at risk for pregnancy are also likely to reject social norms, to have limited knowledge of their own physiology, to have difficulty using information about birth control, to be biologically mature, and to have little structured religious orientation (Brown & Eisenberg, 1995; Haveman & Wolfe, 1994). Finally, a youngster's perception of opportunity and her estimation of how far she is able to go successfully in school and in a career are crucial determinants of her risk for pregnancy. One study, supported by Hofferth's (1991) review of community-based prevention programs, found that girls with greater career and life options were significantly less likely to engage in intercourse and more likely to use contraceptives when they did (Hambright, 1988).

Teens who were born to teenaged parents are also more likely to bear children during adolescence (Haveman & Wolfe, 1994; Wu & Martinson, 1993). Not only do lower educational and career opportunities influence a youngster's risk for pregnancy, but coming from a single-parent family or a family marked by marital strife and instability also increases the risk. Ethnicity, low socioeconomic status, absence of a father, poor school performance, and family difficulties are all associated with teen pregnancy. Among male teens, school difficulties, low socioeconomic status, and ethnicity are associated with fathering a child (Kiselica, 1995). To prevent unwanted pregnancies among teens with these characteristics, schools and communities would do well to implement programs that increase self-esteem, educate students about sex and pregnancy, expand the range of career options that students consider, and provide students with the skills they need to pursue these options.

Interpersonal Influences

One of the primary interpersonal variables associated with adolescent pregnancy is the degree of communication and alienation in the mother-daughter relationship. A close mother-daughter relationship encourages adolescent and preadolescent girls to turn to mother instead of others for nurturance. Communication between mother and daughter about sex, sexual issues, and sexual feelings and behaviors can significantly help daughters learn and practice responsible sexual behavior. Such communication desensitizes the topic of sex; helps teens overcome negative feelings about the changes in their bodies, and provides information about birth control. In addition, girls who feel close to their mothers may work harder to please them; they may be more likely to abstain from sex or to practice birth control when they are sexually active. A good mother-daughter relationship can provide a girl with a model not only for responsible sexual behavior but for forming and maintaining a good relationship with a future partner (Apter, 1990). When communication is absent, a girl is placed at greater risk for premature sexual activity and potential conception, in part because she looks to others, especially male peers, for nurturance and intimacy.

Families with poor interpersonal relationships, ineffective communication, and limited problem-solving skills may inadvertently encourage teens to turn elsewhere for nurturing relationships. Promiscuity and neglect of contraception are not uncommon outcomes of family strife and family estrangement (Apter, 1990; Musick, 1993). Teens turn to peers for relationships that they are unable to find in their families. Pressure from the peer cluster (as we discussed earlier) can lead to norms of risky behavior and irresponsibility. The peer cluster not only provides support, fairly clear norms, and the structure that most adolescents want but, along with the media, becomes the primary source of information about sex. Unfortunately, the adolescents who confidently share information about sex may lack knowledge about their own bodies and about contraception. Without family support, a sense of personal worth, and employment and life goals, young people are much more susceptible to peer influence. Other teenagers, therefore, often become the primary factor in a youngster's decision to engage in sexual activity—a decision that is usually both premature and irresponsible (see Box 8.1).

Finally, once a girl becomes pregnant, her mother usually has the most influence on the outcome. Often the mother pressures her pregnant daughter to keep the child. In this case, the relationships between mother, daughter, and baby tend to become confused, with the new grandmother taking on primary responsibility for the infant. Although these teen mothers may indeed have family support, the pressure to keep the baby in the family usually restricts their educational and occupational attainment (Haveman & Wolfe, 1994). Often this choice locks the babies into a similar situation of restricted future options, and the cycle of "babies having babies" is perpetuated.

Media Influences

Premature and irresponsible decisions are encouraged by the way sexuality is represented in the media. Young people are bombarded with sexual messages and images in

■ ■ ■ Box 8.1

Daddy's Girl

Youngsters and adults often fail to see eye to eye on family support. When 16-year-old Susan and her father came for counseling to work on their relationship, she appeared sullen, depressed, and angry. When I met with her alone, she explained that her father had tricked her into coming by telling her he was taking her shopping. She confided that she was pregnant, that her father did not know, and that she hadn't been able to hold down food for three straight days. Susan's mother had "run off years ago." Susan reported that she had had one abortion already and was very reluctant to have another one. When I saw her father alone, he told me that he knew she was pregnant—"Well, that's why I brought her to you." He emphasized several times, "I'm a hundred percent behind her. I support Susan all the way." He told her the same thing when the two were brought together and she acknowledged her pregnancy. In the same breath he told her, "The decision is totally up to you. But of course, if you decide not to get an abortion, you'll have to live somewhere else."

Susan did not show up for her next appointment. She sounded tearful when she answered the phone.

"Couldn't you make it in today?" I asked.

"No, I'm sick. Well. . . I had an abortion this morning."

Despite repeated calls and letters to her father, he would not bring her in for additional counseling. So far as her "supportive" father was concerned, Susan no longer had a problem.

entertainment, advertising, and in other aspects of their lives. That the media is saturated with sexual material is incontestable. Lowry and Shidler (1993) found an average of 10 instances of sexual behavior per hour on network prime time television, and portrayals of heterosexual intercourse increased 84% (from 1.8 to 3.3 behaviors per hour) from a similar study conducted four years earlier. Promotional messages for other prime time programs included even higher rates of sexual behavior, with networks using sexual bait to increase their ratings. When promotional sexual behavior is added, the rate of sexual behaviors per hour increases to more than 15. Music rock videos, rap music, and cable and video cassette movies tend to be even more sexually explicit. Virtually every R-rated movie contains at least one nude scene, and some favorites contain as many as 15 instances of sexual intercourse in less than 2 hours (Greenberg et al., 1993).

Running parallel to this provocative sexual permissiveness is a prudishness about contraception use. Despite the high level of sexual activity in television programming, the major national networks have adopted the position that contraceptive advertising is not acceptable. ABC believes such advertising offends many listeners; the Fox network is willing to accept condom advertising to prevent disease only, not unintended pregnancy (Lebow, 1994). Interestingly, an early 1990s survey found that two-thirds of adult Americans supported airing contraceptive advertisements (Lebow, 1994). These conflicting attitudes and views about sexual behavior make it difficult to disseminate accurate, clear information about contraception, which may limit contraceptive use.

CONSEQUENCES OF EARLY CHILDBEARING

When a teenage girl becomes pregnant, her physical, social, educational, and career development is significantly altered. An unwanted child has consequences for the mother's socioeconomic status, her educational attainment, her health, and her family development.

Socioeconomic Consequences

A teenage girl who decides to keep her baby is likely to suffer consequences in the form of substandard housing, poor nutrition and health, unemployment or underemployment, an end to her schooling, inadequate career training, and financial dependency (Robinson, Watkins-Ferrell, Davis-Scott, & Ruch-Ross, 1993). She is substantially more likely to live in poverty than a married mother who is older. Furthermore, the average family income of girls who give birth at 16 or younger is approximately one-fourth that earned by families in which the mother is in her late 20s (Moore, Myers, Morrison, Nord, Brown, & Edmonston, 1993). A disproportionately large share of Aid to Families with Dependent Children (AFDC) goes to teenage parents, and the same is true of other forms of public assistance, such as Medicaid and food stamps, a great cost to society. Perhaps most discouraging, teen mothers are rarely able to achieve economic parity with women who postpone parenthood until they are in their 20s.

A truncated education, which frequently accompanies a teenage pregnancy, exacerbates the problem. Young mothers with limited education do not develop the skills, resources, and experiences necessary to overcome their poverty and the pervasive sense of powerlessness that usually accompanies it. Most teenage girls who carry their pregnancies to term decide to keep their babies, cementing the link between adolescent childbearing and poverty. Unlike their more affluent sisters, when poor girls make bad choices, engage in risky behavior, become pregnant, and keep their babies, they are more likely to close doors that can never be reopened. Those who come of age in poverty are given very little margin of error in negotiating the tasks of adolescence. Breaking this cycle and fostering teens' productive participation in society is critical to adolescent parents, their children, and society as a whole.

Educational Consequences

Teen pregnancy is associated with low achievement scores and low vocational aspirations. Clearly, youth at risk for becoming parents are also at risk for dropping out of school and are more likely to be unemployed or underemployed throughout much of their lives, especially if they are minority youngsters. Teen mothers were three times more likely to drop out of school than mothers who delayed childbearing until they were in their 20s. In recent years, the proportion of teenage mothers with high school diplomas has increased, in large part because many school districts now provide alternative high schools or school programs for student mothers. However, few young mothers attend college, and less than 1% complete a college degree (Moore, 1992).

The educational problems faced by adolescent parents are frequently carried over into the next generation. A disproportionate number of the children born to teenagers show more emotional and behavioral problems while growing up (Thomson, Hanson, & McLanahan, 1994; Zill, Morrison, & Cioro, 1993). These children also have more erratic attendance records, lower grade point averages, lower scores on standardized achievement tests, and lower college expectations (Astone & McLanahan, 1991). These consequences have clear implications for school policy. As teens continue to deliver children at the current rate, school systems are confronted with a burgeoning group of children who are themselves at risk for intellectual and social deficits. Ultimately, educators and society are forced to cope with the special needs of the children of teen mothers.

Health-Related Consequences

Pregnant adolescents commonly experience poor nutrition, poor health, and limited access to and use of medical and health services. Prenatal, perinatal, and postnatal problems are more common among them than among older mothers, and more of their babies die, likely because they seek prenatal care infrequently in their first trimester. The younger the mother, the higher the incidence of anemia, toxemia, infections of the urinary tract, STDs, uterine dysfunction, cephalopelvic disproportion, and other complications of labor and delivery (Stevens-Simon & White, 1991). These problems are compounded for teenagers who live in poor socioeconomic conditions. In comparison with older women, younger girls also have problems with premature delivery and are at greater risk of very long labor (American College of Obstetricians and Gynecologists, 1993). Youngsters whose living conditions are poor receive inadequate health care and are in poorer health even before they become pregnant.

Children of teenage mothers also have serious health problems. For example, 15-year-old mothers are twice as likely as older mothers to have low-birth-weight babies, and the baby is three times as likely to die in the first eight days of life. Low birth weight has been related to a number of developmental difficulties and learning disabilities. The mortality rate is twice as high for infants born to mothers under 17 years of age than for infants born to older women. These infants also experience higher rates of injury and illness, and there is a higher incidence of Sudden Infant Death Syndrome (Morris, Warren, & Aral, 1993). Health problems are particularly acute in ethnic minority groups. Hispanic and African American teen mothers in younger age groups are nearly one and a half times more likely than European American teen mothers to receive late or no prenatal care; only 43% got early prenatal care in 1992 (CDF, 1995). Nationally, the ethnic minority infant mortality rate is about twice that of European Americans, and this difference is not explained by the difference in the number of conceptions and births.

Family Development

Few teen pregnancies actually involve marriage. Of the girls who do marry, nearly a third are divorced within five years, compared to 15% among couples who marry later. Most children born to teen mothers will spend at least part of their lives in single-parent homes (AGI, 1994). Indeed, many teenage fathers never acknowledge parenthood. Some of these boys never know that they are fathers, but many more do know and are simply unwilling to deal with the responsibilities of parenthood (Arendell, 1995; Kiselica, 1995).

Teenage mothers are at a great disadvantage when they attempt to create a healthy and stimulating environment for their children. They are often forced to work long hours and may have little time to spend with their babies. These problems may be compounded by neglect, as teen mothers often know little about what babies need to thrive. Teen mothers experience a great deal of stress, and the potential for child abuse is significant (Becker-Lansen & Rickel, 1995). Boyer and Fine (1992) and Walker (1996) suggest that the high rate of maltreatment inflicted by adolescent mothers on their own children is more likely to be associated with the stress of their histories as abuse victims rather than the immaturity associated with their young age. Nevertheless, the baby's underdevelopment in all of these areas lays a foundation for a continued cycle of teen pregnancy.

Children raised by young single mothers exhibit problems with their own family formation and their adjustment to society. They leave home earlier (Kiernan, 1992; Thornton, 1991). If married, they are more likely to divorce, and they are more likely to become teen parents and unmarried parents (Haveman & Wolfe, 1994; Wu & Martinson, 1993). The risk of becoming a teenage mother is 27% for children raised by single mothers compared to 11% for children raised by both parents (McLanahan & Sandefur, 1994). Such children are more likely to have problems finding and keeping a steady job after leaving school and are more likely to be involved with the criminal justice system (Haveman & Wolfe, 1994; McLanahan & Sandefur, 1994; Powers, 1994).

AIDS and Other Sexually Transmitted Diseases

Irresponsible, premature, and risky sexual contact can have serious consequences other than pregnancy. Sexually transmitted diseases (STDs) have extremely serious health consequences for sexually active young people. The rates of STDs are escalating among teenagers, and more than 3 million teens acquire an STD every year (Donovan, 1993). Chlamydia, an infection of the vagina or urinary tract, is the most frequently diagnosed STD among adolescents. Gonorrhea, genital warts, herpes, and syphilis are also common. The health consequences of these STDs can be irreversible, and some (herpes and AIDS) are incurable.

Teens who engage in high-risk behavior—principally unprotected sexual intercourse or intravenous drug use—are vulnerable to contracting HIV, which leads to AIDS. By 1995, nearly 2000 cases of AIDS had been reported among 13- to 19-year-olds. Although teenagers currently make up a small percentage of the total number of AIDS cases, their number doubles every year. More important, this figure does not fully reflect the level of risk because full-blown AIDS takes an average of ten years to develop from initial contraction of HIV (CDC, 1994; Smith, McGraw, Crawford, Costa, & McKinlay, 1993). Teenagers who contract HIV may not be aware that they carry this virus until after they have infected others. By 1995, nearly 17,000 young adults between 20 and 24 years old were diagnosed with AIDS. These individuals represent nearly 80% of the AIDS cases, and these young adults undoubtably contracted HIV in their teens.

Teenagers know at least as much about AIDS as adults, and some have changed their behavior over the last decade, increasing their use of condoms from 21% to 58% (Yondorf, 1992). Perhaps more than adults, teens tend to feel invulnerable to something as catastrophic as AIDS—"It can't happen to me!" That attitude coupled with a risk-taking one (Bell & Bell, 1993), plus high sexual activity, multiple sex partners, and ineffective, sporadic, or no condom use make teenagers very vulnerable for contracting HIV/AIDS. The urgency of dealing with teenage sexual issues as early and as informatively as possible cannot be overestimated.

Vulnerable and Underserved Youth

Among adolescents, ethnic minority and gay youth are particularly vulnerable. Hispanic and African American adolescents are highly overrepresented among persons with AIDS: 14% are Hispanic and 25% are African American (Centers for Disease Control and Prevention, 1994; Jemmott, Jemmott, & Fong, 1992). Three-fourths of all younger children (mostly the babies of infected parents) and more than half of all teens known to have the disease are members of ethnic minority groups (Steel, 1995).

Sexually active adolescent gay males, who are less likely to identify with adult gay communities, are particularly vulnerable to HIV infection (Besner & Spungin, 1995; Cranston, 1991). As adolescents experiment sexually with both male and female partners, teenage boys who experiment with unprotected sex with other males may not see themselves at risk if they do not self-identify as gay, which most do not. This activity causes a chaining or bridging effect, which allows transmission of the virus both to the larger teenage population and especially to teenagers who are gay. Chained or bridged contact rather than direct homosexual or intravenous drug use contact is the cause of HIV/AIDS among most teenagers.

PREVENTION AND TREATMENT STRATEGIES: GENERAL FRAMEWORK

Adolescent pregnancy and HIV/AIDS have such serious consequences for teens, their families, and society that it is tremendously important to encourage responsible sexual behavior. Three general approaches seem most useful: (a) family-life planning and sex education, (b) increased accessibility of contraceptives to teens, and (c) increased life options for teens who are at greatest risk for unprotected sexual activity and pregnancy (Conger, 1988).

In presenting these general approaches we adopt a very similar position to the Institute of Medicine's Committee on Unintended Pregnancy (Brown & Eisenberg, 1995). Abstinence cannot be counted on as the major means to reduce unintended pregnancy or HIV/AIDS among teenagers. However, we unequivocally support abstinence as one of the methods available to prevent unintended pregnancy and STDs. Furthermore, we believe that young people should be counseled and encouraged to resist precocious sexual involvement. Sexual intercourse should occur in the context of a major personal commitment based on caring and mutual consent and on the exercise of personal responsibility, including steps to avoid both STDs and unintended pregnancy. The prevention and treatment interventions presented in this section all reflect this position.

Family-Life Planning and Sex Education

All children and adolescents need appropriate family-life education from the early school years through high school. Unfortunately, many young people receive little information about sexuality from their parents. Family-life education should begin in elementary school and can include sex education. Access to information about human sexuality, reproduction, and birth control is a prerequisite for responsible sexual behavior. The curriculum can effectively include complete and accurate information on human reproductive biology, contraceptive methods, and the place of sexuality in normal adolescent development. Educators should avoid overemphasizing technical detail. They should also avoid misrepresenting facts or omitting essential options. The goal is to provide accurate, complete, and relevant data so that young people can make more informed and responsible decisions. Teaching responsible decision-making strategies is also important. Although sex education is still highly controversial in some communities, Haffner (1994) found that when given the option of excusing their children from sex education in the schools less than 5% of parents do so. Further, there is no evidence that HIV and sex education programs increase the frequency of sexual activity or hasten the onset of intercourse among teenagers (Kirby, Short, Collins, et al., 1994).

Sex education improves factual knowledge, but there is no conclusive proof that behavior is influenced by such information. Neither the rate of sexual activity nor the efficacy of contraceptive use appears to change as a result of information nor has pregnancy been prevented as a result of information alone. Therefore, information and knowledge about sexuality must be combined with other approaches and strategies, such as ways to improve relationships, boost self-esteem, and improve behavioral skills.

Kirby and his colleagues (Kirby, Short, Collins, et al., 1994) reviewed 20 school-based sex and HIV/AIDS education programs and demonstrated that specific programs did have some effect on sexual behavior, contraceptive use, or both. The reviewed programs clustered into three types: (a) abstinence-only programs that avoided discussion of contraception, (b) programs that discussed contraception and abstinence, and (c) programs that provided comprehensive reproductive health education topics, including information about clinical services, abstinence, and contraception. Abstinence-only programs provided insufficienct evidence to determine whether they contributed to delay in age of first intercourse or had an impact on other sexual and contraceptive behaviors. They did appear to affect attitudes regarding premarital intercourse; teens reflected more positive or greater abstinence attitudes than before the treatment. Effects of the second type of program were mixed. Some demonstrated positive changes in behavior, and others only positive changes in attitude. In addition to changing attitudes, the comprehensive programs also appeared to delay the initiation of intercourse, reduce the frequency of intercourse, reduce the number of sexual partners, and increase the use of contraceptives. Thus school-based sex education programs that link reproductive health services to educational components that teach specific facts, norms, values, and skills appear to help young people limit and delay sexual activity and avoid unprotected sex (Kirby, Short, Collins, et al., 1994).

Access to Contraceptive Methods

As mentioned earlier, the United States has higher rates of adolescent pregnancy, childbearing, and abortion than most other Western industrialized countries and contraceptive access may be the primary reason. In those countries reporting more favorable rates, contraceptive services are confidential, widely available, and very inexpensive or free (Brown & Eisenberg, 1995).

Pregnancy and childbearing are too important to be undertaken accidentally, unintentionally, or casually. Sexually active adolescents need access to contraceptive methods. Contraceptives cannot be forced on youngsters, but they should be available. Access can best be provided through community- and school-based clinics that provide comprehensive, easily accessible, and high-quality health services for teens and preteens.

School-based clinics are particularly useful because adolescent sexuality in all its aspects can be dealt with in the context of overall health care by a staff that is aware of the special concerns and needs of this age group. Those few clinics that provide comprehensive health services, including dispensing contraceptives, have had promising results. Among the population served by four such clinics in St. Paul, Minnesota, the overall annual rate of first-time pregnancies was reduced from 80 per 1000 to 29 per 1000 (Kirby, 1985; Schorr, 1988). Further, repeat pregnancies were reduced to 1.4%, compared to 33% nationally. Some evidence (see Dryfoos, 1994) suggests that school-based clinics offered in the context of comprehensive family planning services have had an impact on upgrading the quality of contraceptive use, lowering pregnancy rates, and delaying the initiation of intercourse.

Increased Life Options

When young people feel good about themselves and have a clear vision of a successful and self-sufficient future, they will be motivated to avoid pregnancy. "The best contraceptive is a real future" (Edelman, 1987, p. 58). A future requires opportunities to build academic and work-related skills, job opportunities, life-planning assistance, and comprehensive health services. Young people who move steadily along the path toward personal and economic self-sufficiency tend to make more responsible decisions.

Young people also need skills to avoid pregnancy—skills in decision making, assertiveness, and building self-esteem. (We discuss strategies to teach such skills in Chapter 12.) Young people must learn such skills if they are to know how to regulate intimacy, to behave in accordance with their personal values and boundaries, and to avoid the unwanted consequences of sexual activity.

Any skill-building program designed to alter sexual behavior needs to personalize the information so that young people can apply it directly and concretely to themselves. Knowledge of the fact that intercourse without protection is likely to lead to pregnancy has little impact unless it is translated into a personal statement that applies to one's own situation: "If Kevin and I have intercourse and we don't use protection, I could get pregnant. I don't want to get pregnant. We have to use birth control." Such self-statements transform abstract information into personal knowledge that becomes part of the young person's everyday reality. This personal knowledge helps in the decision-making process.

Self-understanding is another means of personalizing information and increasing motivation. Awareness of the purpose and goals of one's behavior is an extremely important component of self-understanding. Young people at risk for pregnancy need to be encouraged to understand why they are engaging in sexual activity and especially why they are unwilling to use methods that prevent pregnancy. Such understanding helps the young person make better decisions. Adults who work with young people at risk for pregnancy need to understand these underlying goals and purposes as well because they are in a position to help young people make better decisions.

PREVENTION AND TREATMENT STRATEGY: AN ADLERIAN MODEL

One of the best models for understanding a youngster's behavior is found in Alfred Adler's (1930, 1964; Hoffman, 1994) concepts of social interest, mistaken goals, and purposive behavior. Rudolf Dreikurs (1964, 1967), the foremost interpreter of Adler's ideas as they apply to the American scene, added another concept: the goals of misbehavior.

We must emphasize that these concepts are extremely useful to a wide range of adolescent problems and issues. They are helpful in responding to teenagers in the sexual realm (B. T. McWhirter, J. J. McWhirter, A. M. McWhirter, & E. H. McWhirter, 1993), but they apply just as well to young people's school problems, delinquency, drug use, and suicide issues as well as to classroom management and family concerns (Clark, 1994; Manaster, 1990). Equally important, the concepts are especially helpful for younger children. Indeed, Adler, and later Dreikurs, developed child guidance clinics that provided education and counseling to families and parents, not infrequently with very young children. Further, many elementary school counselors use these ideas to assist young children in a wide range of problem areas.

Our primary purpose here is to (a) present a framework for understanding one aspect of teenage sexual behavior, (b) help youngsters understand themselves better, and (c) provide the concerned adult with tools to help prevent and deal with teen pregnancy. We first present a general framework of the model, and then we detail its specific application to issues of sexuality.

According to Adler, much individual behavior is directed toward finding a place or position in the group. All young people need a sense of belonging and an arena in which to contribute. Low-risk children find belonging first in their families and later in the school environment with peers and adults. In their interaction with their social environment, they find ways to contribute to the common welfare. These contributions increase their social interest, build their feelings of self-worth, and solidify their sense of belonging. Unfortunately, other youngsters struggle to belong and are frustrated in their attempts to contribute to the social group. But the need to belong continues, and these youngsters often behave in ways that are less acceptable in the mistaken belief that a particular action will fulfill a certain social need. These mistaken beliefs contribute to what Dreikurs calls the goals of misbehavior. Negative, antisocial, and self-defeating behavior has an underlying purpose—to allow the individual to fit in the group. One way to help at-risk children is to attend to the underlying purposiveness of their behavior: first, to understand their mistaken goals and to respond more appropriately to them, and second, to reveal to the youngsters themselves their own underlying goals and the purposiveness of their actions.

Purposiveness of Behavior

Purpose is not the same as cause. Cause is past-oriented; purpose is future-oriented. Cause implies a need to search through past history to identify what event, person, or situation brought about the youngster's present behavior. It also implies the individual's lack of control over the behavior. Purposiveness reflects the goals the youth wants to achieve and the consequences he or she anticipates. In this sense, the youngster's behavior is a means to an end and is based on his or her perceptions of reality. Young people perform behaviors that they believe will lead to desirable consequences and help them avoid unpleasant ones. Because the causes of behavior are in the past, they usually cannot be reversed, so knowledge of them is of minimal use. Their only significance lies in the fact that they influence the child's expectations for the future and help the adult understand the child's goals. Purpose operates in the present and looks toward the future, toward the outcome of behavior, and therefore is more directly open to intervention.

When researchers analyzed the early recollections, birth order, and personality characteristics of unmarried pregnant adolescents, they found concurrence among judges that becoming pregnant was purposive behavior (Jorgensen & Newlon, 1988). Each girl had a purpose in conceiving that was in accordance with her lifestyle, even if she consciously denied it.

Goals of Misbehavior

In the Adler/Dreikurs model, a youngster's misbehavior may have one or more of four goals: (a) attention (the child wants service and attention), (b) power (the child wants to be boss), (c) revenge (the child desires to hurt others), and (d) inadequacy or assumed disability (the child wants to be left alone). Although young people are usually unaware of the underlying purpose of their misbehavior, they do see their actions as logical. Whether youngsters seek attention, attempt to assert power, take revenge, or capitalize on their inadequacy, the corresponding misbehavior is designed to get special recognition. Their behavior, regardless of their goal, results from the belief that this is the most effective way to function in the group, which includes the family and the peer cluster.

Attention.   When children do not achieve acceptance and belonging through useful contributions to the family, many youngsters seek inclusion through attention. At first they may seek attention through socially acceptable means. If these efforts are unsuccessful, they may try any of a vast array of negative behaviors calculated to get attention. The *purpose* of such attention-getting mechanisms (AGMs) is to engage the adult. The young person's underlying goal is to get adults to pay attention. The adult's intervention reinforces the youngster's desire for attention, because it's better to be punished than to be ignored.

Attention-getting behaviors are usually negative, but overly cooperative behavior may also be a bid for special attention. It is sometimes difficult to distinguish between behavior that stems from a genuine willingness to be helpful and behavior that is aimed primarily at getting attention. If the youth's behavior seems directed to becoming the best or better than the other children (the teacher's pet), this youngster is probably motivated by a desire for attention. Children and adolescents need to be able to derive satisfaction from performing positive, cooperative behaviors rather than simply from the reinforcement that follows. Consider an adolescent girl who gains satisfaction from her pro-social acts only when adults notice them. If her siblings (at home) and classmates (at school) are more successful at gaining adults' attention, she may try to gain attention by being the worst among her peers. Many youngsters behave negatively because the positive roles they really want are already taken.

Recognizing when attention is the goal of misbehavior is not simple, but some clues can be discerned. The first clue is the feeling engendered in the adult toward the misbehaving youth; the second is the child's behavioral reaction to the adult's reprimand. The child's response to corrections depends on the goal of the misbehavior. If the adult's initial feeling is annoyance, irritation, or surface anger, then the child's goal is probably attention. In this case, the child should react to correction by temporarily stopping the disturbing action. Essentially, the scolding, coaxing, helping, reminding, and so forth provide the desired attention, so the behavior stops—temporarily.

Understanding the purpose of irresponsible sexual behavior is a more complex task because the behavior is aimed not only at adults but at peers as well. In some cases, AGMs evoke attention and concern from permissive or indifferent parents. In other cases, AGMs derive from a desire for attention and affection from boys or from a specific boy. Sometimes the AGM is directed toward the idealized infant in the hope that the baby may fill an emotional gap left by rejecting parents or an insensitive partner. In each instance, the need to belong, to feel needed, to be loved, or to feel self-esteem underlies the AGMs.

As part of a research project, one of the authors was debriefing eighth grade students after they filled out questionnaires about stress. One student, a 12-year-old eighth-grader, offered shyly, "well, I don't have a boyfriend, but I met a boy at the mall and I let him put it in me. I know that's how you get a baby, but he said he took it out in time. I hope he's gonna meet me there again." In the course of the subsequent conversation, it was quickly apparent that she was not interested in physical pleasure, nor did she seem to have romantic notions about babies; she simply wanted to feel special.

Boys, too, exhibit purposiveness and mistaken goals in their sexual behavior. Sexual interaction provides affection and attention from girls. Sometimes boys establish desired reputations as their sexual exploits gain the attention of their male peers. In some subgroups, fathering a child increases the boy's status and brings him into what he perceives to be a more mature and powerful stage of development.

Power.   When the goal of misbehavior is power, youngsters appear to believe that their worth is based on their ability to dominate, control, and manipulate adults. They demonstrate their control and power by refusing to be commanded and by breaking rules. Many youngsters use manipulation to assert their feelings of self-worth and to demonstrate to themselves and to the world that they do have power over others.

If the adult responds to the power struggle by exerting more control or power to force compliance, the youngster becomes even more convinced of the value of power. The goal is less to win the struggle than to get the adult involved in it. Once the battle has been joined, the teenager has already won (King, 1991). The youngster, of course, would prefer to get his or her way, but regardless of the end result, getting the adult engaged is the real purpose behind the behavior. Even though teenagers ultimately may not win this struggle, they do score a victory each time they defy a request or break a rule.

If the adult's anger goes beyond mere annoyance and if the anger is coupled with feelings of being challenged and provoked, then the young person's goal is probably to gain power. The sentences that run through the adult's mind at this point also provide clues to the nature of this power struggle ("I'll show you who's boss around here." "I'll make you do it." "You can't get away with that."). When the adult behaves in accordance with these thoughts, the youngster may escalate his or her actions or comply outwardly while subtly sabotaging the adult's efforts. Either way, the teenager wins the power struggle.

The underlying goal of power in sexual acting out may be directed against parents who are inconsistent, too permissive, or too strict. On the surface level the youngster appears to be expressing independence, but in reality the behavior is designed to establish a position vis-à-vis the parents. Willingness or unwillingness to engage in sex may provide the girl with perceived power over males or over a specific partner. Willingness to participate in unprotected intercourse may be based on the mistaken belief that her tenuous relationship with a boy will become more stable and permanent if she has his child.

Boys may also use sexual activity to demonstrate independence and power over their parents. With their partner, boys may use sex as a physical expression of domination or control. Sometimes the boy's macho attitude and his unwillingness to use a condom are attempts to demonstrate power. Assuming that girls are responsible for contraception and denying fatherhood when pregnancy occurs are other ways in which the young male may express domination and power over others through sexual behavior.

Revenge. The youngster who seeks revenge is extremely discouraged and poses the greatest problem. Hostile or aggressive behavior in young children does not necessarily indicate a deep personality disturbance, but among adolescents such behavior may be pathological. If youngsters have not been able to attain and maintain a desired position by gaining attention or power, they may consider that the only other way to gain attention is to hurt someone. It is as if they conclude, "I can't be liked and I don't have power—but I *can* be hated." This often violent antagonism provides youngsters with a specific role to play in the group.

Revenge is sought only after a long series of failures has convinced the youngster of his or her utter lack of belonging. Revenge is frequently the result of an unrecognized problem (depression, say, or a learning disability) and of unrealistic expectations and pressures by significant adults. The unrecognized problem may prevent the young person from accomplishing a particular task. Assuming negative motives, adults punish the youth for "not trying." Youngsters are hurt by such encounters and want to hurt back. In taking this position, they are likely to evoke responses that justify the continuation of revenge, and the cycle escalates.

Feelings of intense anger with underlying hurt and shock in response to a young person's behavior indicate to the adult that the goal of misbehavior is probably revenge. The adult may think: "How could he possibly do that to me?" "This kid is just nasty and unlovable." "How could she be so vicious and cruel?" If the adult's response is full of anger, the youngster will continue trying to get even. If the adult responds with hurt, sadness, and tears, the youth may actually smile (see Box 8.2).

Premature and irresponsible sexual activity is sometimes a way to get back at parents. Sexuality can also be used to obtain revenge on the partner if one feels slighted,

> ### Box 8.2
> ## Lying for Revenge
>
> Some years ago I was co-conducting a consultation with several teenagers and their families. The model* we were using called for a large group meeting that included both parents and teenagers, in which participants discussed family and school concerns. We then broke into smaller groups, the adults in one group and the young people in another.
>
> After several weekly sessions, a girl who had a particularly stormy relationship with her mother used the large group session as an opportunity to tell her parents that she thought she was pregnant. Her mother's horror and embarrassment were vividly expressed. Later, during the session with peers and siblings, the girl reported that she was *not* pregnant and currently wasn't even sexually active. Her earlier, false self-disclosure, she concluded, was intended to hurt her mother: a clear instance of revenge. In a later family session this incident became a springboard that enabled us to help her look at the self-defeating aspects of her behavior and to help her family confront their own dysfunction.
>
> *Note: See J. J. McWhirter, 1966; J. J. McWhirter & Golden, 1975; J. J. McWhirter & Kincaid, 1974.

rejected, or jilted. The person who acts out sexually may intend to get back at the former partner. Some young people also learn early on to use sex as a means to exert power over others, as in the case of rape, including acquaintance rape or date rape. Ultimately, the dynamics of revenge are played out not only within the family but also between partners.

Assumed inadequacy. Children and teenagers who expect failure rely on their assumed inadequacy to escape participation in the group and family system. They want to be left alone. As long as nothing is expected of them, they can still appear to be members of the group. Some children and adolescents believe that by hiding behind a display of real or imagined inferiority, they can avoid even more embarrassing and humiliating experiences. Youngsters who feel inadequate and incapable of functioning will not try, whether their deficiency is real or merely assumed.

This goal poses serious problems for parents, teachers, and counselors because these young people realize that underachievement and lack of effort are the most effective ways to keep adults involved with them. Thus, it is convenient for them to continue their lack of effort even when it is no longer necessary. Adults often fail to distinguish between a real lack of ability and a lack of ability that the child or adolescent merely assumes.

Feelings of despair, frustration, and hopelessness in the adult are good signs that the young person is operating on the assumption of inadequacy. It is mandatory that adults reflect upon the feelings aroused by a youngster's misbehavior, because whatever they feel is often exactly what the youngster intends them to feel. Despair and hopelessness may be what the youngster wants, but such responses encourage continued inadequacy. Once counselors, teachers, and parents understand what the youngster is seeking, they can avoid inappropriate reactions that strengthen the misbehavior and can attempt more constructive responses.

Assumed inadequacy in the sexual realm is expressed in a variety of ways. Lack of assertiveness in saying no to sexual activity is one way. Others are unwillingness to use contraceptives and leaving responsibility for their use solely in the hands of the partner. The term *assumed* suggests that these youngsters have the skills to resist sexual pressure—from a partner or from peers—or to insist on protection if they do engage in sex but that they do not use these skills. Of course, we know that some young people's inadequacy is not assumed; the lack of skill is real. In such situations the concerned adult can use specific cognitive and behavioral strategies to provide success experiences and reduce the young person's sense of inadequacy. In Chapter 11 we provide a model for building skills, and in Chapter 12 we discuss specific cognitive and behavioral strategies from which young people may benefit.

Summary. Having reviewed the four goals, we must emphasize that young people are often in pursuit of more than one goal at the same time and that their goals can shift depending on the people with whom they interact. Some youngsters have not determined their goal orientation; they may be vacillating between attention and power or between power and revenge. Some young people switch from one goal to another, and some actually pursue all four goals at one time, a situation that causes parents, counselors, teachers, and other adults a great deal of distress. Some children or teenagers may have one goal at school, another goal with their peers, and still another at home. If the misbehavior is to be understood, the youngster's actions have to be seen as a whole, as part of the total social environment, not as emanating solely from one situation.

Sexual behavior does not have an underlying negative purpose for all teens. Needs gratification, reinforcement, pleasure, and desire for warmth, closeness, and validation are all components of sexuality. When teens become pregnant, mixed goals are probably the rule rather than the exception. Allie Andrews, for example, appears to use sex to gain attention from boys. Further, lacking a positive position at home, she has progressed from sex-as-attention to sex-as-power to show her stepfather that she counts. Unfortunately, his criticisms and accusations have led her now to use sex to shock and hurt him. She has adopted the goal of revenge (on her stepfather), and uses her sexual behavior at least partly as a way of getting back at him.

Among the methods that have proved helpful in efforts to intervene with young people who are struggling with these four mistaken goals are corrective procedures, logical and natural consequences, and encouragement. We first present the techniques and strategies that are useful for general problems, and then follow these with specific approaches related to managing the problems of teenage pregnancy.

Corrective Procedures

Corrective procedures involve (a) learning to alter one's responses to misbehaving youngsters and (b) helping the young people to interpret the goals of their misbehavior. Altering one's responses begins with identifying the feelings aroused by the youth's behavior (anger, disgust, resentment, despair, whatever) and then not acting on those feelings. Helping young people interpret their goals is a bit more complex. No one is fully conscious of why youngsters behave the way they do. If you ask them why they did whatever they did, the response is likely to be an honest "I don't know." When a young person does give an explanation, it is usually a hindsight rationalization rather than a factual account of motives. The sensitive counselor or teacher can help youngsters gain awareness of their goals by proposing some possible goals of their disturbing behavior. Such a confrontation can be the first step toward change. To confront the behavior, however, is not to label it ("You're aggressive [or lazy, or disturbing]"). Labeling has no meaning for the young person, does not explain the behavior, and does nothing to change it. Confrontation helps youngsters understand their own motivation and gives them the option of continuing or discontinuing their behavior. Often the behavior loses its appeal once the underlying intention has been brought into the open.

The most useful questions begin with "Could it be that. . ." All questions must be asked in a friendly, nonjudgmental way, and the middle of an argument is not the time to ask them. And it is not enough to help youngsters identify their goals; it is important to provide them with alternative and less self-defeating goals. All corrective procedures should be geared toward helping youngsters choose more constructive goals and behaviors.

Corrective procedures for AGMs. We suggest that counselors, teachers, and parents use the following procedures to redirect youngsters whose attention-getting tactics are inappropriate.

- Help youngsters understand the attention-getting aspects of their behavior by asking "Could it be?" questions. "Could it be that you want me to do special things for you?" ". . . that you want to keep me busy with you?" ". . . that you want me to notice you?"
- Ignore the misbehaving youngster and provide attention when the child or teen is not engaging in AGMs.
- Recognize that punishing, giving service, coaxing, and scolding are forms of attention and serve to reinforce the negative behavior.

Corrective procedures for power. The interpretive questions and corrective procedures listed below help power-seekers modify their behavior.

- Ask "Could it be?" questions: "Could it be that you want to be the boss?" ". . . that you want to get me to do what you want?" ". . . that you want to show me that you can do what you want and no one can stop you?"
- Recognize and admit to yourself and to the youngster that he or she does have power.
- Withdraw from or do not engage in conflict.
- Act, don't talk. For example, demonstrate your commitment to family or school rules by consistently imposing consequences when the rules are broken.
- Establish equality through a willingness to negotiate as many issues as you can.
- Redirect youngsters' efforts into constructive pathways by enlisting their cooperation, appealing for their help, and giving them responsibility.

Corrective procedures for revenge.   Youngsters whose behavior is directed toward revenge can be helped to behave more appropriately. Try the following suggestions.

- Identify the revenge goals with "Could it be?" questions. "Could it be that you want to get even?" ". . . that you want to hurt me?" ". . . that you want to hurt the other children?" ". . . that you want to hurt your parents?"
- Avoid punishment and especially retaliation.
- Maintain order with a minimum amount of restraint.
- Do not take the behavior personally or show your hurt. Recognizing the purposiveness of the behavior will make this response easier.
- Spend time and effort to help the young person. Learn to change your own behavior so as not to respond to repetitive provocations.
- Consider extensive professional counseling for the youth.

Corrective procedures for assumed inadequacy.   These suggestions help a counselor or teacher encourage youngsters who see themselves as failures.

- Use "Could it be?" questions to reveal the goal of inadequacy. "Could it be that you feel stupid and don't want people to know?" ". . . that you want to be left alone?" ". . . that you want to give up?"
- Show encouragement yourself. Don't give up.
- Arrange situations in which the youngster can succeed.
- Work on strengthening areas of interpersonal or academic deficiency.

Corrective procedures for risky sexual activity.   When the mistaken goals are in the sexual realm, the following suggestions help redirect at-risk behavior.

- Ask "Could it be questions" that link the problematic sexual behavior to its underlying purpose. "Could it be that you're using sex to get attention?" ". . . that you don't use a condom because you want to seem powerful?" ". . . that you want to get pregnant to hurt your father?" ". . . that you can't say no because you think the boys won't like you?"
- Explore constructive means by which the young person can achieve attention and power.
- Develop skill-building groups and activities to increase self-esteem, assertiveness, and self-efficacy (see Chapter 12).
- Provide individual and group counseling for support, insight, and personal development.
- Encourage boys to assume responsibility for their sexual behavior.
- Encourage family therapy as a means of enhancing family nurturance, understanding, and communication (see Chapter 14).
- Provide straightforward sex education for students *and* for their parents.

In addition to interpreting youngsters' goals to them, alternative goals that are less self-defeating should be identified. One of the authors worked with an adolescent male client who had been having unprotected sex with an older young woman in his father's garage. He quite readily admitted that part of him wanted to be caught, to show his father he was "practically a man" now. After several counseling sessions he decided to, at least temporarily, abandon this tactic and get his ear pierced instead. This action provoked a confrontation with his father that allowed him to express some of his resentment quite directly. When last seen, he and his father had begun a tense but hopeful process of negotiating a new set of freedoms and responsibilities.

All interventions and corrections should be geared toward empowering adolescents to identify and achieve alternative, healthier goals.

Natural and Logical Consequences

Natural and logical consequences are effective ways of dealing with misbehavior. Traditional discipline involves reward and punishment: Adults punish youngsters for unacceptable behavior and reward them for complying with their wishes and commands. Natural and logical consequences differ from reward and punishment in a number of ways and have certain advantages. The goal of consequences is to teach young people responsibility, cooperation, respect for order and the rights of others, good judgment, and careful decision making, and to give them a sense of control and choice. The goal is not to force submission and compliance, nor is it to obtain retribution and revenge (often the real goal of punishment). To some degree, reliance on consequences removes from the adult the function of meting out rewards and punishment, which deemphasizes the traditional authority position of the adult. When authority is deemphasized, youngsters feel more independent, and that feeling itself decreases undesirable behavior.

The adult who lets young people experience the natural and logical consequences of their behavior relies more on the natural order of things than on emotion and arbitrary, one-sided action. As a result, much of the resentment and frustration that so often are associated with discipline are avoided. Consequences are administered and experienced in an impersonal, matter-of-fact fashion, without moralizing, judgment, or excessive emotional involvement.

A few examples will illustrate this approach. In each case, a child or teenager has the choice of continuing the unacceptable behavior and taking the consequences. The choice is of course not offered when physical danger is involved, but the consequence is still logically related to the behavior. Note also that the adults do not react emotionally: They do not lecture, bribe, coax, or demand obedience; they do not make threats or impose an arbitrary punishment.

EXAMPLE 1. Todd and Denise Baker are disturbing the evening meal by kicking each other under the table. Sally calmly gives them the choice of settling down or leaving the table until they are ready to eat properly. She makes no effort to keep their food warm.

EXAMPLE 2. Sixteen-year-old Allie typically turns her alarm clock off in the morning and goes back to sleep. Alice used to call her several times, have her clothes and books ready, fix her breakfast, and, if she missed the bus, drive her to school, all the while scolding her and complaining about her laziness. Now she calls her once, ten minutes after her alarm goes off, then goes about her own business. If Allie does not get up then, she has to scramble to get dressed and may not have time for breakfast. If she misses the school bus, she has to spend her own money for the city bus, and take the penalty for being late at school.

EXAMPLE **3.** Jason Carter has broken a window while playing ball. Doug does not scold him and arbitrarily cut off his allowance until the window is paid for. Instead, he asks Jason for suggestions as to how he might make restitution, working from the assumption that Jason will pay for the damage and is capable of figuring out a way to do so.

EXAMPLE **4.** Ten-year-old Christie Carter has been begging to ride her bicycle to the store down the street, instead of walking. She received permission to do so, provided she stays on the sidewalk. When her mother observed Christie riding in the middle of the street, she told her that because Christie obviously was not ready to abide by the agreement now they would try again in two days.

Here we see that reliance on consequences is intended to help children develop responsibility for their own behavior. It is not meant to be a vehicle to express the adult's displeasure or anger. Care should be taken that the nonverbal aspects of the interaction do not turn it into covert punishment and thereby defeat the purpose of the entire procedure.

Because natural and logical consequences are geared to helping develop responsibility in young people, they are particularly useful in the area of sexual behavior. Unfortunately, the natural consequences of unprotected sexual intercourse are pregnancy and STDs, including HIV infection. Even "protected" sexual intercourse is not without risk. This fact must be communicated, clearly and unequivocally, to young people who are interacting sexually. Again, rather than harsh, judgmental, or punitive communication, the facts and a description of these consequences must be accompanied by encouragement to motivate more healthy behavior.

The use of information generated by students to teach other students is an important tool to help at-risk students. Here is one way to use student-generated knowledge. A student of one of the authors gave a speech on how becoming pregnant earlier in high school had drastically changed her life. She did not "preach" to her classmates, nor was she dramatic in her descriptions. She simply told her story. Her straightforward, unromantic portrayal of daily life had a profound effect on her classmates and generated a lively discussion on the belief that "it could never happen to me." Although the actual effects of her speech cannot be measured, her matter-of-fact and nonjudgmental approach certainly provoked a good deal of nondefensive discussion. Exposing students to the natural and logical consequences of risky sexual behavior through other people's lives may promote some behavior change so they do not have to experience the consequences themselves.

Encouragement

Encouragement greatly enhances the relationship between child and adult and reduces the youngster's need to resort to undesirable behavior to feel significant. Encouragement is the process of increasing youngsters' sense of worth and self-esteem by focusing on their *actual* strengths and assets, not on *expected* or potential strengths. Encouragement is less a set of behaviors than an attitude that permeates behavior. Encouragement conveys to young people that the adult has faith in them, trusts and respects them, and values them as people despite any deficiencies, mistakes, or flaws.

All too often children and teens are exposed to discouraging experiences. Some adults focus only on the mistakes youngsters make, attributing them to basic defects of character or ability ("He's just lazy." "She's always been clumsy."). Some adults set standards that are difficult or impossible to reach; they compare youngsters to each other in such a way that there is always a loser. The discouragement and self-doubt that arise from these practices may be manifested in misbehavior and in useless, inappropriate attempts to gain recognition.

Encouragement should be a regular aspect of interactions with all adolescents and children. When a young person is deeply discouraged, the teacher or counselor has the difficult task of counteracting a host of negative experiences. Adults can offer encouragment by recognizing effort and improvement as well as accomplishment, expressing appreciation, separating the deed from the doer when the deed is unacceptable, focusing on the child's or teenager's unique talents and contributions, and treating youngsters with respect and courtesy. Nonverbal messages are also important. Listening without interruption, using a friendly, nonjudgmental tone of voice, treating mistakes as opportunities for learning rather than as failures, and choosing the right moment for a remark are as important as the choice of words.

Keep in mind that some words that purport to be encouraging have the opposite effect, whether well intentioned or not. Some ill-advised attempts at encouragement include: competitive encouragement ("See what you can do when you try?"), coupling encouragement with expectations ("You got an A; that's great. Now let's keep up that average."), expressing surprise at success ("You *did*? I never thought you could do it!"), using someone else as an example ("If Kristin can do it, you can too, I'm sure."), and blaming someone else for a young person's failure ("If it hadn't been for that referee, I'm sure you'd have won.").

In general, anything that perpetuates low self-esteem, that lowers confidence in a child's ability to master problem situations, or that fosters feelings of inadequacy and insignificance is discouraging. Anything that gives a sense of being an important member of the group and a feeling that the child's participation, contribution, and cooperation are valued is encouraging. Above all, it is important for youngsters to learn that they are good enough as they are. Nowhere is this more critical than in the arena of teenage sexuality. When adolescents are engaged in risky sexual behavior, teachers and counselors need to deliberately set out to increase feelings of self-worth and confidence. Within the current framework, risky sexual behavior is a misbehavior rooted in the need to belong. Encouragement contributes to feelings of belongingness.

CONCLUSION

Premature and irresponsible sexual activity, teen pregnancy, and HIV/AIDS are growing problems. Understanding some of the family and peer dynamics that young people encounter and helping these adolescents change the goals of their misbehavior may help prevent some of these problems. Because of the long-term consequences of teenage sexual activity, it is critical to respond to the needs of young people by helping them improve their feelings of self-worth and by helping them recognize their own strengths and potential, and by helping them build a future for themselves. We must develop comprehensive programs to expand educational and occupational opportunities, provide skills for maintaining constructive group affiliations, and educate young people about themselves and their bodies. Otherwise the problems of teenage pregnancy will continue, and the cycle of babies having babies will be unbroken. In addition, the epidemic of AIDS will continue, and the spiral of early death will remain.

FURTHER READINGS

In addition to those books and articles cited in the reference section, the following books may be useful to readers wishing to know more about teen pregnancy and sexually transmitted diseases, including HIV/AIDS.

Besner, H. F., & Spungin, C. I. (1995). *Gay and lesbian students: Understanding their needs.* Washington, DC: Taylor & Francis.

Boyd-Franklin, N., Steiner, G. L., & Boland, M. G. (Eds.) (1995). *Children, families, and HIV/AIDS: Psychosocial and therapeutic issues.* New York: Guilford.

DiClemente, R. J. (Ed.) (1992). *Adolescents and AIDS: A generation in jeopardy.* Thousand Oaks, CA: Sage.

Hechinger, F. M. (1992). *Fateful choices.* New York: Carnegie Corporation of New York.

Hoffman, E. (1994). *The drive for self: Alfred Adler and the founding of individual psychology.* Reading, MA: Addison-Wesley.

Kiselica, M. S. (1995). *Multicultural counseling with teenage fathers.* Thousand Oaks, CA: Sage.

Miller, B. C., Card, J. J., Paikoff, R. L., & Peterson, J. L. (1992). *Preventing adolescent pregnancy: Model programs and evaluations.* Newbury Park, CA: Sage.

Musick, J. S. (1993). *Young, poor, and pregnant.* New Haven, CT: Yale University Press.

CHAPTER 9

DELINQUENCY AND PROBLEMS OF VIOLENCE

When I feel bad and can't do anything about it,
Don't even know it, maybe,
I can still pound somebody, smash a windshield, maybe.
At least I have a good reason for feeling bad.
And so what if they do too?

When I feel bad, I can do something about it.
Ripping off lunch money, or something from the store shelf, or
    the Jacksons' yard, or even living room, maybe, helps.
The rush covers up bad feelings.
And so what if the feeling becomes me?

When I feel bad, the kids on the street help.
I like colors and coats and bright-green shoelaces.
And so what if I'm bad?
Out here, bad is good.
And being feared is better.

J. J. McWhirter

CHAPTER OUTLINE

As a society, we are plagued by problems of delinquency and violent behavior among our youth. Teachers, counselors, and others are often confronted with young people who are victims of violence or who inflict it on others. Youth violence is a complex problem that takes many forms. Delinquency and violence are often outward expressions of nonconformity, rejection of social and parental norms, and reactions to internal pressures. Many violent children and adolescents learn their behavior from parents who are psychologically or physically abusive. They become caught in a cycle of violence at home and continue it because it seems essential for survival in the world.

In this chapter we discuss (a) the nature and scope of delinquency and violence; (b) the roots of antisocial behaviors that lead to delinquency, focusing on a developmental perspective; (c) the consequences of youth violence; and (d) general intervention strategies that can be used in a variety of environments and a specific intervention based on Glasser's reality therapy.

THE SCOPE AND NATURE OF DELINQUENCY, ANTISOCIAL BEHAVIOR, AND VIOLENCE

We use the terms *delinquency* and *antisocial behavior* interchangeably. Delinquency typically refers to any activity that is illegal or conflicts with social norms, but it does not always imply violence. Violence takes many forms, among them organized gang violence, destruction of property through vandalism, and self-inflicted violence. Antisocial behavior, delinquency, and violence have common roots and consequences. Teachers, counselors, and parents who learn to recognize these common factors have taken the first step toward treating and preventing delinquency. Although not exhaustive, the following list represents the most frequently encountered antisocial behaviors expressed by children and teenagers: (a) expression of aggression and violence within the family; (b) aggression in school, such as fighting and the destruction of property; (c) minor infractions of the law, or "nonindex" crimes (vandalism, substance use, running away); (d) major infractions of the law, or "index" crimes (larceny-theft, robbery, forcible rape); (e) self-inflicted violence, including suicide; and (f) gang membership. Although these areas are clearly related (and some of these relationships are causal), we discuss them separately to make clear their unique characteristics and prevalence.

Family Violence

Family violence occurs with alarming frequency and can lead to the development of severe antisocial behavior. Statistics compiled by the Federal Bureau of Investigation (FBI) reveal that 20% of the murder victims in the United States are killed by members of their own families and that one-third of the female victims are killed by their husbands or boyfriends (Goetting, 1995).

An increasing proportion of assaults within the family are committed by youngsters (Cochran et al., 1994). Furthermore, it is estimated that as many as 4 million Americans may be the victims of physical abuse and neglect each year (Kashani, Daniel, Dandoy, & Holcomb, 1992). Although the true severity and frequency of child sexual abuse is hidden, a conservative estimate places the number of victims quite high, with evidence suggesting that sexually abused adolescents perpetuate their abusive experiences either by victimizing or being revictimized (Koss, Goodman, Browne, Fitzgerald, Keita, & Russo, 1994). In view of the incidence of violence within families, delinquent and violent behavior in so many young people is not surprising.

School Problems

Problem behavior at school is typically a precursor to more severe antisocial behavior. Vandalism accounts for millions of dollars each year in damage to school property (Goldstein, 1996; Patterson, DeBaryshe, & Ramsey, 1989). Fighting and intimidation among students, like vandalism, is increasing. Estimates suggest that at least 15% of all schoolchildren are victims of bullies in grade school, and that approximately 4.8 million schoolchildren in the United States are threatened by other students (Shakeshaft, Barber, Hergenrother, Johnson, Mandel, & Sawyer, 1995). Nearly every school day, 200,000 students skip classes because of fear of physical harm (Kadel & Follman, 1993). Every day there are more than 1000 assaults on teachers; nearly every day 100,000 thefts are reported in schools.

Handguns are also causing increasing problems in schools. The U.S. Department of Justice has reported that more than 27,000 youngsters between 12 and 15 years of age were victims of handguns in 1985, up from an average of 16,500 in earlier years. Of 390 high school students polled in one major metropolitan area, 64% knew another student who had carried a handgun within the last six months, 60% knew someone who had been shot, threatened, or robbed at gunpoint in their school, and almost half of the male respondents admitted to having carried a handgun at least once. This incidence of contact with firearms has tragic consequences: Between 1984 and 1993, the number of juveniles arrested for murder rose 168%, and weapons violation rose 126% (CDF, 1995). Teachers and counselors who strive to create an atmosphere conducive to learning and to the development of pro-social behaviors clearly face an enormous challenge.

Juvenile Crime

According to data released by the FBI, youth crime has actually declined over the last 20 years. Arrest figures from 1992 indicate that the total youth arrested was 16% of all arrests, compared to the all-time high of 26% in 1975 (Sautter, 1994). Nevertheless, most people continue to believe that juvenile crime is increasing. This may be because many young people who engage in antisocial behavior never come to the attention of the justice system. Some evidence suggests that official records may account for as little as 2% of the actual law violations committed by young people, yet the juvenile justice system in the United States spends more than $1 billion a year to process these young criminals (Dunford & Elliott, 1984). Perhaps a more important reason for the public's misconception about juvenile crime is the shift in severity of crime coupled with a younger age of both victims and perpetrators. For example, 1992 saw a record number of violent crimes committed with handguns. The youth murder rate and the diminishing age of many perpetrators has increased dramatically in the 1990s (Sautter, 1994).

Many of the arrests of juveniles are occasioned by the use or possession of alcohol and other substances, the subject of Chapter 7. Because substance use is highly correlated with law violation by youngsters and adults alike, we encourage readers to take particular note of the discussion there.

Self-Inflicted Violence

The rates of suicide and attempted suicide among children and adolescents have increased alarmingly in the United States. As many as 2000 adolescents commit suicide and 700,000 attempt to do so each year (Smolowe, 1995). Suicide is now the third leading cause of death among 11- to 24-year-olds (Centers for Disease Control and Prevention, 1993). In Chapter 10, we discuss suicide in detail and offer suggestions for prevention and intervention.

Gang Membership and Violence

A gang is a group of young people who form an allegiance for a common purpose, usually including unlawful or criminal activity (Lal, Lal, & Achilles, 1993). The typical gang offers a structured and organized way to engage in delinquent or criminal behavior. Estimates indicate that more than 90,000 young people belong to more than 800 different gangs operating in Southern California (Lal, 1991). Not unlike other cities in the United States, Los Angeles recorded more than 350 gang-related deaths in 1987, and gang membership is no longer limited to adolescents and young adults. "Minigangs" of grade-school-aged children are not uncommon in larger metropolitan centers (Boozer, 1989).

As one gang gains power and control in a given area, rival gangs sometimes relocate to other areas of a city or even to other cities. These divisions of power and region are frequently related to ethnicity. The increased prominence and control of Hispanic gangs in Los Angeles, for example, has prompted some African American gangs to move elsewhere. Economic opportunities, such as the availability of new markets for drug profits, may also play a part in the decision to relocate (Spergel, 1995). Many communities and neighborhoods once untouched by organized violence now find themselves threatened by gang activity.

THE ORIGINS OF THE PROBLEM

The origins of delinquent and violent behavior among children and adolescents are complex and multifaceted. The ecological theory of delinquency and the developmental model are two ways to approach this problem.

The Ecological Theory of Delinquency

Ecological theory views the social context and social conditions of a community as predictors of violent and delinquent behavior among youngsters. National prosperity, unemployment rates, and average family income are all accounted for in this perspective and shed light on the problems associated with delinquency and violence. Significant correlations between rates of unemployment and juvenile delinquency have been found in 101 American cities (Winbush, 1988). An understanding of these relationships helps us to identify communities at risk for youth violence and to predict—and possibly to prevent—increases in delinquency on the basis of ecological changes in our communities (Tolan & Guerra, 1994).

A recent analysis of violence among children and adolescents (Eron, Gentry, & Schlegel, 1994) highlights four different individual social experiences that appear to accelerate the pace towards antisocial behavior, conduct disorders, violence, and crime. These experiences are: (a) early involvement with alcohol and drugs, (b) association with antisocial groups, (c) easy access to firearms, especially handguns, and (d) portrayal of violence in film and television media. Extensive and powerful empirical evidence supports the influential role of each of these factors. Lieberman (1994) makes a persuasive case that the media have played a key role in desensitizing society to violence. In much the same way that the tobacco industry has denied the health risks of smoking, media spokespeople continue to deny the overwhelming empirical evidence that such exposure increases aggressive and violent tendencies among children and adolescents. Lieberman (1994) points out that hundreds of empirical studies have documented that exposure to media violence makes children more likely to behave in aggressive ways, desensitizes them to violent acts, and increases the likelihood that they will commit violent acts themselves. She argues that media violence should be thought of as a highly addictive lethal drug, which requires ever higher exposure to more graphic violent acts to satisfy the addiction. She concludes that it is very unlikely that the problems of violence in our society can be solved until the violence portrayed in a glamorous way by the media is somehow limited. Ironically, even as the media glamorize violence they perpetuate a climate of fear about adolescent violence (Bortner, 1993). Effective interventions must address the economic and social factors that foster discontent, a fact that challenges us to expand our notions of intervention and treatment.

Ethnic minority youth.   Ecological theory considers historical and social changes as well as the broader perspective of society, community, and cultural norms. The civil rights movement of the 1960s, for example, created expectations in African Americans that have been largely unfulfilled. Hacker (1992) contends that racism continues unabated in this country, and its effects are still as insidious and negative. A primary effect of racism is that it consigns some people to the margins of society. Violence within the African American community is seen as a reaction to the frustrations caused by continued economic and educational marginalization (Winbush, 1988).

Hispanic American young people faced this same pattern of unmet expectations in the 1980s. Other ethnic minority groups, such as Asian Americans and Native Americans, face similar difficulties. Social conditions, economic patterns, and marginalization from the mainstream opportunity structure provide a framework for understanding the increase in criminal behavior among minority children and teenagers.

Parents of ethnic minority youth who are repressed by economic and social circumstances may be less able to provide the structure that young teenagers need as they separate from the family. Perhaps this is part of the reason that inner city minority youth are drawn to gangs. Gangs provide structure (that is, rules and norms) and a sense of belonging as well as a sense of group and individual identity. Ethnic minority adolescents living in inner cities have reported levels of personal victimization and weapons carrying that far exceed those reported in national surveys (Sheley, McGee, & Wright, 1992). For both female and male African Americans between the ages of 15 and 34, homicide has been the leading cause of death since 1978 (Hammond & Yung, 1994).

Gay and lesbian youth.   Gay and lesbian youth are at high risk for conflict with the law largely because of substance abuse, truancy, running away, and prostitution (Savin-Williams, 1994). Rotheram-Borus et al. (1991) found that 23% of their subjects had encountered trouble with police, and 14% had been jailed. Although there is little documentation regarding the reasons that lesbian and gay youth engage in criminal activity, they probably commit crimes for many of the same reasons as do heterosexual youth as well as for reasons specific to their sexual identity (revenge against society and their parents for rejecting them, for example).

Probably more important than crime done by gay and lesbian adolescents is the violence done to them. Lesbian and gay youth are uniquely subject to violence resulting from societal homophobia. In the Rotheram-Borus et al. (1991) study, a significant number of youth reported that they had been physically assaulted, sexually abused, raped, and robbed. Forms of violence in school and in the community range from name calling to "gay bashing" or physical attacks. Reported violence based on sexual orientation has risen 127% in the last six years (d'Augelli & Dark, 1994; National Gay and Lesbian Task Force Policy Institute, 1994). This amplified vulnerability to victimization of lesbian and gay youth is especially problematic because of the distinctive character of their adolescent years (Savin-Williams, 1995).

The Developmental Perspective on Delinquency

Developmental models of antisocial behavior can help to explain some of the root causes of delinquency. Winbush (1988) has argued, for example, that counselors should use such theories as Kohlberg's (1981) six stages of moral development to gain a better understanding of the way young people reason and act. Although Kohlberg's theory has been effectively criticized (Gilligan, 1993), using a developmental framework to conceptualize moral reasoning and its relation to delinquency can be helpful to teachers, parents, counselors, and other mental health professionals. Teachers and counselors can foster more sophisticated moral reasoning and greater self-awareness by challenging young people to resolve problems that represent moral dilemmas. Such activities help young people evaluate their thoughts and actions, beginning a process that ultimately may help youngsters to improve their skills in moral reasoning.

Patterson, DeBaryshe, and Ramsey (1989) argue that antisocial behavior is a developmental phenomenon that begins early in life and continues through childhood and adolescence into adulthood. Chronic delinquency emerges in a series of predictable steps that place young people at increasingly greater risk for long-term criminal behavior. This model incorporates four variables to explain the role of social influences on delinquent behavior: (a) the influence of the family and home environment; (b) social rejection and school failure; (c) membership in a deviant peer group; and (d) the age of onset of delinquent behavior. Each of these variables contributes to the development of antisocial behavior in a distinctive way.

Family and home environment.   The family environment can mitigate against delinquency or encourage it. Parents whose discipline is harsh and inconsistent, for example, who have little positive involvement with their children, and who do not monitor their children's activities foster early aggressive behavior, which is strongly related to later delinquency (Baumrind, 1993; DeBaryshe, Patterson, & Capaldi, 1993). When parents and grandparents are negative and inconsistent in their parenting styles, when grandparents are explosive in the home, and when both parents are antisocial themselves, aversive and aggressive behavior is reinforced (Fry, 1993). Finally, family stressors, such as family violence, marital discord, and divorce, all contribute to the development of a youth's antisocial behavior (Patterson et al., 1989).

Certain family demographic features are also highly correlated with delinquency. SES is not directly related to the incidence of delinquency, but ethnicity, the type of neighborhood, and the parents' education, occupation, and income in combination can influence the type of delinquency children exhibit (Tolan & Guerra, 1994). The children of minority families who live in poor communities and whose parents have unskilled jobs or are unemployed are at greatest risk for violent forms of delinquent behavior. The risk is partly attributable to the difficulty of raising children in a poor environment and to the parents' lack of education, resources, and problem-solving skills. Parents with this profile often monitor their children less, show little involvement with them, and provide less educational stimulation and positive reinforcement for pro-social behaviors. (Family influences are described in more detail in Chapter 3.)

Patterson and his colleagues (1989, 1992b) suggest two ways in which some of these early parenting activities can lead to antisocial behavior. First, control theory suggests that a negative and violent interaction style and inconsistent discipline lead to poor bonding between parent and child. A lack of bonding contributes to the child's failure to accept society's values and to develop internal control mechanisms. Second, social-interactional theory suggests that family members may actually train children in antisocial behaviors. Coercive and violent behaviors are modeled and reinforced by grandparents, parents, and siblings. Children learn to use aversive and violent behaviors to counteract the hostile and violent behaviors of other family members. Learned aggressiveness, in such an environment, is functional for survival. Hitting and other aggressive behaviors are sometimes accepted as normal early in life.

Families that reinforce aversive and violent behavior also frequently fail to provide the socially appropriate skills that children need for survival in the school and social environment. The significance of positive parental involvement, healthy parent-child interaction, and consistent discipline is supported by the fact that when parents change their discipline and monitoring styles to become more consistent, more positive, and less physical, their children's antisocial behavior almost invariably declines significantly (Cunningham, Bremner, & Boyle, 1995; Forgatch, 1988). Conversely, if youngsters receive training in antisocial behavior in the home, they will most certainly experience significant difficulties in school and out of it (see Box 9.1).

Social rejection and academic failure.   Coercive and aggressive behavior learned at home frequently leads to academic failure and rejection by nondelinquent or normal peers (Patterson et al., 1989, 1992b). Uncontrolled behavior adversely affects a child's ability to concentrate, to stick to a task, and to complete homework. The correlation between antisocial behavior and poor academic performance is clear (Catalano & Hawkins, 1996).

As young children become socialized to the behavioral standards and norms of society, they gradually reduce their level of aggressive and acting-out behavior. However, older children with antisocial behavioral patterns display rates of aggression that are more typical of younger children. They are usually not cooperative or helpful in their social interactions. Indeed, antisocial students seem to have a particular disinclination to cooperate with others in peer-related activities.

Aggressive and antisocial behavior also leads to nonacceptance and eventual rejection by normal peers (Fraser, 1996). Rejected children are usually deficient in social and cognitive skills. They experience difficulty entering peer groups and accurately perceiving peer group norms, and they inappropriately interpret the reactions of their peers (Cole, 1990). Uncontrolled and aggressive behavior ultimately forces many young people to join deviant peer groups as a means of achieving support and acceptance.

The relationship between inappropriate and aggressive behavior and academic failure and peer rejection may be circular. That is, school failure and social rejection may in fact stimulate behavior problems, enhance aggressiveness, and contribute to delinquent and violent reactions by the struggling student. This relationship needs to be assessed more carefully, however. Some studies suggest that training in academic and

■ ■ ■ Box 9.1
Training for Violence

At one time I was a school counselor for two brothers, Tom, a freshman, and John, a sophomore. Almost every week one or the other or both got into a fistfight at school—sometimes with each other, more often with another student. The vice principal provided appropriate discipline, which progressed from talking to detention to more detention to in-school suspension to suspension. Because the parents refused to attend parent-teacher or parent-administrator conferences, and because I worked with the boys in a counseling relationship, the vice principal asked me to make a home visit to discuss the problem with the parents.

The boys' father was home when I arrived. It quickly became clear that the boys' problem was their dad. The overriding family value he expressed was: "Don't take nothing off of nobody. If someone bothers you, hit him." In this family, aggression and violence were not only being modeled and reinforced, they were being actively encouraged through verbal instruction.

Now that I understood the situation, I was able to work with the boys to help them understand their aggression, to develop different standards of behavior at school, and to learn more appropriate problem-solving skills.

social skills can be effective but must be introduced early in the child's life to prevent or reduce antisocial behavior (Goldstein, Harootunian, & Conoley, 1994; Kazdin, 1994).

Conduct disorders. Conduct disorder (CD) and its less severe diagnostic cousin oppositional defiant disorder (ODD) encompass most of the antecedant, precurser behaviors that predict and lead to delinquent and violent behavior in juveniles. CD in particular refers generally to clinically severe antisocial behavior including aggression, stealing, fire setting, truancy, and running away. The risk factors discussed later in this chapter are particularly salient for CD and ODD children.

Membership in a deviant peer group. Aggressiveness and antisocial behavior learned at home and exacerbated by academic failure and rejection by normal peers is a precursor to membership in a deviant peer group. As we discussed in Chapters 4 and 7, the peer cluster is a major training ground for the development of a youngster's attitudes, beliefs, and behaviors. Peers supply the attitudes, motivations, rationalizations, and opportunities for engaging in antisocial and delinquent behaviors. Further, delinquent peers reinforce deviant behavior and punish behavior that is socially conforming (Patterson et al., 1989, 1992b). Pressure from the peer cluster makes it difficult for children and adolescents to modify antisocial behavior once they have started to engage in it. Many delinquent youngsters actively resist efforts to change their behavior. If they adopt more positive social behavior, they may alienate themselves from their major source of companionship and acceptance.

Onset of delinquent behavior.   The age of a child when aggressive and delinquent behavior begins is an important factor in the severity of the problem. Aggressive children in the preschool and early school years are at risk for future antisocial behavior. Youngsters who begin delinquent activities early are at greatest risk for becoming chronic offenders (Patterson et al., 1992a; Walker et al., 1995). Boys who are first arrested between the ages of 6 and 10 have more criminal charges and convictions than late starters. "Late starters" are youth who commit their first offense in middle adolescence. About one-half of antisocial children become adolescent delinquents, and about one-half to three-fourths of adolescent delinquents become chronic adult offenders (Blumstein, Cohen, & Farrington, 1988). These data argue for the importance of early assessment of the risk factors in a young person's life. They also argue for early intervention.

Focusing on the developmental perspective proposed by Patterson and his colleagues (1989, 1992b), Figure 9.1 shows how economic, ecological, and cultural factors place external pressure on families, schools, and young people. As youngsters make their way through their developmental milestones, their interactions with families, schools, and peer groups change. For youngsters who are at risk for antisocial behavior, identification with and commitment to a deviant peer cluster encourages delinquent behavior and, for some, eventual membership in a gang.

ASSESSMENT OF ANTISOCIAL BEHAVIOR: RISK FACTORS

Instruments devised to assess personality traits are also useful for measuring the potential for antisocial behavior in children and teens. Self-report testing can be used to assess antisocial characteristics. The Minnesota Multiphasic Personality Inventory–Adolescent (MMPI–A), for example, can provide information about violent and delinquent tendencies of teenagers. Although the MMPI is useful, especially in conjunction with behavioral reports, family and school histories, and clinical observations, its effectiveness is limited primarily to non-Hispanic European American older teens and adults. The MMPI was not developed for use with children, younger adolescents, or members of ethnic minorities. Alternative means of assessment must be used for these groups, and familiarity with some high-risk warning signs in the family, school, and social environments is one alternative.

Risk Factors in the Family Environment

Patterson and his colleagues (1989, 1992b) have identified factors in a child's early life that make delinquency likely later on:

• Both parents and grandparents exhibit negative, aggressive, and inconsistent parenting and discipline styles; the grandparents have explosive outbursts in the home.

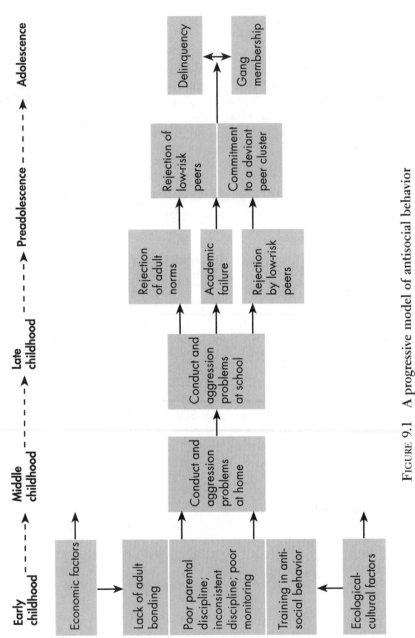

FIGURE 9.1   A progressive model of antisocial behavior

Source: Adapted from Patterson, DeBaryshe, and Ramsey, 1989.

- One or both parents are antisocial or have a history of delinquent and violent behavior; the risk is higher when both have a history of these behaviors.
- The parents are uneducated and work in unskilled occupations, live in a poor neighborhood, and earn little money.
- The child is subjected to family stressors, such as family violence, alcoholism, drug abuse, marital problems, or divorce.

Risk Factors in the School Environment

Many of the risk factors that emerge in the school environment are symptomatic of other problems, such as learning disabilities, emotional problems, or a temporary difficulty in the family's situation. Nevertheless, some of the following risk factors in the school environment lead to or are symptomatic of more severe violent or delinquent behavior expressed outside of school. In school, children and teens may:

- behave aggressively or violently toward other students and toward teachers in the classroom or on the playground
- use money as a means of winning other students' approval and acceptance
- disrupt the classroom by failing to attend to the tasks of the class, stay in their seats, respond appropriately to the teacher, or participate in appropriate classroom behavior (such as raising a hand before speaking)
- vandalize school property and classroom materials
- make sexual gestures toward other students and teachers
- perform poorly in academic work, regularly scoring low on tests and consistently failing to complete classroom and homework assignments
- spend free time with older students who behave aggressively in and out of the classroom
- describe themselves as "bad" or "dumb," or in other ways deride their ability to do the required schoolwork and behave appropriately around other students and teachers

Risk Factors in the Social Environment

Although the primary social environments for most children are family and school, children also interact with others in their neighborhood, with peers who attend other schools, and with other adults. Children develop a set of expectations about themselves and others in these social contexts and are faced with many challenges. These social interactions may be positive or they may enhance the risk that a youngster will develop delinquent and criminal behavior. Among other things, effective assessment depends on recognizing:

- the degree of poverty, racism, and frequency of violence and gang activity in the neighborhood
- the economic prosperity of the community and the nation as a whole
- the rates of unemployment and underemployment and the likelihood of economic hopelessness
- the level of family income

- the degree to which the economic and educational expectations of the community are being met and the nature of a community's response to economic and educational marginalization

Risk Factors for Gang Involvement

Some specific characteristics warn that a young person may be involved in a gang (National School Safety Center, 1988, p. 10):

- rumors or more reliable information that a youngster has not been home for several nights
- evidence of increased substance use
- abrupt changes in behavior and personality
- newly acquired and unexplained "wealth," often showered on or shared with peers
- requests to borrow money or reliable evidence of borrowing
- "hanging around," but no discussion of problems with others
- evidence of mental or physical abuse
- a dress style or other symbol of identification adopted by only a few

Gangs have significant negative consequences not only for society but also for their young members. The majority of adult criminals began their careers as juvenile delinquents. However, a gang may be the only means many young people have to satisfy their need for affiliation and affirmation (Prothrow-Stith & Weissman, 1991). Gangs also provide an opportunity for economic gain and an image of success for young people who have no other means to establish it. Gangs provide security, protection, companionship, and opportunities for excitement. Thus gang membership gives young people ways to enhance their perception of their worth and acceptance (Boozer, 1989). These consequences of gang involvement make intervention a complicated and challenging task and further highlight the importance of early detection and intervention.

GENERAL INTERVENTION APPROACHES

Both broad-based and specific intervention models can be effective in dealing with delinquency. General approaches focus on family, school, and community issues (Tolan & Guerra, 1994). Specific intervention models, such as Glasser's reality therapy, help young people establish the healthy relationships they need to be able to avoid delinquency and remain in school (Comiskey, 1993). Let's first examine some general approaches to intervention.

Family Intervention and Prevention

The family's cooperation in minimizing the risk of gang involvement, delinquency, and violence is critical. Parent training in child management is a promising family intervention strategy (Kazdin, 1994). It is most effective, however, if parents learn to recognize and deal with the signs of risk before their child reaches adolescence. Training in behavior modification, in management of rewards and consequences, and in communication skills is most effective with younger children whose behavioral problems have not yet developed into violence or delinquency. If children are already violent and delinquent, parent training is relatively ineffective in reducing the children's offenses, perhaps because the youngsters' delinquent behaviors have already become part of their repertoire or because they have already identified with deviant peers (Tate, Reppucci, & Mulvey, 1995).

Current research supports the use of multiple interventions aimed not only at the family but also at the school and social environments. Behavior modification procedures used in halfway houses, for instance, have immediate results but produce no long-lasting changes after teenagers return to their natural environments (Patterson et al., 1989, 1992b). A combination of efforts designed to improve the young person's academic performance and social skills, to modify the youngster's peer cluster, and to train the parents for better family management offers the greatest promise for averting or reducing the problems of youthful violence and delinquency (Patterson et al., 1989, 1992b).

School Intervention

Educational interventions such as cooperative learning and teaching learning strategies (discussed in Chapter 15) are extremely helpful, especially if they are introduced early. Training in social and cognitive skills (discussed in Chapter 12), especially conflict resolution and mediation programs (discussed in Chapter 13), are critically important. Children can learn to behave more responsibly if they are taught to do so.

We have encouraged development of anger reduction groups (J. J. McWhirter, Herrmann, Jefferys, & Quinn, 1997). Such programs seem most effective when children and adolescents are taught that others are controlling their temper and that there are advantages to controlling one's own temper. The child or adolescent is encouraged to develop an individualized cognitive strategy of calming self-talk to employ when he or she becomes provoked and to employ relaxation behaviors that are incompatible with anger and acting out behavior. In short, anger management programs are effective primarily because they provide strategies that allow the child or adolescent to control his or her aggressive impulses.

The school can also play an effective role in limiting and mitigating the influence of gangs. The effectiveness of such efforts depends on the level of communication among school personnel and the speed of their response. School personnel must be in constant communication with one another, each employee must have a clearly designated response role, and employees must respond rapidly to any threat of gang activity (Lal, Lal, & Achilles, 1993). The National School Safety Center (1988, pp. 33–34) suggests the following actions to limit gang activity in schools:

- Acknowledge the problem immediately and get help from local police and community groups.
- Educate security personnel.
- Establish informed communication networks with students.
- Institute a strict visitor/trespasser policy.
- Control points of access to the school.
- Remove graffiti as quickly as possible.
- Work closely with local police, and establish procedures to share information with them.

- Consider the use of cameras to take pictures of suspicious visitors or trespassers.
- Maintain a high profile: Consider posting uniformed security personnel in strategic places to ensure maximum visibility.
- Form or access a community network.

These procedures will help to restrict many gang-related activities and may keep some students from being influenced by gangs.

Community Intervention

Schools can play a crucial role in developing communication with the community and in building coalitions with community organizations and government agencies. Community groups that are recruited and educated by schools can help to minimize violence and gang activity. Community organizations that can meet a youngster's need for inclusion, affirmation, and acceptance also discourage involvement in a gang. Youth service centers, recreational centers, and religious organizations can all fill this role and help to prevent gang activity and delinquency (Boozer, 1989). School personnel, juvenile parole counselors, community social workers, and specialists in neighborhood crime prevention must encourage community organizations to provide young people with educational, economic, and social opportunities to offset the attraction of gangs.

All of these approaches are designed to confront a general situation. To deal with delinquency in a specific individual, a specific intervention, such as reality therapy, is called for.

REALITY THERAPY

Reality therapy, one of the more promising approaches to the deterrence of delinquency, was developed by Dr. William Glasser and Dr. G. L. Harrington. When Glasser was a resident in psychiatry at the Veterans Administration Neuropsychiatric Hospital in West Los Angeles, California, in the 1950s, both he and his supervisor, Dr. Harrington, were frustrated by the inability of traditional psychotherapy to solve the problems of many of their patients. Harrington was in charge of a "back" ward that had a very low success rate. The 210 patients averaged 17 years of confinement; the last discharge had occurred two years earlier, and the patient had returned within a short time. Although the staff was compassionate and well intentioned, the patients were not getting better. Harrington began to confront the patients, chiding them for their unacceptable behavior and supporting them when their behavior improved. Nurses and aides began to follow suit; they became more involved with the patients and less tolerant of their "crazy" symptoms.

At this time Glasser was taking a similar approach to delinquent girls at the Ventura School for Girls, an institutional facility of the California Youth Authority. In view of the populations they were serving, both men were achieving a remarkable degree of success. Forty-five patients on Harrington's ward went home the first year. They were followed by 85 the second year and 90 the third. Many returned, of course, as they were encouraged to do, but only a very few remained more than a month after their return. The others reentered mainstream society immediately. Glasser obtained similar results at the Ventura School. Roughly 400 girls, with offenses ranging from "incorrigibility" to murder, were confined there for six to eight months for rehabilitation. After applying the new therapy, Glasser reported that 80% of the girls were released and did not return.

Reality therapy grew out of the experiences and discussions of Glasser and Harrington. Glasser first described this treatment in *Reality Therapy* (1965) and has continued to elaborate and expand his approach through numerous publications (Glasser, 1972, 1976, 1986).

Assumptions of Reality Therapy

Reality therapy is based on the assumption that human beings must have human communication and contact. We have a basic desire to be with other people, to care for others, and to be cared for in return. Individuals who seek help or who are sent for help suffer from one basic inadequacy—they are unable to achieve such contact successfully.

Striving for human contact reflects two fundamental needs: (a) to love and be loved and (b) to be worthwhile as a person. Low risk young people are able to satisfy these needs in an appropriate way. They develop a success identity that allows them to be involved with respected people who care for them and for whom they care. They have the capacity to give and receive love. They have at least one other person who cares about them and one person whom they care about. They also develop a feeling of personal self-worth. They believe they have a right to be in the world, and they behave in socially responsible ways.

High-risk young people are unable to satisfy these two basic needs. Instead, they either ignore or deny reality. In the process, they develop a failure identity. Young people who ignore reality cope with life by acting as if the rules did not include them (see Box 9.2). They are described as antisocial, sociopathic, delinquent, or criminal. Those who deny reality cope in one of two ways, through substance abuse or mental illness. The young person who says "The world is no good, so I must change it" and proceeds to change the world by getting "high" or "wasted" is essentially denying reality. The high is intended to provide feelings of importance or self-worth. Another way of denying reality is to withdraw from the world through delusions and other symptoms of mental illness.

The reality therapist assumes that all problems result from an inability to fulfill essential needs. Individuals must fulfill their needs without preventing others from fulfilling theirs. The person who cannot do so is irresponsible, not mentally ill or bad. Individuals must learn to deal responsibly with their world. Perhaps more than any other approach, reality therapy holds that it is impossible to maintain self-regard while living irresponsibly. The practice of reality therapy is based on teaching at-risk individuals satisfactory standards of behavior, praising them when they act appropriately, and correcting them when they are wrong. Self-respect comes through self-discipline and closeness to others. In learning to face reality, youngsters fulfill their needs. In doing so they become socially responsible people who can achieve honest human relationships.

Theoretical Components of Reality Therapy

Reality therapy has three basic components: involvement, rejection of unrealistic behavior, and relearning. Each component must be implemented if the youngster at risk is to be helped. First, an adult must become involved with the youth and develop a deep emotional relationship. This relationship becomes the vehicle that allows the adult to

■ ■ ■ Box 9.2
Mikey the Menace

When Mikey arrived at the classroom door each morning, the atmosphere changed. A subtle wave of tension would pass among the children as he entered the room shouting, "Hi everybody!" Within minutes, someone would be crying, complaining, or retreating from his awkward overtures and fast-moving fists, and he would be temporarily relocated to the time-out chair. He would beam at me from the chair. "Teacher, I'll be good." And he tried.

Mikey was the youngest of seven children. His father was in prison for selling drugs, and his mother had described her current boyfriend as a "damn scary alcoholic." Child Protective Services closely monitored the family and was close to taking the younger children away from the mother. During one home visit, I observed her grab Mikey roughly, pull his hair, and hit him on the head, all in response to appropriate attention-seeking behavior. Each time he was punished, Mikey scowled and then quickly turned his sunniest smile back on; each time, his mother failed to notice.

One evening I was still working in my classroom as darkness fell, and I was suddenly startled to hear him shout, "Hi, every . . . Where's the kids?" There was Mikey in the doorway, cheerful as ever, having just walked seven long blocks through projects so crime-ridden that the classroom mothers had warned me to "never go in there." Mikey was very disappointed to learn that "the kids" had gone home. His desperate efforts to gain affection and attention were all that a 4-year old could do. Mikey should be 13 years old now. What new methods has he learned?

reject the young person's unrealistic, unacceptable, and irresponsible behavior. The adult then teaches the youngster a more realistic way to fulfill his or her needs without interfering with the needs of others. Let us consider each of these components in detail as they might apply to Todd Baker of Chapter 2.

Involvement.   Involvement is the initial and most difficult phase of the counseling process and requires the most skill. The process is a prerequisite to the other steps and forms a consistent theme running through the entire counselor-client or teacher-student relationship. Glasser is not very explicit in his suggestions as to specific methods for demonstrating involvement, although he does suggest that the counselor or teacher neither give up nor push too hard.

In Todd's case, the helper must be able to become emotionally involved with him and must be able to accept him uncritically at first. The adult cannot be frightened by or angry about Todd's behavior, thoughts, or attitudes. By demonstrating interest, warmth, and sensitivity while discussing Todd's values, interests, hopes, and fears, the adult helps Todd grow beyond his problems. The counselor must know and understand Todd and express interest in him as an individual with great potential.

Further, the helper must be open and present him- or herself as a model of transparency and integrity. Glasser says that helpers must be willing to have their own values tested. The helper must be tough and able to withstand Todd's intense criticism and anger. In addition, the helper must be willing to admit imperfection and yet demonstrate to Todd that he has the ability to act responsibly. The helper, in effect, supports and strengthens Todd's conscience by demonstrating honesty, concern, and personal authenticity.

The counselor develops an "I/you" pattern of interaction. The personal "I," Glasser says, must be used instead of the more impersonal "we," "the school," and "they." The adult says: "I'd like you to do your homework for me." "It's important to me that you're here every day." "I'm concerned about you and interested in you." "I want to explain how your life can go better." Such statements emphasize the personal; they lead the adult to involvement not only as helper to client but as person to person. They communicate that the adult cares enough to risk an emotional, personal involvement. This allows Todd to look at his unacceptable behavior and to learn better ways to lead his life. By being responsible, tough, and sensitive, the helper shows confidence that Todd can change his irresponsible behavior.

Rejection of irresponsible behavior.   In the second phase of treatment, the client's irresponsible behaviors are rejected first by the counselor and later by the client. The counselor ignores the past and works in the here and now with a view to the future. The focus is on Todd's behavior rather than on his feelings and attitudes. In fact, the feelings and emotions that accompany deviant behavior are deemphasized.

The counselor working with Todd insists that he recognize and assume responsibility for his own behavior. Todd is helped to evaluate and to judge his behavior against an established standard of social responsibility. The counselor does not accept excuses or help Todd justify irresponsibility. Todd is helped to "own" his behavior and to view that behavior in light of his values and needs and of society's system of values and needs. "The skill of therapy is to put the responsibility upon the client and, after involvement is established, to ask him why he remains in therapy—if he is not dissatisfied with his behavior" (Glasser, 1965, p. 29).

The key theme in reality therapy is responsible satisfaction of needs. The critical question is, "Does this behavior help you get what you need and want?" The result of forcing Todd to think about his behavior in relation to his needs is that he begins to think about how he can satisfy those needs in a more socially acceptable way. Given the assumption that Todd needs to love and be loved and to feel worthwhile as a person, a standard of responsible behavior is necessary. The counselor helps Todd judge the quality of his own behavior.

Emphasizing responsibility is fruitless if the client is not ready. Irresponsibility is discussed with stubborn clients only when they are ready to change. Even then, the counselor should discuss only the fact that the client's behavior is irresponsible and that only the client can do something about it. Todd's recognition that his current behavior is irresponsible or wrong and therefore not effective in getting his needs met provides powerful motivation for positive change. Consequently, the counselor is free to pose such questions as: "Are you taking the responsible course of action?" "Are you doing right or wrong?" Questions of this sort underline the unrealistic aspects of negative behavior and set the stage for the next level of interaction.

Relearning.   The third procedure employed by the reality therapist is to help clients learn more realistic ways to fulfill their needs. By modeling consistently responsible behavior, the counselor can guide Todd toward an understanding that happiness results from responsibility.

Counselors instruct clients to examine their "constructive" thinking about the present and future. That is, counselors encourage clients to evaluate their plan for getting what they want out of their current situation so that they can be where they would rather be (Glasser, 1965). By working out this plan of action with Todd, the counselor helps identify alternatives to his negative, self-defeating behavior. Developing a realistic plan of action that accords with Todd's previously articulated values serves as a means for the counselor to teach responsibility. The focus of the plan is the client, Todd, and not other people in the environment. Ultimately, Todd must realize that only he can solve his problems.

After the counselor and the client jointly agree upon a plan, they make a mutual commitment to resolve the problem. Todd's plan, for instance, must lead to behaviors that will allow him to satisfy his needs for acceptance and connection with others. The mutual planning and mutual commitment demonstrate that the counselor does not accept Todd's negative behavior but cares about him and is willing to help him do something definite that will lead to the fulfillment of his needs. The plan and the commitment always involve much positive reinforcement for Todd's responsible behavior and the rejection of excuses for irresponsible, self-defeating behavior.

When Todd behaves irresponsibly, the counselor refrains from punishing him. The helper does, however, freely express praise when Todd behaves responsibly and shows disapproval when he does not. In varying degrees, then, the counselor teaches Todd more realistic ways to meet his needs.

The Seven Principles of Reality Therapy

Glasser has elaborated his three-stage framework by providing seven principles of reality therapy. These principles constitute the essential mechanics of reality therapy, and we list and briefly describe them here with sample statements that reflect the interactions of client and counselor.

It should not be assumed that every session will incorporate all seven principles. Involvement is essential in every session, but the other principles emphasized will depend on the particular client, the circumstances, and the progress of counseling. Early sessions tend to focus on identification and evaluation of current behavior. Later sessions tend to deal with planning and commitment issues.

Involvement.   Involvement means development and maintenance of a close, emotional relationship between client and helper. It implies a positive, caring attitude and gives the relationship a warm, personal quality. The thread of involvement is woven throughout the therapeutic process and intertwines with all other principles. (Client: "I'm going out of my head. I've got to get some help quick." Helper: "I'd really like to help you.")

Current behavior.   The focus is on behavior here and now. The counselor helps the client become aware of his or her current behavior and its ramifications. The client is also helped to see that this behavior is self-selected and therefore the consequences of the behavior are self-inflicted. (Client: "My mother is always angry at me. She's always been angry at me. I never do anything right." Helper: "What are you doing now about that situation?")

Evaluating behavior.   The client is made to look critically at his or her behavior and judge whether or not the behavior is in his or her best interest. The counselor helps the client make value judgments about what is contributing to a lack of success. At this stage, the client realistically determines what is good for him- or herself and what is good for people the client cares about or would like to care about. (Client: "To keep her off my back, I don't stay home much." Helper: "Is that productive for you?")

Planning responsible behavior.   The counselor helps the client develop a realistic plan to implement the identified value judgment. At this stage the counselor is strongly involved in teaching responsibility to the client. Working with the client to develop a realistic plan for changing behavior is an important step in teaching responsibility. (Client: "It's not productive because when I do come home she complains even more." Helper: "Is there a plan that we could make together that would keep your mother from complaining so much?")

Commitment.   When the plan of action has been agreed upon, the client and counselor make a commitment to follow it. The commitment may be a written agreement, but usually it consists of an oral exchange. Equivocations—"I'll try," "Maybe," "I think I can do it"—are not acceptable. (Client: "Yes, I guess I could stay home a couple of nights a week." Helper: "Are you willing to make a commitment to stay home two nights next week?")

The principles of reality therapy are designed to help clients learn to become involved with others in a responsible way and to learn to say yes and no at appropriate times. Clients are also encouraged to try new patterns of behavior to fulfill their needs, regardless of fears that these behaviors may not work. Essentially, clients learn not only to face reality but also to fulfill their needs. They commit themselves to a plan that has no loopholes. In the process they evaluate their current behavior and develop a plan for the future. Reality may be painful, but when clients can admit to the irresponsibility of their actions, the last phase of counseling—the relearning process—can begin. Then there is potential for growth, fulfillment, and self-worth.

Accept no excuses.   The helper must help the client gain the experience that will enable the client to keep the commitment he or she made. In addition, the new behavior needs time to become satisfying and thus self-reinforcing. Consequently, the helper cannot accept excuses for failure to keep a commitment. Glasser makes it clear that counselors, teachers, parents, and other adults who care about youngsters must not make excuses for them. Nor should adults tolerate the excuses that youngsters offer. (Client: "Yes, I'll stay home unless something more important comes up." Helper: "If you make the commitment, no excuses are acceptable. You have to decide now whether to commit yourself or not.")

No punishment. A counselor will not implement sanctions that have not been agreed upon in the commitment. Punishment changes the relationship that is necessary for success and reinforces the client's loneliness and isolation. (Client: "What will happen if I don't stay home two nights?" Helper: "Well, then we'd have to restudy the plan and the commitment. I would be disappointed; you wouldn't have helped your situation. It would be better to come up with a plan you can live with than not to follow through on your commitment.")

Engaging youngsters in a process that reflects the assumptions and principles of reality therapy can be very helpful to counselors, teachers, and parents. Adults who use this approach can effectively confront a potential or current delinquency problem. Although the principles of reality therapy were developed in a structured, controlled setting, they can be applied successfully in many less controlled environments.

CONCLUSION

Youngsters have to cope with many interpersonal, personal, and environmental pressures. Some children react to these pressures by aggressive acting out. Unless they are helped to control such behavior, they are likely to go on to antisocial behavior, gang involvement, and criminal activities as teenagers. The problems of delinquency are multifaceted, so assessment of the problem and treatment interventions must focus not only on the individual youth but on the family, school, peer cluster, and community environment. The principles of reality therapy can be usefully applied to help youngsters understand the consequences of their actions and form a plan for changing these self-defeating behaviors.

FURTHER READINGS

In addition to those books and articles cited in the reference section, the following books may be useful to readers wishing to know more about youth violence and antisocial behavior.

Barbaree, H. E., Marshall, W. L., & Hudson, S. M. (Eds.) (1993). *The juvenile sex offender.* New York: Guilford.

Bloomquist, M. L. (1996). *Skills training for children with behavior disorders: A parent and therapist guide.* New York: Guilford.

James, O. (Ed.) (1995). *Juvenile violence in a winner-loser culture: Socio-economic and familial origins of the rise in violence against the person.* London: Free Association Books.

Lykken, D. T. (1995). *The antisocial personalities.* Hillsdale, NJ: Erlbaum.

Olweus, D. (1993). *Bullying at school: What we know and what we can do.* Oxford, England: Blackwell.

Patterson, G. R., Reid, J. B., & Dishion, T. J. (1992). *Antisocial boys.* Eugene, OR: Castalia.

Prothrow-Stith, M. D. & Weissmann, H. (1991). *Deadly consequences.* New York: Harper Collins.

Ross, D. M. (1996). *Childhood bullying and teasing: What school personnel, other professionals, and parents can do.* Alexandria, VA: American Counseling Association.

Straus, M. B. (1994). *Violence in the lives of adolescents.* New York: Norton.

Walker, H. M., Colvin, G., & Ramsey, E. (1995). *Antisocial behavior in school: Strategies and best practices.* Pacific Grove, CA: Brooks/Cole.

CHAPTER 10

YOUTH SUICIDE

Wet the top of the glass
and run your finger around the rim.
That's me in the shimmering squeal; the sound of
glass.
Drop the vase to the floor
and listen to it shatter.
That's me in the piercing shatter; the sound of
glass.
Crush the mirror and watch the image
crack and splinter.
That's me in the crack, the splinter; the sound of
glass.
There is not much left of me.
Why not just silence the sound of glass, too?
If only I could find
Some meaning for myself that
Death won't take away.

J. J. McWhirter

CHAPTER OUTLINE

The problem of youth suicide is widespread and complicated. In the last two decades the number of people 15 to 24 years old who committed suicide rose 200% (Garland & Zigler, 1993). To prevent suicide we must understand the influences that culminate in suicidal behavior, which may range from a young person's family life to the realities of living in a technological culture, from feeling left out of the possibilities of adulthood to not knowing how to manage interpersonal relationships, from a child's perception that the future is doomed to a teenager's feeling that the present is hopeless. Those involved in the lives of young people can help prevent suicide when they know the warning signs and treatment strategies.

Among the aspects of suicide that we discuss in this chapter are (a) the incidence of childhood and adolescent suicide; (b) precursors to suicide and the characteristics of suicidal children and teens; (c) identification and assessment of suicide ideation; (d) common misconceptions of suicide; (e) warning signs and behaviors, and (f) prevention and intervention strategies, including early intervention, crisis intervention, and follow-up treatment. Particular attention is given to childhood and adolescent depression. Finally, for each intervention, we focus on the potential role of the teacher, counselor, and psychologist and the role of the school, family, and inpatient settings in effecting change.

THE SCOPE OF THE PROBLEM

Suicide is the third leading cause of death among adolescents in the United States after unintentional injury and homicide (Centers for Disease Control and Prevention, 1993). It is estimated that as many as 2000 young people commit suicide each year, and for every success, up to 350 teenagers attempt to do so (Smolowe, 1995). Some research suggests that 11% of young people attempt suicide (Andrews & Lewinsohn, 1992; Lewinsohn, Rhode, & Seeley, 1994). This rate climbs to about 33% among troubled adolescents (Tomlinson-Keasey & Keasey, 1988) and to 61% in some groups of juvenile offenders (Alessi, McManus, Brickman, & Grapentine, 1984). Actual suicide among some categories of exceptional students is thought to be higher than that of the general population (Guetzloe, 1991). In the last two decades, the suicide rate among children has increased two and one-half times (McDowell & Stillion, 1994). Obviously, suicide is a growing problem among young people. Over the past 30 years or so, the suicide rate among adolescents has increased by 300% and the number of youngsters who attempt suicide is predicted to continue to increase (Robertson & Mathews, 1989).

These estimates are probably low, because many suicides are not reported due to the family's embarrassment or religious beliefs or the discomfort of the school and the community (see Box 10.1). Consider also that accidents, the leading cause of death among adolescents, are often associated with recklessness and use of alcohol. Both alcohol use and reckless behavior are related to suicide ideation. The reckless behavior of people who seem to be courting death but do not acknowledge such an intention is termed *passive suicide*. Many accidental deaths may be a result of a wish to be dead. Similarly, drug overdoses, recorded as accidental deaths, may be unrecognized or unreported suicides. Researchers are unable to determine the number of passive suicides that occur each year.

Gender-related differences have been found in the rates and the lethality of suicide attempts. Three times as many females as males attempt suicide, but about three times as many males as females are successful (Canetto & Lester, 1995). Differences can be partially attributed to the lethality of the method. Men tend to choose more violent means to kill themselves, such as firearms. Guns are more immediately effective than the pills and poisons favored by female would-be suicides. This trend may be changing, however, as some evidence indicates that women are beginning to use more lethal methods in their suicide attempts (Rogers, 1990). Regardless of method, suicide by young people is a severe and complex problem that is assuming epidemic proportions.

Vulnerable and Underserved Youth

Ethnic minority children and adolescents.   Although relatively little research has been done on ethnic minority child and adolescent suicide, some evidence suggests that Hispanic children and adolescents may have a higher rate of suicide than do European American youth. J. C. Smith, Mercer, and Rosenberg (1989) and Queralt (1993), in two

■ ■ ■ Box 10.1
Case of Heart Failure

Rhonda was a senior in high school who loved to play the guitar and compose songs. She had dreamed of being a musician for as long as she could remember. It was a dream her parents did not share. Rhonda was the oldest child in the family, and she had been led to expect that she would go to college. But her parents registered her in a business school because they didn't want to "send good money after bad." Rhonda expected a lot of herself, and she knew that her parents also expected a great deal of her. She had few friends, but the friendships she had were quite intense. Her friends looked up to her and had high expectations for her career in music. They were disappointed about her parents' plan to send her to business school and told her so. Feeling unable to live up to her friends' expectations, she retreated from them. That spring Rhonda was sleeping only 3 to 4 hours a night. She alienated herself from her friends and her parents, and grew increasingly distraught over her seeming inability to please the people she loved. Four days after her high school graduation, local newspapers reported that Rhonda, age 18, had died of "coronary failure."

different locations in the United States, demonstrated that Hispanic teenagers had higher rates of completed suicide than adolescents from other groups. For some years, African American youngsters, especially boys, had been less susceptible to suicide. For example, Kempton and Forehand (1992) found that suicide attempts were reported approximately three and half times more often by European American youth than by African American youth. However, recent increases in suicide attempts in African Americans are quite dramatic, with the rate tripling within one decade (Summerville, Kaslow, & Doepke, 1996).

Although there is considerable variability from tribe to tribe, Native Americans have the highest adolescent suicide rate of any ethnic group in the United States. The high suicide rate has been associated with factors such as substance abuse and alcoholism, child abuse and neglect, unemployment, the availability of firearms, and lack of economic options that lead to hopelessness (Berman & Jobes, 1991). Little data exist for Asian American adolescents.

Gay and lesbian youth. Suicide among gay and lesbian youth has received considerable attention during the last several years. According to Gibson (1989), suicide is the leading cause of death among gay and lesbian youth, primarily because of the debilitating effects of growing up in a homophobic society. Gay and lesbian youth are two to three times more likely than heterosexual youth to kill themselves, and in fact they constitute 30% of all adolescent suicides. Several researchers (Remafedi, Farrow, & Deisher, 1991; Savin-Williams, 1994) suggest that suicide attempts by this population are frequently linked with sexual milestones, such as coming out to others or self-identification as homosexual. Male suicide attempters adopted a homosexual identity at a younger age and expressed more feminine gender roles. They also came from dysfunctional families (Savin-Williams, 1994). Family problems are the most cited reason for attempting suicide, and many attempters use illicit drugs and express other antisocial behaviors (Savin-Williams, 1994).

Attempts were most likely to occur after same-sex sexual activity or when individuals were questioning their heterosexual identity. These youth experience more gay-related stressors and experience feelings of social isolation, self-revulsion, disenfranchisement, and rejection from family and peers (Remafedi, Farrow, & Deisher, 1991; Savin-Williams, 1994). This particularly high-risk group of young people needs special attention to prevent them from killing themselves.

CAUSES AND CHARACTERISTICS OF YOUTH SUICIDE

Many adolescents of all cultures enjoy life, are happy most of the time, and are able to develop nurturing friendships (Diener & Diener, 1996). They feel positive about their development and their future. They experience physical changes and new social roles without undue trauma, even though they may regularly experience situation-specific anxiety. For the most part, these youngsters are able to cope with the rapid changes that are taking place in their lives.

For many children and adolescents, however, this period of change and growth is filled with stressful events and adjustments. Depression, aggression, and divergent thinking are common during this transitional period. These personality characteristics are exacerbated by low socioeconomic status, poor living conditions, and lack of educational and economic opportunity. Girls tend to experience more negative feelings than boys and are more lonely, sad, and vulnerable (Metha & Dunham, 1988). These experiences do not necessarily lead to suicide, but they may provide fertile ground for suicide ideation and future attempts.

Parents, teachers, and mental health professionals must be able to differentiate the "normal turmoil" that occurs during childhood and adolescence from turmoil that is life-threatening. Too many youngsters at risk for suicide have been mistakenly and sometimes tragically viewed as simply "going through a stage" (Metha & Dunham, 1988). Let's look at the psychological and relationship characteristics that may distinguish between youngsters who are able to cope with their world and those who are at risk for self-destructive behavior.

Interpersonal, Family, and Psychosocial Characteristics

Troubled relationships can contribute to suicidal thoughts and behaviors in children and adolescents. Other interpersonal, family, and psychosocial characteristics and experiences are associated with suicide ideation and attempts as well.

Loss and separation.   Suicidal youth are more likely than other youth to have experienced the loss of a parent through separation, divorce, or death (Marttunen, Aro, & Lonnquist, 1993). Suicidal thoughts also may arise in response to the loss of a friendship. Although separation and differentiation from parents is an important developmental task of adolescence, death and divorce are life-changing events over which a young person has no control. The natural feelings of grief, abandonment, and anger call for coping skills that not all youngsters have developed. The surviving parent may be going through tremendous emotional adjustment as well and may be unable to provide the direction and support the child needs. It is important to encourage the autonomy that comes with adolescence, but it is also important to refrain from pushing youngsters toward adulthood before they are ready. Youngsters who feel expendable as sons or daughters are at risk for suicide.

Dysfunctional and disintegrated families.   Suicidal youth often come from dysfunctional or disintegrated families (Fergusson & Lynskey, 1995). The rise in single-parent households as well as a lack of skill and experience in parenting, communication, and discipline (see Chapter 3) exacerbate the risk of suicide. Family interactions that are characterized by anger, emotional ambivalence, and rejection are also associated with self-destructive behavior in youngsters. Single parents, usually overloaded with work and financial obligations, sometimes have little energy to devote to the parent-child relationship. "Blended" families or stepfamilies can also suffer from uncertain, inconsistent, and confusing family interactions. These family dynamics may leave children and adolescents feeling isolated, unwanted, and expendable.

Violence is common in the families of many suicidal youngsters. In one study, attempters were three to six times more likely to have experienced sexual or physical abuse at home (Blumenthal, 1990). Suicide is also more prevalent among young people whose families have a history of suicide (Pfeffer, Normandin, & Kakuma, 1994). One study found that nearly 38% of adolescent suicide attempters had a close relative who committed suicide (Metha & Dunham, 1988). The age of a child is also significant: As many as 75% of children who were under 11 years old when a family member committed suicide attempted suicide themselves when they became adolescents (Roy, 1983), which is a greater percentage than older children who experience this tragic event.

Poor communication skills.   Children who grow up in a dysfunctional family system frequently "inherit" inadequate communication skills. Young people who grow up in an environment where communication of their thoughts and feelings is unsafe do not learn to express their distress to others. As feelings and thoughts fester and become increasingly negative, these young people may withdraw into themselves, making it difficult for others to recognize and respond to their increasing pain, depression, and possible suicidal feelings. The progressive isolation that results from poor communication skills can be a warning sign of self-destructive behavior (Marttunen et al., 1993).

Under- and overachievement.   Underachievement is related to suicide, although impaired academic functioning may follow and be a consequence of suicidal behavior rather than causative (Lewinsohn, Rohde, & Seeley, 1994). Nevertheless, poor achievement in school often signals a spiral of self-doubt, failure, and negative thoughts about the future. This signal may hint at a suicide crisis.

Youngsters who do very well in school but face a great deal of pressure to perform can be at risk for suicide too. Some gifted students face a suicidal crisis if they receive a C on a test—a grade that other youngsters would be relieved to get. Perfectionism and living up to high expectations is characteristic of many academically talented suicidal youngsters. Some researchers suggest that suicide among youth is related to high intellectual ability (Tomlinson-Keasey & Keasey, 1988). Deterioration in the academic performance of one of these youngsters can be a warning sign.

Catastrophic worldview. Many young people view the world as an unpredictable, dangerous, and hostile place. These intimations of catastrophe are exacerbated by threats of nuclear weapons, the AIDS crisis, racism, poverty, regional wars and civil violence, and a declining standard of living. Some youngsters also believe strongly that society has no power to effect any positive change. Consequently, some young people feel desperate and helpless and are potential victims of a suicide crisis. Unfortunately, many films and television shows validate these catastrophic feelings by modeling and glorifying violence and death (Levine, 1996).

Cluster suicides. Cluster suicides are suicides that follow or imitate another suicide. They may also follow a television program or movie that depicts teenage suicide (Capuzzi & Golden, 1988; Gould & Shaffer, 1986). When one youngster commits suicide, the act somehow becomes normalized for others, and youth who are experiencing despair may begin to see suicide as a viable response to their stress and feelings of hopelessness. Youngsters who are at risk for self-destructive behavior are even more vulnerable after someone they know or know of commits suicide (Lewinsohn, Rohde, & Seeley, 1994). Suicide clusters, often trivialized as "copycat" suicides, are a particular problem on Native American reservations (Tomlinson-Keasey & Keasey, 1988). Their incidence suggests that one youngster's suicide is a powerful model that can influence other youngsters to take their own lives. For this reason, postvention or follow-up treatment after a suicide crisis is essential.

Intrapersonal and Psychological Characteristics

Certain internal traits or intrapersonal and psychological characteristics may account for suicide ideation and motivate some youngsters to attempt suicide. These issues deserve specific attention.

Hopelessness and Depression. Depression is clearly a strong contributing factor to suicidal behavior in adults, with 35 to 80% of adult suicide attempters reporting depression before the attempt. Although the traditional relationship between depression and suicide is less clear for younger populations (J. J. McWhirter & Kigin, 1988; B. T. McWhirter, J. J. McWhirter, & Gat, 1996), current research indicates that depression is linked to suicidal thoughts and behaviors among youngsters in both clinical and nonclinical settings. Depression is a significant problem among children and adolescents, and we will return to it later in this chapter when we consider a major prevention program, teaching optimism.

Hopelessness, one component of depression, is a solid predictor of the feeling or state that leads some young people to self-destructive behavior (Levy, Jurkovic, & Spirito, 1995; Metalsky & Joiner, 1992; Whisman & Kwon, 1993). Children and teens do not need to feel hopeless or depressed to feel suicidal or to have suicidal thoughts, but depression, although not present in all cases of youthful suicide, remains an important common denominator (J. J. McWhirter & Kigin, 1988; B. T. McWhirter, J. J. McWhirter, & Gat, 1996). Other psychological disorders, such as anxiety disorders, obsessive-compulsive behavior, hostility, and psychosis, also play important roles in some teenage and child suicides. Recognition of the signs of depression and other psychopathology in youngsters may help to avert a suicidal crisis.

Impulsivity and risk-taking.   Impulsivity is often related to a suicidal response in young people. Teenagers and preteenagers who are part of a peer cluster, for example, may attempt suicide out of an impulsive reaction to someone else's self-destructive actions. Impulsive youngsters are also influenced by others' responses to suicide and by the impact that a suicide has on others (Lipschitz, 1995).

Impulsivity is also related to a risk-taking style. Although young people may be ambivalent about ending their lives, an impulsive or daredevil reaction to stressors often leads to suicide. High-risk behaviors and impulsivity, actually fairly common during adolescence, allow young people to test their fears of death against their feelings of immortality (Bell & Bell, 1993). Impulse control may be the one variable that determines the outcome of a suicidal crisis. Some youngsters who contemplate suicide will call for help, but others may make the attempt before they have time to think of an alternative response. The results of such impulsivity can be catastrophic.

Loneliness.   Loneliness and isolation are clearly implicated in suicide (B. T. McWhirter, 1990). Most suicidal youngsters are described as lonely or as "loners," and they tend to be withdrawn (Tomlinson-Keasey & Keasey, 1988). They generally have problems with their peers and are sensitive to rejection. Loneliness usually begins in childhood and continues into adolescence. Teenagers who are lonely and isolated in a period marked by developing social relationships feel expendable and unnoticed— feelings that often lead to a suicide crisis.

Self-image.   Low self-esteem, poor self-concept, and feelings of worthlessness are typical of suicidal youngsters and may predispose a child or adolescent to suicide ideation. Poor self-esteem and self-concept often lead to feelings of hopelessness and depression (Bagley, 1992; Stivers, 1990). A distorted view of the self can also lead to irrational and unrealistic expectations of others, the world, and the future. Youngsters who dislike themselves and who are unable to see themselves in positive ways should be of special concern to counselors and teachers.

Thinking patterns.   Faulty thinking and irrational beliefs, consistently found in conjunction with depression and low self-esteem, are prevalent among suicidal youngsters (Metalsky, Joiner, Hardin, & Abramson, 1993). If faulty thinking can be modified at an early age, many suicide crises may be avoided. Here are some thinking patterns common to suicidal youngsters:

Cognitive constriction: inability to see options for solving problems, which leads to dichotomous thinking, common in the critical stages of suicide ideation. The youngster is able to see only two solutions to the problem: continue to exist in a living hell or find relief through death.

Cognitive rigidity: a rigid style of perceiving and reacting to the environment that restricts a person's ability to cope with stress and to formulate realistic alternative approaches to problems. Cognitively rigid individuals see the problem, their inability to solve it, and the future, as catastrophic.

Cognitive distortion: overestimation of the magnitude and insolubility of problems. The difficulty of a problem is also generalized to all situations. Distorters assume that they are the cause of their problems. The past is forgotten, and the future is unimaginable.

These consuming negative beliefs about the self, the insolubility of problems, and the future are pervasive. They can lead to withdrawal, to an inability to create change, and ultimately to a suicide crisis. Unfortunately, faulty thinking patterns have a self-defeating spiral effect in which youngsters' problems grow increasingly worse and their ability to conceive solutions becomes increasingly limited (see Figure 10.1). In Chapter 13 we present an extremely important and useful prevention program developed by Seligman (1990, 1995) and his colleagues that is designed to modify faulty thinking patterns among children.

Motivations for attempting suicide. Out of these faulty thinking patterns arise motivations for attempting suicide. Suicide can be a method of *self-punishment* to deal with guilt or shame. Self-punishment is not uncommon for a young girl who discovers she is pregnant, for a teenager who begins to have memories of sexual molestation, or for an adolescent in conflict about sexual identity. Suicide may also seem to provide *absolution* for past behaviors; this motivation is not uncommon among alcoholics who end their lives. Suicide is sometimes *perverted revenge*, a perceived means to get back at those who caused the youngster pain, such as parents who got divorced and destroyed the

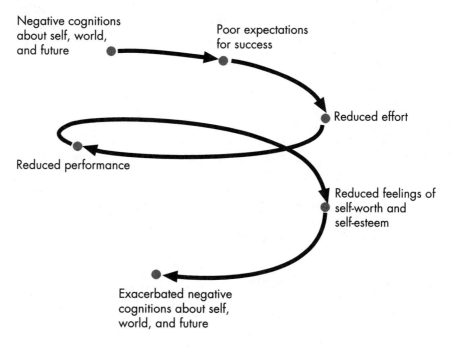

FIGURE 10.1 **Spiral of self-defeating cognitions**

■ ■ ■ Box 10.2
The Girl Who Had Everything

Shelley was an intelligent, beautiful, and popular high school senior. She was dating the Homecoming king, was earning straight As, was the star of the girls' softball team, and was liked by everybody. She seemed to have everything her girlfriends wanted without even trying. When her parents went through a sudden and angry divorce, Shelley continued to be the same smiling, fun-loving friend; her girlfriends believed that this "courage" was just another strength that their talented friend possessed.

One weekend Shelley got into a fight with her mother just before her mother and brothers were to leave for an overnight visit with friends. In what was probably an attempt at revenge, Shelley called a large number of her friends and had a party at her mother's house. After several hours of drinking, Shelley got into another argument, this time with her boyfriend, and he broke off the relationship. Her girlfriends reported that Shelley seemed to be her "normal, laughing self" for the rest of the evening; at the time, they assumed she thought the breakup was only temporary. When her family arrived home the next morning, the car was running in a closed garage, and Shelley had been dead for hours.

Shelley left no note. She had not done or said anything to her friends to suggest that she wouldn't be around the next day. It appeared to be an impulsive decision, carried out in haste. Clearly, her outgoing high spirits and bravado were masking despair and anger. Perhaps they also masked the fact that this girl who "had everything" had never really learned how to cope with disappointment and pain.

family. *Retaliatory abandonment* is another motivation for suicide. A boy who has been dumped by his girlfriend can "retaliate" by showing her how awful she was to cause him to end it all. He would rather leave than be left by someone. Both perverted revenge and retaliatory abandonment may have been operating in the case of the girl described in Box 10.2. Finally, *fantasy of omnipotent mastery* is a desire to have absolute control over the self and others, to control life and death itself, and to be completely autonomous.

These motivations can be assessed and a suicidal crisis averted if effective strategies are used to identify a potential suicide.

IDENTIFICATION AND ASSESSMENT STRATEGIES

Very useful assessment strategies have been devised to determine a youngster's suicide ideation and risk of acting on suicidal thoughts. Two such methods are (a) clinical interviews, which can disclose the severity and lethality of suicide ideation; and

(b) self-report measures. When these approaches are taken early, family members, friends, the community, and the school can respond appropriately.

Interviews for Suicide Lethality

Interviews are probably the most effective and informative way to assess suicide risk (J. J. McWhirter, 1993). Interviews are conducted with parents, teachers, and the child or adolescent who appears to be at risk of suicide. Suicidal youngsters are typically angry at themselves and at the world and are caught up in emotional turmoil; it is therefore critical to establish a professional relationship that expresses confidence, helpfulness, and trust. Interviews are used to determine the potential risk of suicide and the lethality of this risk.

So far as possible, the interviewer should assess (a) the history of the presenting problem (depression, anxiety, loneliness, and so forth); (b) the family constellation and family relationships; (c) a developmental, medical, and academic history; (d) the status of interpersonal relationships; (e) verbal and behavioral warning cues; and (f) any current stressors that may trigger a suicide attempt. Changes in behavior, in sleep and eating patterns, and in emotional status should also be noted along with any previous suicide attempts. It is important to identify any discrepancies between the parents' and the youngster's reports; this may indicate a problem. An effective interview will reveal any warning signs of suicidal ideation and behavior.

Once suicide ideation has been identified, the lethality of the risk must be assessed. The severity of the threat depends on the specificity and the lethality of the method of choice. Ideation alone is not a great risk. Progressively worse are (a) ideation with a plan, including a time, place, and method; (b) a lethal method (such as a gun or a leap from a tall building); (c) accessibility of a means to commit suicide (such as a loaded gun in the house); and (d) a history of previous suicide attempts (Pfeffer, Hurt, Kakuma, Peskin, Siefker, & Nagabhairava, 1994). This last factor is particularly important. In one study, adolescents with a history of suicide attempts were almost 18 times more likely than those with no such history to attempt suicide (Lewinsohn, Rohde, & Seeley, 1994). Some of the following high-risk factors should also be determined:

- symptoms of *clinical depression* and *hopelessness*
- *recent loss* of an important relationship or life goal
- serious *family problems,* such as divorce, alcoholism, physical abuse, or incest
- *personal history* of physical disability, alcohol or drug abuse, or psychiatric treatment
- *interpersonal impoverishment,* or the absence of friends, family, church members, or others who can provide direct emotional support in a crisis

Holinger, Offer, Barter, and Bell (1994) have devised useful guides for determining many of these risk factors. Readers are encouraged to consult their work and other sources, such as J. J. McWhirter (1993), for sample interview procedures.

Self-Report Inventories

In view of the relationship between depression and suicide, the use of depression inventories is warranted in efforts to determine the risk of suicide. Two that are useful for children and adolescents are the Beck Depression Inventory (BDI) (Beck, Ward,

Mendelson, Mock, & Erbaugh, 1961) and the Child Depression Inventory (CDI) (Kovacs, 1981; Kovacs & Beck, 1977). The BDI, frequently administered to adolescents, contains 21 items that yield a single score reflecting whether an adolescent may be severely depressed and at risk for suicide. The CDI was modified from the BDI for use with children between the ages of 8 and 17. The 27 items on the measure are couched in language appropriate for that age group.

Other instruments by Aaron Beck and his associates are the Scale of Suicide Ideation (Beck, Kovacs, & Weissman, 1979) and the Beck Hopelessness Scale (BHS) (Beck, Weissman, Lester, & Trexler, 1974). The Scale of Suicide Ideation is designed specifically for suicidal persons and is useful with adolescents. It includes questions related to attitudes about living or dying, the characteristics and specificity of suicidal ideation, and background factors such as previous suicide attempts. This measure, like the depression instruments and the BHS, can be used to determine the severity and manifestations of depression and suicidal thoughts in youngsters.

These assessment techniques increase our understanding of both the warning signs of suicide and some of the reasons youngsters see suicide as an option. They may also help to dispel some of the common and pervasive misconceptions of suicide.

COMMON MISCONCEPTIONS OF SUICIDE

Mental health workers need to be aware that misconceptions or myths about suicide are common (Capuzzi, 1994). Understanding some of the causes of suicide and the characteristics of young people who are at risk for taking their own lives will help to dispel some of these myths. Here are some of the most common ones:

• *A person who has considered or attempted suicide will always be suicidal.* In fact, most young people think about suicide. Most suicide attempts are a means of crying out for help. The cry is not for "attention"; rather, it is directed at receiving desperately needed understanding and help. If a young person's feelings are dealt with immediately and in an effective way, a suicide crisis can be positively resolved. Many people who consider suicide do so only once and fleetingly.

• *After a suicide crisis has passed, the youngster is no longer at risk for suicide.* Youngsters may not continue to feel suicidal after an attempt, but neither are they out of danger. Suicide attempters have already overcome a social taboo by trying to kill themselves once; subsequent attempts are easier for them. If parents, counselors, psychologists, and school personnel do not attend to the young person and the reasons for the attempt, a subsequent attempt is possible. Suicide takes a great deal of emotional energy. A child or adolescent who displays a calm reaction after an initial suicide attempt may be gaining strength for another. This period, especially if it is marked by a lack of overt emotional turmoil, should be treated with caution because the risk of suicide may not be over. Later suicide attempts frequently involve more lethal methods.

• *People who commit suicide always leave a note.* Actually, only a small proportion of children and teenagers who commit suicide leave a note, even though they may leave numerous clues or hints. This misconception can perpetuate a family's bewilderment after a suicide. Not only are they helpless to change what happened, but they are also uncertain about the reason for the suicide. Many suicides are classified as accidents because no note has been found and the deaths may not be recognized as suicides.

• *Suicide happens without warning.* Few people intent on suicide actually spell out their intention directly, but most do give numerous clues and hints of despair and suicidal ideation. After a youngster has committed suicide, it is not uncommon for friends and family members to recognize many behaviors and words that indicated the youngster's vulnerability. Accident-proneness, increasing dosages of medications or sleeping pills, withdrawal, declining academic performance, and hints about not being around much longer are suicide warnings. Concerned adults and young friends need to recognize even the most indirect and subtle warnings.

• *The person who talks about committing suicide never actually does it.* Nearly every suicide has been preceded by some kind of warning. Even if such threats seem to be bids for attention, it is better to respond to a youngster's potential risk than to regret a completed suicide. Always take threats seriously.

• *Suicide occurs more frequently among the lower socioeconomic groups than among the more affluent.* Although age, gender, and ethnic differences persist—suicide is on the rise among children and adolescents, and Native Americans have the highest suicide rate—suicide is a problem in all socioeconomic and cultural groups.

• *Suicidal people are mentally ill or severely depressed.* Suicide is an ineffective, maladaptive solution to a dysfunctional living situation. Suicidal youngsters are not mentally ill, nor can any genetic markers for the incidence of suicide be distinguished from ineffective coping mechanisms learned from others in the environment. And although many suicidal youngsters are depressed, not all are. Some children and adolescents who are not depressed consider suicide in the absence of adequate problem-solving skills.

Parents, counselors, teachers, and other professionals who are free of misconceptions about suicide are in a position to predict suicidal behaviors and risk among young people. They can also help to prevent many suicides by teaching young people the facts about suicide and the warning signs to look for.

WARNING SIGNS OF SUICIDE

Among the warning signs that a child or adolescent may be contemplating suicide are behavioral changes, verbal messages, and cognitive preoccupations.

Behavioral Changes

Behavioral changes that suggest the risk of suicide include:

• mood swings or fluctuations
• a change from happy and positive interactions with others to withdrawal and negativity
• apathy or a lack of activity, such as neglect of hobbies that once were important to the person
• changes in sleeping or eating patterns—lack of appetite or ravenous hunger, insomnia or lethargy

Such changes are common warning signs. In addition, school personnel may recognize:

• a decline in the youngster's productivity and performance

- an increase in truancy
- more acting out in class
- possible drug or alcohol use with "the wrong crowd" at school and after school hours

Suicidal youngsters also give away prized possessions, because they expect to have no use for them in the future. This is a clear warning sign. The verbal cries for help that accompany these behaviors are also warning signs.

Verbal Messages

Most youngsters who feel self-destructive give verbal hints that life is too difficult to handle or not worth living. Youngsters who say things like "I don't see how I can go on," "I wish I were dead," "There's only one way out of my problems," "I won't be around much longer," "I'm tired of living," "You'll be sorry you treated me this way," or "Pretty soon my troubles will be over" are hinting or saying directly that they are considering suicide. Suicidal youngsters also talk about death, wonder aloud what it will be like to be dead, and may be preoccupied by thoughts of others who have died. They may also joke about killing themselves. Many messages that are communicated as jokes are actually indications that a suicidal crisis is imminent. In an effort to get help or to find out how others will respond, some youngsters make direct threats of suicide. Verbal warnings should be taken seriously and not seen as just a "stage" that youngsters go through. Failure to respond to a verbal warning or to a direct threat of suicide may be interpreted as confirmation that the youngster is worthless, expendable, and unloved. These feelings only increase the risk of a suicide attempt.

Cognitive Preoccupations

As we observed earlier, suicidal youngsters typically have a rigid and unrealistic style of thinking. The content of their preoccupations may also be a warning sign. When youngsters seek to escape from a situation, to join a dead friend or family member, to be punished for their actions, to get revenge or to hurt someone else, to control their death, or to solve a problem that they see as intolerable or unresolvable, they are at risk for self-destructive behavior (Capuzzi, 1994; Capuzzi & Gross, 1996). A negative outlook and poor self-image are also warning signs. Adults and other youngsters must try to be aware of what other children and teens think about. Most youngsters will express their thoughts in some way. Knowing the state of mind and the style with which a youngster resolves or fails to resolve problems is the first step in preventing suicide. (Strategies for cognitive change are discussed in Chapter 12.)

As we saw in Chapter 1, Paul Andrews exhibits many of the warning signs of suicide. The conflict with his parents, although less focused than that of his sister Allie, can be a precursor to a suicide attempt. Paul's stepfather, Burt, is either overtly aggressive toward him or ignores him completely. His mother passively encourages him not to upset Burt. Paul acts out in school, is aggressive with other children, and yet at times is very withdrawn. He also receives attention (and subsequent rejection) from other youngsters by repeating gory news stories related to death and human pain. Paul's interactions with his peers therefore reinforce both his aggressiveness and his feelings of guilt, worthlessness, and anger at himself and at the world. In short, Paul is a very depressed youngster whose strategies for getting attention are ineffective, and the attention he does receive is almost always negative.

One night, after being berated by a teacher for a poor performance on a test and after a dinner "conversation" that consisted of Burt's upbraiding of Allie, Paul swallowed all of the sleeping pills in his mother's medicine cabinet; the bottle was almost full. Later, when Alice reached for the bottle and found it gone, she ran to his room and found him only partially conscious, the empty bottle on the floor next to his bed. The paramedics rushed Paul to the hospital, where his stomach was pumped.

Depression

Had knowledgeable teachers, counselors, or other adults observed Paul closely and talked with him, they would have discovered that the warning signs were there. Paul demonstrated changes and intensity in those areas that serve as red flags—behavioral changes, verbal messages, and cognitive preoccupations. Unfortunately, Paul's behavior reflects trends that have been increasing steadily over the last several decades: the increase of depression in the general American population, and the increase of depression among children and adolescents.

Building on research focusing on adults in the mid-1980s, two recent studies focused on the increase of depression among children and adolescents (Garrison, Addy, Jackson, et al., 1992; Lewinsohn, Rohde, Seeley, & Fisher, 1993). These researchers found that depression affects approximately 30% of the adolescent population; in fact, one in five youngsters reports a minimum of one episode of *major* depression by the age of 18. Similar trends are present in young children, and it is assumed that the precursors of depression begin quite early in a child's life. Seligman (1995) suggests that this trend among both adults and younger people is of epidemic proportions and that considering our time as an Age of Melancholy is very appropriate. Having a clearer understanding of depression in childhood and adolescence is helpful in developing prevention programs for suicide. Furthermore, the prevention of depression in childhood and adolescence is critical to reducing the higher costs of treating this disorder among adults (King, 1991).

Later, we present strategies for early intervention, crisis intervention, and postvention for child and adolescent suicide. Interventions to prevent depression itself and depression as a precursor to suicide are extremely important.

PREVENTION

Where suicide is concerned, the traditional distinctions between treatment and prevention can be somewhat confused. Treatment for severe suicide ideation, for example, is aimed at preventing an actual suicide, so treatment and prevention become one and the same. In general, efforts to prevent suicide focus on the factors that lead to a suicide crisis; treatment is intervention after an unsuccessful attempt, such as Paul's, or even before, in response to acute suicide ideation. Postvention, or follow-up treatment, consists of interventions for the surviving family members, friends, and community after a completed suicide. One of the goals of postvention is to prevent cluster suicides. Prevention strategies and treatment (that is, crisis intervention) could have been helpful to Paul, and may still be helpful to him.

Primary prevention involves the removal or modification of environmental and interpersonal characteristics that are commonly associated with suicide and usually takes the form of a generic program carried out in all grades of an elementary or secondary school. Many primary prevention programs focus on developing affective skills, such as building self-esteem, and learning social and problem-solving skills (Hyson, 1994; Seligman, 1995; Shure, 1992a, b, c). It is quite possible that such a program could have prevented Paul's suicide attempt.

Education in the schools about suicide and death is an appropriate method of suicide prevention (Capuzzi, 1994; Grossman, Hirsch, Goldenberg, & Libby, 1995). Through education a child's distorted view of mortality can be modified to reduce the likelihood of accidental death or experimentation with suicide. Workshops, staff and teacher outreach programs, and direct classroom instruction can focus on stress, family communication, cognitive distortions, and other factors associated with suicide.

One such program uses puppets to teach children about death (Bernhardt & Praeger, 1985). Puppets are a useful medium for the communication of feelings and ideas and have been used successfully for a variety of educational purposes (J. J. McWhirter & A. M. McWhirter, 1987). Puppet skits give information and generate questions about death so that children gain a more realistic perspective on death and on suicide. Puppet skits can encourage children to discuss their feelings and give presenters a chance to validate the feelings that children share. Teachers and school counselors play key roles in this type of preventive education program.

A primary prevention program can lessen the need for early intervention and treatment, but because the risk of suicide is never completely eliminated, schools and community agencies must institute early intervention programs and be prepared to respond to crises.

EARLY INTERVENTION, CRISIS MANAGEMENT, AND POSTVENTION

Early intervention programs target early detection and treatment of depressive disorders, anxiety, loneliness, stress, and family problems. Parents and teachers, the adults most accessible to the child and adolescent, play crucial roles in early intervention, but other school personnel and community professionals are also important. Early intervention programs in the school minimize the frequency and severity of the suicide ideation experienced by high-risk youngsters. Early detection can be managed conveniently and inexpensively through group screening devices. Had such an early intervention program been in place in Paul's school, he might have been identified as at risk earlier and appropriate interventions could have been implemented before the suicide crisis emerged.

Early intervention is focused on deterring a suicide by dealing with its causes. Researchers (Kalafat, 1994; McKee, 1993; Vidal, 1989) argue, for example, that schools must have a response-ready crisis team available to deter suicides and to deal with a suicide crisis should it emerge. Response teams are made up of teachers and administrators, school counselors, school nurses, and social workers, as well as parents and community members. Although response teams are designed for crisis intervention, part of their purpose is to provide education and intervention before an actual crisis emerges.

Four early intervention activities are central to the response-ready crisis team (McKee, 1993; Vidal, 1989).

1. The school must develop a prevention and early intervention plan. Referral resources should be prepared, and a procedure of action has to be established so that team members can take direct, immediate action when it is needed. Schools should involve families and parents in this program.
2. Teams coordinate their activities with those of mental health agencies and other organizations that serve families and youngsters in the community. They may also engage law enforcement agencies, private therapists, medical professionals, and church and hospital personnel. Developing a network is critical for preventing suicide and for dealing with attempts.
3. Response teams can participate in education and training. Educational presentations and seminars should be directed not only to students but to teachers, other school personnel, and parents as well. Public awareness of suicide and its risk factors will increase the effectiveness of any prevention effort. Response teams can also maintain appropriate audiovisual materials and a library of information on suicide and intervention resources.
4. Response teams should review and maintain the entire program to ensure that referral resources are updated, procedures are efficient, and the prevention and early intervention activities are appropriate for the students.

Finally, response teams must avoid certain procedures when they develop and institute a prevention and early intervention program. Vidal (1989; see also Capuzzi, 1994) suggests the following don'ts regarding suicide prevention:

1. Don't wait for a crisis before planning a response. Response plans need to be instituted before a crisis.
2. Don't avoid talk about suicide. Suicide issues should be dealt with openly and honestly.
3. Don't prepare students to deal with suicide before significant adults are prepared. Teachers and other school personnel who must deal with a crisis need preparation first. Capuzzi (1994; Capuzzi & Gross, 1996) argues that it is unethical not to prepare school faculty and staff in advance of the presentation of suicide information to students.
4. Don't show an educational film or video on suicide without first discussing the content with students. After the film or video, allow time for students to discuss their thoughts and feelings about it.

Crisis Management and Response

Suicide treatment is a response to a threat of suicide with severe and acute ideation or to a failed attempt at suicide. A suicide crisis is managed with the same concern and immediacy as any other emergency. Counselors, teachers, and administrators who are members of the response-ready crisis team should free themselves from normal duties to respond to such an emergency. Mental health professionals, such as school counselors, play primary roles in a crisis response.

First, counselors assess the lethality of the suicide threat (Holinger, Offer, Barter, & Bell, 1994; J. J. McWhirter, 1998). If a suicide plan is specific and lethal or after an attempt has been made, counselors must assess whether or not the child or adolescent is stable. If they are uncertain about this, counselors must use referral procedures to provide the intervention needed. Hospitalization may be called for. The response team can help in making this decision.

Second, a written contract is developed between the student and the counselor. This contract establishes an agreement that the student will call and talk to the counselor or will wait until his or her next counseling appointment before attempting suicide. Most youngsters who sign a contract comply with it. Providing the youngster with an emergency crisis number is also important. Paul's self-destructive behavior seems to have been motivated by a need for acceptance and attention. If caring adults provide the support he needs, he would probably respond well to a contractual agreement not to attempt suicide again.

Third, observation is critical. The youngster must be monitored during the crisis for a period of at least 24 to 72 hours. Counselors can hospitalize the potentially suicidal young person or can recruit family members and friends to participate in a "suicide watch" to keep track of the youngster's affect and behavior (Capuzzi, 1994; Capuzzi & Gross, 1996). Counseling should be action-oriented and directive and aimed at dealing first with the danger of suicide. Once a youngster is stabilized, the underlying causes of the suicide crisis can become the focus of intervention.

Finally, counselors must notify parents of the danger of suicide when they are aware of suicide ideation. Parent-counselor contact may be, in fact, the first part of a crisis response. *Although this contact breaks confidentiality, it is an ethically and legally appropriate response to a youngster's suicide threat.* If youngsters are to develop trust in the counselor, the counselor must make clear to them the limits of confidentiality. The counselor who informs others of the danger of suicide shows concern for the youngster's welfare.

Crisis intervention steps.   Six steps must be taken to defuse a suicide crisis:

1. Listen and show respect for the feelings a suicidal youngster expresses. Suicidal youngsters feel that their problems are severe, and their feelings should not be brushed aside.
2. Reinforce the young person for seeking help. Admitting suicide ideation or attempting suicide brings shame and embarrassment. These feelings should be acknowledged. The counselor can also help the youngster recognize and voice the part of him or her that wants to survive. This can help to deter a later attempt.
3. Be specific about assessing lethality. Ask direct questions: "Are you thinking about killing yourself?" Be particularly specific about assessing the concreteness of the plan. Ask: "How do you plan to kill yourself?" "Do you have the necessary means?" "Have you attempted suicide before?"
4. Make decisions for the client. Youngsters who indicate that they will attempt suicide within the next few hours should be hospitalized for consistent care and monitoring, and parents must be notified.
5. Have the client sign a written contract. An oral contract may be adequate, but a written contract is more powerful. Sometimes the suggestion of hospitalization is enough to persuade a youngster to sign a written contract, but be very careful about using this tactic. *The youngster who feels coerced into signing a contract may feel under no obligation to abide by its terms.*
6. Use the resources that are available. Community mental health agencies and private therapists are often the primary resources for helping youngsters and their families after a suicide attempt or acute suicidal ideation.

Immediately after a crisis.   After a nonfatal attempt, school personnel or the crisis team should attend to a number of other issues. As most suicide attempts are not made at school, a member of the crisis team should call the parents to verify the suicide attempt. The call also provides an opportunity to offer assistance to family members. After this call, a team member should notify teachers and administrators, emphasizing confidentiality. It is also important to monitor the attempter's friends, to follow up on others who are perceived to be at risk for suicide, and to respond to friends who may be traumatized by the attempt. While the student is recovering, a team member should keep the student informed about what is going on at the school and encourage the parents and other professionals involved to report on the young person's progress.

This collaborative relationship is continued when the student returns to school. Members of the crisis team should help to make the student's return to school as comfortable as possible. Both individual and group counseling have been effective in helping a youngster deal with the aftermath of a suicide attempt, although group counseling should be postponed a few months so that the attempter is not the primary focus of the group (Robertson & Mathews, 1989). Medications for depression and anxiety are also effective after a suicide attempt and may be used in conjunction with therapy.

Family interventions.   A maladaptive, homeostatic family system is maintained when one child performs the role of the "sick" one in the family, and other family members may resist positive change in the child or adolescent because it threatens the family's homeostasis (as you shall see in Chapter 14). This reality necessitates family treatment in addition to individual interventions after a suicide gesture. An attempt at suicide by any member of the family is very stressful for all the other members, even when the family is not homeostatic. Teachers, counselors, and other mental health workers must be aware that normal nurturance and family care may not be adequate to deal with a youngster's stress, anxiety, depression, and suicide ideation.

When working with families, counselors must emphasize certain key issues (McLean & Taylor, 1994). First, counselors must establish the significance of the problem. Although parents may see their child's concerns as minimal, they may be overwhelming to the youngster. To the youth, suicide may seem to be a realistic solution. Parents must understand that a suicidal young person's problem is a family problem. Paul's parents, for example, must become involved in efforts to help him, because much of his despair is rooted in family problems.

Second, counselors must deal with the shame, guilt, and anger that parents often experience when their child is suicidal—and with the denial that may be operating within the family. Counselors need to identify these denial patterns and make them a focus of discussion and treatment.

Third, the family must begin to recognize that the problems that led up to the suicide crisis have developed over a long time and reflect family dynamics. Families should be encouraged to recognize, understand, and modify these dynamics as a means of managing a suicide crisis and of effecting long-term change.

Finally, counselors must be flexible and work with a variety of combinations of family members: the suicidal youngster alone, the parents as a couple, other siblings, and the entire family unit. This is especially important because other family members may reflect suicidal thoughts and behaviors that need to be identified and attended to. Family counseling is probably the most effective method for dealing with the primary causes of self-destructive behavior. For example, modifying the communication styles and helping each family member to clarify and modify his or her role in keeping the dysfunctional family in balance would be useful for Paul and his family. (Family counseling interventions are discussed in Chapter 14.)

Postvention and Follow-Up Treatment

A great deal of suffering goes on in the aftermath of a teen's or child's suicide. Surviving family members, friends, and schoolmates of the suicide victim often need follow-up treatment, or postvention. Individual, group, or family counseling may be needed to help them deal with the event. Sharing information about the suicide and discussing it with community members and with fellow students helps to prevent cluster suicides. Indeed, mental health professionals and school personnel have important responsibilities after a successful suicide. Most postvention efforts involve the school and the family.

Schools. The school is the major setting not only for prevention and early intervention but also for attention to the aftermath of a student's suicide. School personnel can provide information about suicide, help survivors cope with their loss, and offer counseling to students who may need special attention. Suicide should be discussed; a fear of discussing self-destructive behavior actually increases the risk to other students. In discussions of the suicide, the dead youngster should not be glorified or romanticized, but students should be allowed to grieve. Neglect of these factors may increase the possibility of cluster suicides.

Postvention, like crisis intervention, is the responsibility of the crisis team. The response team should take the following steps after a student has committed suicide (Grossman, Hirsch, Goldenberg, & Libby, 1995; Vidal, 1989):

- Administrators should call an emergency faculty meeting to relay the facts and to encourage class discussions.
- A designated team member needs to inform others, who should call parents and offer their assistance. They need to contact the mental health department and the district office to inform them of the incident.
- The school should not hold an assembly to announce the suicide or issue a public statement about it. Some students may perceive these actions as positive consequences of suicide.
- The school should *not* hold a memorial service, nor should it prepare a memorial statement for publication in the student newspaper. These activities can increase the perception that suicide is an acceptable form of death.
- Opportunities should be provided for friends and schoolmates to meet to share their grief, and emergency or crisis hotline numbers should be made available to students. The school may need to enlist community resources to manage these groups and to provide emergency and information services.
- The school should hold a "critical incident stress debriefing" of staff members (E. H. McWhirter, 1994). This process includes a structured review of the event and allows personnel to ventilate their feelings, fears, and frustrations.

Families.   Some of the strategies used in working with families after a suicide attempt are also useful for postvention. Besides experiencing feelings of guilt, shame, and embarrassment, family members also feel grief, loss, and helplessness after a suicide. Therapists should recognize and work with these feelings. They become the focus of the family interventions discussed earlier. We discuss specific interventions in Chapter 14; here, we simply encourage those who must deal with a youth suicide to pay particularly close attention to the needs of the surviving family members.

CONCLUSION

The behaviors associated with suicide can have a catastrophic effect on adolescents and on those around them. The prevention of suicide and the provision of early intervention in the presence of suicide ideation is essential. Because teachers, school counselors, and other school personnel play primary roles in the lives of young people, they must be especially aware of and responsive to the symptoms, causes, misconceptions, warning signs, and related problems of adolescent and child suicide. Understanding child and adolescent depression and instituting depression immunization can help greatly. Identification, awareness, and quick response by school personnel and mental health professionals, especially as members of a response-ready crisis team, may be of paramount importance in avoiding the devastating and potentially long-lasting effects of self-destructive behavior.

FURTHER READINGS

In addition to those books and articles cited in the reference section, the following books may be useful to readers wishing to know more about child and adolescent depression and youth suicide.

Capuzzi, D. (1994). *Suicide prevention in the schools: Guidelines for middle and high school settings.* Alexandria, VA: American Counseling Association.

Gilliland, B. E., & James, R. K. (1997). *Crisis intervention strategies.* 3d ed. Pacific Grove, CA: Brooks/Cole.

Holinger, P. C., Offer, D., Barter, J. T., & Bell, C. C. (1994). *Suicide and homicide among adolescents.* New York: Guilford Press.

Naom, G. G., & Borst, S. (Eds.). (1994). *Children, youth, and suicide: Developmental perspectives.* San Francisco: Jossey-Bass.

Roberts, A. R. (Ed.). (1991). *Contemporary perspectives on crisis intervention and prevention.* Englewood Cliffs, NJ: Center for Alcohol Studies, Rutgers University.

Reynolds, W. M., & Johnston, H. F. (Eds.). (1994). *Handbook of depression in children and adolescents.* New York: Plenum.

Prevention, Intervention, and Treatment Approaches

■ In this section we provide a systematic framework and model of prevention, early intervention, and treatment of children and teenagers at risk. In Chapters 11 and 12 we suggest ways to address the roots of the problem in the social environment. Chapter 12 specifically focuses on components of intervention that draw on social skills, cognitive-behavioral strategies, and other strategies aimed at decreasing negative behaviors and attitudes and increasing positive ones. In Chapter 13 we include several exciting intervention programs that can be used to help young children either at home or at school, or to help young adolescents by harnessing pro-social peer group influences. Chapters 14 and 15 focus on family-based and school-based interventions, respectively. We conclude Part 3 with a discussion of legal and ethical factors that must be considered by helping professionals who work with children and adolescents.

CHAPTER 11

A Prevention/Early Intervention/Treatment Framework and Other Environmental Considerations

The teacher says, "If it weren't for
those parents . . . counselors . . . "
The counselor says, "If it weren't for
those teachers . . . parents . . . "
The parent says, "If it weren't for
those schools . . . agencies . . . society . . . "
Society says, "If it weren't for
those kids . . . "
The kids say—
But who listens to kids anyway?
The spiral of blame and guilt,
incrimination and rationalization,
circles like buzzards over a
gritty desert.

Can we ever find a way to straighten
the spiraling circle—to roll up our
sleeves and get to work?

J. J. McWhirter

CHAPTER OUTLINE

In this chapter we introduce a multifaceted prevention and treatment framework that helps integrate concepts addressed throughout the book and that provides an overall context for the interventions described in later chapters. We precede our description of the framework with clarification of the relationship of prevention, treatment, and risk and a brief history of prevention strategies. After a thorough description of the framework, we address relationships, empowerment, and social activism as factors that can reduce the problems of children and adolescents at risk.

A COMPREHENSIVE PREVENTION/EARLY INTERVENTION/ TREATMENT FRAMEWORK

Prevention, Treatment, and Risk

What serves as a *treatment* intervention for one problem frequently serves as a *preventive strategy* for a more advanced problem. In a sense, problem behaviors form a continuum. If we involve Todd Baker (of Chapter 2) in a smoking-reduction group, for example, we are providing a treatment for his cigarette smoking; but because cigarette smoking puts Todd at risk for the use and possible abuse of alcohol, marijuana, and other drugs, our treatment also serves as a prevention strategy. If we engage the Carter family (of Chapter 3) in treatment for their dysfunctional family system, we are providing treatment for their ongoing negative interactions. We are helping Jason Carter deal more effectively with both his maladaptive and his self-defeating behaviors, and we are also potentially preventing Jason's further progression toward one or more of the at-risk categories.

Risk, too, forms a continuum, from remote risk to imminent risk. Factors that contribute to risk include demographic characteristics such as social class and economic conditions; family, community, and school stressors; and personal characteristics. As we discussed in Chapter 5, some youngsters are resilient enough to flourish even though demographically they are at risk. Unfortunately, other young people develop specific personal behaviors that increase their potential for problems and place them at further risk. As more and more factors and characteristics associated with dropping out, teen pregnancy, delinquency, and so forth become evident, the young people are considered to be at imminent risk. Our framework incorporates the relationship between prevention and treatment as well as the continuum from remote to imminent risk.

Any model that incorporates prevention, early intervention, and treatment raises complex issues. The role of the school, the linkage between the problems of young people and prevention, and the interplay between treatment and prevention are all important considerations (Lowenthal, 1996). Equally important are outcomes of previous attempts to prevent problems. Only if we understand previously unsuccessful efforts can we overcome past problems.

History of Prevention Programs

Programs designed to prevent problems that can blight young people's lives include attempts to modify the use and abuse of tobacco, alcohol, marijuana, and other drugs. During the 1960s, drug education programs focused on providing information. Early efforts were based on scare tactics, moralizing, and often inaccurate information. Many programs contained fear-arousal messages regarding the social and health consequences of drug use. The emphasis was on the drugs themselves rather than on the reasons people used them. Perhaps even more significant, youth reported that the information lacked credibility. This approach was not effective. In some cases, drug use actually increased among adolescents during this time. The consensus is that relying on knowledge alone to change problem behavior is misguided (Dielman, 1994; Montagne & Scott, 1993).

By the 1970s, drug-prevention programs began to address personal and social factors that correlated with drug abuse and to provide more accurate information. Affective education became the major preventive approach. Rather than focusing on drug abuse, educational efforts focused on factors associated with the use of drugs and attempted to eliminate the presumed reasons for using drugs. Affective education programs targeted self-esteem on the assumption that if young people understood their motivations for drug use and had greater self-esteem they would not want to use drugs. This approach also failed to lower substance-abuse rates. Indeed, trying to eliminate most problem behaviors by focusing on self-esteem alone is not effective. Seligman (1995) provides an interesting discussion of "feel-good" self-esteem versus "do-good" self-esteem and their relative contributions to childhood depression and other problems. "Do-good" self-esteem is helpful; "feel-good" self-esteem is not.

During the 1980s, prevention efforts began to include affective, cognitive, and behavioral strategies. These programs focused on developing social competency and pro-social coping, subsumed under the rubric of "life skills." A solid body of research has been conducted across many of the at-risk areas to test the efficacy of these broad-based prevention and early intervention programs. The results of this research have been promising (Durlak, 1995). The implications of the drug-prevention experience are that our model must incorporate affective, cognitive, and behavioral approaches that emphasize development of skills and pro-social attitudes as well as comprehensive, broad-based, and extensive applications (J. J. McWhirter, 1993).

Description of the Framework

The framework we describe here is based on the assumption that comprehensive prevention, early intervention, and treatment programs are essential to ameliorate the problems of at-risk children and adolescents. This comprehensive framework is conceptualized as operating along several continuums and provides appropriate intervention components that encompass society/community, family, and school concerns as well as generic primary prevention programs. Secondary prevention/treatment programs (that is, early intervention and target programs) and second-chance treatment intervention strategies are also included. Figure 11.1 shows the several continuums that comprise the framework.

The Risk Continuum

The risk continuum introduced in Chapter 1 is at the top of the figure. Recall that problems faced by youngsters are conceptualized as following a continuum from minimal risk to actual participation in an activity in one of the at-risk categories. Beginning at the left of Figure 11.1, a remote degree of risk is associated with certain demographic characteristics. As young people develop and mature, personal characteristics that lead to increasingly higher risk may become evident. If these personal characteristics are not modified, young people may soon be beyond remote risk and high

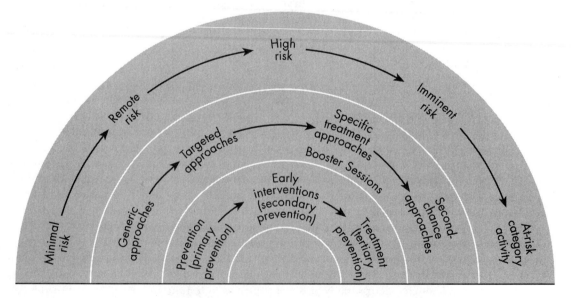

Figure 11.1 **Risk approaches, and prevention continuums**

risk and considered at imminent risk for many problems. Finally, at the end of this continuum, children or adolescents may behave in a manner consistent with one or more of the five categories discussed in earlier chapters (that is, they may become pregnant, engage in delinquent behaviors, use drugs, drop out of school, or attempt suicide).

The Approach Continuum

The second strand in the arch in Figure 11.1 identifies various intervention approaches to the problems that may appear at each level of risk: generic approaches, target approaches, specific treatment approaches, booster sessions, and second-chance approaches. The relative placement of each approach between the anchors of the risk continuum above reflects the relation of the approach to the level of risk. Thus, a generic approach is the most appropriate type of intervention when a youngster exhibits minimal or remote risk. As a youngster moves from remote risk to high risk, a target approach is more desirable. As a youngster moves from high risk to imminent risk and then to at-risk category activities, a specific treatment approach and then a second-chance program become more useful interventions. Each of the approaches in the second strand of the arch can operate in the domain of the community, family, or school, but we will focus here on the school setting.

Generic approaches.   Generic preventive strategies are considered to be appropriate for all children, not just those who are presumed to be at risk. All children within a given catchment area (a community, a neighborhood, a school) may receive a common or generic intervention. All children in a low-income neighborhood, for example, are given access to a program even though some are at only minimal risk and some of their families are more affluent. Or perhaps all children in a given classroom are engaged in interactive and cooperative learning groups rather than just those who are educationally deficient.

In generic school approaches, the intent is to maintain or increase the educational achievement, pro-social coping skills, and mental health of large numbers of children. Ideally, generic content is integrated throughout a comprehensive health-oriented school curriculum. Basic life-skill competencies (discussed in the following two chapters), such as problem-solving and decision-making skills, communication and other social skills, and impulse control, help young people respond to a variety of social situations. Developmentally appropriate personal, social, and cognitive skills are important components of a generic life-skills program. These programs can be beneficial at any time in the life of a young person, but they have the greatest influence early in life. Ideally, generic programs should be an integral part of preschool, elementary, and middle school curriculums.

Target approaches.   Target approaches are aimed at groups of young people who share some circumstance or experience that increases the probability that they will develop problems in the future. Demographic parameters, specific environmental stressors, and skill deficits indicate the need for target prevention programs. Perhaps the best example of a targeted group defined by demographic factors are the children from low-income families who qualify for a Head Start program. Because of their economic situation (which presumes other stressful circumstances), they are provided with an enriching preschool experience that increases their chances for later success.

Specific environmental stressors also provide a useful way to target young people either when they appear to be in a vulnerable situation or during specific developmental stages. Children of divorced, pathological, or alcoholic parents, for example, are quite vulnerable. Individual or group counseling or school support programs are very useful interventions for these students. The transitions from elementary school to middle school and from middle school to secondary school are stressful developmental periods that are often followed by a significant increase in absenteeism, increased susceptibility to substance abuse and delinquency, and a sharp decline in psychological well-being (Felner, Brand, Adan, Mulhall, et al., 1993; Lord, Eccles, & McCarthy, 1994; Reyes & Hedeker, 1993; Walsh-Bowers, 1992).

A third group of youngsters appropriate for target programs are those whose behaviors indicate deficits in skills. Sometimes these children are identified in psychological terms, such as lonely, depressed, anxious, aggressive; sometimes by educational categories, such as learning disabled or behavior disordered; and sometimes in terms of their limitations in the five Cs (critical school competencies, concept of self, communication, coping, and control skills, discussed in Chapter 5).

The risks, problems, and needs of the targeted group must be identified before an appropriate intervention can be designed and implemented. The appropriate content for a target approach often consists of the same social and cognitive skills that are addressed in generic approaches. Some youngsters need increased attention, more intensive emphasis, and more applied practice to acquire these life skills. This is the case in any classroom, but school personnel need to give particular attention to pupils in special education classes. Because of their emotional, behavioral, and learning problems, they are especially suited for target approaches. Indeed, special educators will recognize indications of risk in the behavior of many children in their resource rooms or classrooms.

Booster sessions.   Prevention efforts should be intensive, sequential, and comprehensive, with continued involvement over a long time period. One-shot prevention efforts are not very effective because program effects dissipate in a relatively short time (Elmquist, 1991). Short-term interventions achieve, at best, short-term results. Consequently, periodic and sequential "booster" follow-up sessions should be added to help maintain the effects of the initial intervention (Elmquist, 1991). Such sessions are important for generic approaches, and they are critical for target and specific treatment approaches. Few programs without booster sessions have achieved positive long-term results (Durlak, 1995).

Specific treatment approaches.   On the right-hand side of the middle continuum in Figure 11.1 are specific treatment approaches for individuals who are at imminent risk for (on the brink of) some problem behavior or who have actually begun to engage in the behavior. Specific treatment approaches must be developed for young people whose underlying characteristics, problems, and behaviors are associated more directly with at-risk activity. A smoke-reduction treatment group, for example, is a specific treatment for problems associated with smoking as well as an attack on a major gateway to the use of even more hazardous substances.

Specific treatment approaches also include interventions that deal directly with at-risk activity. Situation-specific attitudes and skills that have particular relevance for each at-risk category are addressed. The goal of a specific treatment approach is to increase youngsters' knowledge of the problem category, to teach them alternative behaviors and coping skills, and to help them resist various forms of social pressure to drink or do drugs, to become involved in delinquent behaviors, to engage in unprotected premature sex, to withdraw from school, or to kill themselves.

Second-chance approaches. Finally, "second-chance" interventions are needed for those children and adolescents who are already engaging in substance use, have dropped out, have become pregnant, or are engaging in the other behaviors of concern. Young people who have made poor choices need an opportunity to change those choices to more constructive ones; they need a second chance. In the five chapters of Part 2 we provided concrete examples of both specific treatment interventions and second-chance approaches for each of the specific at-risk categories.

The generic, target, treatment, and second-chance approaches address, in sequential order, those risk factors that are the most salient contributors to young people's problems. These intervention efforts are most successful when they are comprehensive and cover a broad range of risk factors. The problems of children and youth at risk have multiple antecedents, and interventions must focus on many causal factors if they are to be effective. The intent of such approaches is to set individuals on new developmental paths as early as possible, to open opportunities, to modify life circumstances, and to aim for long-term change.

The Prevention-Treatment Continuum

Prevention, early intervention, and treatment programs also form a continuum, which is represented by the bottom strand of the arch in Figure 11.1. Conceptually, these three terms are closely allied to the nearly three-decade-old formulation of primary, secondary, and tertiary prevention that Caplan (1964) used to define prevention in the psychiatric field. Caplan used these terms to describe efforts for "reducing (1) the incidence of mental disorders of all types in a community (primary prevention), (2) the duration of a significant number of those disorders which do occur (secondary prevention), and (3) the impairment which may result from disorders (tertiary prevention)" (pp. 16–17). Caplan's traditional terms are included on the continuum; however, we use the prevention, early intervention, and treatment designations more appropriate to at-risk issues to anchor the framework.

Environmental Settings

In our comprehensive framework we attend to the environment by including society/ community, family, and school settings, and we acknowledge the relationship between these components. Intervention in each of these settings is also conceived as following a continuum from (a) early broad-based prevention to (b) early intervention efforts to coordinate support and training activities, and ultimately to (c) treatment approaches that include a variety of education, training, and counseling efforts. The three rectangles in Figure 11.2 represent the three settings, and each is divided by a diagonal line to indicate that some strategies and programs are best implemented earlier in the risk continuum and some are more appropriate later. The diagonal line also suggests that some aspects of prevention need to be maintained and supported throughout the model. In some circumstances treatment begins early and may accompany prevention. Early intervention falls in the middle of Figure 11.2 and has elements of both prevention and treatment.

Society/community.   The society/community continuum interacts with both family and school continuums but encompasses the community and larger society. Prevention efforts in this setting consist of improving socioeconomic conditions; increasing the supply of low-cost housing, child care, job opportunities, and career options; providing community social support programs; and developing nonrisk community norms and values.

Along the early intervention portion of the continuum are community programs that involve family members and school personnel. That is, there is a need to provide social support and coordinated programs that enable community members to assist young people. There is a need to strengthen existing support for families in the schools and in community organizations. There is a need for schools to work with the community. Below the diagonal line are treatment strategies that include system-level interventions, such as empowerment and social activism. Empowering clients and helping them develop plans for social action are a preventive approach on the individual level, but they serve as treatment on the society/community level. The target here is not individuals or even groups of individuals but rather the norms, structures, and practices of organizations, communities, society, and the nation.

Family.   Prevention, early intervention, and treatment for families and family dysfunction also form a continuum. This continuum begins with strategies designed to strengthen families—strategies that encourage interaction, communication, stability, support, and pro-social values. Prenatal and health care programs are included as well. As family problems increase, social and emotional support programs and training in parenting skills are implemented. Counseling is critical for dysfunctional families. At the extreme end of the continuum, programs designed to address child abuse and neglect, parental dysfunction, and family violence are especially important. (We discuss the prevention and treatment of family dysfunction in Chapter 14.)

School.   Because we have focused on the school as an important delivery system for prevention, early intervention, and treatment programs for young people at risk, this portion of the diagram and Figure 11.3 are very important. Prevention in schools begins with adequate comprehensive preschools, compensatory programs (such as Head Start), and before- and after-school programs.

Generic school programs for teaching social and cognitive-behavioral skills to all children begin early in this model, although the diagonal line indicates that they can be implemented at any point. In Chapter 12 we provide detailed information about teaching these skills. The need for target programs increases chronologically; specific early intervention is necessary for targeted youngsters in specific problem situations or for those who exhibit problem behavior. Figure 11.3 depicts some of these approaches and suggests the need for treatment and second-chance programs.

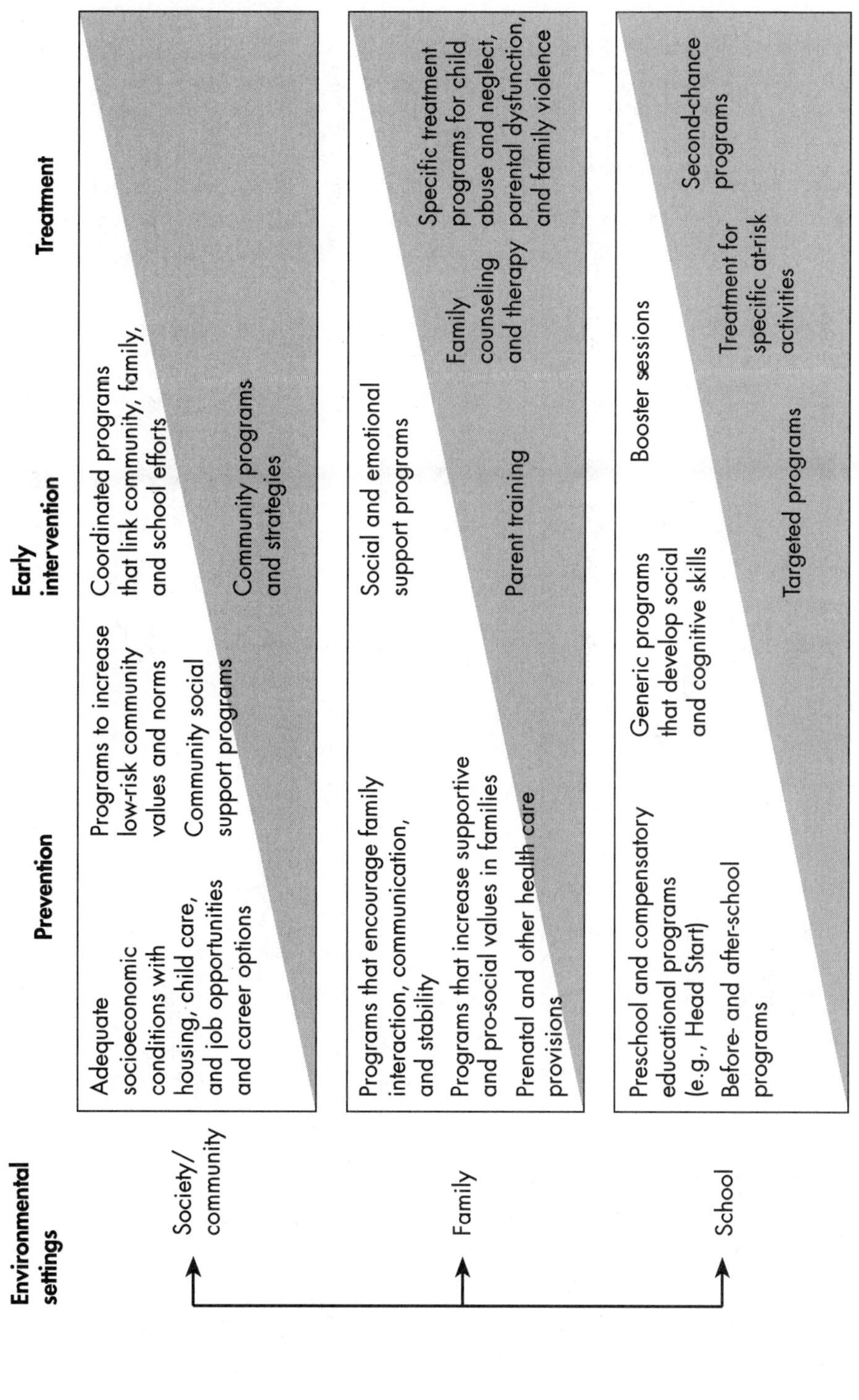

Environmental settings	Prevention	Early intervention	Treatment
Society/community	Adequate socioeconomic conditions with housing, child care, and job opportunities and career options	Programs to increase low-risk community values and norms	Coordinated programs that link community, family, and school efforts
		Community social support programs	Community programs and strategies
Family	Programs that encourage family interaction, communication, and stability	Social and emotional support programs	Specific treatment programs for child abuse and neglect, parental dysfunction, and family violence
	Programs that increase supportive and pro-social values in families		Family counseling and therapy
	Prenatal and other health care provisions	Parent training	
School	Preschool and compensatory educational programs (e.g., Head Start)	Generic programs that develop social and cognitive skills	Booster sessions
			Second-chance programs
	Before- and after-school programs		Treatment for specific at-risk activities
		Targeted programs	

FIGURE 11.2   Environmental settings for prevention/early intervention/ treatment framework for at-risk children and youth

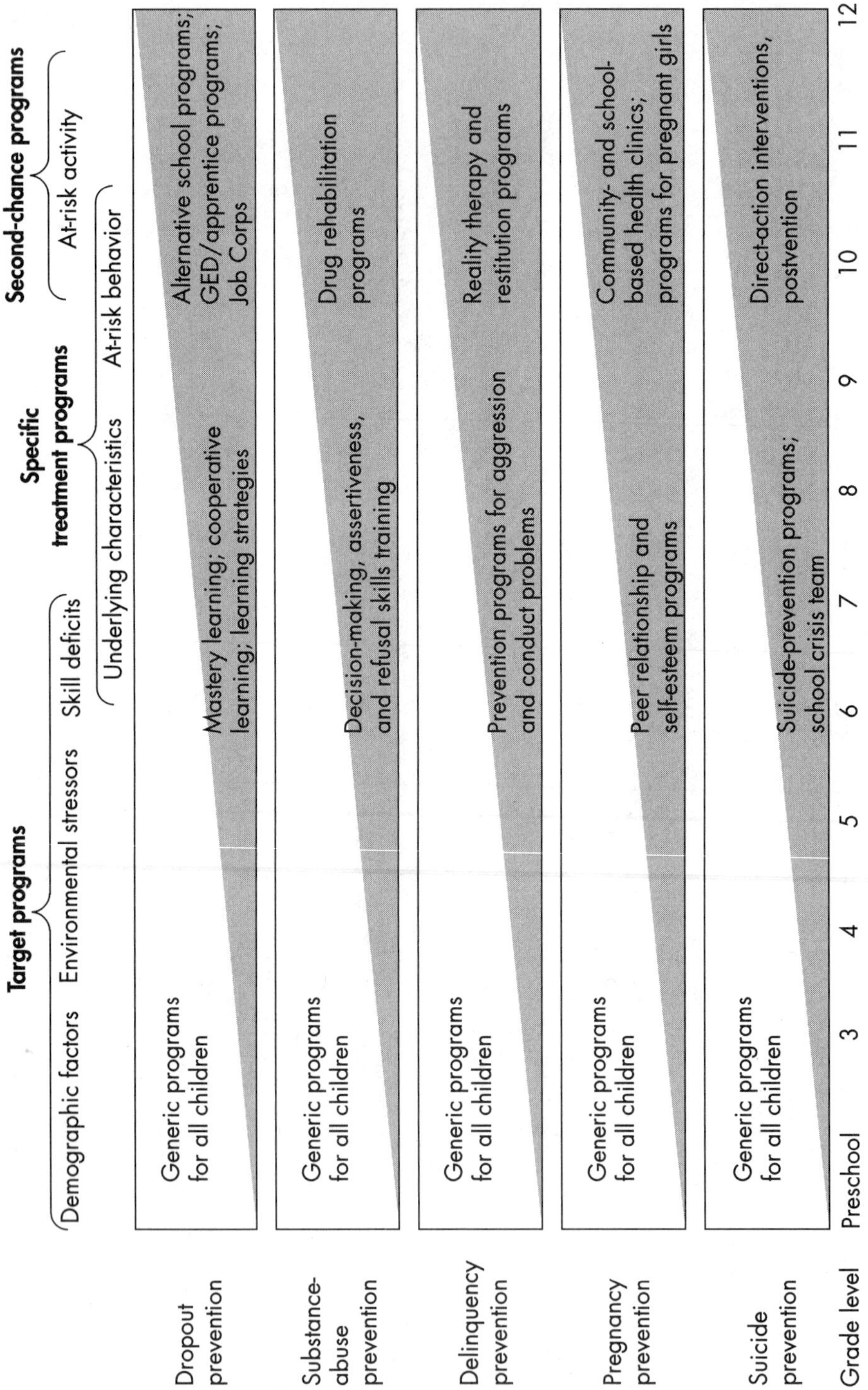

FIGURE 11.3 Early intervention and treatment for five at-risk categories

Many of the programs identified in Figure 11.3 reflect the early interventions and treatments discussed in Chapters 6 through 10. The generic programs specified at the left in each box represent the preventive efforts that are directed toward all youngsters. As children develop chronologically and behaviorally, efforts shift from generic approaches to programs aimed at specific target groups or individual children.

Even before they enter kindergarten, children whose demographic characteristics make them vulnerable deserve special attention. As they progress through school, children who undergo such traumas as poverty, injury, abuse, neglect, or divorce or death of their parents should be identified and provided with appropriate support and counseling.

Target interventions should begin at least by grade 3 for children who engage in risky behavior (aggressiveness, withdrawal, suicide gestures) or who exhibit such negative emotions as depression, anxiety, or hostility. In a given third-grade classroom, quite accurate predictions can be made as to who will drop out of school before graduation (Rumberger, 1987; Slavin, 1994). Evidence also suggests that delinquency in adolescence can be predicted on the basis of early behavior patterns. Researchers have shown that a pattern of antisocial behavior established by fifth grade (Walker, Colvin, & Ramsey, 1995) or even earlier (Patterson, Reid, & Dishion, 1992) is the single best predictor of criminal behavior in adolescence. This is especially the case if the antisocial behavior occurs in a wide variety of settings and involves more than one type of act.

As young people progress through school, specific treatment programs need to be developed. Figure 11.3 also highlights second-chance programs for adolescents in more serious trouble.

We believe that all children should receive comprehensive life-skills training as part of their regular curriculum from preschool onward. Such a curriculum, modified and adapted for initial skill level, cultural appropriateness, and social class variables, should be progressive and developmental as students move through school. Training programs, corresponding with predictable developmental stages and environmental pressures, should include information on study skills and time management, how to study for tests, how to make friends, how to manage emergencies when home alone, how to avoid or report abuse, and, as the young adolescent matures, how to prepare for intimate relationships, how to prevent pregnancy, how to avoid drug abuse and resist peer and media pressure to engage in behavior that has negative consequences, and other life events. These programs should be ongoing components of the curriculum rather than one-session classes. Training in problem solving, decision making, empathy, communication, assertiveness, and coping skills should also be ongoing. All teachers, with support from and in consultation with school counselors, psychologists, and social workers, should be prepared to teach cognitive and life skills, avoidance of substance use and delinquency, and sex education. Implementating such a model will have far-reaching effects for young people and for society as a whole.

PRACTICAL CONSIDERATIONS

Cost

Would such a comprehensive program be expensive? Certainly. But consider the social costs of the behaviors the program addresses. We are losing too many of our young people to drugs, to delinquency, to suicide. Too many are becoming pregnant; too many are dropping out of school. The costs of such a program must be weighed against the sometimes overlooked costs of residential treatment programs, medical bills, the criminal justice system, property damage, and welfare and food-stamp programs. The lost productivity of these young people continues to limit our ability to compete on the world market (Slavin, 1994), and the social cost of ruined and crippled lives affects us all. When we calculate all of these costs, the expense of prevention and early intervention programs shrinks considerably.

Two principles are embedded in American culture: (1) It is better to do something than to do nothing; (2) an individual can make a difference. If we succumb to discouragement, depression, and apathy, no one is helped, and the problems will continue to get worse. All of us need to be alert to programs and strategies that might help youngsters with problems. The second principle is based on individual efforts. In each of the chapters on at-risk category behaviors we have mentioned the need for more nurturing personal relationships between at-risk youth and caring adults. We share with many readers the belief that each individual teacher, counselor, psychologist, or other human service professional can make some difference in the lives of the children and adolescents with whom he or she interacts.

Counselor/Psychologist/Teacher Interface

Many of the techniques we discuss can be used by a school counselor or school psychologist as an intervention with elementary, middle, or secondary school clients. Mental health counselors, social workers, and psychologists employed in public and private agencies and hospitals can incorporate aspects of these strategies and interventions in their practice. Many of the suggestions can be used by a teacher with an individual child, a group of children, or an entire classroom. These interventions, with appropriate modifications, lend themselves to both individual and group work. They are most effective when concerned adults work together.

When teachers, counselors, and psychologists collaborate in their efforts, putting the needs of an individual youngster uppermost on their agenda, they increase the effectiveness of their work. One problem that plagues teachers, counselors, and psychologists alike is lack of time. It takes time to develop a collaborative relationship among people. The structure of the school can support or detract from such efforts. Even if it is not supportive, it is still worth the effort to develop a means of working together to reduce overlap, increase efficiency, and enhance the well-being of the affected children.

Teachers.   Teachers, especially those in special education, can incorporate aspects of the suggested programs in their classrooms. There is an increasing need for adults to serve as mentors, to become positive role models for young people, and to provide practical information about communication and human relationships. Comprehensive life-skills training programs (discussed in Chapter 12) effectively meet this need. Teachers, perhaps with help from counselors, are in an excellent position to implement these programs. They need to be encouraged and supported in their efforts to do so.

Counselors and psychologists.   The school or agency counselor or psychologist is in a good position to consult with teachers about implementing life-skills programs. Counselors and psychologists have the training to apply cognitive-behavioral approaches, small-group processes, and other developmental, psychoeducational strategies in the effort to improve youngsters' social skills. Not the least of the counselor's many professional responsibilities is direct training of clients in psychological skills.

Psychoeducation involves training individuals in psychological skills or knowledge. Psychoeducation can be preventive or remedial; it can be provided individually or in groups. The developmental and educational role of the counselor is crystallized in the concept of the counselor as a psychoeducator. Psychoeducation has been used to improve general coping skills and transition to work (P. T. McWhirter & J. J. McWhirter, 1996), to reduce anxiety and other emotional stressors (J. J. McWhirter, 1995), to reduce anger and aggression (J. J. McWhirter, Herrmann, Jefferys, & Quinn, 1997), to improve interpersonal skills (Wenz & McWhirter, 1990), to decrease loneliness (B. T. McWhirter & Horan, 1996), and to increase study and assertiveness skills. Psychoeducational treatment is applicable in a wide variety of problem areas and is especially useful for at-risk children and youth.

ADDITIONAL ENVIRONMENTAL ISSUES

As we noted earlier, the prevention/early intervention/treatment model represents one approach to altering the environment that produces at-risk young people. Three other environmental issues are of particular importance: *relationships* between caring adults and at-risk youth, *empowerment* as a central component of efforts to help, and direct participation in the process of social change, or *social activism*.

Relationships

Relationships between at-risk youth and stable, nurturing adults provide a means by which young people learn academic skills and knowledge as well as necessary social skills. Adults can increase a sense of self-worth in children and adolescents.

The importance of relationships is particularly critical in prevention efforts. Recall from Chapter 5 that resilient, invulnerable children are consistently found to have established a significant, positive relationship with at least one adult, not necessarily a parent. Relationships make a difference. Caring relationships with at-risk children and adolescents can prevent or disrupt the negative spiral and raise self-expectations. They provide a model of appropriate behavior. They provide mentoring to help guide young people to more healthy and happy life experiences.

Relationships also increase the social interest of the child or teen. Given the learning and adjustment problems facing at-risk children, teachers and counselors must be sensitive to issues related to social interest. Human life is social life. Feelings of belonging, along with the ability and desire to cooperate, participate, and contribute, are critical to the common welfare. Social interest is also necessary for good mental health, and the degree to which it is present is a measure of the individual's adjustment. Experiences that increase a child's feelings of belongingness and that convey social status and significance foster social interest. Conversely, whatever makes a child feel inadequate, inferior, or humiliated decreases his or her social interest.

The potential for social interest is present in the infant but it must be developed through interaction with the social environment. Children learn effective or ineffective social behavior in their relationships with family members, school personnel, and other significant adults. Through this socialization process, children learn to adapt their interests to those of society. Children must learn to accomplish tasks and overcome obstacles in a way that benefits not only themselves but all those around them. Thus, children whose private interests are in agreement with general human interests have the best chance for success. The constructive approach for increasing a child's social interest is to maintain order without conflict. This is of fundamental importance. In learning to accept order willingly, the child learns to cooperate with others and develops feelings of belonging and social interest. It is essential that the overall atmosphere be one of mutual respect, kindness, and tolerance for mistakes and failures. Equally important are firmness, regularity, and the maintenance of order. Positive relationships between concerned, caring adults and at-risk children and adolescents help create an environment that allows the young person to acquire and express social interest.

Empowerment

Empowerment is another way in which adults can help at-risk children and adolescents address limiting environmental conditions. Empowerment helps people actively confront their environment rather than passively accept their conditions as unalterable (E. H. McWhirter, 1991, 1994).

The term *empowerment* has been used with increasing frequency in education, social work, and counseling literature. We have elsewhere defined empowerment as "the process by which people, organizations, or groups who are powerless or marginalized (a) become aware of the power dynamics at work in their life context, (b) develop the skills and capacity for gaining some reasonable control over their lives, (c) which they exercise, (d) without infringing on the rights of others, and (e) which coincides with actively supporting the empowerment of others in their community" (E. H. McWhirter, 1994, p. 12). For young people this means learning how their lives are influenced by family, school, and the larger society, developing the skills to combat negative influences and make positive choices for their lives, and supporting the healthy choices of other young people in their families, schools, and communities. We will discuss three aspects of empowerment in more detail: power analysis, skill development, and exercising new choices and behaviors.

Power analysis.   Young people are empowered when they develop a critical awareness of systemic power dynamics. Classroom discussion of the roles in which many children are cast by dysfunctional families (mascot, hero, lost child, scapegoat) can facilitate recognition of how family systems can influence both healthy and unhealthy behaviors. Even young children can be taught in simple ways to examine their behavior in its context and to identify their choices. For example, "I guess I was mean because Sarah pushed me, but I didn't have to be mean, did I, Teacher?" is a statement of awareness youngsters can easily achieve. Adolescents are often quite willing to explore how their behavior is shaped by peers, by the school, and by their community. When they understand how they are influenced and can explore the situation in a nonjudgmental atmosphere, they have a basis for choosing different attitudes and behaviors. Power analysis can be integrated into a variety of standard subjects, such as history, language arts, government, creative writing, and literature. Power analysis can focus on family dynamics, school and community factors, and local and national government policies; it can also be applied to racism, sexism, ageism, ecology, nuclear weapons, and a multitude of other topics. The key is to help students understand how these issues affect them as individuals. Better understanding of power dynamics helps individuals refocus their efforts to change and may provide important clues to help in the change process.

Skill development.   Empowerment also involves development of the concrete skills necessary for responsible choices. Teaching children more effective social skills increases their power over their personal environment. Learning cognitive-behavioral skills helps them control and cope better with their internal processes. Providing them with learning strategies facilitates their intellectual growth. Decision-making and assertiveness training, imagery and relaxation techniques, and other psychological tools enhance people's ability to cope effectively with their environment. Training in other skills, such as research, writing letters, organizing meetings, public speaking, and leadership, enable at-risk youth to take more active roles in confronting or joining various power structures influential in their lives. Much of the discussion in the following chapters is designed to help teachers and counselors empower their students and clients through the development of important skills.

Exercising new choices and behaviors.   Through power analysis, the teacher or counselor helps at-risk youth realistically appraise the impact of socialization, economic stratification, and discrimination on their lives. To ignore the political, economic, and social context within which the young person operates and survives is to risk identifying the source of the problems as the individual. It is the responsibility of the teacher or counselor to help individuals identify contributing factors, for most young people are all too willing to shoulder all the blame themselves.

If young people are led to believe that "the system" caused all of their problems, however, their apathy and withdrawal may simply increase. Growing awareness of power dynamics must be accompanied by the development of concrete alternatives. Empowerment suggests that although problems are often rooted in systems, individuals can and must share the responsibility for addressing and alleviating the problems. Identifying new choices and behaviors is essential, as is providing students with opportunities to practice those behaviors and actively pursue those choices. Otherwise, teachers and counselors will leave their students and clients feeling even less in control of their lives. The need for social activism among teachers and counselors is equally important.

Social Activism

One hindrance to the development of adequate services for youth is the fact that so many of the solutions require fundamental sociopolitical changes (E. H. McWhirter, 1994; J. J. McWhirter & E. H. McWhirter, 1989; B. T. McWhirter, E. H. McWhirter, & J. J. McWhirter, 1988). Poverty, inadequate nutrition and housing, discrimination, and lack of information on birth control cannot be prevented with crisis-oriented programs. One means of prevention is to change the environment that fosters such problems. Thus, some aspects of prevention must involve critical analysis of the structure of society and reflect the results of such analysis in planning, programming, and action.

The issue of action is critically important. From an empowerment perspective, we need to develop awareness of existing community organizations, support groups, neighborhood action committees, and other channels of collective effort. We need to inform our clients of opportunities to participate in social and community affairs. We also need to look for opportunities for involvement ourselves. We have suggested elsewhere (J. J. McWhirter & E. H. McWhirter, 1989; E. H. McWhirter, 1991, 1994) that it is time to add a new dimension to the traditional roles of counselor and teacher. Traditionally, both teachers and counselors have been advocates of individual development and growth. With the growing acknowledgment of the role the environment plays in human development, however, social activism is the natural arena into which counselors and teachers must move if they are to remain faithful to that advocacy. As social activists, counselors and teachers can promote awareness of the damaging effects of poverty, poor housing, overcrowding, undernourishment, and discrimination. Counselors especially can urge adoption of mental health programs that address specific environmental circumstances, limitations, and inadequacies. Teachers and counselors can make their views known to local and national leaders through votes and letters, publications and seminars. Both can be more aware of how local politics is affecting mental health policy in their communities. Teachers and counselors can enhance awareness of the influence of the environment, encourage recognition that change is possible, and facilitate development of resources and skills for creating change.

The social and economic risk factors in the larger society can be directly modified by mental health and school personnel only modestly at the grassroots level. However, educational and mental health policy and practice at every level of government, pre-service training, school district and building, and agency service can be modified to improve the health and learning of students at risk. Further, teachers and counselors need to be involved in the process of seeking change at the level of those who have the power to fund, to legislate, and to affect the structure of the environment. Teachers and counselors have both the resources and the knowledge to address the needs of the poor and to break the cycle of poverty.

CONCLUSION

Understanding the interventions needed by children and youth at risk requires that we clearly recognize the environmental issues that youngsters face. The comprehensive prevention/early intervention/treatment framework presented in this chapter highlights how intervention is related to and modified by the developmental sequence through which youngsters progress as they become increasingly at risk. Specifically, prevention efforts include generic approaches and sometimes target programs for all youngsters. As children come to be increasingly at risk, they may require early intervention or specific treatments focused on special problem areas. Finally, for youth already engaged in an at-risk category activity, treatment that includes second-chance programs may be necessary. Each of these interventions, provided for children and teenagers at a specified level of risk, can be offered in the society/community, family, and school settings. Furthermore, the interventions described in this comprehensive framework consider cost issues and the relationship or interface of counselors, other mental health professionals, and teachers.

Additional environmental issues include helping youth examine the relationships at work in their lives and fostering positive, healthy relationships between youth and nurturing adult role models. From an empowerment perspective, helping children and teens assess the power dynamics in their lives, teaching them skills not only for self-improvement but for the advancement of other similar youngsters, and helping them to exercise new choices and behaviors allow them to recognize and use their own internal resources as human agents. Finally, for full effectiveness, counselors, teachers, and other human service professionals must be socially active. Their activism should be focused on improving resources and the accessibility of resources to all children and youth at risk. Indeed, modeling social activism alone can serve as a powerful tool to help young people recognize their own potential to change or improve the course of their lives.

FURTHER READINGS

In addition to those books and articles cited in the reference section, the following books may be useful to readers wishing to know more about prevention programs for high-risk children and youth.

Bloom, M. (1996). *Primary prevention practices.* Thousand Oaks, CA: Sage.

Bryant, D. M., & Graham, M. A. (1993). *Implementing early intervention: From research to effective practice.* New York: Guilford.

Cowen, E. L., Hightower, A. D., Pedro-Carroll, J. L., Work, W. C., & Wyman, P. A. (1996). *School-based prevention for children at risk: The primary mental health project.* Hyattsville, MD: American Psychological Association.

Durlak, J. A. (1995). *School-based prevention programs for children and adolescents.* Thousand Oaks, CA: Sage.

Goldston, S. E., Yager, J., Heinicke, C. M., & Pynoos, R. S. (Eds.). (1990). *Preventing mental health disturbances in childhood.* Washington, DC: American Psychological Association.

McWhirter, E. H. (1994). *Counseling for empowerment.* Alexandria, VA: American Counseling Association Press.

CORE COMPONENTS OF PROGRAMS FOR PREVENTION AND EARLY INTERVENTION

To change your way of thinking is to move great,
huge trunks around in the attic.
To change your way of acting is to push toothpaste
back into the tube.
To change your way of feeling is to take a great,
irretrievable leap of hope into the dark void.

To change means to develop and grow.
And to develop and grow
You have to
move the trunk,
push the paste,
and leap.
If you don't change, develop, grow
You lie in the muck down in the dark hole.

The truth and reality of your existence
will continue to bury you.
If you do not work to execute your past,
how shall you construct your future?

J. J. McWHIRTER

CHAPTER OUTLINE

LIFE SKILLS
Overcoming Deficits in Life Skills
Training in Life Skills
The life-skills model
School peer mediation
Peer tutoring
Peer facilitation

INTERPERSONAL COMMUNICATION
Training in Interpersonal Communication
Assertiveness Skills
General assertiveness training
Resistance and refusal training

STRATEGIES FOR COGNITIVE CHANGE
Problem Solving and Decision Making
Self-Management and Self-Control

Self-assessment
Self-monitoring
Self-reinforcement
Cognitive Restructuring
Rational-emotive therapy
Cognitive therapy

COPING WITH STRESS
Beneficial Relaxation
Progressive Relaxation
Visual Imagery
Affirmations

CONCLUSION

FURTHER READINGS

Specific affective, cognitive, and behavioral skills play a large part in a youngster's personal and social success. Resilient youngsters develop social competencies that help them negotiate life's vicissitudes and emerge as healthy, strong, and contributing individuals. High-risk youngsters do not develop such competencies and frequently find themselves on a downward spiral of lowered expectations, deviant behavior, rejection by society, and a dead-end future. They have not mastered those fundamental life skills that allow them to survive and thrive in the world.

LIFE SKILLS

Social competence can be described as the ability to make use of personal resources to influence the environment and to achieve a positive developmental outcome. Social competence is made up of a variety of skills that provide effective ways of living with others. Such skills include the formation of relationships and friendships, nonviolent resolution of conflicts, assertiveness, resistance to peer pressure, and negotiation of relationships with adults. In other words, social competence consists of critical life skills. Without certain life skills, children and adolescents are susceptible to high-risk problem behaviors. Life skills are not just useful or handy, they are virtually essential (Botvin, Schinke, & Orlandi, 1995; Wagner, 1996).

Overcoming Deficits in Life Skills

Deficits in specific personal, cognitive, and social skills are an underlying cause of social incompetence. As we discussed in Chapter 11, a good prevention program provides skills during the critical period of early childhood or at the time of entry into school. Early intervention programs overcome deficits early in a child's school life. Training in life skills is the formal teaching of skills needed to succeed, to live with others, and to survive in a complex society. People do not learn these skills automatically. Young people, especially those at risk, need help to acquire the social competence to cope with academic work, to make good decisions about life's options, to adopt health-promoting behaviors, to form stable human relationships, and to maintain hope about their future.

Life-skills training programs emphasize the acquisition of generic social and cognitive skills. The theoretical foundation of these approaches consists primarily of Bandura's (1977) social learning theory and Jessor and Jessor's (1977) problem-behavior theory. From these perspectives, at-risk deviant behaviors are seen as socially learned, functional behaviors that result from the interplay of personal and environmental factors. Programs typically employ some combination of interpersonal communication and social skills, strategies for cognitive change, and coping mechanisms.

Training in Life Skills

The life-skills model.   With its emphasis on education and training rather than counseling and therapy, the life-skills model is ideal for use in elementary and secondary schools. Programs that include a few core elements are useful, but comprehensive programs are more effective (Dryfoos, 1994; Durlack, 1995; Lowenthal, 1996). The life-skills model enlists the efforts of mental health counselors, psychologists, social workers, teachers in such varied fields as physical education and home economics, school nurses, nurse practitioners, and health educators. School counselors, psychologists, and special education teachers are key participants in this plan. Life-skills modules can be incorporated into the curriculum at all developmental levels, from kindergarten through high school. Life-skills training can also be included in adult and continuing education programs and in parent education programs offered by the school system as well as by community colleges and community service agencies.

Procedures for teaching life skills resemble those used in teaching any other skill. The overall task is broken down into small stages or component parts, which are taught systematically, step by step, from the simple to the more complex. Training in each session follows a five-step model: (1) instruction (teach), (2) modeling (show), (3) role-play (practice), (4) feedback (reinforce), and (5) homework (apply). Specific tasks are presented in sequence, and frequent rewards are given for desired behavior. In this model, directed practice and an emphasis on influential models play equal parts. Although the order may vary somewhat, all five training steps are important in teaching specific skills.

1. *Teach.* Explanations and instructions are provided. A rationale for the skill is provided, and students are given oral instructions on how to perform it.
2. *Show.* The specific skill is modeled for the student. The skill can be "shown" by a videotape, or the trainer or another youngster can demonstrate it.
3. *Practice.* The child is encouraged to imitate and use the skill by role playing in the training session. The performance is evaluated with emphasis on the correct aspects of the student's imitative behavior.

4. *Reinforce.* As the student role-plays additional problem situations, feedback and encouragement are given. Further coaching is provided as needed to shape and refine the performance.
5. *Apply.* Students are requested to perform the newly acquired skill in various real-life situations. They record their experiences and report back at the next session. The characteristics of successful and unsuccessful performances are reviewed and refinements introduced as needed.

Life-skills programs are most effective when they are carefully designed and well implemented. Following the five steps helps ensure their effectiveness.

Components of the life-skills program can be included in regular and special education classes and in a program designed for use throughout a school or a district. School peer mediation, peer tutoring, and peer facilitation are especially applicable to such programs.

School peer mediation.   School peer mediation (Lane & McWhirter, 1992, 1996) is a mode of conflict management employed by students for the purpose of resolving conflicts. Trained peer mediators work as a team of two to facilitate problem solving between disputants. Students' involvement in the mediation process ensures practice with critical thinking, problem solving, and self-discipline. Students' participation in efforts to change their own and their peers' behavior is directly related to the developmental construct of self-regulation. Awareness of socially approved behaviors is a critical feature.

Peer tutoring.   Peer tutors are students who teach other students in formal and informal learning situations that are delegated, planned, and directed by an educator. The term *peer tutor* has been used to describe situations in which a person provides instructional assistance and guidance to another person (Tansy, Santos de Barona, McWhirter, & Herrmann, 1996). Peer tutoring alters the environmental and social climate in a school and can enhance and increase learning. It provides a cost-effective way to meet the individual needs of students and to improve the performance of students who need help with their studies. Peer tutoring improves social interactions, self-concept, motivation, attitudes toward the school, peer status, and overall school experience. The concept of peer tutoring has deep roots in our educational system.

Peer facilitation.   Peer facilitation (sometimes referred to as peer leadership, helping, or counseling) is very helpful in increasing the impact and efficiency of professional counseling. Peer facilitation is a process in which trained and supervised students perform interpersonal helping tasks—listening, offering support, suggesting alternatives, and engaging in other verbal and nonverbal interactions—that qualify as counseling functions with similar-aged clients who either have referred themselves or have been referred by others. Like peer tutoring and peer mediation, peer facilitation appears to be a useful way to counter negative peer cluster influence. It also reinforces and supports the use of life skills.

Of the several components of a basic life-skills program, three are most critical: interpersonal communication skills, including skills in assertiveness, resistance, and refusal; strategies for cognitive change that encompass skills in problem solving and decision making, self-management and self-control, and cognitive-behavioral restructuring; and strategies for coping with stress, including relaxation, visual imagery, and affirmations.

INTERPERSONAL COMMUNICATION

Interpersonal communication skills are among the major components of most comprehensive life-skills training programs. Sometimes termed *social skills, social competence,* or *human relations,* skill in interpersonal communication is generally taken to mean effectiveness in interpersonal relationships. As we mentioned in Chapter 5, interpersonal communication skills are necessary for responsive, confident, and mutually beneficial relationships. A lack of good communication skills often leads to social isolation and rejection, which in turn results in poor psychological adjustment. Positive peer reactions and peer acceptance are related to friendly, positive interpersonal communications.

Training in Interpersonal Communication

Acquisition of basic communication skills begins in early childhood; by adolescence most individuals have acquired a complex repertoire of social skills. Most programs designed to promote communication skills offer training in verbal and nonverbal communication, creation of healthy friendships, avoidance of misunderstandings, and development of long-term love relationships.

In designing a program to promote interpersonal communication skills and prevent problems from arising, the teacher or counselor needs to be particularly sensitive to the developmental age and skill level of the student. The variables that seem to play a role in the development and maintenance of interactions from age 1 to 3 years are: attention to the listener, to the speaker, or to the object of interest; proximity and turn-taking with others; relevance of content; and provision of feedback from the listener (Keane & Conger, 1981). From age 3 to 5 years, behaviors that may be incorporated in training programs include the use of attention-getting cues, listener responses, reinforcement of turn-taking and mutual attention, and the use of routines to maintain attention. Mutual attention and feedback are still important skills for 6- to 8-year-olds, and appropriate role taking is developed during this age period. From ages 9 to 12, the use of positive, cooperative, and helpful communication, as opposed to negative statements, appears to be important. (Gazda, 1989, provides a comprehensive list of interpersonal communication and human relation skills and indicates the approximate age at which each skill is usually acquired.)

Interpersonal communication skills represent the major thrust of the many useful training programs that have been proposed. Shure (1992a, b, c) provides extensive modules designed to improve communication among children. Another particularly useful package is an integrated program of training in communication skills for adolescents (Goldstein, Sprafkin, Gershaw, & Klein, 1980) and younger children (McGinnis & Goldstein, 1984, 1990), described as "one of the most highly delineated and descriptive programs to date" (Cartledge & Milburn, 1986, p. 303), although "more time is needed for an unequivocal endorsement" (p. 154). Other useful programs have been developed for elementary school students (Cartledge & Milburn, 1986; Jackson, Jackson, & Monroe, 1983; Wiig, 1983) and for secondary school pupils (Kelly, 1982; Wilkinson & Canter, 1982). Stephens's (1992) social skills program is appropriate for both children and adolescents.

Jason Carter (of Chapter 3) could profit from training in communication skills. His difficulty in dealing with his dysfunctional family has extended to his classroom interactions. Although parent training and family counseling approaches are probably necessary to help modify the family dysfunction, Jason's ineffective interpersonal communication is contributing to the aversive nature of his school experience. Better interpersonal communication skills would allow him to interact more positively with classmates and adults at school. This improvement could bring greater acceptance by Jason's peers and increase his self-esteem.

Assertiveness Skills

Some at-risk young people get into trouble because they are timid and withdrawn and appear to be incapable of dealing with other students, teachers, and family members in effective ways. Others express themselves in hostile, angry, aggressive ways that cause problems for people around them and ultimately for themselves. Still others find themselves going along with the crowd because they are overly susceptible to influence by their peers. They do not recognize pressure or have the skills to resist it. Many at-risk children and youth need training in general assertiveness and in specific ways to resist peer pressure.

General assertiveness training.   Assertiveness training is a psychoeducational procedure designed to reduce deficits in specific social skills and to help the individual interact more effectively with others. Assertiveness training also reduces the maladaptive anxiety that prevents young people from expressing themselves directly, honestly, and spontaneously.

Assertiveness training usually includes modules on the expression of positive feelings, the expression of negative feelings, and the ability to initiate, continue, and terminate general conversations. Besides these basic interpersonal communication skills, assertiveness training focuses on limit-setting and self-initiation. The person who knows how to set limits can say no to unreasonable requests. Self-initiators have the capacity to ask for what they want and actively to seek opportunities for enjoyment, advancement, and intimacy.

Nonverbal communication is also an important aspect of assertiveness training. The way a message is delivered is given as much attention as the message itself. Loudness of voice, fluency of spoken words, facial expression, body expression, interpersonal distance, and method and degree of eye contact all deliver their own messages. Students are taught to look others squarely in the eye during both positive and negative social confrontations. Looking people in the eye is a sign that one is sure of one's position, knowledge, or attractiveness in mainstream United States culture. Students are taught that passive behavior can be replaced by assertive techniques and that assertive responses are more adaptive than aggressive ones in handling conflict and anger. All assertiveness training programs should attend to students from cultural backgrounds in which direct eye contact is considered disrespectful or aggressive. Rather than exclude "eye contact," this component of the program as well as others should acknowledge cultural differences and provide guidance in exploring when using assertive behavior may be more or less effective.

One school-based assertiveness training program has been reported to yield extremely positive results (M. J. Smith, 1986). The children trained in assertiveness had better school attendance records than their untrained counterparts, were ill less often, scored higher in reading and math, had better self-images, and showed positive changes in those negative attitudes that predict future drug abuse. Three years after completing the program, the trained students were more resistant to peer pressure to use tobacco, alcohol, and illicit drugs. The assertiveness-trained youngsters also achieved higher grades than the students who were not trained in assertiveness. This social thinking and reasoning program, called STAR (Benn, 1981), provides techniques and methods to train children from grades 3 through 5 in how to respond more effectively in social conflict situations. Another program for promoting learning and understanding of self, called PLUS (Benn, 1982), is an adaptation of STAR for high school students and has demonstrated similar success.

Resistance and refusal training.   Specific resistance and refusal skills help at-risk students resist negative social influences (Herrmann & J. J. McWhirter, 1977). Resistance training focuses on helping young people (a) identify and label social influences and pressure situations and (b) develop behavioral skills to resist such influences. Skills are needed to resist various types of pressures, from those exerted by the entertainment media and advertising to those of peers. Students are taught to identify and label various forms of pressure. Peer pressure, for instance, can take the form of teasing, friendly pressure, tricks, dares, lies, physical threats, social threats, or silence. Typical examples of each kind of pressure are demonstrated.

Students are then taught strategies for resisting pressure and for refusing to succumb to it. Particular techniques are described, demonstrated, and modeled. Students practice and observe others practicing each resistance or refusal strategy. They engage in role playing to develop competence in each technique. All of them are given opportunities to rehearse and refine their performances so that in real-life situations they can respond with confidence.

STRATEGIES FOR COGNITIVE CHANGE

Cognitive-behavioral techniques have been devised to help children and young people develop control over their internal reactions and overt behavior. Three points in cognitive-behavioral theory are particularly important in this respect:

1. Cognitive events mediate behavior; therefore, a focus on cognition can be an effective approach to changing behavior.
2. Young people are active participants in their own learning and can exercise control over it.
3. Cognition, behavior, and the environment are related: each affects and is affected by the others.

Among the cognitive-behavioral strategies with demonstrated utility are techniques to be used in problem solving and decision making, which help youngsters develop less rigid ways of dealing with their interpersonal problems and encourage alternative solutions. Self-management and self-control techniques draw upon very effective cognitive-behavioral operations to empower young people. Cognitive-restructuring approaches help at-risk youngsters modify their negative and self-defeating beliefs (Durlack, Fuhrman, & Lampman, 1991).

Problem Solving and Decision Making

Human beings must solve problems to survive. Among the problems to be solved are difficult interpersonal and social situations. At-risk young people are more likely to engage in rigid thinking and perceive fewer alternatives. Thus, their ability to generate and select from alternatives needs to be improved.

Early models of problem solving and decision making were based on the assumption that adequate and accurate information would lead to better choices. There was an implicit assumption that prudent choices would flow from a rational review of options. We now know that accurate information is necessary but not sufficient. Even for adults with substantial life experience and mature cognitive skills and abilities, the processes of problem solving and decision making are far less rational than they were once thought to be. Children and adolescents are at least as irrational as adults in their problem solving and decision making.

Young people have the potential to make competent decisions. Dodge and Price (1994) suggest that children who accurately perceive and effectively solve interpersonal problems use a five-stage sequential problem-solving decision-making process. In stage one, they attend to relevant environmental cues. During stage two, they accurately encode and interpret these cues. In stage three, they generate many and varied solutions to the problems. During stage four, they accurately evaluate each of the solutions and determine the best possible solution. Finally, in stage five, they plan the steps necessary to carry out and actually perform the favored solution. For high-risk youngsters several things stand in the way: the emotional component of most problems, the tendency to appraise situations from an egocentric perspective, the perception of limited alternatives, and the lack of systematic decision-making procedures. For example, social-cognitive deficits in aggressive children have been reported in the area of social attention and recall (stage 1), generating multiple solutions to interpersonal problems (stage 3), and performance of favored responses (stage 5). Social-cognitive distortions in antisocial children occur when errors are made in the interpretation of social stimuli (stage 2) and misjudgments are made concerning the consequences of hostile acts (stage 4) (Dodge & Price, 1994).

Explicit instruction in problem-solving and decision-making processes helps to avert problems in the at-risk areas. The steps involved in problem solving require specific skills, which need to be learned and practiced. We have adopted a model for general problem-solving training that we call DECIDE, which is similar to that of the DECIDES model of career counseling developed by Kinnier and Krumboltz (1984) but contains some variations for problem solving and was developed separately. As Kinnier and Krumboltz point out, "there is significant overlap between the steps in most models" of decision making (p. 32).

We developed the DECIDE model specifically for improving the skills in general problem solving for at-risk children and adolescents. DECIDE stands for the steps to be taken: (1) define the problem, (2) examine variables, (3) consider alternatives, (4) isolate a plan, (5) do action steps, and (6) evaluate effects. Teaching at-risk children and adolescents these six problem-solving steps will contribute to a more internal locus of control—that is, students will feel that their behavior is under their own control—and will help modify impulsive, self-defeating behavior. An internal locus of control, in turn, can improve self-esteem, increase a sense of self-efficacy, and strengthen resistance to problem behaviors. Let us consider each of the steps.

1. *Define the problem.* The problem is defined as clearly as possible and is stated as a goal to be achieved. This goal is assessed: Will it address the problem? If it is attained, does it help the individual achieve satisfaction?

2. *Examine variables.* The specifics of the total situation are examined. Background issues and environmental factors are considered, so it may be necessary to gather and appraise additional information. It is particularly important to identify the feelings and thoughts of the youngster at this step. In both this step and in step 1, questions and suggestions from other students in the classroom or the group are useful.

3. *Consider alternatives.* Various means of solving the problem are considered. The strengths and weaknesses of each possibility are evaluated. Again, the teacher or the counselor may call for brainstorming to generate ideas from other students about alternatives and strategies.

4. *Isolate a plan.* The alternatives are gradually narrowed down until what seems like the best response or solution remains. A plan for carrying out this alternative is prepared, and the potential consequences are considered in more detail.

5. *Do action steps.* After a plan is decided upon, action must be taken to implement it. Youngsters are systematically encouraged to follow through on the necessary steps to carry out their plan. They perform the behaviors that make up the solution plan.

6. *Evaluate effects.* Finally, youngsters need to evaluate the effectiveness of the solution. Teaching them to look for effects in their thoughts and feelings is important. They analyze and evaluate the outcome, review the decision, and if necessary develop another plan to achieve their goal.

Spivack and Shure (1974; Shure & Spivack, 1978), D'Zurilla (1986), and Bransford and Stein (1984) have also contributed useful models for problem solving and decision making. Teachers, counselors, and psychologists may wish to consult these and other resources as they prepare to implement problem-solving training with their at-risk young people.

Self-Management and Self-Control

Self-management is the ability to maintain or alter goal-directed behavior without depending on discernible external forces. Youngsters with good self-management skills are able to respond to situations based on their internal standards and goals. They continuously modify either the environment or their behavior to produce a match between performance and desired level of functioning.

Self-control is an important component of self-management and refers to control over one's affective, cognitive, and behavioral reactions. It is particularly important for at-risk children and adolescents because it helps them prevent problem situations, limit negative emotional reactions, delay gratification, and resist problematic behaviors (Shapiro & Cole, 1994).

Self-management and self-control help in the educational process too. Self-management training produces both short- and long-term gains in achievement. Students who have received this training have been found to raise their levels of academic aspirations, increase their efforts on future tasks, improve their nonacademic skills, and decrease their disruptive behaviors (D. J. Smith, Young, Nelson, & West, 1992). Self-control skills help students make adaptive attributions: Students are encouraged to take responsibility for their successes and failures by learning when failure is attributable to their own lack of effort and when success results from their own ability, efforts, and skills. These modified attributions result in enhanced efforts in similar tasks in the future.

Training in self-management and self-control includes the following skills: (a) self-assessment (being able to compare present functioning with internal standards and evaluate significant differences between the performance and the standard), (b) self-monitoring (being attuned to and aware of one's present functioning), and (c) self-reinforcement (providing positive consequences when performance meets standards and negative consequences for failure to perform adequately).

Self-assessment.   Self-assessment is the systematic evaluation of one's own behavior to determine whether or not it has been adequate. Young people need to be able to evaluate and assess their behavior to improve it. Most young people evaluate themselves on the basis of standards acquired from significant others in their environment. Both parents and teachers provide young people with standards against which to evaluate their behavior in various situations. For a variety of reasons, many at-risk young people fail to acquire clear standards for self-evaluation.

Self-ratings can be used to teach youngsters to assess their behavior. First, student and teacher decide together which specific behavior needs to be changed. After a target behavior is identified, the next step is to devise a rating system—a scale of 0 to 10, say, or 0 to 100—by which the specific behavior can be assessed and evaluated. Paul Andrews of Chapter 1, for example, might be asked to rate his classroom outbursts by rating his underlying mood and behavior: 0 (no desire to hit or to explode) to 10 (several outbursts). Number 5 on his rating scale might be "resisted desire to hit or explode." Such a rating scale would provide Paul with a subjective measure of mood and behavior, and the self-assessment would help him to develop self-control. Although Paul has several behaviors that need to change, he needs to deal with only one behavior at a time. An attempt to change too many behaviors simultaneously would lower the probability of success and serve to confuse him. If he started out by attempting to change a single behavior, Paul's chance for success would be increased. (Workman, 1982, is an excellent source of self-assessment techniques.)

Self-monitoring.   Self-monitoring is focusing attention and awareness on one's characteristics, emotions, thoughts, or behavior and is closely related to self-assessment. Self-monitoring requires students to observe their own behavior and to record it. Essentially, students are taught to collect data on their own behavior. (Kaplan, 1991; Shapiro & Cole, 1992; and Workman, 1982, provide useful information on observation and record-keeping forms for the self-monitoring process.) Self-monitoring helps students become more aware of their own negative and positive behaviors, putting their behavior more firmly under their own control (DiGangi, Maag, & Rutherford, 1991).

Self-reinforcement.   Self-reinforcement is the act of supplying one's own consequences for performance. Such consequences may be intangible and intrinsic (such as silent self-praise for meeting a personal goal) or tangible and external (such as buying oneself a present after meeting a personal goal). Consequences may also be negative. A negative consequence might be self-criticism or forgoing a particular pleasure.

Self-reinforcement energizes the self-management process. People anticipate and work for possible positive consequences. Self-reinforcement keeps the person on the track of establishing and pursuing goals. The effects of self-reinforcement on school performance are found to be as beneficial as those of external reinforcement (Kaplan, 1991). The self-reinforcement of behaviors conducive to learning works powerfully to improve school achievement and personal performance.

In summary, when young people are taught to assess their own behavior, to monitor their academic and personal performance, and to reinforce their improved behavior with positive consequences, their school performance is likely to improve, and their personal problems will be minimized.

Cognitive Restructuring

The term *cognitive restructuring*, as we use it here, simply means modification, changing, or restructuring one's beliefs. A belief is a rule that a person applies to all situations regardless of his or her current experiences; it is a cognitive pattern that the individual has learned. When the belief is maladaptive, it can be unlearned to produce a new and better cognitive pattern. As more adaptive cognitions replace incomplete or faulty ones, behavior changes too.

The best-known approaches to changing inappropriate cognitive patterns are rational-emotive behavioral therapy (REBT) (Ellis, 1962, 1996) and cognitive therapy (CT) (Beck, 1976, 1991). Both approaches are based on the assumption that faulty cognitions cause detrimental self-evaluations and emotional distress and that these experiences lead to behavioral problems. The goal is to help people develop their cognitive ability to recognize faulty self-statements and to substitute more positive ones. There is growing evidence that children and adolescents can understand the principles of REBT (Vernon, 1983, reviews the evidence) and CT (Garber, Deale, & Parke, 1986).

Rational-emotive therapy.   Ellis's rational-emotive behavioral approach, the oldest and probably best known of the cognitive therapies, is based on the belief that people need to change their faulty thinking and correct irrational beliefs to lead healthier, happier lives. Ellis (1996) suggests that emotional disturbances are the result of illogical and irrational thinking in the form of internalized beliefs. Thus, emotional disturbances arise from cognitive or thinking processes. Ellis recognized, however, that emotion is a complex mode of behavior that is tied to a variety of sensing and response processes and states.

The major assumption of REBT is that thoughts create feelings. In other words, it is not events or other people that make one feel upset or inadequate but one's belief about them. A young boy who does not succeed at football and feels depressed, for example, may assume that his poor performance has caused the depressed feeling. Ellis argues, however, that it is the assumptions about the event or the failure—the thoughts about it, not the event itself—that cause the depressed feeling.

Ellis (1985) proposes an A-B-C-D-E model as a cognitive intervention strategy. The child or adolescent learns to recognize the activating event (A), the corresponding belief

(B) about the event, and the emotional and behavioral consequences (C). The counselor or teacher then helps the young person to dispute (D) the old belief system and attend to the new emotional and behavioral effects (E) of more rational thinking.

At-risk children and adolescents develop many irrational ways of thinking. These irrational thoughts lead to inappropriate or maladaptive behavior. Cognitive restructuring efforts are designed to help young people recognize and change these irrational beliefs into more rational ones. Attainment of this goal requires a confrontive and supportive counselor or teacher who is able to engage the client or student actively (Ellis, 1996).

Cognitive therapy.   Beck (1976, 1991) suggests that cognition and affect are interactive. Like Ellis, he believes that an individual's cognition about an event determines the affective response to the event. If cognitions are distorted or inaccurate, the individual's emotional response will be inappropriate.

Three elements are central to Beck's CT model: the cognitive triad, cognitive schemas, and cognitive errors. The cognitive triad is composed of thoughts that focus on three major aspects of life. Disturbed individuals have a negative view of the world, the self, and the future. When the cognitive triad is negative, the individual has no way to win, and depression and despair result. The assumption is that sadness, loss of motivation, suicidal wishes, and other disturbing thoughts or behaviors are related to concerns in one or more of the three domains.

A schema is like a personality trait; it is a stable cognitive pattern that an individual creates from the cognitive triad. Schemas are underlying cognitive structures that help the individual organize and evaluate information, events, and experiences. At-risk children and adolescents develop schemas that distort environmental stimuli in a negative way. Often their schemas include a derogatory self-image. Because these schemas are a person's "core beliefs," they influence both behavioral and affective responses to an event.

Dysfunctional or negative schemas are often maintained and exacerbated by faulty information processing or consistent errors in logic. These are called cognitive errors. At-risk young people make these automatic cognitive errors when they evaluate events. These errors—negativistic, categorical, absolute, judgmental—cause the person consistently to misread or misinterpret even benign experiences.

Treatment and training strategies flow directly from Beck's cognitive model. His cognitive therapy has both behavioral and cognitive components that are designed to reduce automatic negative cognition. The client learns to challenge the assumptions that maintain the faulty cognitions. Behavioral strategies are used first in the therapeutic or training process. Positive activities are established and augmented through role playing, graduated task assignments, activity schedules, assertiveness training, and behavioral rehearsal. After these strategies are successfully used, cognitive interventions are introduced to identify, test, and modify the cognitive distortion. Clients are taught (a) to recognize the connections between cognitions, affect, and behavior; (b) to monitor negative automatic thoughts; (c) to examine evidence related to distorted automatic cognitions; (d) to substitute more realistic interpretations for distorted cognition; and (e) to learn to identify and modify dysfunctional beliefs.

Cognitive therapy is dedicated to the goal of helping clients discover maladaptive thoughts, recognize their negative impact, and replace them with more appropriate and positive thought patterns. Cognitive restructuring techniques have been successfully applied in clinical settings and are used increasingly in training modules to help at-risk young people make cognitive changes so that they can lead more productive lives.

Todd Baker (of Chapter 2) could benefit from cognitive change strategies. Interpersonal problem solving could help him make better decisions. Self-assessment, self-monitoring, and self-reinforcement could provide him with tools to help him delay gratification. Through cognitive restructuring, he could modify his irrational thoughts, the nature of his cognitive triad, and his negative schemas. Cognitive errors could be corrected to modify and improve his negative behavior.

COPING WITH STRESS

Many at-risk young people are affected by stress and anxiety. Anxiety is associated with a number of undesirable intrapersonal and interpersonal characteristics: lack of responsiveness, inability to perform independently, overdependence on conformity, excessive concern about evaluations, and self-critical and self-defeating attitudes. Anxiety from such sources leads to chronic stress. Because many aspects of the educational process are greatly affected by anxiety and stress, providing coping methods to deal with them is particularly beneficial.

Relaxation and imagery are helpful tools to offset some of the negative aspects of anxiety and stress. These two techniques are combined in relaxation and imagery training (RIT), a program that promises to help at-risk children realize more of their potential (J. J. McWhirter, 1988; J. J. McWhirter & M. C. McWhirter, 1983).

Beneficial Relaxation

Relaxation techniques alone can reduce stress and many of its negative psychological and physical effects. Relaxation has been reported to help clients overcome fatigue, avoid negative reactions to stress, reduce anxiety, improve social skills and interpersonal relationships, and improve self-assurance (Burns, 1981). Relaxation can also help to reduce depression and improve self-esteem (Kahn, Kehle, Jenson, & Clarke, 1990). Relaxation is both effective and efficient in helping students to behave more appropriately in school, to think more positively about themselves, and to interact more positively with their peers. Relaxation also reduces anxiety—an especially important effect because anxiety is associated with dependence, hostility, low peer status, poor relationships with teachers, and aggression (McReynolds, Morris, & Kratochwill, 1989). Anxious people magnify normal events into threats. Because the anxious person remains mobilized even after the anxiety-provoking event has passed, the threshold is already low when the next normal event occurs. This self-perpetuating sequence of inappropriate reactions to neutral situations frequently leads to heightened interpersonal discord.

Relaxation techniques are useful in schools as well as in the social arena. A variety of studies have demonstrated the positive effects of relaxation techniques on reading, spelling, mathematics, music, and athletics (Carter & Russell, 1980; Frey, 1980; Glantz, 1983; Oldridge, 1982; Olrich, 1983; Proeger & Myrick, 1980; J. J. McWhirter & M. C. McWhirter, 1983; Zenker, 1984; Zenker & Frey, 1985). In addition to improving social and academic performance, relaxation has been used successfully as an intervention strategy for hyperactivity. Relaxation is a viable tool for increasing attention to task and decreasing impulsiveness.

Relaxation training teaches youngsters to use the relaxation response when anxiety and fear arise. Students exposed to disturbing emotional situations can use natural biological processes to reduce negative consequences.

Relaxation training promotes anxiety reduction and self-enhancement by teaching the individual to reduce muscle tension. Essentially, relaxation training accomplishes two objectives. First, it is a means to countercondition the anxiety associated with a stressful environment. Second, it is a self-management tool. Through the self-regulation training of relaxation, children can increase their control over their lives, be responsible for their behavior, and improve their academic performance. This tool has a spinoff effect. As children gain confidence in the ability to become calm in learning and social situations, they gain approval from adults and peers, improve their attention span, are less distractible, and learn more. This procedure shows considerable promise for improving the self-management skills of children (Brennan, 1984; Brenner, 1984; Rivera & Omizo, 1980).

Progressive Relaxation

Several techniques are useful in relaxation training, including biofeedback, autogenic training, meditation, the quieting reflex, and progressive relaxation. Most training in relaxation uses a procedure originally outlined by Jacobson (1938), which he referred to as progressive (deep-muscle) relaxation. Merely telling an individual to relax is not enough. Jacobson developed a more structured and concrete procedure by which the individual achieves a state of deep muscular relaxation. To achieve relaxation in a specific muscle or muscle group, the client lies down comfortably and alternately tenses and relaxes the major muscle groups. The contraction phase is then gradually decreased until it is eliminated as the individual develops awareness of and releases muscle tension.

In the relaxation technique used in RIT, the youngster tenses and then relaxes various muscle groups. This procedure continues until the person is aware of the contrast between a tense and a relaxed state. Early in relaxation training it is necessary to repeat the tension and relaxation phases several times during several sessions. Eventually the need for tensing is eliminated and the individual achieves relaxation quickly. Once students develop this technique, they can relax on their own without instructions from the adult, thereby exercising a greater degree of self-control. After practice, most individuals can learn to achieve a relaxed physical and mental state within a few minutes. Lazarus (1971) and Carkhuff (1969) have published guides for conducting relaxation sessions. Koeppen (1974), Monaco (1982), and J. J. McWhirter (1988) have developed relaxation strategies for younger people. To varying degrees, all use the systematic procedure of tensing and relaxing various muscle groups.

At least some of the problems faced by Paul Andrews (of Chapter 1) can be attributed to his stressful environment. The tension in his dysfunctional family and his intense dislike of school have led to angry, hostile, aggressive acting out. Adults' reactions to his behavior increase his stress. His aggressiveness and anger appear to be methods for coping with underlying anxiety. Relaxation training would enable him to cope better with his own emotional reactions to his situation. Relaxation would provide Paul with the skill needed to redirect his aggression and attend to his underlying apprehension and anxiety.

Visual Imagery

Visual imagery is an important adjunct to relaxation training. It is used to lessen tension and to enhance comfort, to engage various muscle groups, and to cue a relaxation response. The counselor or teacher might ask the child to imagine a peaceful scene, such as waves lapping on a shore at night, rocking on a porch swing, or sitting in front of a warm fireplace. Many excellent scripts and audiotapes are available to set imaginary scenes for students (Davis, Eshelman, & McKay, 1988). Commercial tapes have music, narrative, and distinctive environmental sounds (bird songs, flowing water, rustling leaves). Of course, the subject matter of the tape or script must be appropriate to the age and environment of the targeted youngsters. For example, an ocean scene may be outside the experience of many students. Students must be given ample time and practice to develop skill in imagery.

Visual images in the form of guided fantasies allow the child or youth to confront areas of difficulty, to learn tasks, and to develop self-control. Through imagery, the child is guided through an event as if the activity were actually happening. The child enters a rich world of internal experiences where imagination is recruited to promote specific psychological and physiological changes to aid performance or behavior. In addition, imagery should include positive suggestions, especially when a youngster is anticipating a negative outcome or condition. Positive imagery is obviously important for an at-risk child or adolescent such as Paul Andrews, who has come to expect failure and negative reactions.

Several key elements go into guided fantasy scripts for young people. The scripts should be as realistic and focused as possible and incorporate words, phrases, and situations that apply to the individual. Paul Andrews's counselor might enlist other adults as collaborators. Paul's mother could become a technical consultant and suggest words, language, and fantasies as well as key events and details that would make the fantasy a rich and realistic experience. If we were to construct a fantasy for Paul, we would follow these guidelines:

1. Help Paul use all his senses—touch and hearing as well as vision. Internal emotional and muscular cues that are experienced before and during a scene should not be neglected.
2. Set the scene as vividly as possible by describing it clearly. If specific details are available, provide them. If not, ask Paul to supply them.
3. Work from the outside environment (the classroom, the home) to the inside environment or the emotional state.
4. Guide the fantasy from Paul's viewpoint, as if he were actually in the situation. Paul is not simply observing himself as a spectator but is actually participating in the event—feeling the emotion it arouses, thinking about it, observing others in the situation, and so forth.
5. Use positive statements and autosuggestions to help Paul develop self-reinforcing statements. Be sure to close the fantasy with a positive image.

Imagery improves learning and retention of materials in most academic subjects (J. J. McWhirter, 1988). It seems to be useful in all areas of the curriculum, as it can create an appropriate readiness and mental set for learning. In the sciences and mathematics, imagery aids creative problem solving and memory. It promotes learning in the language arts by lending vitality to poetry and prose. In educational contexts imagery (a) creates a readiness to learn, (b) aids comprehension, (c) enhances memory and recall, and (d) facilitates problem solving and creative thinking.

Helping students prepare their minds, emotions, and bodies for learning may be as important as the instruction itself. Anticipation of a mental event and openness of mind create a state of readiness for whatever is to be learned. We have had success using imagery, along with other techniques, to enhance group experiences of high school students (Wenz & J. J. McWhirter, 1990).

Affirmations

RIT, with its twin pillars of relaxation and imagery, is a helpful procedure for at-risk children and youth. In view of the generally negative cognitions of these young people, a liberal dose of positive affirmation to acknowledge and to increase personal strengths is critical. RIT provides an opportunity for the teacher or counselor to encourage the child by making positive affirmations. These affirmations should be used consistently and frequently throughout both the relaxation and imagery segments of the program. Most children know the story *The Little Engine That Could*, with its refrain of "I think I can, I think I can, I think I can." This saying can be the basis of a class discussion of other positive sayings. Children repeat these sayings to themselves to reduce stress and to build confidence and self-esteem. Several phrases seem particularly useful: "I can do it"; "I've studied for this test, and I'll do my best"; "I am special because. . ."; "I can relax and remember the right answer"; "I have lots of strengths." Specific phrases and sentences need to be developed from the repertoire of the at-risk children and adolescents.

Under the RIT program, children will begin to understand that they have the power and self-control to overcome the effects of stress and anxiety and get on with living and learning. Counselors and teachers can facilitate development of that power and that self-control.

CONCLUSION

Communication skills, cognitive change strategies, and coping techniques are critical elements in programs for prevention and early intervention. Young people who have acquired these tools have the ability to avoid at-risk behavior. Ideally, comprehensive training programs to teach these techniques need to be instituted early for all youngsters to prevent future problems. For youngsters whose demographic and personal character-istics place them at risk, intervention programs to teach these skills are needed as early as possible—ideally before third grade—and should continue through secondary school if necessary. For long-term benefits, young people need reinforcement over time and from a variety of people.

For older children and adolescents who are further along on the risk continuum, the skills need to be included in special education classes, school counseling programs, and community treatment programs. In addition to treatment groups focused on category behavior and specific deficiencies, school mediation programs and peer (and cross-age) tutoring and facilitation programs provide useful vehicles for helping at-risk young people. Besides enlisting the positive influences of the peer group, they help to reinforce the necessary skills throughout the school environment. Youngsters can be taught the core skills that will enable them to improve their interactions with others, their performance in school and in life, and their potential for a positive future.

FURTHER READINGS

In addition to those books and articles cited in the reference section, the following books may be useful to readers wishing to know more about program strategies to help at-risk children and teenagers.

Aponte, H. J. (1994). *Bread and spirit: Therapy with the new poor: Diversity of race, culture, and values.* New York: Norton.

Elias, M. J., & Tobias, S. E. (1996). *Social problem solving: Interventions in the schools.* New York: Guilford.

Hibbs, E. D., & Jensen, P. S. (Eds.). (1995). *Psychosocial treatments for child and adolescent disorders: Empirically based strategies for clinical practice.* Hyattsville, MD: American Psychological Association.

Prochaska, J. O., & Norcross, J. C. (1994). *Systems of psychotherapy: A transtheoretical analysis.* Pacific Grove, CA: Brooks/Cole.

Reinecke, M. A., Dattilio, F. M., & Freeman, A. (Eds.). (1995). *Cognitive therapy with children and adolescents: A casebook for clinical practice.* New York: Guilford.

Shapiro, E. S., & Cole, C. L. (1994). *Behavior change in the classroom: Self-management interventions.* New York: Guilford.

CHAPTER 13

CHILD AND PEER INTERVENTIONS

It's three A.M. again and she wakens full of dread
another day coming
another endurance test to mark
how many taunts, snubs, stares
a girl can bear in silence.
The clock ticks on relentlessly
then in its rhythm she begins to hear

"I   think   I   can   I   think   I   can"

She smiles, remembering stories and laps, comfort
Smiles at herself for this lapse into silly optimism
Smiles at the thought of her teacher—
trying so hard to push this "positive thinking"
That no one will ever use . . .

Sleep finds her
Still smiling.

E. H. MCWHIRTER

CHAPTER OUTLINE

The life-skills training described in the previous chapter is presented in terms of curriculum-based developmental programming across school level. Young people will not benefit from such training, however, if they drop out of school. In this chapter, we describe a series of interventions designed to prevent dropout and to enhance school success. Of course, the social, personal, and success components of the dropout problem begin in preschool and continue through kindergarten and the primary grades and into the intermediate grades. In the next section, we present major prevention strategies to preempt school dropouts. These include the Interpersonal Cognitive Problem Solving (ICPS) program of Spivack and Shure, Training for Optimism by Seligman, peer and cross-age tutoring programs, and school peer mediation programs. Each provides a major impetus to preventing school dropouts, and each is helpful in other problem areas as well.

PREVENTION STRATEGY FOR CHILDREN: INTERPERSONAL COGNITIVE PROBLEM SOLVING (ICPS)

Shure and Spivack (1988) point out that rebelliousness, aggressive and antisocial behavior, poor peer relationships, and poor academic achievement are important early predictors of later delinquency, alcohol and substance abuse, psychopathology, and school dropout. Often by the third grade, schoolchildren exhibiting poor coping skills exhibit behavior that indicates a high-risk pattern for subsequent behavioral maladjustment, special school placement, academic problems, and grade retention. Considerable evidence exists to suggest that some children do not have adequate problem-solving skills. Available evidence suggests that problem solvers draw on and appear to be limited by their repertoire of social behavioral and social cognitive competencies (for example, role-taking and assertiveness skills), as well as by their store of social knowledge (for example, familiarity with social roles and conventions) in generating, evaluating, and applying potential solutions to social and interpersonal dilemmas that confront them.

Several generally accepted models for social problem solving were discussed in Chapter 12. Others include "think aloud" (Camp & Bash, 1985a, b, c), "skill streaming" programs (Goldstein et al., 1980; McGinnis & Goldstein, 1992, 1984), and "I can problem solve" (Shure, 1992a, b, c). This last program includes recently published interpersonal cognitive problem-solving or "I can problem solve" manuals for preschool, kindergarten and primary grades, and intermediate elementary grades. This cognitive problem-solving program is the result of more than 25 years of research by Spivack and Shure and their colleagues at Hahnemann University. It is designed to enhance interpersonal thinking skills to reduce or prevent high-risk behaviors. The underlying goal of the program is to help children learn *how* to think, not *what* to think.

Spivack and Shure (1974) investigated how these cognitive interpersonal skills might be taught and how early they could be successfully absorbed. They assumed that the earlier these skills could be learned the greater the cumulative benefit and the broader their usefulness for confronting life challenges. Focusing on African American inner-city nursery school children, these researchers found that children as young as four could benefit from the program. The interpersonal cognitive problem-solving program (ICPS), later nicknamed by the children "I can problem solve," was the result.

The researchers also investigated whether the level of effective problem solving was correlated with level of intelligence, asking, in essence: Do smarter people make better problem solvers? Results suggest that general verbal skills and IQ scores are not related to effective problem solving (Spivack, Platt, & Shure, 1976). Another investigation focused on how overly impulsive (impatient, quick to act) or overly inhibited (passive, very shy) children would respond to problem-solving training. Both of these extremes are examples of children deficient in the ability to foresee the consequences of their actions and to generate solutions to interpersonal problems. Both impulsive and shy children responded well to training in interpersonal problem solving. Apparently, the ICPS approach is broadly useful. The program has even been successfully implemented with parents being trained to work with their children on problem solving (Shure, 1990). The program is applicable to different age groups, social classes, and to children of diverse ethnic and racial backgrounds.

Program Description

The format of the preschool program is a script (Shure, 1992a), which is upgraded in sophistication for use in kindergarten and early elementary school (Shure, 1992b) and even further upgraded for intermediate grades (Shure, 1992c). The program has a particularly strong advantage as an intervention strategy in that it is easily implemented by teachers in a typical classroom context, preferably mixing quiet and talkative youngsters in smaller groups. Ideally, teachers work with small groups of six to ten students for about 20 minutes per day.

As a school-based program, the ICPS intervention includes all the children in a class. The assumption is that no matter how good a problem solver a child is, he or she can always get better, and that the ICPS approach would do no one harm. The classroom-based approach has several advantages: No students feel left out; youngsters initially competent in problem solving help avoid group silence; it helps those children incorrectly identified as being at low risk (the unidentified false negatives); and more youngsters can be reached in a shorter period of time.

It is recommended that the formal classroom curricula be implemented on a daily basis for four months. However, informal use of the approach should continue throughout the time the children are in school. The ICPS manuals include formal lessons as well as specific suggestions for incorporating problem-solving approaches into ongoing classroom curricula and interactions. Each lesson includes a stated purpose, suggested materials, and a teacher's script. The teacher's script is intended to be a flexible guideline for implementing the basic steps of the lesson. Lessons are grouped into two major categories: pre-problem-solving skills and problem-solving skills.

Pre-Problem-Solving Skills

Pre-problem-solving concepts set the stage for the acquisition of problem-solving skills by teaching the ICPS vocabulary, teaching cause-and-effect relationships, encouraging listening and paying-attention skills, and helping children identify feelings.

The first and second weeks of the program focus on basic word concepts that lay a foundation for problem solving. For example, the words *different* and *same* help children develop a habit of thinking about a variety of different alternatives. Kicking and hitting are the same in that they both hurt; asking is different from hurting. The words *all* and *some* help children learn to recognize that certain solutions may not be successful with all people but with some. The word *or* helps children think about more than one way to solve a problem: "I can do this," or "I can do that."

Cause-and-effect relationships are also taught. For example, "Lidia hit Denise because Denise hit Lidia first." Children learn to understand cause and effect but also to think in such a way that they will see the cause-and-effect connection between an act and its consequence. The words *because* and *why*, *might* and *maybe*, *now* and *later*, and *before* and *after* are all included and set the stage for problem-solving consequences that come later in the program.

Approximately 20 lessons are included that teach children the concept of emotions and about how people feel. Children are encouraged to identify another's feelings in a problem situation; they learn to be sensitive to feelings. Obviously, they must learn a language for emotions, and they are encouraged to learn "if . . . then" logic. For example, a child learns to identify and label emotions: "If he is crying, then he is sad." Teaching feelings is important; if people's feelings are to be considered in decision making, it is necessary to identify, understand, and verbalize them.

Problem-Solving Skills

Problem-solving skills are taught through lessons on alternative solutions, consequences, and solution–consequence pairs. The intermediate grade school program also includes a

Box 13.1
The Birthday Party

As we walked up the sidewalk, the front door opened and Mary exclaimed, "Grandma, Papa . . . Thank you for coming to my birthday party!"

At three years old, her social and interpersonal skills were in stark contrast to the group of inner-city children I had worked with that afternoon. Too bad all children don't have a mother that teaches them what to say. And if parents don't, teachers must.

section on means–ends thinking, which is believed to be too advanced for the younger students.

Alternative solutions lessons are designed to help children recognize problems and generate possible solutions. The goal is to stimulate children to think of as many different solutions as possible to everyday interpersonal problem situations that are presented to them. All solutions are accepted equally. Solutions are never evaluated for being "good" but are praised for being "different." Later, the children evaluate for themselves whether an idea is good or not, and why.

The objective of the consequences sessions is to help children learn to think sequentially and to engage in consequential thinking. Children are guided to think about what might happen next if a particular solution is carried out. Children are encouraged to identify consequences for their own solutions and then to decide whether the idea is good or not.

The lessons for solution–consequence pairs are designed to give children practice in linking solutions with consequences. Children are encouraged to suggest a solution to a problem and then follow it up with a consequence. They then return to the same problem for a second solution and look at the consequence of that solution, and so on. These exercises provide experience in linking a variety of pairs of solutions and consequences. For example, in trying to get a friend to leave the room, a child might say "Push him if he won't go" (solution), "but he might hit me back" (consequence). "If I ask him" (solution), "he might go" (goal).

The curriculum for older children includes means–ends thinking. Means–ends thinking is a higher order skill that does not emerge until sometime in middle childhood. In these sessions, children are taught to elaborate or plan a series of specific actions to attain a given goal. They are encouraged to recognize and devise ways around potential obstacles. They are helped to develop a realistic time frame in constructing a means to the goal.

In addition to the formal curriculum, the teacher is encouraged to extend the approach from helping children think about hypothetical situations and their problems to helping them think about actual problems that arise during the day, including those that occur in the classroom (see Box 13.1). This informal problem-solving dialogue technique, which focuses on the real-life world of the child, contributes to another advantage of the program—generalization—which is built in as an integral part of treatment.

In addition to the preschool and elementary school programs, ICPS curricula have been developed for adolescents through high school and young adulthood (Spivack, Platt, & Shure, 1976). Taken as a whole, available findings suggest that ICPS training has beneficial effects going beyond improved cognitive test performance (Shure, 1993; Shure & Spivack, 1988). Changes in social behavior have been noted, including decreases in aggressive and impulsive behavior and increases in cooperative and pro-social behavior. Behavioral gains have been achieved with numerous groups, ranging from preschoolers showing early signs of behavioral maladjustment to disturbed school-children in residential treatment to juvenile delinquents. Long-term follow-up data are sparse, but initial findings suggest substantial holding power for behavioral treatment effects, at least in the early years. ICPS interventions have wide applicability and potential to prevent more serious behavioral dysfunctions, and we believe that these techniques are helpful in reducing the number of potential school dropouts.

PREVENTION STRATEGY FOR CHILDREN: TRAINING FOR OPTIMISM

One of the best early primary prevention programs was developed by Seligman and his colleagues (Peterson, Maier, & Seligman, 1993; Seligman, 1990, 1993, 1994, 1995) at the University of Pennsylvania. For nearly 30 years, Seligman has been a major researcher in the general area of depression, with his first contributions identifying, clarifying, and establishing the concept of learned helplessness. While continuing this work, he also devoted major effort and energy to the opposite side of the coin, *learned optimism*, establishing a robust link between pessimism and eventual depression. The Penn Prevention Program (PPP) sought to inoculate children against the effects of pessimism—with spectacular results. The children in the Penn Prevention Program spent a total of 24 hours in a course learning and practicing cognitive-behavioral skills. They were also asked to practice the skills in homework assignments. Because the PPP worked so well in preventing depression when it was taught to children in schools, Seligman (1995) developed an approach to teach it to parents. This program is not a dropout prevention program per se, but we include it here because of the strong links between depression, substance abuse, and other at-risk behaviors.

Building on group interventions that utilized cognitive therapy to successfully treat depression in children and adolescents, Seligman and his colleagues (Jaycox, Reivich, Gillham, & Seligman, 1994) developed a cognitively based social problem-solving program to prevent depressive symptoms in children. Children who reported parental conflict, depressive symptoms, or both were targeted because these factors increase childrens' risk for future depression (Jaycox & Repetti, 1993; Nolan-Hoeksema, Girgus, & Seligman, 1992). Children who participated in the prevention program reported fewer depressive symptoms than did children in the control group immediately after the program and at a six-month follow-up. A later study explored the program's effects after a two-year delay (Gillham, Reivich, Jaycox, & Seligman, 1995). Surprisingly, the effects of the prevention program actually grew stronger after the program was over. Apparently, psychological immunization against depression can occur by teaching social and cognitive skills to children.

The PPP contains two major components: a social problem-solving component and a cognitive component. The social problem-solving component focuses on interpersonal and conduct problems that are often associated with depressed children. Children are taught to think about their goals before acting. They generate lists of possible solutions for various problems. They are encouraged to make decisions by weighing the pros and cons of all the options. The cognitive component is based on the theories developed by Ellis (1962, 1985, 1996) and Beck (1976) and Seligman (1991). Briefly, children are taught to identify negative beliefs and to evaluate these beliefs by examining evidence for and against them. Children are taught explanatory style and how to identify pessimistic explanations. They learn to generate alternative explanations that are more realistic and more optimistic. Finally, children are also taught behavioral techniques to enhance assertiveness, negotiation, and relaxation, as well as techniques for coping with parental conflict.

Optimism

The PPP also focuses on the notion of optimism. Optimism is a style of engaging in or adapting to a situation that follows from the belief that what one does has an effect of achieving one's desired goal or making the possibility of achieving that goal more likely. It is a set of skills on how to talk to oneself when suffering a setback. When people do badly, they ask themselves, "Why?" There are three components to the answer to this question: Who is to blame? How much of life will be undermined? How long will it last? The distinctions among these three aspects are critical. The first issue attaches blame to the self or to the world. The second and third questions—how pervasive is the cause and how permanent is the cause—govern what people do to respond to failure. Feeling bad about yourself does not directly cause failure. However, the belief that problems undermine everything in life and will last forever cause people to stop trying. Giving up leads to more failure, and more failure leads to an even more pessimistic explanatory style. Thus, in the face of a bad event, a pessimist characteristically thinks that it is pervasive and permanent and that he or she is personally at fault. For example, a child may attribute a poor school performance to a personal failure or inability and begin to believe that all school efforts will result in failure. This explanatory style leads to destructive actions and becomes a kind of self-fulfilling negative prophecy. Positive events are believed by pessimists to be temporary, limited, and caused by something other than their own actions.

By contrast, optimists characteristically employ an explanatory style in which they think the bad event is temporary, limited to the specific event, and with many possible causes other than themselves. This cognitive mind-set saves the person from stress and mobilizes energy toward constructive goals. When a positive event occurs, an optimist characteristically thinks that he or she had a personal hand in causing the outcome and that it is pervasive and permanent. Thus, the three critical dimensions used to explain why any particular good or bad event happens are personal, permanent, and pervasive.

Internal versus external: Personal.   When events happen, children either blame themselves (internal) or they blame circumstances or other people (external). Pessimistic children have a habit of blaming themselves when bad things happen and frequently explain good events by attributing them to other people or to the situation. To change the explanatory style from pessimism to optimism and thus inoculate against future depression, this order must be reversed. We want children to take appropriate responsibility for events that occur in their lives, but children at risk for depression blame themselves when things go wrong—even though most real problems are caused by a complex set of contributing factors. Some children shoulder the entire blame and think of things in black-and-white terms. This leads to overwhelming feelings of worthlessness and guilt, causing them to withdraw and further increasing their risk for depression.

Sometimes versus always: Permanent.   Pessimistic and depressed children believe the cause of bad events and the reasons for their failure are permanent. Because the cause will persist forever, bad events are always going to occur. Optimistic children believe that the causes for bad events are temporary; this serves to inoculate them against depression. For the pessimistic child, mistakes, rejections, failures and so forth are thought of in terms of *forever* and *always*. The optimistic child explains bad events with words such as *sometimes* or *lately* or another time-limiting term.

Pessimistic and optimistic children react differently to positive events in their lives as well. Children who believe that good events have temporary causes tend to be more pessimistic than children who believe that good events have permanent causes. This is just the opposite of the explanation for bad events.

Specific versus global: Pervasive.   If the cause of the event is pervasive, its effect is distributed across many different situations in life and becomes global. Children who focus on global explanations for bad events give up on everything when they fail in one area. Pessimistic and depressed children tend to let a bad situation expand into all parts of their lives. This limits the number of positive outlets available to them. Everything is under a dark cloud, and they catastrophize.

Children who attribute global causes to bad events need to learn to be more specific in their explanations. Instead of a test failure meaning "I am stupid," children can learn to say "I didn't prepare very well this time." Children who think about good events as having more global causes do better in more areas of their lives. When it comes to good events, the optimist believes that the causes enhance everything they do. Pessimists believe that good events are caused by specific factors: "That just happened because she felt sorry for me." Global negative causes are pervasive and lead to despair and passivity. Seligman (1995) argues that the dimension of pervasiveness is not easily taught to children, although it is routinely taught to adults. It is not included in the PPP but is mentioned here in case aspects of this program are used for middle and secondary school students.

Basic Skills of Optimism

The PPP has incorporated the main techniques that cognitive therapists use to treat depression and has adapted them for people who are not depressed. These techniques decrease the future risk of depression because they help the individual develop new skills of thinking that can be used the next time something bad happens. There are four basic skills of optimism:

Thought catching. People must first learn to catch the negative things they say to themselves, about themselves, and about events that occur. These almost imperceptible thoughts affect behavior and mood. By learning to recognize the thoughts that flutter across the mind, these thoughts can then be changed.

Evaluation. The second skill is to evaluate the automatic and habitual thoughts that have been identified. These thoughts can be acknowledged as being hypotheses that need to be tested, and evidence can be gathered and considered to determine the accuracy of the beliefs.

Accurate explanations. When bad events happen, more accurate explanations can be developed to challenge the automatic thoughts. By interrupting the chain of negative explanations, attitudes and mood can improve.

Decatastrophizing. Catastrophizing, or thinking about the worst possible case, is counterproductive. Most often, the worst case is very unlikely. Ruminating on potential terrible implications and the worst possible consequences creates frustration, drains energy, and interferes with correcting problems.

Identifying automatic thoughts, searching for evidence, generating alternatives, and decatastrophizing are extremely important in developing optimism and lowering pessimism and depression in children.

Application for Dropouts and Problem Prevention

Early primary prevention programs can be very helpful to children. Skills for optimism can serve as a means of problem prevention. Children who drop out, and even children who attend school but have given up on themselves academically and personally, lack hope that school will benefit their future or that they can succeed in school. They may internalize their lack of success as their own fault, due to pervasive personal characteristics ("I'll never be able to read. I'm stupid."), as well as blaming it on pervasive global factors ("Teachers don't care." "School is useless."). Teachers or school counselors could initiate classroom discussions to identify thoughts students face in response to negative school experiences (thought catching). The class can assist in evaluating sample thoughts, helping to generate accurate explanations to substitute for sample negative thoughts. Decatastrophizing can be illustrated. When working individually with students, the same series of steps can be followed, reinforcing and further personalizing optimism skills. With practice, students will begin to utilize these skills to encourage each other.

Teaching these skills to children is important, but it is equally important for the helping adults to learn and practice these skills themselves. Using these skills may improve the mental health of the helper—not an unimportant consideration given the nature of the work, the consistent drain of personal resources and energy, and the constant stress of budget cuts, limited resources, and "broken" children, adolescents, and families. Increased optimism gives the helper more energy and greater impact.

Optimism can be taught to parents as well. Parental (and other adult) criticism often reflects the bad habits and biases of the adult and contributes to increased pessimism in children. If they are aware of their children's attributions, parents can provide more helpful feedback and criticism to their children. Children view ability as permanent, so blaming failure on lack of ability fosters pessimism. In contrast, blaming lack of success on conduct, effort, or attention is less malignant because these are temporary and changeable. Children can be challenged and supported in their efforts to improve conduct, increase effort, or focus attention. If they believe they lack ability, they will be at greater risk of dropout and other problems.

PEER INTERVENTIONS: PEER AND CROSS-AGE TUTORING PROGRAMS

Peer influence is powerful. In this section we will describe strategies that utilize peers to prevent dropout and other problems by enhancing academic and social success in school settings. Peer and cross-age tutoring programs are designed to aid at-risk children by improving their academic performance and their emotional well-being (Garcia-Vazquez & Ehly, 1992; Tansey, et al., 1996). Peer tutoring is a one-to-one teaching process in which the tutor is of the same academic age as the partner. Cross-age tutoring involves matching an older student tutor with a younger student learner.

Systematic planning is a critical component of successful peer or cross-age tutoring programs. Programs that attend to readiness, preparation, selection, implementation, supervision, and evaluation components have been found to be more readily accepted by administrators, teachers, students, and families. Well-planned programs can be integrated into schools more effectively than programs that are not well articulated from the outset (Greenwood, Carta, & Maheady, 1991). Elements essential to implementing a successful peer or cross-age tutoring program include considerations of cost, school readiness, and teacher, student, and parent preparation. The following sections outline these considerations.

Cost Effectiveness

Cost effectiveness is an important consideration for administrators in the implementation of academic interventions. Levin, Glass, and Meister (1984) studied the cost effectiveness of four educational intervention strategies designed to raise student achievement in reading and mathematics: (a) computer-aided instruction; (b) cross-age/peer tutoring; (c) reduced class size; and (d) a longer school day. When student gains and program costs were compared, peer tutoring produced math and reading gain scores more than twice those resulting from computer-aided instruction, three times those achieved through reducing class size from 35 to 30 students, and almost four times more than lengthening the school day by one hour. Information regarding the relative utility of peer or cross-age tutoring interventions is vital to administrators in a time of reduced resources, increased demands, and increased accountability.

Readiness

Much of the success of peer tutoring depends on the readiness of the school to accept the program. Readiness is a function of both attitudinal factors and availability of resources to support the program. As administrator of the school, the principal is instrumental in allowing for program adjustments such as release time, schedule modifications, allocation of space, and active encouragement of peer tutoring. Teachers support the peer tutoring program by participating in peer selection, curriculum development, ongoing evaluation, and program development activities. Teacher readiness requires thorough training in peer tutoring methods through in-service training and ongoing consultation and supervision (Hawryluk & Smallwood, 1988). Specialized training and instruction in peer and cross-age tutoring methods for teachers are often available from school psychologists and counselors. Counselors may encourage teachers to acquaint themselves with tutoring methods and materials through published resources, including the *Cross-Age Tutoring Handbook* (S. Johnson, 1977), *Tutoring for At-Risk Students* (Gaustad, 1992), *Increasing Student Productivity Through Peer Tutoring Programs* (Pierce, Stahlbrand, & Armstrong, 1984) and *Peer Tutoring: A Guide for School Psychologists* (Ehly, 1986).

Preparation

Sufficient preparation of participating individuals increases the likelihood that the peer/cross-age tutoring program will be successfully established and accepted in both the school and the community. Students may be readied for peer tutoring through written and oral information about the program. Because peer/cross-age tutoring is a nontraditional means of instruction, presenting the program and its participants in a positive light is important.

Teachers play a central role in determining the content to be tutored, explaining how learning is approached by tutors, monitoring student progress, and facilitating student interaction. To increase teachers' acceptance of and commitment to the program, training and preparation of teachers should encompass several components, including: (a) understanding the purpose, advantage, and features of the peer tutoring program; (b) planning lessons and material preparation for student use; and (c) developing competence in teaching interactional and problem-solving skills to students. This training is accomplished through consultation, exposure to written material on peer tutoring, and in-service training. Teacher training includes instruction of tutoring methods, simulation exercises to familiarize teachers with student and teacher roles, modeling strategies for social and conflict resolution skills, and discussion of anticipated problems that may interfere with implementation. Our experience suggests that training programs developed for this purpose can accomplish these objectives in a minimum of three to five 40-minute training sessions if ongoing in-service, consultation, and coordination for maintenance purposes is provided.

The degree to which students are prepared to tutor is another critical element of an effective peer tutoring program. Children who have a fuller understanding of a task and its rationale are better prepared to perform the task themselves and better equipped to teach it to others (Barron & Foot, 1991). Students planning to tutor are better prepared when trained in various aspects of tutoring, including: (a) developing and presenting instructional material, (b) recognizing and reinforcing correct learner responses appropriately, (c) providing corrective feedback effectively, (d) redirecting off-task behavior, (e) communicating with learners, and (f) working closely with teachers. Tutor preparation includes a mix of didactic instruction, practice in specific skills, and group discussion of possible problems. Tutors also benefit from ongoing training to strengthen their skills and reinforce the purpose of the program. Ongoing training can be accomplished through brief refresher training sessions offered periodically during the peer/cross-age tutoring program.

Advance preparation of parents is essential to the program's acceptance. If not properly informed, parents may perceive their child's participation in the peer/cross-age tutoring program negatively. If their child is being tutored, they may believe that their child is receiving instruction from a less-than-qualified instructor and that their child's participation in the program is at the cost of valuable instruction in the regular curriculum. Parents of tutors may worry that their child is losing the benefit of teacher instruction, and worse, is being exploited by school personnel by providing instruction to others without payment.

Advance preparation of participating parents in the form of written information, group discussions, and personal contact may convert potentially doubting parents to agents of support. Because peer tutoring activities involve individual students selected from the entire class, parental consent is needed. Parents should be provided with a clear explanation of the program, reasons for their child's involvement, and safeguards against possible negative effects. Parent preparation may be accomplished through letters to the parents, meetings between parents and school personnel, and presentations at meetings such as the PTA and the PTSO.

Sample Method: Pause, Prompt, and Praise

To illustrate the nature of peer tutoring, we selected one method for fuller description. We have had considerable success with the "pause, prompt, and praise" method for tutoring oral reading. Rather than giving immediate attention to errors—that is, attention that occurs within five seconds of the error—a delay of five seconds or until the end of the student's sentence yielded greater improvement. Specifically, learners were more likely to self-correct errors, and reading accuracy improved. Thus, the first part of the tutoring procedure, "pause," requires the tutor to delay attention to the student's reading error for more than five seconds or until the end of the sentence. The second part of the procedure, "prompt," requires the tutor to supply a prompt if no self-correction occurs. The prompts are the self-correction strategies that the student learner has already learned as part of program preparation. They are often graphic or contextual clues that provide meaning. If no correct response is elicited following two prompts, the tutor supplies the correct word and moves on.

The final part of the procedure, "praise," requires the tutor to verbally reinforce positive behaviors and to encourage development of independent self-correcting skills. Therefore, in addition to the general praise for behaviors such as finishing a whole page, the tutor praises self-corrections and prompted corrections made by the learner.

This method supplies the tutor with a procedure for dealing with both correct and error behavior by the reader. It encourages him or her to reinforce the desired behaviors. Perhaps more important, it allows the reader to develop independence and independent self-correction strategies.

Program Implementation

Educational interventions such as peer or cross-age tutoring often emerge from a need to remediate students who are failing or at risk of failure. The impetus to develop new programs often reflects a sense of urgency. Initially, however, a modest peer/cross-age tutoring program is most viable. Avoid overtaxing available resources during the initial implementation stage of a program, and expand later when the program is well established.

In spite of how thoroughly a program has been planned, unforeseen problems will arise. After initial start-up, slight adjustments will be necessary. Administrative support is essential to the program. As well, teachers will need some release time and other forms of support to develop materials, assess and supervise program participants, and provide ongoing training (in-service and discussion groups) related to the program. Now let's take a closer look at the elements of a successful peer tutoring program.

Tutor selection. In cross-age tutoring programs, older tutors are matched with younger partners. In peer tutoring programs, tutors and student learners (or partners) are the same age, class, or grade. When selecting tutors, consideration may be given to students with a variety of characteristics, including those who are academically accomplished and able to instruct, those who are positive role models and influential with their peers, and others who are at greater risk of school failure and may benefit academically and emotionally from their role as tutors. Each type of tutor offers a degree of assurance that the program will be accepted. The academically accomplished tutor will bring mastery of the subject matter to the tutoring session, the influential peer will popularize the program within the peer culture, and the "at-risk" tutor will provide evidence that the program is of benefit to those who tutor.

When choosing whom to include as student learners, educators might consider the degree of learning difficulties, motivation, and behavioral adjustment the learner presents. Learners with severe problems may not be good candidates for initial implementation of the program. These students may be introduced to the peer tutoring program in subsequent years, once introductory concerns are resolved and the program is established.

Once matched, it is advisable that tutor-learner interactions be observed and pairs assessed for compatibility. Supervising teachers or coordinating counselors should intervene in difficult relationships and reassign unworkable matches. This kind of support will prevent tutors and learners from feeling frustrated or discouraged with the program and will increase their enjoyment of the process.

Tutoring sessions. A tutoring schedule should be developed by the program coordinator, scheduling several 20- to 30-minute sessions each week. Tutoring schedules must be followed consistently. Failure to hold tutoring sessions at their scheduled times conveys the message that the program is unimportant relative to other activities.

Tutoring sessions typically are held in a designated area within the classroom, isolated somewhat from other student activities. This seating arrangement allows for privacy and reduces distractions but enables the teacher to directly monitor the tutoring session.

Materials. Tutoring materials are generated by the teacher or adapted from published sources. With supervision, experienced tutors can learn to develop materials for the learner, resulting in increased understanding of the materials by the tutor and decreasing the teacher's required time commitment somewhat.

Student incentives. Students' motivation to participate in a peer or cross-age tutoring program will not be sustained without some form of incentive. Incentives for participating in the program can be provided for both tutors and their partners on a regular basis. Although some students are motivated through praise and verbal approval, activities such as social events and learning games can be initiated by schools along with efforts to recognize student involvement such as making schoolwide announcements. Time set aside for personal reflection and discussion of students' experiences in the program are especially useful. In some schools, tutors receive elective credit for their participation in the program. Some programs recognize tutors and their partners by awarding certificates of completion and recognition. School newsletters and plaques hung in the administrative office are other ways to recognize students for their involvement. Strategies for motivating students are numerous and varied. Creativity on the part of school personnel will enhance the possible incentives available to students for their involvement.

Teacher supervision.   Teachers need to meet with tutors before each session to review instructional materials. Prior to the session, the teacher ascertains that the tutor has a clear grasp of the content of the instructional material and the objectives for the learner. These meetings become shorter as the tutor demonstrates competence in the tutorial role.

Initially, after each session, the tutor meets with the teacher to discuss how the session went, the partner's progress, and any difficulties encountered. The teacher reinforces and instructs the tutor at this time. Post-session supervision is reduced as the tutor establishes competence. The motivational aspects of these meetings, however, must be kept in mind; reinforcement of tutors is an ongoing activity and is extremely important. As part of their supervisory role, teachers should directly observe the tutoring session about one in every three or four sessions to monitor the tutoring process.

Evaluation.   Program evaluation is important to a tutor program for several reasons. Ongoing evaluation of student progress can be used to motivate both the student receiving tutoring and the tutor. Also, feedback from student performance can be used to determine aspects of the program that are effective and those that could benefit from modification. Evaluation results can be used to demonstrate the value of the program to interested parties, such as administrators faced with decisions about funding special programs or parents who express doubts about the quality of alternative educational approaches.

Evaluation activities should be linked to the goals and objectives of the program. Tutoring programs are often designed to improve the academic achievement of both the tutor and the student learner in the specific area tutored. Another common goal of tutoring programs is enhancing both students' academic self-concept. The effectiveness of a tutoring program may be gauged by whether the tutor and the learner have achieved gains in academic performance in the subject being tutored and in academic self-concept.

The use of global measures of academic achievement or self-concept for evaluating the effectiveness of the program may result in ambiguous feedback on student progress. Overall academic achievement is a composite of several academic areas (mathematics, reading, spelling, and so forth). It is unrealistic to expect change in overall academic achievement through tutoring in only one academic area. It is equally unrealistic to anticipate change in global self-concept as a result of improved performance in a specific academic area (Craven, Marsh, & Debus, 1991). Efforts to evaluate program effectiveness using global indices will underestimate the actual benefits of the program. The best way to measure the effect of the tutoring program is to evaluate academic and self-concept change specifically related to the subject tutored.

Students participating in the tutoring program should be assessed before, during, and after participating in the program. Academic achievement can be assessed through teacher-developed curriculum-based measures that are inexpensive, directly related to the academic subject matter, and sensitive to improvement in academic performance (Marston, 1989).

Several tests designed to measure children's self-concept have academic self-concept factors (Harter, 1985; Piers, 1984). Each of these tests mixes academic self-concept items among the other self-concept items, which does not readily allow measurement of academic self-concept alone. The Multidimensional Self-Concept Scale (MSCS) is well suited to isolating academic self-concept as its 25 academic self-concept items are not woven into the body of the instrument; rather, they are presented on a separate page and may be administered, scored, and compared to national norms without giving or scoring the entire test (Bracken, 1992). The academic scale of the MSCS, about a five-minute test, can be used throughout the course of program participation as a measure of academic self-concept.

PEER INTERVENTION: PEER MEDIATION

Peer mediation is a mode of student conflict management. Two trained peer mediators work as a team to encourage problem solving between disputants. The setting for this mediation process is often the playground. Used in conjunction with traditional means of discipline, such as suspension for serious violent acts, peer mediation provides a structured forum for the resolution of in-school disputes. Student involvement in the mediation process provides practice in critical thinking, problem solving, and self-discipline. "The process of peer mediation is a self-empowering one—it enables students to make decisions about issues and conflicts that affect their own lives" (Maxwell, 1989, p. 150). This element of student participation in self- and peer behavior change is directly related to the developmental construct of self-regulation. Awareness of socially approved behaviors is a critical feature of self-regulation, which involves the ability to postpone acting on a desired object or goal. Self-regulation requires being able to generate socially approved behavior in the absence of external monitors. The ability to self-regulate is a developmental skill that must be practiced regularly. School peer mediation programs provide daily opportunities for reinforcement.

Background

School peer mediation programs have sprung up across the nation in the last decade, and many of them are based on community mediation models such as the San Francisco Community Board Program (1982). Developers of the San Francisco Community Board Program had five years of experience settling disputes between neighbors and businesses before introducing this school-based Conflict Manager program. In this program, students receive 16 hours of training and role-play practice. They eventually become team mediators on the playground and in the lunchroom. Similar programs now exist in almost all major cities in the United States. The assistance of a community mediation school initiative trainer, although not essential, may be valuable in training school personnel and students.

Models for both adults in the community and children in schools promote conflict mediation through the application of communication skills, listening to evoke varying perspectives, eliciting mutual contributions to the problem's eventual solution, and attending to feelings—all in an atmosphere of respect for the parties involved.

Theoretical Assumptions

Advocates of peer mediation in the schools assume that "children helping children" is a valid perspective from which to view program implementation and outcome. A wealth of research literature supports this perspective. Peer leaders have been found to have greater credibility regarding student social interactions. They serve as potent role models and can demonstrate pro-social behaviors. Peers can create and reinforce norms supporting the notion that certain behaviors are deviant rather than acceptable, and they can promote alternatives to deviant behaviors. The student mediators themselves derive great benefit from the programs as well (Cahoon, 1988; Maxwell, 1989; T. Roderick, 1988).

Another strength of such programs is that they emphasize student involvement and student management. Thus, participants tend to feel more committed to program goals and more interested in producing change among their peers. A more specific description of benefits follows.

Benefits to Students and to the School

Both student behavior and school discipline problems improve as a result of peer mediation. McCormick (1988) reported that at-risk disputants (students who had been referred frequently for discipline problems) were observed by teachers to exhibit shifts to cooperation after experiencing peer mediation, a change supported by a 47% decrease in self-reported aggressive conflicts. Also, "at-risk students who directly participated in the program developed more 'prosocial' attitudes towards conflict, but those who had only indirect exposure to the collaborative process maintained their 'antisocial' attitudes towards conflict" (McCormick, 1988, p. 73). For example, when one at-risk student was trained as a peer mediator, his previous preference for resolving conflict in an aggressive style was replaced (over one semester as a mediator) with a reported preference for a collaborative style of dispute resolution. Such metamorphoses are also described by McCormick: "'Troublemakers' were just as enthusiastic about the problem-solving process and just as competent to guide others through it as those peer mediators who were thought to be ideal students" (p. 63).

Araki, Takeshita, and Kadomoto (1989) found that peer mediation increased empowerment and volunteerism, with both mediators and disputants developing increasing capacities for self-control. Disputants who were nonlisteners became listeners through participation in the mediation process. All students—both disputants and mediators—found a place for talking about problems, learning more about the views of others, and practicing better communication in a nonviolent, nonjudgmental atmosphere. The words of one student summarize peer mediation's impact:

> All I ever wanted to do was to fight. If someone said something to me I didn't like, I didn't think about talking, I just thought about fighting. I came into a mediation session as a disputant with four girls on the other side. I thought, "Who needs this? What am I doing here?" I just wanted to punch these girls out. I figured that the mediator would tell me what I was going to have to do. But she didn't. Instead she drew me out, listened to me. It felt so good to let it all out; then I wasn't angry anymore. I thought, "Hey, if this can work for me, I want to learn how to do it." (McCormick, 1988, p. 54)

Peer mediation also provides benefits for schools by reducing the number of discipline events. In one Hawaii school, the number of on-campus fights dropped from 83 to 19 over a two-year period (Araki, Takeshita, & Kadomoto, 1989). At a New York school, these events declined by 50% (Koch, 1988), and an Arizona school reported a 47% decrease in the average number of aggressive incidents per month (McCormick, 1988). Finally, out of 69 mediated cases at a Milwaukee high school, 60 agreements were reached, and researchers recorded an 80% success rate for disputes mediated during the 1986–87 school year (Burrell & Vogel, 1990). As more instruments for program evaluation become available, the benefits to students and to school climate will become increasingly apparent.

Training Staff Members

The training sequence begins with presentation of the mediation program to the entire school staff. The school counselor and principal often conduct this introductory session. Given the time and resources required to implement a peer mediation program, it is very important that the initial presentation include evidence of the benefits to students and to the school. After the presentation, each staff member completes a level-of-interest questionnaire to determine his or her degree of commitment to the process. If staff support for mediation is adequate (usually 80%), training for teachers and support personnel is initiated. Elementary and middle school staff training usually requires about eight hours. The content of this training includes communication skills that encompass active listening, reflection of feeling, message clarification, body language, giving "I" messages, brainstorming, types of questioning, and effective problem solving. The mediation sequence is identified, and adult responsibilities are delineated. Role-play is used extensively with the adult staff members, as it is later with the students.

Training Student Peer Mediators

Once the adults have been trained, they plan and implement an orientation assembly to motivate students and alert them to the qualities of a good mediator. Role-plays and skits are used to outline aspects of the program and the process.

As the time for implementation nears, students who wish to become peer mediators nominate themselves or are nominated by others. Nominations may also come from counselors, teachers, and administrators. Final selection of mediators is completed by student vote. Selected students are then trained by adult staff members, sometimes with the assistance of a community mediation training consultant. Training for elementary and middle school students consists of five half days. The adult staff members teach the communication skills that they reviewed in their own training. They guide the students through role-plays not unlike those they engaged in during the adult training.

The mediation sequence is introduced and practiced until it becomes a comfortable process for the children. This sequence involves four basic stages: introduction, listening, wants, and solutions.

In the first stage of the peer mediation sequence, the student mediators introduce themselves, offer their services ("Do you need a mediator?"), and walk to a different area to cause physical and psychological separation from the initial point of conflict. When the disputants and mediators are ready, the rules are reviewed and commitment to them is elicited. An assurance of confidentiality is given to disputants by the mediators.

In stage 2 of the mediation sequence, the peer mediators listen to each disputant in turn. They reflect and restate content and feelings as they address each disputant.

Because no interruptions are allowed, disputants have the opportunity to hear the others' perspective of the conflict and their resultant feelings.

With guidance from the peer mediators, disputants express their wants in stage 3 of the sequence. As the requests are heard and restated by mediators, clarity reduces anxiety about possible hidden agendas.

In stage 4, disputants are asked what they can contribute to the resolution of the problem. The peer mediators restate and check solutions for balance. Then each disputant is asked if the proposed solution is acceptable. An important step in this phase is asking if the problem is solved. Disputants may wish to express a need to receive or to give an apology to smooth hurt feelings. The mediators then ask disputants how such a conflict could be handled differently in the future. Peer mediators close the sequence by asking former disputants to tell their friends that the conflict has been solved, thus reducing the potential for rumors. After congratulating the students on solving their problem, the peer mediators complete a mediation report form. In this last step of the sequence, the peer mediators have an opportunity to review the quality of their guidance as they do their record keeping together.

When training is complete, student mediators receive recognition and uniform T-shirts, banners, or hats at an assembly. They are then assigned to recess duty in pairs. They meet twice a week with a staff program coordinator to discuss their successes and problems, to maintain and build new skills, and to handle scheduling problems. School counselors often introduce classroom guidance curriculum activities to promote general student awareness of the peer mediators and the services they offer.

Implications

The simplicity of the peer mediation process contributes to its success. The student mediators can easily implement the steps. They also provide support for each other. In the San Francisco Community Board Program (1982) demonstration video, a young man who was formerly a "conflict maker" became a "conflict manager." Sonny had this to say about his peer mediation experience:

> I used to be a bully. I think because I wanted to get the authority—the power. Now, as a conflict manager, I get the authority and status I used to take. I've changed. Now I can feel what the kids feel, and I can help them solve their problems.

Cahoon (1988), an elementary principal, noted that her "mediators learn valuable problem-solving skills: to think logically about processing the information presented to them, to see issues impartially, and to advise without censoring. They also gain recognition for their efforts" (p. 94). Roderick (1988) emphasized a valuable aspect of school mediation programs: "Young people have many choices besides passivity or aggression for dealing with conflict . . . [through mediation] we give them the skills to make those choices real in their own lives" (p. 90).

The Ripple Effect

Program implementation results in fewer playground problems and fewer referrals to the nurse or the principal's office. Families may also experience the program's impact. Parents and students in peer mediation schools report that conflict in the home is resolved in new and more productive ways. Perhaps this supports the research conclusions of Frey, Holley, and L'Abate (1979), who emphasized that a by-product of mutually and peacefully resolved conflict is often a new intimacy in the family. They advocated teaching children to be vulnerable—to share their fears and hurts, not just their anger. This concept is built into the mediation sequence, as elicitation of feelings as well as information is part of the mediation process.

Program trainers in the Phoenix area serving more than 70 schools have compiled a list of reported benefits (Terros, 1988). Although empirical evidence is lacking (Maxwell, 1989), reports by administrators, teachers, and school counselors confirm many of these benefits:

- pressure for staff members to be constant disciplinarians decreased
- staff time saved
- tension reduced
- overall improvement in school climate
- students' leadership skills developed
- student language skills enhanced
- academic improvement of mediators
- increased status among peers for mediators
- improved self-esteem for mediators and disputants
- valuable problem-solving skills learned
- practice received in self-regulation
- improvement in self-discipline of mediators
- more openness in sharing of feelings reported
- greater assumption of responsibility
- student needs are met more positively
- families report improved self-discipline at home
- families note better listening all around
- home conflicts resolved more effectively

In society, the effects of teaching mediation skills will be cumulative as more children learn positive ways to resolve conflicts. An eventual reduction of violence is hypothesized, which will help to reduce the burden on our court system.

Counseling Ramifications

Elementary and middle school counselors are in key positions to institute peer mediation programs. Self-regulation and many other skills and concepts are directly related to a developmental counseling philosophy. "Positive self-esteem and self-regulation can be fostered in students when they are given the opportunity to participate in decisions relating to their own lives" (Maxwell, 1989, p. 150). School counselors can promote this developmental process through implementation of peer mediation programs. Furthermore, counselors are in a position to open up mediation training to parents as part of a school–community outreach program. Conflict resolution through peer mediation is a preventive program as well—in the form of leadership training. It is also an integral component of a school's discipline plan. Finally, it is a way to meet the communication objectives of a guidance curriculum. Regardless of its placement in the overall picture of school pupil development, its importance for children and its implications for society are clear.

The conflict resolution model of peer mediation addresses the skills of listening, problem solving, oral language expression, and critical thinking. These identified skills are directly taught in the process of mediation training. They are modeled and reinforced by the peer mediators. If children are to mature into adults who know how to solve problems while respecting the views of others, then mediation is not only a positive school program but an essential survival skill.

Carlos Diaz would benefit in several ways from being trained as a peer mediator. The experience of being nominated by a peer, teacher, or counselor would bolster his confidence. The skills he learns as a mediator would help him to reduce the number of fights he has with peers. Providing a valuable service to his school would help him view himself as more a part of the school community. This participation might influence teacher perceptions, increasing the amount of support and positive feedback he receives from teachers. The verbal skills learned and utilized by peer mediators might enhance Carlos's language acquisition efforts. Finally, Carlos could be an effective mediator for monolingual Spanish-speaking children at the school. Given Carlos's responsibilities at home, however, staff would have to ascertain whether the time demand of the program would hinder Carlos more than the benefits would be an enhancement. Nevertheless, a young man reinforced for his contributions to the school community who is being supported in the development of useful life skills is a young man with a lowered risk of dropout.

CONCLUSION

In this chapter we have described several programs designed to directly or indirectly prevent student dropout. ICPS, training for optimism, and programs utilizing peer influence such as peer and cross-age tutoring and peer mediation are effective means of reducing some of the correlates of dropout and other at-risk categories: depression, interpersonal conflict, reading and communication deficiencies, loneliness, and lack of purpose. Although requiring the resources of teachers, counselors, psychologists, and administrators in a time of increasing demands and fewer resources, these school-based programs have positive effects that outweigh the costs. The benefits for young people now and in the future are enormous.

FURTHER READINGS

In addition to those books and articles cited in the reference section, the following books may be useful to readers wishing to know more about prevention and intervention programs for children and young teenagers.

Dettre, J. H. (1980). *1, 2, 3 Read! A step-by-step tutoring plan for teachers, parents, and friends.* Carthage, IL: Fearon Teacher Aids.
Erwin, P. G. (1993). *Friendship and peer relations in children.* Chichester: Wiley.
Jindall, J. A. (1995). *Peer programs: An in-depth look at peer helping.* Bristol, PA: Accelerated Development.
Johnson, D., & Johnson, R. (1991). *Teaching students to be peacemakers.* Edina, MN: Interaction Book Company.
Schmuck, R. A., & Schmuck, P. A. (1997). *Group processes in the classroom.* (7th ed.) Madison, WI: Brown & Benchmark.
Schrumf, F., Crawford, D., & Usadel, H. C. (1991). *Peer mediation: Conflict resolution in schools.* Champaign, IL: Research Press.

FAMILY INTERVENTIONS

*In some families words are like
barbed wire, they cut and puncture.*

*In some families messages are like
exploding shrapnel, they rip and tear.*

*In some families secrets are like
land mines, step on one and they
erupt in explosion.*

*In some families even love and affection
are tools in the battle.*

*All war, especially the war in families, is
at once horrible and dehumanizing—
and obscenely senseless.*

J. J. McWhirter

CHAPTER OUTLINE

In the 1950s the family was the number one influence on children, but by 1989 the family had dropped to third place behind peers and television (Parham, 1991). Family structure has also shifted in response to social, political, and economic conditions. Divorce, remarriage and stepchildren, and the loss of the extended family network—even negotiating the inevitable developmental changes that are part of the family life cycle—can be highly stressful and can generate conflict within a family.

The symptoms of family distress may emerge when a reasonably healthy family goes through a difficult transition, such as the marriage of the first child. In other cases, family symptomology reflects ongoing dysfunction and emerges in response to everyday stresses. A father's alcoholic binges, for example, may occur whenever the extended family gathers, when the mother confronts him, when the children fight, or when the traffic is heavy. The patterns of behavior that various family members use to cope with (and often to maintain) the father's drinking may in themselves represent symptoms of family dysfunction. Devine and Braithwaite (1993) and Brooks and Coll (1994) have described and researched the roles frequently assumed by members of families with an alcoholic parent. One role, the scapegoat or the acting-out child, may be played by a son or daughter whose acting-out behavior draws attention away from the alcohol problem and causes the parents to unite to deal with the "problem child." The youth whose behavior appears to be self-destructive and irrational is often actually serving to keep the dysfunctional family together, inadvertently helping to perpetuate its dysfunction (see Box 14.1). When teachers and counselors become frustrated by the destructive and aggressive behaviors of their students, it is helpful to keep in mind that these behaviors are often goal-directed and represent attempts to meet basic human needs. Much of this

■ ■ ■ Box 14.1
The School Slut

He was always angry with her. Every aggressive retort, every call from the school, every violation of curfew drew his rage like flies to butter. But the failing grades, her reputation as the "school slut," the constant battles—they were all worth it. As long as his attention was focused on his anger with her, it would not be directed at her sister, the "good" daughter, and he wouldn't come into her sister's bedroom. Her sister wouldn't be forced to endure those long nights, the hideous emptiness, the vomiting afterward. At least this much she could control.

And that's one reason why the rage overwhelmed and consumed her ten years later; that's one reason why the tears in my office were so torrential that her whole body convulsed with agony. Because ten years later, her sister said, "It was happening to me too."

sort of behavior originates in response to the dynamics in the families to which the students return every night.

In this chapter we attend to interventions for individual families as one point of entry for addressing the problems of at-risk youth. The model we presented in Chapter 11 illustrates our view that addressing the problems of at-risk youth is a multifaceted endeavor. In addressing family interventions, we do not intend to "blame the victim," but ultimately we hope to empower family members by providing suggestions that may enable the family to chart new directions for all the members, especially the children.

A variety of options are available for the teacher or counselor who decides that the at-risk student would most benefit from family involvement in problem solving. We will discuss four of those options: family counseling, parent support groups, parent education, and parent training.

FAMILY COUNSELING

Treating the entire family is often the optimal approach for dealing with young people at risk for dropout, substance use, pregnancy, delinquency, suicide, and other problems. When a child or adolescent is contemplating or engaged in life-threatening behavior, it is of utmost importance that the family be involved in efforts to avert or solve the problem. In general, family therapy is appropriate when (a) the presenting problems are affected by and affect the family system; (b) the child or adolescent is living in the family or is working through unfinished business with the family and is in contact with them even though not living at home; and (c) both the counselor and the client agree that family therapy is an appropriate intervention.

Family counseling is not always a viable option. In some schools, the school counselor, social worker, or psychologist is allowed to function as a family counselor.

However, this role is not always feasible, and referral to a private or public agency may be the only available alternative. The following questions often are considered in exploring the option of family counseling: Does the family have resources such as transportation? Are there any language or cultural factors that might prohibit or discourage family members from availing themselves of counseling services? Does any family member have access to counseling services through an employee assistance program or some other work benefit? Discussion of these questions with the family and familiarity with community resources will facilitate appropriate referrals.

Referring the Family for Counseling

It's a rare family that responds with delight when a teacher or counselor suggests family counseling. For many family members, attending a counseling session is tantamount to acknowledging severe mental illness within the family. When a teacher or counselor has determined that a particular family might benefit from a referral to family counseling, several steps can be taken to lay a foundation for success (E. H. McWhirter, J. J. McWhirter, B. T. McWhirter, & A. M. McWhirter, 1993). First, the family needs to know why: On what basis has the referring professional made this decision? The identified problem—that is, the behavior of the child that attracted the teacher's or counselor's attention—should be explained in specific and concrete terms. For example, Ramona Diaz's teacher (Chapter 4) might say: "For three weeks now, Ramona has been withdrawn and quiet. She seems to be avoiding her school friends. She's refusing to participate in class, and she has cried at school three or four times this week. When I asked her how things were going at home, she simply stared at the floor and said, 'It's probably my fault anyway.' This is so different from Ramona's usual behavior that I thought it was important to contact you to talk about some possible ways to help her." Notice that Ramona's teacher does not assign blame or sound judgmental, nor does she draw conclusions from her observations.

A second step in family referral is to help the family understand that family counseling may help in the achievement of mutual goals. Counseling provides an opportunity for the family to work as a cohesive unit; the needs of all family members are considered in developing solutions to problems. Potential benefits include more appropriate behavior by the "problem child," increased responsibility among family members for voicing their opinions and feelings, better grades for the children, and more support and less stress for all family members. The teacher or counselor who knows the general nature of the problem can identify the benefits appropriate to the specific situation.

Family members are often more accepting of recommendations for counseling if they have a sense of what to expect. When Jason Carter (of Chapter 3) was first seen as a client, he asked the family counselor, "Where's your black couch? Aren't you going to write down everything I say?" Adults, too, have many misconceptions. The teacher or counselor can dispel some of the mystique surrounding counseling by discussing some of the reasons families go to a counselor and what the process might be like. Common reasons include problems with discipline and communication, lack of trust among family members, school problems, and tension related to divorce, dating, or remarriage of a parent. There are many approaches to family therapy, and individual therapists vary in style even if they subscribe to the same approach. We discuss several approaches to family therapy later in this chapter.

◻ ▪ ■ Box 14.2

In the Waiting Room

Recently, a tragedy occurred in one of Kansas City's local hospitals. A woman of Hmong descent (the Hmong people are from Vietnam) was standing in the waiting room of the hospital with her seriously ill infant. As she stood reticent in a corner waiting to be helped, the baby died in her arms. When the staff behind the reception desk realized what had just happened, they were aghast. They wondered why she had not approached them to ask for assistance. The simple truth was this: Hmong people do not approach a majority group without first being summoned (Maltbia, 1991, p. 26).

Families should be encouraged to ask potential counselors, "What do you expect of your clients?" "How long have you been practicing and what are your credentials?" "What can we expect of you?" "How do you structure your counseling sessions?" "How can we make best use of our time and money here?" A family that has a sense of its own role in the therapeutic process may be more willing to consider the option of counseling.

Some families resist counseling because they are unsure how to begin the process. Let them know that once they call for an appointment it may be anywhere from a day to a month or more before they have their first session. This first session may be an intake session during which a counselor gathers information about the family's background and history. The family may work with the intake counselor in later sessions or be assigned to a different counselor. If families are unprepared for this sometimes drawn-out process, they may become frustrated and discontinue the process prematurely.

Some parents want to meet with the counselor alone before their child or children enter the room. Some counselors may request such an arrangement, but others may refuse it. This decision depends on the theoretical orientation and judgment of the counselor. Encourage parents to let the counselor know their preference.

Teachers and counselors are more likely to be successful in referring families for counseling if they are knowledgeable about a variety of local counseling agencies and practitioners. It is especially important to make referrals that are consistent with the family's cultural and language needs. Not all counselors have multicultural training; such training is not yet a requirement for certification by the Council on Accreditation of Counseling and Related Educational Programs. And certainly not all agencies have counselors fluent in Spanish or Vietnamese. When a counselor or a teacher approaches an ethnic minority family, it is important to consider that counseling as we know it has historically been a Western, white, middle- and upper-class phenomenon. Recent immigrants in particular will need a thorough explanation of the nature of counseling and may need time to consider whether it is consistent with their cultural values and practices (see Box 14.2).

When individuals are referred for family counseling, they should be provided with accurate information about the various agencies and practitioners—their current names, addresses, and phone numbers, their specializations, and whether they adjust their fees to the client's ability to pay. Follow up with the family and find out what might help them to take action if they haven't followed through with the referral. For those who follow through, ask for feedback regarding the counseling facility for the benefit of future families.

The Nature of Family Counseling

In family counseling, people's problems are examined within the context of the family's interactions. Problems are viewed not as the result of individual issues but as the consequence of the complex dynamics that characterize every family. Often, the family comes to a counselor expecting that the person the family has identified as the "problem" will be fixed. Family members expect to have minimal involvement in the process. The family counselor's first task is to assist family members to recognize that a family system is composed of a number of both positive and negative interlocking relationships. Family members must be helped to understand their contribution to the maintenance of the identified client's symptom. Finally, the family must agree to work together to change their situation.

Working with the entire family is advantageous in many ways. It enables the counselor to establish a more accurate perspective on the problem. The counselor may discover, for example, that what has been portrayed by a 15-year-old son as cruel authoritarianism is a belated attempt by his parents to impose control over curfew limits and homework completion. A mother who describes herself as loving and affectionate may truly believe she is so, in comparison with her own unavailable mother. But the verbal objections or behavioral expressions of disagreement demonstrated by family members can be invaluable and immediate means to begin dealing with definitions of the words *loving* and *affectionate* and the expectations that surround them. Watching arguments in progress provides the counselor with a picture of the family's interaction that no series of descriptions could convey. In addition to enhancing problem identification, working with the whole family makes problem solving a more cohesive, efficient, and timely process. The outcome of family therapy depends on many variables, including the therapist's skill, the willingness of family members to exert effort and take risks, their willingness and ability to take responsibility for their behavior, and the range of coping skills they possess. Each approach to family therapy will reveal and attend to potential problems for which children and youth are at risk in different ways.

Approaches to Family Counseling

The work of Virginia Satir, Jay Haley, Murray Bowen, and Salvador Minuchin is at the forefront of family therapy. Many others have also made valuable contributions. By focusing on the theoretical perspectives and practices of these four, we hope to convey a sense of the variety of particularly effective family therapy approaches and to encourage further reading and exploration of this area.

In the 1950s Gregory Bateson and others at the Mental Research Institute (MRI) developed a communication framework for working with families. Communication theorists in family therapy focus on the verbal and nonverbal interaction styles of family members. Notable members of this group include Watzlawick, Weakland, and Don Jackson, as well as Satir and Haley. Jackson, Satir, and Haley, as well as most other family systems theorists, share four core concepts:

1. Two major tasks are involved in the process of forming and maintaining a relationship; deciding *what* the rules of the relationship are and negotiating *who* actually makes the decisions regarding the rules.
2. The exchange of messages is accomplished through the task of setting rules and negotiating who has control over the rules.
3. The basic elements of the interactional process are the messages that form the substance of communications between people in the relationship.
4. Messages have two major aspects: the communication (content of the message) and the metacommunication (message about the message). The latter seeks to impose behavior or to define the self and the nature of the relationship.

Communication theorists attempt to understand the family by analyzing the communication and metacommunication aspects of their interactions. An outline of four approaches to family counseling is particularly useful for understanding how family therapists help families and youngsters at risk.

Virginia Satir. Virginia Satir, a social worker, believed that the emotional system of the family is reflected in the family's communication. She based her work with families on the concepts of maturation and self-esteem. Maturation is the process that results in taking full responsibility for one's choices and behaviors. Maturity is possible only when a person has high self-esteem, and self-esteem is expressed in family communication. Satir believed that people with low self-esteem often feel disillusioned and let down by their marriage partners. They are also unable to provide what their mate expects. They put pressure on their children to accomplish what they could not, but ambivalence about the children's success causes their messages to be confusing and incongruent. One or more children eventually develop a problem, which serves temporarily to unite the parents in an effort to deal with the behavior.

Satir usually met with the parents alone at first, then brought the children into subsequent sessions (Satir, 1967; Satir & Baldwin, 1983). She also worked with various combinations of family members in the course of therapy. One assessment technique she often used is the "family life chronology," an in-depth exploration of how the parents met, characteristics of their families of origin, the early days of the marriage, the births of the children, and current family dynamics.

Satir focused on teaching the family to communicate with clear and congruent messages. This goal is consistent with her view that dysfunction is rooted in the incongruence between communication and metacommunication. Self-esteem rises when the family is able to communicate feelings and ultimately results in healthy and congruent family interactions as well as maturation of family members. In addition to teaching communication skills directly, Satir devised a number of family games. Treatment is completed when

> family members can complete transactions, check, ask; when they can interpret hostility; when they can see how others see them; when they can see how they see themselves; when one member can tell another how he manifests himself; when one member can tell another what he hopes, fears and expects of him; when they can disagree; when they can make choices; when they can learn through practice; when they can free themselves from the harmful effects of past models; when they can give a clear message. (Satir, 1967, p. 176)

Satir stands out from other family therapists because of her emphasis on growth and self-esteem rather than on problem solving or symptom removal. Her emphasis on family history and on communications training also distinguishes her from other communication theorists. She was an active and directive therapist, relating to the family as a caring friend and teacher. Satir died in 1988, but her theories and methods continue to have a strong influence in the field of family counseling.

Jay Haley.   A communication theorist, Jay Haley also believes that relationships are defined by communication. Haley began his work with Bateson and the others at MRI. He believes that all relationships are characterized by power struggles, and the struggle is not for control of one by the other but for control of who defines the relationship. "Maneuvers" are messages that attempt to change (to control the definition of) the relationship. Haley is interested in learning how symptoms (the "individual" problems) maintain or challenge the power balance within the family system.

He begins therapy by defining a problem that is solvable and "discovering the social situation that makes the problem necessary" (Haley, 1976, p. 9). He views the problem as a sequence of acts between people, and his goal is to change those sequences and thereby solve the problem. It is the task of the therapist to identify the problem through observation of the family's interactions, including such behaviors as seating arrangement, control of the children, and who speaks most and least frequently. According to Haley (1976, 1984), the therapist does not share his or her observations with the family members. Therapy is oriented toward symptom removal, with no attempt to enhance insight. The therapist is responsible for change; the family is responsible for following the directives of the therapist. Thus, the therapist's role is that of a powerful expert who intrudes freely into the family interaction.

Techniques commonly employed by Haley are "paradoxical messages" and "prescribing the symptom." Paradoxical messages direct the family to do something that seems opposite to the stated goal; they are particularly useful with resistant families. For example, a family might be directed to refuse to cooperate during a session. The family has the choice of either cooperating (to maintain control vis-à-vis the therapist) or continuing their lack of cooperation and thereby give the counselor therapeutic leverage because they are following his or her directive.

The therapist who "prescribes the symptom" asks the family to continue their problem behavior, perhaps because "I don't yet understand it well enough." This technique is also beneficial with resistant families—to resist they must change their problem behavior. Haley also uses "relabeling," which consists of describing the problem behavior in such a way that it sounds positive. A therapist might relabel an adolescent's use of foul language, for example, as a creative way of directing her parents' attention away from her school performance. After establishing that this teen is creative and purposeful, the therapist can draw upon her creativity to devise more effective means of getting what she wants.

Haley focuses exclusively on solving the problem, which he defines as disappearance of the symptom. He plays the role of a directive and human expert without revealing himself personally to the family. In contrast to Satir, Haley is manipulative and controlling in his sessions, believing that no intervention should be spontaneous but must be carefully planned. Whereas Satir often took a careful history of the family, Haley focuses exclusively on the present. Both view diagnosis as unimportant, and both believe that it is essential to establish a warm and trusting relationship with the family. Although Haley and Satir share an emphasis on communication, Satir focused on changing the way people in the family interact, particularly in the expression of feelings, whereas Haley seeks to change the way the family fights over defining relationships.

Murray Bowen. In contrast to Satir, Haley, and other communication theorists, Murray Bowen focuses on the structural context of the family interaction. Structural theorists examine the organizational dynamics and boundaries both within the family system and between the family and the environment. Boundaries can be seen as a manifestation of the rules and regulations governing the system and separating the system from its environment. How the family regulates and modifies these boundaries is of prime interest to the family therapist with a structural orientation.

Bowen, a psychiatrist, developed his theory throughout the 1960s and 1970s. Two of his fundamental concepts are "differentiation of self" and "triangulation." Bowen (1978) postulates that a chronic high level of anxiety within a family causes tension to escalate. If unchecked, this tension eventually exceeds the capacity of the family's normal coping mechanisms, and a variety of family symptoms result. Differentiation of self is the individual's ability to discriminate between emotional and cognitive processes and to achieve independence from the emotional climate of the family. Highly differentiated family members can respond to conflict on a cognitive level, on the basis of conscious beliefs and values. The undifferentiated individual responds in an emotional and unstable manner. The greater the differentiation of self, the more effectively the family member can cope with anxiety. The failure of family members to differentiate is termed *fusion*. Fusion—that is, a low level of differentiation—is characterized by an inability to separate emotional from intellectual interaction; the person is vulnerable to being "sucked into" a family dilemma. Poorly differentiated family members are more likely to be part of a family triangle.

Triangulation occurs when the anxiety in a two-person system is more than the system can handle, and a third person is brought into the system to diffuse the tension. Triangulation is a specific type of enmeshment. Frequently, a child is caught in a tug-of-war between the parents. The resolution of the anxiety results in close identification (enmeshment) with one of the parents, and this dyad functions to exclude the other parent. Thus, a parent and child collude to exclude the other parent.

Bowen's primary goal is to help individual family members differentiate themselves from the "family ego mass." Because all operating family triangles interact, modifying even one part of a triangle will result in change throughout the system. Bowen attempts to de-triangulate the family by understanding which parts of the triangle are enmeshed and "undoing" them. He does so by arranging for two family members to interact with a third person (the therapist) who does not succumb to emotional maneuvers and thus forces the two to change. Bowen will even work with a single family member, because a change in any part of a triangle will change the rest of the family system. He minimizes the expression of emotionality and affect, modeling for family members a rational, cognitive communication style.

Bowen contends that the extent to which family therapists have achieved differentiation in their own family ego mass will determine their ability to avoid triangulation with the families with whom they work. His role with families is that of a calm, emotionally detached coach (Bowen, 1978; Kerr & Bowen, 1988).

Salvador Minuchin.   Salvador Minuchin, a psychiatrist, believes that individuals are shaped by the specific demands of their family as well as by the larger societal context. As a family moves through the stages of the family life cycle, it must change structurally to accommodate changing roles and tasks. Such adaptation occurs through renegotiation and modification of boundaries. Boundaries are the rules that define who participates and how they do so. Minuchin (1974; Minuchin & Nichols, 1993) describes three types of boundaries: enmeshed, disengaged, and clear. Clear boundaries fall between enmeshed and disengaged and allow for optimal functioning. Minuchin views family subsystem boundaries that are pervasively enmeshed or consistently rigid, especially those between the parent and child subsystems, as the primary basis for dysfunction.

Minuchin contends that there are four primary family stressors to which families respond with a range of functional and dysfunctional interactional processes:

- an external stress that affects one family member (such as conflict on the job)
- an external stress that affects the entire family (such as gang violence in the neighborhood)
- a developmental transition (such as the last child leaving for college)
- an idiosyncratic problem (such as the birth of a mentally retarded child)

Minuchin begins his work by joining the family and identifying the boundaries and transactional patterns within the family system and subsystems. The goal of therapy is to change the structure of the family so that it is more consistent with the developmental needs of its members. Minuchin works toward this goal by maneuvering the family into new transactional patterns, a technique that requires the therapist to become an active and controlling participant in the family system.

Some of the therapeutic techniques that Minuchin employs to restructure the family system are dramatic. He may deliberately increase the stress in the family in the course of a session to experience what the family is going through and to magnify the role that the symptom plays in maintaining family homeostasis. As he gains understanding of the family structure, he identifies points of entry for changing the balance. Minuchin sometimes deliberately escalates stress to the point of precipitating a family crisis; he then uses the crisis as a means of forcing the family to change. Another of his techniques is to present the family with a scenario and assign roles to the individual members. The roles require them to act out new patterns of behavior. Minuchin attempts to change the behavior patterns that support the symptom and to alter the sequences between family members, thereby restructuring the family system.

As a therapist, Minuchin is dynamic, manipulative, and controlling. He joins the family system, confronting and challenging family members in accordance with carefully constructed plans. Minuchin characterizes dysfunction as the inability to respond to stress through renegotiation of boundaries, whereas Bowen views dysfunction as a result of family members' failure to differentiate themselves. Bowen adopts a multigenerational perspective on dysfunction, whereas Minuchin emphasizes the effects of sociocultural factors on families. Both focus on the structure of the family and the maintenance of family boundaries.

Comparison of the four approaches.   Let us see how the four family therapists we have discussed might conceptualize the problem if the Carter family (of Chapter 3) came to them for family therapy.

Satir would focus on the Carters' patterns of communication. She might help Lois Carter recognize that her expressions of guilt in regard to her husband also convey anger and blame for Jason's school problems. While assisting Doug Carter to express his frustration with his wife and son, Satir would help him clarify and express the feelings of hopelessness, aloneness, and inadequacy that he experienced in his family of origin and that he continues to feel in his present family. She might also help him to become more clear and consistent about his expectations regarding Jason's behavior and in implementing a system of consequences for misbehaviors. With Jason she would emphasize the importance of his unique feelings and opinions, modeling for the others how Jason's anger, fears, and concerns are just as valid as everyone else's. Satir would help Christie express the fear and anxiety about the family tension that she hides beneath her "perfect child" exterior. She would relate to each of the Carters in a sincere, congruent manner, consistently modeling clear messages and encouraging the family members to be open and honest as well. As the Carters' self-esteem increased, their ability to take responsibility for their choices and behaviors would also increase. Their new means of communicating would help the family address tensions and difficulties in a healthier manner.

Haley would begin work with the Carter family by identifying the sequence of acts in which the family's problems are embedded. He would note the relationships among Lois's constant negative affect, lack of eye contact with her husband, fatigue, and refusal to ask for what she wants and needs; Doug's telling Jason, "If you . . . I'll . . ." without ever following through, his black-and-white view of Jason, the "bad one," and Christie, the "good one," and his sarcastic tone when he talks to his wife; Jason's feeble attempts to cheer up his mother, his belligerence toward his father, and his rapt attention whenever his parents interact; Christie's subtle teasing of Jason, her aloof primness when asked a question, and her fingernail biting. Haley would attempt to understand how these behaviors maintain or threaten the power balance in the family. He would view each symptom as a tactic employed by one person to deal with the others. He would see Jason's acting out as his way of defining his relationship with his parents: Jason sets the pace and they respond. Haley might direct Jason to continue to misbehave at school and at home and ask him to keep a log of each misbehavior and to note why he chose each behavior when he did. This use of symptom prescription gives Jason the choice of cooperating with the others, setting the stage for change, or resisting the therapist by reducing his symptoms. Haley would continue to use a variety of maneuvers with each family member until the symptoms abated.

Bowen would focus on helping each of the Carters to differentiate from the family ego mass and encourage their ability to separate emotionality from objective thinking. He would begin by assessing the degree to which objective thinking overrides emotionality and look for clear and well-defined boundaries between family members. Bowen might view Doug's anger at his wife and his feelings of inadequacy as overriding his cognitive knowledge of the importance of consistency and consequences in discipline. He might view Lois's guilty feelings partially as an indication of her inability to separate her own feelings and behavior from those of her son. The unexpressed anger between Lois and Doug is diffused and focused on Jason, with the result that Doug feels excluded by both his wife and his son. Bowen would step in and replace Jason as the "third person," but instead of allowing the tension to be diffused through him, he would help the couple express and explain their feelings to each other objectively. As the process of triangulation diminished, the members of the family would achieve a greater degree of differentiation.

Minuchin would acknowledge the sociocultural context in which the Carter family operates. He would conceptualize the problem in terms of two stressors: a developmental transition (Jason is entering adolescence) and an idiosyncratic problem (Lois is chronically depressed). The family's dysfunction is a result of their failure to renegotiate boundaries in response to stress. In light of the enmeshed boundaries between Jason and his mother and the lack of a defined parental subset, Minuchin might work to increase the strength of the parental subset by engaging Doug and Lois in tasks together. He might ask Jason and Christie to reverse roles as a means of unbalancing the homeostasis and creating an opportunity for change.

Although each of these family therapists takes a unique approach to the families that seek help, emphasis on the family as a system is common to them all.

ALTERNATIVES AND ADJUNCTS TO FAMILY COUNSELING

Some families referred for counseling refuse to follow through. Counseling may cost more than they are able or willing to pay. Family members may have had negative experiences with counselors in the past, or they may perceive the time commitment as too demanding. Underlying these reasons are a variety of others. Parents may be insecure about their child-rearing practices and fear exposure. Family members may be concerned that such issues as alcoholism, domestic violence, incest, and neglect will come to the surface. Often, these fears are expressed as: "We can deal with these problems alone," or "My family doesn't need some stranger getting into our business."

When the family declines counseling, the family system can still be changed. Counseling for an individual family member may improve the family system. Recall that the family as a system struggles to maintain homeostatic balance. The changes wrought by individual counseling can have a positive influence on the rest of the family. When one person changes, the others will usually try to change that person back to restore the system to its original state. If these efforts are unsuccessful, other components of the system must change to arrive at a new balance.

Interventions other than family counseling may be equally effective in modifying the family system, especially if the family dysfunction is not extremely serious. In such cases parent education, family support groups, and parent training programs have proved very beneficial and may be the interventions of choice (Alvy, 1994).

Parent Education

Teachers and counselors can often provide effective interventions in the form of psychoeducation. A few basic principles of parenting can go a long way to help parents be more effective. Other family-oriented programs designed to prevent chemical dependency and to teach parents behavioral management and discipline, sex education, nutrition, and family budgeting are reviewed in Kumpfer and Alvarado (1995).

The Premack Principle. The Premack Principle, or Grandma's Rule, is a relatively simple and highly effective guide that parents can quickly put to good use (J. J.

McWhirter, 1988). The Premack Principle tells us that "for any pair of responses, the more probable one will reinforce the less probable one" (Premack, 1965, p. 132). In other words, behaviors that youngsters are quite likely to perform (playing outside, riding a bike, watching television, talking on the telephone) can serve as reinforcements for those behaviors that they are less likely to perform (completing homework, drying dishes, caring for younger siblings, cleaning their rooms). As Grandma might put it, first you work, then you play. The parent's task is to identify what the child or adolescent likes or wants to do and then require that a less favored activity occur first: "Clean your desk, and then we can play a game." "Pick up the room before you go out to play." "Do the dishes before you watch television."

Application of the Premack Principle is most effective when parents break down tasks into subtasks (clean desk = put away all loose books and papers + put away all crayons, pens, pencils + dust desktop + water plant on desk) and reward the performance of each subtask. Frequent small rewards provide more effective reinforcement than infrequent large rewards. Parents should provide rewards immediately after the behavior is accomplished; and they should reward the behavior *only* after it occurs. This last point is very important. Parents will hear rationalizations ("But my show will be over by the time I finish the dishes!"), and they are guaranteed to hear many more if they give in to them.

Logical consequences. Setting up a system of logical consequences not only encourages children to take responsibility for their behavior but can greatly reduce the amount of arguing that goes on at home. Consider the Carter family (of Chapter 3). Doug Carter is unhappy with the fact that Jason stays up very late on weekends watching television. Because he stays up so late, he sleeps late the following morning, leaving his chores undone until the afternoon or forgetting them altogether. Jason's behavior is only one of the problems here; the other problem is that his behavior has no logical consequences. A logical consequence of staying up very late is to be quite tired when one is roused from sleep to do one's chores. By allowing Jason to sleep late, his parents condone his late-night TV habits. By requiring Jason to get up and do his chores no matter what time he went to bed, his parents would give him responsibility for deciding how late to stay up (reducing the likelihood of a "But I'm 13 years old!" argument) and still have the satisfaction of knowing his work is done (reducing the likelihood of a "You live in this house too" argument).

Parents once brought to us a 4-year-old who stubbornly clenched her teeth and refused to eat when she didn't like the food she was served. By the time her parents came for counseling, this behavior had evolved one step further—she threw her dinner on the floor when she was pressured to eat. In response, her parents were yelling at her, arguing with each other over what to do, cleaning up the mess, and providing her with an alternative food. At first, the parents were horrified when we informed them that the logical consequence of such behavior was to go without eating until the next meal. But finally they conceded that she really would not be harmed by her hunger pains and agreed to try this approach. Upon their daughter's next refusal to eat, they explained to her that if she threw her dinner on the floor, she would get nothing to eat until breakfast. When she promptly flipped her dinner to the floor, her parents were prepared. They didn't yell or argue or rush to clean it up. Instead, they calmly reminded her that it would be a long time until breakfast and finished their own dinner before attending to the mess she had made. She kept them awake most of the night with her tearful cries, but they didn't back down. Two evenings later she once again overturned her plate and endured the same logical consequence. She cried for only two hours that night. Two months later her parents reported that she had never again overturned her plate and was eating at least a small portion of everything they served her.

If logical consequences are to work, parents must be prepared to apply them without fail and consistently. Table 14.1 provides some sample behaviors and their logical consequences. Each consequence must be modified according to the severity of the misbehavior and the number of times the behavior recurs after consequences have been applied. If a child continues to leave toys about the house, for example, the parents may remove the toys for two or more days at a time. Children should always know the logical consequences of their misbehaviors and be informed when the consequences are changing. With older children, parents may draw up a contract that specifies, for example, rules for using the family car and consequences of failure to follow those rules. By signing the contract, families formalize the agreement and establish a clear standard of conduct.

Teachers and counselors may also assist parents by referring them to books and articles on parenting. Such literature offers parents the opportunity to refine techniques and strategies to enhance their parenting skills.

Parent Support Groups

The challenges faced by parents seem to increase daily. Each new generation of parents must deal with issues that their own parents never imagined. Your grandparents, for example, are unlikely to have had a son who wanted an ear pierced. Many of the underlying issues are the same, however, and are related to the movement through the family life cycle: dealing with stress, loss, and anger; problems of communication, discipline, and authority; and passing down values and traditions. Especially in light of the decline of the extended family network, a parent support group is an ideal way for parents to express their concerns and learn what other parents have experienced and attempted (Allen, Brown, & Finlay, 1992). It also allows parents to share the pain and

TABLE 14.1   Sample of logical consequences

Action	Consequence
Leaving toys out	The toys are taken away for one day; only one toy allowed out at a time
Talking on the phone too long	All calls are limited to three minutes for two days
Fighting over a bike	The bike is taken away for a day, and the children must play peacefully together for 30 minutes
Violating family curfew	The teenager must stay home the next evening or weekend
Stealing from a store	The child must apologize to the store manager; return the item; work to earn the cost of the item and give the money to the store, a church, or a charity organization

frustration as well as the joys and successes of raising children in the 1990s. Parent support groups are available through local churches, YMCAs, schools, counseling agencies, day-care centers, and workplaces. Many areas of the country also have local parent crisis lines or Parents Anonymous groups, which can provide information about parent support groups.

One parent support group that is active throughout the country is ToughLove. ToughLove is a self-help group for parents of teenagers who are uncontrollable, addicted, abusive, or otherwise in trouble with the school or the law. With more than 1500 groups, this organization provides ongoing support, assistance in crises, and referrals to professionals, as well as many practical ideas for helping teenagers stop their self-destructive behavior. Parents are encouraged to make their own plans for addressing their teenager's behavior. The group functions as a sounding board, a source of suggestions, and a backup support team. One ToughLove mother we know enlisted the help of other ToughLove parents in planning a constructive confrontation with her drug-abusing daughter. One of the other couples provided an alternate place for the daughter to stay for a week in case she decided she could not stay with her mother after the confrontation. The same mother had just posted fliers for a ToughLove parent in another part of the country whose runaway son had been seen locally. Further information about ToughLove can be obtained from the organization itself. The address and phone number are in Appendix A.

Alateen and Al-Anon Family Group (see Appendix A for addresses) are broad-based teen and family support groups that operate throughout the country. Teens or families of alcoholics meet together much like the members of Alcoholics Anonymous. Participating teens and families learn about alcoholism and are helped to achieve a loving detachment from the alcoholic, to increase their self-esteem and independence, and to rely on a "higher power." By sharing common problems, members of alcoholics' families discover that they are not alone and that they have the ability to cope with their situation.

Parent support groups can provide invaluable information and support for parents who feel hopeless, angry, and alone in dealing with the problems of their troubled children. ToughLove, Alateen, and Al-Anon provide support for family members who may feel trapped in an impossible situation (see Box 14.3). These are only three such groups; there are literally thousands of others. There are support groups for parents of children with problems ranging from spina bifida and cerebral palsy to manic-depressive psychosis and schizophrenia. Teachers and counselors can assist families by keeping informed about these resources and by encouraging families to contact local chapters of these support groups. (Refer to Appendix A for more information.)

PARENT TRAINING

Often, the behavior that brings a family to the attention of a teacher or a counselor can be addressed through parent training (Alvy, 1994). For example, the parents of a student who is acting out sexually may shy away from discussing sex, birth control, and sexually transmitted diseases. The parents of a student who doesn't turn in homework may lack a consistent system for monitoring school progress. The parents of a student who is belligerent and aggressive may have lost control of their child. Each of these issues and many others may be effectively addressed by a classroom format in which parents are

Box 14.3

Mother Gets a Head Start

When her first child was 4, she shyly volunteered to help out in the classroom. Just for an hour. Over the weeks it became two and three hours, and she even started looking children in the eyes. She was quiet, worked very hard, and seemed quite bright in a clandestine kind of way. When her next child turned 4 a year later, she was working on her GED. Her home, she told me, had been a smelly, dirty shack; her children were always barefoot and always hungry. When they weren't hungry, it was because she had given them change for candy bars and pop. "I weighed 250 pounds and I was still growing," she said, laughing. "I was disgusting even to me." And she had bruises, and permanent nerve damage in her left hand, and a husband who got mean when he drank.

She had bruises on her arm the first time I met her, and a welt under her eye, and she had been a Head Start teacher's assistant for three months. She was bringing her youngest to work and taking home a paycheck for the first time since she got married at age 18. Her husband didn't much like it, but he had a little more beer money now. He really got mean when she insisted on cooking carrots one night. For the first time, she pressed charges. One incredible year, 82 pounds, and a divorce later, she was considering a community college course, "so I can be a teacher someday." And several years after she left Head Start, I heard she had done it.

educated together on dealing with specific aspects of their children's behavior. Parent training may be a prevention measure as well as a treatment approach. We first focus on those parent training approaches that are specifically geared to ethnic minority parents and then conclude with Parent Effectiveness Training (Gordon, 1970, 1977).

Vulnerable and Underserved: Ethnic Minority Parent Training

An important focus for the teacher, counselor, or parent-trainer in getting acquainted with the family is perceiving cultural and ethnic considerations and appreciating their meaning to the family. Expectations regarding child behavior and accepted modes of child discipline often vary among groups, but cultural stereotypes must be avoided. Nevertheless, teachers, counselors, and psychologists should be sensitive to the implications of particular backgrounds. The following parent programs have been developed for specific ethnic minority groups (Bickel & Ertle, 1991; Pines, 1991).

The Effective Black Parenting Program. The Effective Black Parenting Program, developed by the Center for Improvement of Child Caring, is most appropriate for African American parents with children ages 2 to 12. The program contains 15 two-hour sessions; each session includes a review, demonstration, role playing of skills, and homework assignments. Parents are taught a variety of management strategies, including African American self-discipline, the family rules guidelines, effective phrase and verbal confrontation, time-out, and the point system. The importance of African heritage and pride and the courage and strength of African American families are continually reinforced.

The program is intended to foster effective family communications, healthy African American identity, extended family values, child growth and development, and healthy self-esteem.

Black Parenting Education Program.   The Black Parenting Education Program is a comprehensive, competency-based, culturally relevant parenting program designed to meet the needs of young, high-risk African American parents. It is designed to address issues of nurturing and raising children from an African American perspective and is intended for economically and educationally disadvantaged parents of high-risk students who lack the skills, motivation, and self-confidence necessary to raise children successfully.

The focus of this curriculum is to teach young parents how to care for children ages 0 to 6 by systematically preparing them for a successful school experience. It is based on the concept that by empowering African American families parents can raise children who are competent individuals.

Positive Indian Parenting.   The Positive Indian Parenting curriculum is a practical, brief, culturally specific training program to help Native American parents explore and apply the values and attitudes expressed in traditional Native American child-rearing practices. Parents are helped to develop positive and satisfying values, attitudes, and skills that have roots in Native American cultural heritage.

Because there is no one child-rearing tradition among Native Americans, the curriculum draws examples from numerous tribes and is designed to be adapted to fit various tribal cultures. It does, however, build on universal values, attributes, and customs that include the oral tradition, storytelling, and the role of the extended family. The curriculum consists of eight sessions, each with specific learning objectives. Each session is designed to take two or three hours.

Family effectiveness training.   Szapocznik and his associates (1986a, 1989) present a prevention model for Hispanic families of preadolescents who are at risk for drug abuse. This program is based on the premise that intergenerational family conflict related to the acculturation process may exacerbate existing maladaptive patterns of interaction in families and contribute to drug use. It is one of only a few *empirically tested* programs that directly address cultural differences. The three components of family effectiveness training (FET) are designed to change maladaptive interactional patterns and to enhance the family's ability to resolve intergenerational and intercultural conflict.

The first component, family development, helps the family to negotiate their children's transition to adolescence. Family members learn constructive communication skills and take increased responsibility for their own behaviors. Parents develop the skills to direct their children in a democratic rather than an authoritarian style. This component also includes drug education for the parents so that they can effectively teach their children about drugs.

The second component, bicultural effectiveness training (BET) (Szapocznik et al., 1984, 1986b), is designed to bring about family change by temporarily placing the blame for the family's problems on the cultural conflict within the family and by establishing alliances between family members through development of bicultural skills and mutual appreciation of the values of their two cultures. Through BET the family learns to handle cultural conflicts more effectively and reduces the likelihood that they will occur. BET is itself an excellent parent training program of obvious value to families of nonmajority cultures.

The third component of FET is brief strategic family therapy, based on the work of Salvador Minuchin (1974). This is the most experiential aspect of this didactic/experiential model. The FET therapist meets with the family for 13 two-hour sessions. The FET model may be modified to deal with issues other than drug use.

Los Niños Bien Educados. This program was also developed by the Center for Improvement of Child Caring specifically for Hispanic parents. This cognitive-behavioral program fosters positive family communication, healthy Hispanic American identity, child growth and development, and healthy self-esteem. It is designed to play a role in the prevention and intervention activities in community efforts to overcome high-risk behavior in children and adolescents.

The program focuses on one of the dominant goals Hispanic parents often have in carrying out their parental functions: raising children to be academically, socially, and personally well-educated. It emphasizes child management skills, family meetings, effective praise, problem assessment, time-out, increasing respectful behaviors, and other approaches. Los Niños Bien Educados consists of 12 three-hour training sessions with a suggested group size of about 15 to 20 parents.

Parent Effectiveness Training

Parent effectiveness training (PET) (Gordon, 1970, 1977) is a method of parent training based on two principles stressed by the psychologist Carl Rogers: unconditional positive regard, and empathy. A fundamental premise of the method is that everyone in the family can "win," with power negotiated and shared by parents and children. Although the program was originally designed for parents of problem children, parents of well-functioning children have enrolled across the country in increasing numbers. The PET program teaches parents skills in confrontation, conflict resolution, active listening, and giving "I" messages. Training provides parents with an opportunity to practice and refine those skills throughout the sessions. These skills enable parents to communicate more effectively with their children and to resolve problems constructively. PET parents are able to apply these skills to their children with positive effects for the entire family (J. J. McWhirter & Kahn, 1974).

Gordon's program has also had an impact in training school personnel (Gordon, 1974) and businesspeople (Gordon, 1977). These effectiveness training approaches are designed to enable people to attain their goals without being overpermissive or overcontrolling and without bribing or forcing people to do it a specific way.

A PET training course is typically 24 hours in duration, ordinarily presented in eight weekly three-hour sessions, although variations in the schedule often occur. Brief trainer presentations, group discussions, audiotapes, dyads for skill practice, role playing, workbook assignments, and textbook reading are among the training methods used.

Gordon (1989), who continues to develop new applications for his core ideas, emphasizes several major dimensions of parenting for which his prevention method is proposed.

Problem ownership.   In all relationships, particularly parent-child, PET parents are taught that problems are "owned" either by the parent or the child; that is, the individual is responsible for performing and for changing these behaviors. Other people in the family may find a given behavior undesirable from their point of view. In PET, parents are taught to analyze problems by attaching ownership of responsibility to them. "Who owns the problem" is of critical importance. The adult must be able to decipher the situation, because a particular response is called for depending upon who owns the problem. If the adult "owns" the problem, a particular set of skills is employed. If the child "owns" the problem, another set of skills is used. If the child and the adult mutually "own" the problem, still another set of skills is used. The first job of the adult, then, is to define just who does own the problem.

When the child owns the problem, he or she is blocked from satisfying a need; however, the behavior does not interfere with the satisfaction of the parents' needs. When the parent owns the problem, the child is satisfying his needs and by so doing interferes with the satisfaction of the parents' needs. The relationship is said to "own" the problem when both the child and the adult directly affected are in conflict about the situation.

To determine who owns the problem, adults ask themselves who will reap the results of the problem in some tangible way. Thus, the adult asks the question, "Do the results of the problem tangibly or directly affect my ability to meet my own needs?" If so, the adult owns the problem. If not, probably the child owns the problem. If both the parent and the child are directly affected by the results of the problem, it is mutually owned "by the relationship."

One of three different communication skills is used, depending on problem ownership: active listening when the child owns the problem, sending "I" messages when the parent owns the problem, and mutual problem solving when both own the problem.

Active listening.   Active listening is used if the adult determines that the child owns the problem. The purpose of active listening is to communicate a deep sense of acceptance and understanding to the child. The listener tries to understand what the child is feeling and what the message means by putting that understanding into words and checking back with the sender. For example, a parent speaking to a distraught child who has just come home from a day at school might say: "Sounds like you think your coach is mean to you." Child: "Well, not mean exactly. It's just that he keeps yelling at us in practice."

In active listening the adult listens with empathy to the child's feelings about the problem. Communication involves more than just the words exchanged between people. The affective and emotional dimensions of the communication process are reflected in eye contact, tone of voice, and body movement. The parent employs a technique of listening that allows the child to confirm that the parent really does understand what is being felt and that the parent is "with" him. When the child talks more about his feelings, amplifies his thoughts and feelings, goes from surface to in-depth feelings, or fully expresses the feelings that are at the heart of the problem, the parent knows that the child is moving toward the desired goal, being freed from the emotion of the problem, understanding it, and therefore being able to deal with it on his own. After active listening has occurred, the child may begin to suggest his own solutions. This is a sign to the parent that the child has approached the goal of solving his own problem. Sometimes active listening helps the child accept an unchangeable situation, giving the child a chance to get his feelings out and experience acceptance for them.

Active listening is accomplished by parents who go out of themselves in search of significant clues emitted by the child. The active listener is receptive to all nuances of the child's personality and expression and truly works to understand the child's message. The active listener goes even further than this. The proof of good listening lies in the way the adult responds to the child. Active listening requires getting inside the child, viewing the world through the child's eyes, and communicating that understanding back to the child. The parent must respond to the words that the child uses as well as to the feelings that lie behind the words. The following examples demonstrate this skill.

CHILD: Guess what, Mom? I made the basketball team.
PARENT: You're really feeling great about that.
CHILD: I am!

CHILD: (crying) Tommy took my truck away from me.
PARENT: You sure feel bad about that. You don't like it when he does that.
CHILD: Yeah.

CHILD: Boy, do I have a lousy teacher this year. I don't like her. She's an old grouch.
PARENT: Sounds like you are really disappointed with your teacher.
CHILD: I sure am.

In each of these illustrations, the parent has accurately understood and communicated feelings—what was "inside" the child. The child in each case then verified the accuracy of the parent's understanding by some expression indicating "You heard me correctly."

Detrimental to active listening is the parent's frequent manipulation to control the child. Parents also too frequently begin active listening at first to open the door but subsequently slam it shut because their own attitudes get in the way or because of lack of time. Interference also occurs when parents simply echo back a message to the child without trying to understand it, or when they send a message back that is devoid of empathy.

Active listening is not an appropriate skill at all times. Sometimes a child just wants information. Then, giving him information is the appropriate response. When there is lack of time because of the press of other duties, active listening is not useful. Most of all, active listening is inappropriate when the parent "owns" the problem.

Sending "I" messages. When the parent determines that he or she owns the problem—that is, his or her needs are directly and tangibly affected—several options are available. The parent can modify the environment, him- or herself, or the child, directly. With younger children, changing the environment often promotes a change of the child's behavior, thereby solving the adult's problem. Such changes may include enriching the environment or simplifying it as well as substituting one activity for another. It is helpful to prepare older children for changes and to help them plan ahead for such shifts in the environment or upcoming events.

To limit serious conflicts, a parent can change him- or herself. If parents can grow to accept themselves and satisfy their own needs, they don't need to achieve gratification through their children to feel they are people of worth. If parents can believe that children are separate from themselves, they are bound to be more accepting of the children. They can better accept their children by letting them be themselves and by liking them all the time, not just when they behave like the kind of children they value. Of course, this implies liking the child although some of the behavior is unlikable.

Finally, the parent can seek to modify the child directly. Sometimes this is accomplished by spanking or some other form of corporal punishment; sometimes it is accomplished by another type of punishment. The problem with punishment is that it is often not very effective and can lead to avoidance or escape. Even if the punishment does stop the annoying behavior, the child may resent the adult, and the child's self-esteem may be negatively affected. Adults often choose verbal punishment. Frequently, this takes the form of derogatory or put-down statements, which are sent in "you" message form (that is, "you are lazy"; "you are a bad person"; "you are a pest"). Unfortunately, messages of this nature are often just as bad as physical punishment. In addition to lowering the child's self-esteem, they also communicate only part of the message and are thus inexact.

In contrast to ineffective "you" messages, a simple "I" message is the most powerful tool in confronting a child. In an "I" message the adult clearly expresses to the child the problem and the feelings about the problem, letting the child know that the adult owns the problem. Often, the child is willing to modify behavior based on the adult's feelings. An "I" message is less apt to provoke rebellion and resistance, and it places the responsibility on the child for changing behavior. The following examples demonstrate the contrast between "you" messages and "I" messages.

"YOU" MESSAGE: You didn't do your chores this morning. You are really a lazy kid.
"I" MESSAGE: I'm angry because you didn't do your chores, and I had to do them after you left.

The focus is on the problem of the chores and not on the character or personality of the child. The parent's feelings of annoyance and anger are not openly shared in the "you" message; the anger is clear in the "I" message.

"YOU" MESSAGE: You are a pest. You're always interrupting your mother and me when we are talking.
"I" MESSAGE: I get frustrated with you because Mother and I can never finish a conversation without your interruption.

The "I" message communicates the parents' feelings, puts responsibility on the child for the behavior, and does not lower the child's self-esteem.

By sending an "I" message, the adult anticipates that the child will understand the adult's problem, respect his needs, and discontinue acting in a negative way. Frequently, an "I" message is adequate for modifying the child's behavior. Occasionally it is necessary to follow the "I" message with a change in the environment. For example, after communicating frustration at being interrupted, the father could require the child to leave the room so that he and the mother might finish their conversation. Modifying the parent's own attitude by allowing the child to participate in the conversation or by talking with him at a later time may be necessary for less conflict. Sometimes mutual problem solving is necessary.

Mutual problem solving. Frequently, conflicts arise between adults and children because both are tangibly affected by an interaction. Mutual problem solving is employed when it is determined that the needs of both the child and the adult are being blocked by a problem.

Too often, solutions to problems and conflicts occur in one of two ways, both of which are based on a power struggle: (1) The adult wins and the child loses; (2) the child wins and the adult loses. In both situations, one person goes away feeling defeated and usually angry. In the first instance, the child is denied opportunities to develop self-discipline and inner-directed responsible behavior. In the second solution, children learn to manipulate others, which encourages them to be selfish, and leads to difficulty in social adjustments.

Gordon (1970) recommends the "no-lose" method whenever adult and child encounter a conflict-of-needs situation. Essentially, the adult requests that both participate in a mutual exploration for a solution to the conflict. A solution acceptable to both creates a "no-lose" situation for both the adult and the child. Gordon's six problem-solving steps are:

1. *Identify and define the conflict.* It is important to determine if the disagreement is actually over the issue at hand. Perhaps the conflict is really over a different matter, and the current problem reflects another concern. Both parent and child need to be clear on the conflict.
2. *Generate possible solutions.* Both adult and child need to indicate as many alternative solutions as possible.
3. *Evaluate the alternative solutions.* Once the partners have mentioned potential solutions, their effectiveness needs to be critically evaluated. Both the adult and the child have to decide which solutions they can live with.
4. *Decide on and get commitments for the most acceptable solution.* Both must agree to commit themselves to the solution, possibly modifying their own behavior.
5. *Work out ways of implementing the solution.* The adult and child must decide who is going to do what, and when it is to be done. Both must agree on the practical, concrete issues.
6. *Follow up and evaluate how the solution worked.* After some time has elapsed, it is important to review the solution to determine satisfaction with it.

This method avoids the detrimental side-effects of other approaches. By engaging the child in the process of mutually solving the problem, both parent and child are able to fulfill their needs. Thus, conflicts can be resolved in a healthy manner that builds a mutually satisfying, friendly, deep, and intimate relationship.

Effective parenting derives from a philosophy in which respect for the child is uppermost. This means respecting individuality, uniqueness, complexity, idiosyncratic potential, and capacity for making choices. Effective communication between adult and child is expressed through cognitive, affective, verbal, and nonverbal modes. Useful parenting requires open communication that is encouraged and facilitated by a nonthreatening atmosphere. The preceding skills help create this climate. Of course, these skills are just as important to the effective teacher or counselor as they are to parents (Gordon, 1989), which is why they are included here.

CONCLUSION

A systems framework is a realistic and viable way to view the problems of troubled children and adolescents. Individual interventions too often provide only partial solutions. All young people live in a montage of overlapping systems: families, schools, neighborhoods, larger communities, the nation. Family therapists address the family as a system to change dysfunctional patterns of behavior and communication.

Parent education, parent support groups, and parent training are alternatives and adjuncts to family counseling. Counselors, teachers, and other helping professionals can be of invaluable assistance by providing these services themselves or by helping families gain access to such programs.

FURTHER READINGS

In addition to those books and articles cited in the reference section, the following books may be useful to readers wishing to know more about interventions to help at-risk families.

Becvar, D. S., & Becvar, R. J. (1996). *Family therapy: A systemic integration* (3rd ed.). Boston, MA: Allyn & Bacon.

Glenwick, D. S., & Jason, L. A. (Eds.). (1993). *Promoting health and mental health in children, youth, and families.* New York: Springer.

Kagan, S. L., & Weissbourd, B. (Eds.). (1994). *Putting families first: America's family support movement and the challenge of change.* San Francisco: Jossey-Bass.

McAdoo, H. P. (1993). *Family ethnicity: Strength in diversity.* Newbury Park, CA: Sage.

Sherman, R., Shumsky, A., & Roundtree, Y. B. (1994). *Enlarging the therapeutic circle: The therapist's guide to collaborative therapy with families and schools.* New York: Brunner/ Mazel.

Walsh, F. (Ed.). (1993). *Normal family processes* (2nd ed.). New York: Guilford.

Weber-Stratton, C., & Herbert, M. (1994). *Troubled families–problem children: Working with parents: A collaborative process.* Chichester, England: Wiley.

CHAPTER **15**

EDUCATIONAL INTERVENTIONS

When children are taught
Not merely to know things
but to know themselves

Not merely to achieve
but how to help others to achieve

Not merely to know facts
but how to think and reason

Not merely how to do things
but how to compel others to do things

They may be said to be truly educated.
And the result of a child's education is what is left
once all that was learned is forgotten.

J. J. McWhirter

280

CHAPTER OUTLINE

The Diaz children (of Chapter 4) face many of the social, educational, and economic problems typically encountered by at-risk students. Ramona is unable to discuss issues with her classmates and must work to help support her family. Carlos is having difficulty in class and is misunderstood by some of his teachers. Lidia is in danger of being retained. All the Diaz children are considered to be second-language learners (that is, their first language is not English), and all have some problems with self-esteem.

In this chapter we focus on specific areas of school and classroom interventions designed for at-risk students such as Ramona, Carlos, and Lidia. First, we discuss programs designed to meet the needs of all such students that can be implemented throughout the school. We then document classroom practices that help meet the needs of students at risk—interventions that can be implemented by a single teacher and that are valuable in combating the problems of youth at risk.

EDUCATIONAL PROGRAMS: COMMON FEATURES

Literally thousands of school programs have been designed to improve education, many specifically for the at-risk population. Successful programs have several features in common (Cuban, 1989), and these features coincide with those that experienced teachers have found to be effective with at-risk students.

One feature of successful programs is their small size. A student population of between 50 and 100 fosters enduring relationships among adults and students. Also, students enrolled in a small program are more likely to participate in school activities.

Another feature is inclusion by choice. Many successful programs are staffed by people who have volunteered to participate in them. The teachers, administrators, and district officials involved are highly committed to helping students at risk who are willing to experiment with new ideas.

A third feature common to successful programs is flexibility. Nontraditional educational and problem-solving approaches are usually employed because the goal is to assist students who are not learning effectively in their present situation. Successful programs also tend to be flexible with respect to individual needs and time frames, and enlist the support of social services as the occasion requires.

Closely related to small size, self-selection, and flexibility is a view of the school as a community. That is, small, flexible programs tend to promote a sense of belonging. Such programs consciously seek ways to develop self-esteem through a caring, extended-family atmosphere (Cuban, 1989; Wehlage, 1991).

A final feature of successful programs is involvement of the community outside the school. Many successful programs enlist the help of community members, parents, and business leaders. The involvement of these people helps young people identify and adapt to positive adult norms and expectations. It also links the school program with the parents and the community, thus increasing social capital. We would add one other feature to this list. Many successful programs provide general and focused training in life skills as either prevention, early intervention, or treatment (see Chapters 11 and 12; Dryfoos, 1994; Durlak, 1995; O'Hearn & Gatz, 1996).

SCHOOLWIDE INTERVENTIONS

All of the intervention strategies discussed here are designed to offer support to students at risk for school failure. Because the kind of support students need varies with their ages and developmental levels, separate programs are tailored to fit students in elementary, middle, and secondary schools. The type of program required by Allie Andrews and Ramona Diaz, both teenagers, differs considerably from a program appropriate to the needs of Denise Baker and Christie Carter. With their special needs, students with disabilities require still other sorts of programs. Finally, all programs need to be culturally relevant for ethnic minority students.

Elementary-Level Interventions

Because serious academic problems can occur early in a student's career, it is not uncommon for middle school students to drop out of school before many at-risk programs even begin. In fact, teachers in the primary grades often can identify students who will be at risk of failing high school (see Slavin, Karweit, & Wasik, 1994, for a summary and a review). Schools must provide intervention programs at the elementary level. Such interventions focus on parent involvement, small class size, development of language skills, and specific educational strategies.

The Student Development Program (SDP) developed by Comer (1996) for elementary schoolchildren emphasizes language skills and improved teaching in all disciplines, applies learning to everyday situations, and uses both cooperative learning groups and peer tutoring techniques. Parents are encouraged to interact with school personnel and to provide assistance for their children. The school day is extended to provide physical and arts activities, in which adult volunteers work with students one-on-one. A unique feature of the Comer SDP model is the mental health team designed to attend to the affective and social needs of children (Winfield & Millsap, 1994).

Some interventions are tailored specifically for the primary level (that is, kindergarten through third grade). The Success for All program was initiated to provide immediate and intense prevention. The best available classroom program, along with parental support, includes, among other things, one-on-one tutoring, small classes, and a family support team (Slavin, Karweit, & Wasik, 1994).

Another elementary-level intervention, School to Aid Youth (STAY) (Peck, 1989), is aimed at creating a positive attitude toward school and building self-esteem, thereby increasing at-risk children's ability to learn. This pull-out program serves first grade students identified as being at risk during their year in kindergarten. Project STAY allows for one-on-one tutoring and small classes (approximately ten students) and for intensive reading and math instruction. Communication between teachers and parents is stressed. Because this program has been in operation for 17 years, some long-term effects are known. A ten-year longitudinal study demonstrated that 80% of the STAY graduates were performing at or above grade level. The key to these results is the program's goal of building on students' successes.

At this level, counselors and psychologists should implement life-skills preventive programs that are designed to reach all children. Consistent and effective communication with families, including parent training, is particularly important. Finally, providing a link between the school, the home, and the larger community for family counseling and other services is critical. Denise and Jerome Baker, Christie Carter, and Lidia Diaz would be well served if they were offered such support.

Students with Disabilities

The incidence of students with disabilities who drop out of school is significantly higher than that for students without disabilities (Diem & Katims, 1991), yet relatively few research studies have focused on students in special education classes who are at risk of school failure. This issue is best addressed as a schoolwide concern. Schools are under increasing pressure to excel academically. As a result, special education students may be shunted aside. Schools must recognize their obligation to students with disabling conditions; indeed, the Individuals with Disabilities Education Act (IDEA) and Americans with Disabilities Act (ADA) make it mandatory that they do so.

Potential dropouts should be identified early, and positive intervention should begin immediately with remedial programs, extensive interpersonal counseling, and reevaluation of individual education programs for their relevance and effectiveness in the lives of special education students.

Middle-Level Interventions

The needs of young people at the middle school level vary as widely as the rates at which they are developing. In a typical pre–high school classroom, some students may be banging their desks with their pens and reciting a rap while others groom themselves with hairbrushes and apply makeup. One student might be trying to shoot the lead for a mechanical pencil into the air with a hypodermic needle. Many will be absorbed in passing, reading, and writing notes to classmates. Some students stand 4 feet 10 inches and others are 6 feet tall. They read everything from comic books to the *Wall Street Journal*. Some are able to solve difficult geometry problems; others have trouble with whole numbers. One 13-year-old may still play with dolls, and another may be a mother already. Students at this age go through dramatic physical changes in a short time. The obvious differences in physical attributes are matched by even greater mental, emotional, and social differences (A. M. McWhirter, 1990).

Some interventions have been designed to meet the varied needs of at-risk students in this age group—that is, before they enter high school. The interventions at this level focus on teachers who work together as a team with a specific group of students. The emphasis is on the relationships between students and teachers.

The middle school was devised to meet the special needs of students in this age range. Middle-level education is not a new concept in the United States. Schools "in the middle" (that is, between elementary and high school) have been around since 1910. However, there are fundamental differences between middle schools and junior high schools. In fact, the goals of true middle schools tend to be related directly to the at-risk population.

Several factors led to the emergence of middle-level schools in this country. Enrollment increased in the 1950s and 1960s, just at the time when schools were attempting to eliminate racial segregation. Of equal importance was the obsession with academic achievement brought about by the launch of the Soviet space satellite Sputnik in 1957. Criticism of American schools in the wake of the Soviets' spectacular achievement in space led to an interest in specialized high school courses. An intermediate school for grades 5 through 8 promised to strengthen instruction by allowing a specialist in some subject area (biology, say, or mathematics, or French) to work with these younger students. Junior high school was born.

There is a difference, however, between junior high schools and the middle school trend that is currently sweeping the country. Junior high schools essentially function as miniature high schools—"junior" high schools. A true middle school, however, is meant to function as a bridge between elementary school and high school. Activities and programs are oriented toward and appropriate for students who are in transition from childhood to adolescence. Further, the concept of the teacher team is an important component of the middle school. Teams of teachers working with a group of students can adjust their homework and testing schedules, provide better teaching strategies, and build a learning community more effectively. The middle school is one way to meet the varied needs of young adolescents and help students who are at risk for school failure.

The programs of middle schools are designed to meet the needs of students who are maturing at widely varying rates. In a true middle school, students are grouped in accordance with their developmental level, not their chronological age (as in an elementary school) or the area of study (as in a junior high or secondary school). Neither grouping by chronological age nor by area of study takes account of the extreme differences among students in this age range.

The emphasis of the middle school curriculum is on exploration rather than skills (as in the elementary grades) or depth (as in junior high and secondary schools). A focus on exploration enables teachers to tailor their instruction to fit their students' developmental level. It helps to validate students' interests, which builds self-esteem, and it provides for a smooth educational transition from elementary school to high school.

Interdisciplinary teams of teachers can focus more readily on the students themselves than can the lone teacher in an elementary school classroom or the teachers organized in departments in a junior high or secondary school. Many middle schools schedule a period when teams of teachers can meet to prepare their strategies. The role of the teacher in a middle school is that of an adviser, not a parent, as in an elementary school, or strictly an instructor, as in a junior or senior high school. Carlos (of Chapter 4) could benefit if his teachers became advisers as well as instructors. If his teachers were to work together as an interdisciplinary team, they could discuss individual students and could learn more about Carlos's situation—and perhaps could find better ways of addressing his needs. The social studies teacher and the bilingual teacher have already begun to collaborate on their own initiative. The school counselor has also begun to provide the support his teachers need. The structure of the middle school would enable all of Carlos's teachers to meet as a team and work together to help him and other students.

Because of its organizational structure and curricular focus, the middle school provides a particularly fertile environment for counselors. Counselors can effectively implement an early intervention program that provides training in life skills as a component of the school's instructional offerings. Training in communication skills, for example, can be included in the language arts class. Training in refusal skills can supplement a health unit on the effects of tobacco, alcohol, or other substances. Goal-setting skills can be added to every part of the curriculum (see Chapter 12). When teachers work in interdisciplinary teams, they can collaborate on ways to incorporate such training in their own areas of academic instruction.

An example of this is our CAP program (J. J. McWhirter & Santos de Barona, 1995). CAP stands for Cross-Age Peers and involves eighth grade students at Percy E. Julian and Caesar Chavez schools in the Roosevelt School District (Phoenix, Arizona) who are trained in a variety of helping skills: cross-age tutoring, peer teaching, conflict resolution, peer mediation, and individual and small group facilitation. These older students then support, mentor, and tutor younger students—mostly fifth and sixth graders. They also visit classrooms to deliver lectures on social competency life skills, resistance and refusal approaches, and the unhealthy consequences of tobacco, alcohol, and other substance use. This program has been quite beneficial to the younger students in the two schools, and we have evidence to support the positive changes that have occurred for the older students (Lane-Garon, 1997).

Middle school counselors need to develop programs that serve as a transition from the elementary school to the high school. They need to coordinate the efforts of the school and the family. The parent training programs discussed in Chapter 14 are very pertinent to the role of the middle school counselor. Counselors can be of particular help by consulting with teachers in their team-building efforts. A true middle school organizational structure with the components we have identified would help Carlos Diaz, Jason Carter, and Paul Andrews succeed at school.

Secondary-Level Interventions

Many interventions at the high school level focus on ways to get students through school. Most emphasize support systems designed to help students overcome certain obstacles (such as poverty or large class size) and to accumulate credits. Their ultimate goal is to increase the graduation rate of these students. Because of the age of the student and the imminent risk of withdrawal from school, most of these approaches are directly related to the school dropout problem (discussed in Chapter 6). A large number of programs were developed and reported on in the late 1980s, and many continue to be used through the 1990s.

Project AVID (advancement via individual determination) is one such program (Swanson, 1989). Project AVID, a four-year elective credit class, is designed specifically for minority and economically disadvantaged high school students. Participating students receive instruction in writing concurrently with advanced university preparation courses. Students are encouraged to think about what they are learning in their classes, to write down any questions they may have, and to discuss them in their AVID class period. The experiences as well as the education of AVID students are enriched by the involvement of all segments of the community.

A program designed to intervene with at-risk students at one high school is called RAD (Responsibility and Determination) (White, 1989). Low-achieving students who choose to participate are instructed in study skills and are tutored on immediate assignments. If they need financial support for school activities, they receive it. The success of the RAD class is attributed to the students' commitment to the program and to the consistency of requirements for remaining in the class. Small class size is also instrumental in RAD's success.

The Young Adult Education Program (YAEP), designed to help at-risk high school students who are working, offers evening academic courses for high school credit (Davis, 1989). Students who complete the program receive a high school diploma rather than a GED. The program differs from a regular high school in its flexibility. Classes are offered on a quarterly basis to allow for easy entrance to and exit from the program. Class size is generally low (from 5 to 15 students). Teachers treat students as adults but still enforce the program rules. By providing a respectful relationship between student and teacher, by insisting that students take responsibility, and by allowing for flexibility in class size and scheduling, YAEP gives dropouts and students at risk for dropping out a needed second chance to graduate from high school.

At the secondary level, intervention programs focus on alterable school conditions. They emphasize flexibility in regard to course requirements and grading systems, school climate and culture, support from teachers and administrators, teacher-student contact strategies, and instructional approaches, as well as provisions for vocational and school-community educational programs (Cohen & de Bettencourt, 1991). School counselors and psychologists in particular need to develop and implement training in the life skills that specific young people need (see Chapter 12). School mediation programs (Lane & McWhirter, 1992, 1996), peer and cross-age tutoring and peer facilitation/leadership programs (Tansey, Santos de Barona, McWhirter, & Herrmann, 1996), small-group counseling, and coordination with community agencies and support programs for specialized treatment, job training, and mentorship are extremely important for intervention at the secondary level. Counselors, teachers, and administrators need to identify school conditions that are alterable and work to modify those conditions. Both Ramona Diaz and Allie Andrews could profit from many of the features of such programs. Unfortunately, no such program is available to them, and they are likely to leave school without the skills necessary to compete in a technological society, whether or not they stay to graduate.

INTERVENTIONS AT THE CLASSROOM LEVEL

Alongside schoolwide interventions are classroom practices that can be undertaken by a single teacher, perhaps with counselor or psychologist support. Among them are direct instruction, language acquisition and holistic approaches, metacognitive learning strategies, second-language interventions, and moral discourse. An especially important classroom intervention is cooperative learning. We highlight it in the following section, with special attention to the development of peer support networks.

Direct Instruction

Direct instruction is a technique currently used in many schools. This is a form of teaching that provides teachers with a highly structured method of presenting information to students (Hunter, 1991). Direct instruction is based on the belief that necessary skills can be broken down into subskills, which are then taught directly. The student's performance on these subskills is then practiced, observed, and evaluated. Because direct instruction provides teachers with a way to structure their lectures on a topic, teachers can evaluate their students' performance with relative ease. The approach has also been suggested as a useful strategy for at-risk students (McLaughlin & Vacha, 1992). For these reasons, direct instruction has become quite popular.

Some researchers (Gersten & Carnine, 1984; Rosenshine, 1986; Stevens, Slavin, & Farnish, 1991) indicate that direct instruction results in gains in students' academic performance. A longitudinal study that tracked the progress of two groups of low-income children who received direct instruction, one from first through third grades and the other from kindergarten through third grade, found that direct instruction produced positive effects in achievement and graduation rates years later (Gersten & Keating, 1987). Other researchers found that a carefully sequenced direct instruction program in kindergarten generated student gains in total reading and math scores. Third and ninth grade students were still above grade level after being in such a program (Carnine, Silbert, & Kameenui, 1990; Silbert, Carnine, & Stein, 1990).

Direct instruction has not escaped criticism. Some critics maintain that the effects of direct instruction dissipate if students are left on their own (Gersten & Keating, 1987). Others claim that direct instruction in the early grades is harmful to students' performance in high school, and particularly to their social behavior (Schweinhart, Weikart, & Larner, 1986). Berg and Clough (1990–1991) recommend that before direct instruction is used teachers should give careful thought to both their students and their objectives. They claim that direct instruction is more effective in some teaching situations and with some students than with others.

Perhaps the problem is that direct instruction is teacher-centered and oriented toward large groups. Some critics (Rigg, 1990) maintain that such educational practices reinforce the mug-and-jug view of education: The teacher is a jug containing knowledge, and students are empty mugs waiting to be filled. Moreover, direct instruction can represent a teacher's attempt to control the students' behaviors (by monitoring and insisting on attention and persistence) rather than encouraging students to control their own behavior. Such efforts are of limited effectiveness, particularly with students who have difficulty exercising self-control and whose behaviors cause problems for themselves and for other students.

Language Acquisition and Holistic Approaches

Another argument against the use of direct instruction alone stems from research on language acquisition (that is, observations made as children are first learning to speak). Language educators and researchers have resisted the idea of dividing subject matter into subskills to be taught and tested (Edelsky, 1991; Edelsky, Altwerger, & Flores, 1991; Hudelson, 1989). They maintain that language is one subject that must not be broken down to isolated bits and pieces. When it is, it is no longer language because it no longer conveys meaning.

Children all over the world learn their native language by interacting with others in natural settings. It was once widely believed that parents actually taught their children language, perhaps by pointing to a book and saying "Book. Book. Say it, book." Research, however, indicates otherwise (Plunkett & Marchman, 1993). Indeed, children do not generally receive feedback on the form or syntactical structure of the things they say. Parents focus instead on the meaning of the utterance. Verbal approval of a child's statement ("That's right," "Very good," "Yes") is contingent on the accuracy of its content, not on the correctness of its form. Parents voice approval of such statements as "He a girl," uttered in reference to the mother and "Her curl my hair," spoken as the mother curls the child's hair. But parents express disapproval ("That's wrong," "No") of statements that are grammatically correct but factually wrong: "There's an animal farmhouse," when the building is a lighthouse, or "Walt Disney comes on Tuesday," when the program airs on another day of the week. These observations indicate that parents do not provide direct instruction of language to their children. They do not "teach" their children how to use language. Instead, children learn it as they use it (Pinker, 1991).

Research on language acquisition yields several insights into the learning process that are particularly valuable to teachers of at-risk youth. This research suggests that children experiment with language in their efforts to convey their meaning. For example, 3-year-old Jerome Baker (Chapter 2) said that his preschool teacher was in her classroom "desking." Jerome was using a word form that he had never before encountered. His utterance was original and apparently invented. Furthermore, it indicates a logical hypothesis. When one uses a mop, one is mopping; when one uses a desk, one must be desking.

Marcus (1996) found that these hypotheses become more and more refined as children develop. That is, children use many adult forms early on, only to abandon them for less adult forms before eventually reverting to the adult forms they used originally. At first, for example, a child uses adult irregular verb and noun forms: came, went, ran, men, feet. Later the child substitutes overregularizations: comed, goed, runned, mans, foots. Later still the child goes back to the appropriate forms, indicating that she or he has refined his or her hypotheses enough to be able to distinguish between regular and irregular word forms (Pinker, 1991).

There is evidence that the acquisition of written language parallels the acquisition of oral language. Bissex (1980) reports that her 5-year-old son began to use the conventional "s" to indicate a possessive. For example, he wrote PAULS GABJ (Paul's garbage) and PAULS TALAF ONBOOTH (Paul's telephone booth). The next week he wrote PAULZCIDERMUSHEN (Paul's cider machine); his explanation was that "it sounds more like a z-z-z" (p. 10). Eventually he returned to the standard "s" form for possessives. Children overgeneralize the rules for noun and verb forms when they learn to write just as they do when they are learning to use language orally.

What does all this have to do with children at risk for school failure? The majority of at-risk children have learned to speak some language before they enter school; so it is logical to assume that something about that learning process has been successful. Perhaps children who are at risk of difficulties in learning other kinds of skills (particularly reading) could be helped greatly if educators identified the elements that enabled them to learn to speak initially, and then incorporated similar elements in their teaching practice (Serna & Hudelson, 1993).

Several basic principles have emerged from research on language acquisition that are helpful to classroom teachers. First, children learn their native language in natural, interactive community settings. Therefore, teachers must make learning in the classroom as natural as possible. They must set up communities in their classrooms within which children can interact trustingly as they try out the new skills they are acquiring.

Children learn to speak by using language to meet their needs; language is functional. Students in the early grades should be provided with the opportunity to use language to fulfill genuine purposes rather than merely to complete workbook pages of language exercises at their desks. A native speaker of English who wants to describe a frog that is both green and big, for example, will say "the big green frog," not "the green big frog." No thought goes into the formulation. How many English speakers are aware of the rule that in English, adjectives of size come before adjectives of color? Precious few. And it's doubtful that most native English speakers who faithfully follow that rule learned to do so by reciting it over and over, or by doing worksheet after worksheet. Instead of doing workbook pages, children can be recording their observations from a science project in a notebook, or writing a letter to their teacher or classmates. Here the purpose of the writing is genuine. The child has a need to communicate through written language, much the way a younger child uses oral language to communicate a message.

Finally, children experiment with language as they use it. Teachers must hold such experimentation in high regard. A young child who says "And then she goed to the store" has hypothesized that "ed" is attached to the end of a verb to indicate that the action took place sometime in the past. The child's message is clear, and most adults find such language forms charming. Yet when analogous hypotheses are evident in written language, the charm quickly evaporates. If a child writes "sed" for "said," we ignore the process (the hypothesis that *said* rhymes with *bed* and therefore must be spelled similarly) and pronounce the *product* wrong. Rather than react negatively, teachers, administrators, and counselors should regard such experiments positively. Teachers can identify the language rules a child has already developed and adjust their curriculum accordingly. All school staff must have faith in school-aged children. More important, they must communicate this faith to the students and to their parents.

These principles apply to other areas of the school curriculum as well. Teachers can help children to manipulate fractions by setting up a genuine problem for them to solve (say, doubling or halving a recipe). Science experiments and projects can be structured around things the children are curious about. Having a class list all the things the children want to learn about during the coming month or semester helps to pique their interest and motivate them. Now their activities in science, social studies, and language arts have a meaningful purpose. This practice also provides an opportunity for students to learn new ways to communicate with each other and solve problems within the classroom community. These principles also apply to students with learning disabilities (Keefe & Keefe, 1993).

Teachers need to think about the things they do. They need to ask themselves whether the activities they expect students to engage in make sense. They need to evaluate whether their curriculum is relevant to the real lives of their students.

Metacognitive Learning Strategies

One consistent difference between academically successful and unsuccessful students is their awareness of their own learning strategies. Many at-risk students are unaware that their learning strategies are limited or ineffective. Another way for teachers to intervene in the learning process is to teach successful learning strategies to at-risk students.

A learning strategy is a plan for merging cognitive skills and metacognitive ability in the process of acquiring information (Cohen & de Bettencourt, 1991; Zigmond, 1990). This educational approach is closely related to the training in cognitive skills discussed in Chapter 12. Here students are taught to observe, monitor, and think about their learning strategy or plan.

Cognition is thinking. Cognitive skills are the steps necessary to perform a specific thinking task. Carrying or borrowing a number to solve a math problem, for instance, is a cognitive skill usually learned in elementary school. Metacognition is thinking about thinking. Thus metacognitive strategies allow students to monitor their cognitive skills in arithmetic when they work on that math problem. Lenz (1992) and Shapiro and Cole (1994) provide reviews, discussion, and examples of interventions.

Students, especially poor students, must be taught strategies in metacognition. The older children are, the more effectively they apply cognitive strategies. Children's awareness of their cognitive strategies is correlated with enhanced performance on reading measures. That is, children who can describe the thinking processes they use as they read are able to comprehend more than students who cannot. Duffy and his colleagues recommend that teachers model their own mental processes to stimulate metacognitive skill in their students (Duffy, Roehler, & Hermann, 1988). The purpose of instruction in metacognitive strategies is to increase students' awareness of themselves as learners, place students in control of their own learning activity, and provide them with a method to use to improve their own learning. Instruction in metacognition is a worthwhile tool for confronting problems of children at risk of school failure.

Reciprocal teaching is a similar learning strategy that is successful with poor learners. To implement this strategy, the teacher and a small group of students talk about the texts they read. The students take turns being "teacher" and practicing the four components of reciprocal teaching: They (a) generate questions about the content of the reading material, (b) summarize the content, (c) clarify points, and (d) predict future content on the basis of prior knowledge or clues within the text. Reciprocal teaching has improved achievement of low achievers (Lysynchuk, Pressley, & Vye, 1990; Palincsar, Ransom, & Derber, 1988; Rosenshine & Meister, 1991), providing the experience of success for students with learning problems.

Interventions for Second-Language Learners

Students who are at risk for school failure and dropout typically have low self-esteem and lack control (Jessor, 1991, 1993; Mruk, 1995). Logically, students who are weak in English-language skills have low self-esteem and feel a lack of power or control. Among these students are children whose first language is English but whose dialect differs from the English used in the schools. In fact, what to most of us is a "dialect" is a "language" to a linguist (Hudson, 1980). Therefore, whether the child speaks Spanish, Korean, or African American English, the effect is the same: The child essentially must operate in a foreign language in school (see Box 15.1). Weakness in school language can be a

■ ■ ■ Box 15.1
Bilingual African Americans

African American students who succeed in school learn to function in two languages—the language of school, and the language of the home and street. Maya Angelou discusses this issue in her brilliant autobiography, *I Know Why the Caged Bird Sings* (1969). In the process she reveals not only an acute awareness of second-language problems but also a fine awareness of her own metacognition. In school, she writes,

> we all learned past participles, but in the streets and in our homes, the Blacks learned to drop s's from plurals and suffixes from past tense verbs. We were alert to the gap separating the written word from the colloquial. We learned to slide out of one language and into another without being conscious of the effort. At school, in a given situation, we might respond with "That's not unusual." But in the street, meeting the same situation, we easily said, "It be's like that sometimes." (p. 191)

tremendous barrier to success in social relationships and schoolwork. As we indicated in Chapter 5, academic success and social relationships are both related to self-esteem.

Students who fall two or more grade levels behind their peers are more prone to dropping out. Children who must learn English as a second language spend so much time learning the language of instruction that they fall behind their same-age peers in content areas. Indeed, many students who are at risk of school failure are ESL or bilingual students (Watt & Roessingh, 1994).

Webster's Ninth New Collegiate Dictionary defines *bilingual* as "using or able to use two languages esp. with equal fluency," but this is not a practical definition for students in bilingual classrooms. One college class of graduate-level teachers, a number of whom work in bilingual settings, generated the following list of terms to define bilingual students:

balanced bilingual	limited proficiency in English
multicultural	oral fluency only
oral monolingual	regional oral fluency
literate monolingual	culturally deprived
limited language proficient	

This list has some obvious flaws, but in the educational setting, *bilingual* often connotes deficiency. Students who fit into this educational niche are seen as having limitations not only in English-language skills but in language skills in general. They are often seen as deficient in culture rather than being admired for the richness of skills they have acquired by learning two languages. Perhaps if we called them ESL students or second-language learners, bilingual might regain its positive connotation.

Earlier we identified several warning signs that signal school failure (see the checklist in Chapter 6). Unfortunately, many of the items in that list coincide with learning a second language. For example, lack of proficiency in English may cause second-language learners to have difficulty relating to their peers. Students' performance may not reflect their ability simply because of their language difficulties. If students are denied the opportunity to learn material in their first language, they are likely to fall behind in school. Clearly second-language learners may be at risk of school failure simply by virtue of their language situation.

Several programs have been devised to meet the needs of second-language learners who are at risk of school failure. Some of these programs include counseling approaches (peer facilitation, using teachers as advisers, parent counseling, student hotlines, group counseling); incentives to encourage attendance, achievement, and healthy social interactions; work-related approaches (career education, collaboration between the business community and the school, career fairs); and alternative curriculums (schools without walls, environmental programs, theme or magnet schools).

Because students with low proficiency in English are more likely to drop out of school, the proportion of dropouts whose first language is not standard English will increase considerably in the next several years. Ironically, it is the minority population that is on the upswing. Very soon people of color will be in the majority, especially in diverse states such as California (Banks, 1997). Thus, the portion of the youth population that is increasing most rapidly is also the one most at risk for dropping out of school.

Moral Discourse

Up to this point, we have focused on interventions that aid students who are at risk of failing in school. As we indicated in Chapter 4, classroom teachers view "risk" primarily from an educational perspective. A third grade teacher who works with at-risk students, for example, is concerned mainly with enabling them to succeed academically even though they may also be at risk of teen pregnancy, drug abuse, delinquency, or suicide. Strangely, all these social problems seem less important than academic success, perhaps because the teacher's job is to ensure that his or her students reach the objectives set forth by the school district's curriculum director. Yet teachers can implement another intervention that addresses the needs of students who are at risk of more than just academic failure. This intervention is moral discourse.

Moral education and values education are complicated issues. Parents and educators alike generally agree that everybody should be morally informed about both negative and positive moral imperatives. That is, one should not lie, cheat, steal, or kill; one should help the poor and the sick. In fact, educators as far back as John Dewey (1916, 1944) have expressed concern about positive social characteristics and values, such as social adjustment, cooperation, and democracy. Educators and parents are also concerned with children's ability to apply moral reasoning in making decisions.

Values education is similar to moral education. Values education teaches various types of values (social, political, religious, aesthetic), whereas moral education is generally concerned with justice. Students are helped to reason about justice and to see that morality lies in giving as much weight to the interests of others as to their own interests (Lickona, 1991).

Controversy arises when education in morality and values turns into inculcation of any group's particular morality and values. Citizens of a democratic and pluralistic society rightly shun such "education." A distinction must be made between personal morality and general morality. Personal morality consists of personal values and beliefs and is formed by family orientation, religious commitment, and individual perspective. Teaching personal morality in the public classrooms of a pluralistic society is simply not acceptable. General morality, however, always involves universal human principles. The United States Constitution with its Bill of Rights provides clear statements of universal human principles that need to be taught to children. Wilson (1993) suggests that four innate concepts provide a universal moral platform: sympathy, fairness, self-control, and duty. Although cultures may vary on how the values attached to these traits are applied, these concepts can be found across all cultures—and most Americans believe that they should be taught.

The practice of moral discourse teaches children to judge justly and act morally; the practice activates Wilson's (1993) four traits. Moral discourse consists of conversation about a situation that involves a moral choice. The morality involved is minimal at the outset but becomes maximal as the conversation progresses. In the course of moral discourse, a child learns to develop his or her own point of view while considering and respecting the viewpoints of others. In line with our national ideals of democracy, this approach reflects solid educational practices that meet the needs of students at risk because it encourages them to use higher-order thinking skills in making decisions.

COOPERATIVE LEARNING AND PEER SUPPORT NETWORKS

The practice of grouping students by their ability to learn, as determined by some objective measure, has a negative impact on the children in low-ability groups, and it tends to reinforce initial inequalities (Barr, 1992; Berliner & Biddle, 1995). Teachers treat high-ability groups differently from low-ability groups. Students in low-ability groups have been found to receive fewer opportunities to answer analytical questions, to be given less time to respond, and to receive less praise than the students in high-ability groups. These students begin to think little of their own ability. Overall, current research points to ability grouping as a practice with decidedly negative effects for children in low-ability groups.

Still, teachers are frustrated by the wide range of skills and abilities they confront in heterogeneous classrooms. Cooperative learning groups are one solution to this problem (Johnson & Johnson, 1988, 1989a; Slavin, Karweit, & Wasik, 1994). Cooperative learning is implemented in various ways. First, it can vary in task structure. In some programs, students work independently on a task that has been divided up. In others, students work on the task as a group. The latter format encourages peer tutoring (see Chapter 13) and a truly cooperative learning environment. Second, cooperative learning can vary according to incentives. For example, the group's grade or reward may be the sum or average of the individual members' performances, or it may be contingent on the product that the group as a whole has produced. In most cooperative learning implementations, students work in small, heterogeneous groups (usually numbering between four and six) and are rewarded according to the group's performance.

Cooperative learning groups also have the potential to provide at-risk students with a peer support group. In this section, we present cooperative learning groups as a major intervention approach, and we discuss the deliberate adaptation of them to augment a peer support network.

■ ■ ■ Box 15.2

Getting Smart

One teacher recently experimented with cooperative learning groups. She joined two children of middle ability with one child of high ability and one of low ability for a social studies project. They worked together cooperatively on the reading material. When they were finished with their project, she quizzed each child on the material.

The next day, when the low-ability child received his score on the test, he looked perplexed and said, "I'm not this smart." The teacher smiled and replied, "I guess you must be." She decided to continue to organize cooperative learning groups in her classroom.

Positive Effects of Cooperative Learning Groups

Cooperative learning has several aims. First, a cooperative model is a healthy alternative to an individual competitive model. Individual competition can have devastating effects on the motivation of at-risk students. Membership in a successful group permits students to experience success with all its attendant advantages—perceptions of themselves as able to perform well, satisfaction in their performance, and the esteem of their peers—regardless of each student's personal individual performance. This experience is of particular benefit to at-risk students who have known few academic successes (see Box 15.2).

In cooperative learning groups, students are encouraged to help and support one another rather than to compete. As in most athletic activities, individual excellence is encouraged because it benefits the whole team. Both high- and low-ability children profit from the experience. The low-ability children benefit from the assistance of their peers, and the high-ability children achieve a higher level of understanding after providing that assistance. Incidentally, high-ability students in cooperative learning situations, compared to those in individualistic competitive ones, demonstrated higher achievement on factual recall and high-level reasoning measures and had higher academic self-esteem and greater cohesion (Johnson, Johnson, & Taylor, 1993).

Cooperative learning increases academic performance (Stevens & Slavin, 1995). Whether students are questioning factual information, discovering new concepts, or solving problems, a cooperative learning approach has been shown to develop academic skills. Students, especially those from diverse linguistic and cultural backgrounds, make significant academic gains compared to student gains in traditional settings. Classroom interaction with peers offers students many chances to use language and improve speaking skills, especially important for ESL students.

Cooperative learning encourages active learning. Extensive research and practice have indicated that students learn more when they are actively engaged in discovery and in problem solving. As students talk and reason together to solve a problem or complete a task, they become more involved in communicating and in thinking. These activities automatically engage a child in an active way that is quite different from the passive listening and learning required by most approaches.

Cooperative learning prepares students for work in today's world. Team approaches to problem solving, individual efforts to accomplish group goals, interpersonal harmony, and the work setting are all valued skills in today's society of interdependent workplaces. Cooperative learning teaches students how to work together and builds students' social nature, social understanding, and personal efficacy.

Finally, cooperative learning groups provide an opportunity to improve race relations in the school. Students who work together in cooperative learning groups are more likely to value mixed racial and ethnic acquaintances and friendships. Students develop a respect for diversity, including greater acceptance of students with physical and learning disabilities. When students cooperate to reach a common goal, they learn to respect and appreciate each other. Ms. Basset, Carlos Diaz's social studies teacher, is working toward this goal by placing her students in cooperative learning groups. As her students of different ethnic backgrounds work with each other, prejudice diminishes. Consequently, Carlos is now establishing friendships with other students. Dividing a class into interracial learning teams reduces prejudice by undercutting stereotypes and encouraging group members to pull together (Costa, 1991). Davidson and Worsham (1992) have found that cooperative learning groups are particularly beneficial for African American, Hispanic, and other ethnic minority students. Many minority cultures embed strong values of group interaction and cooperation, and cooperative learning builds on these home and community experiences. Any strategy that improves intercultural relations in the school ultimately enhances such relations throughout the society and into the future.

Cooperative learning takes numerous forms. Programs are known by names such as Learning Together, Group Investigation, Team Assisted Individualization, Student Teams-Achievement Divisions, Teams-Games-Tournaments, and Jigsaw (Devries & Slavin, 1978; Johnson & Johnson, 1988, 1989a; Sharan, 1994; Chap. 2 of Slavin, 1983, provides a complete review of these cooperative learning methods).

Cooperative learning programs have demonstrated positive affective outcomes that directly address the needs of at-risk youth: motivation, peer support, self-attributions, and self-esteem (Slavin, Karweit, & Wasik, 1994; Stevens & Slavin, 1995). After 25 years of research, the evidence is impressive supporting the claim that cooperative learning groups enhance academic achievement; increase positive self-esteem, internal locus of control, altruism, and perspective taking; improve intergroup relationships between students without and with disabilities, as well as the relationship between students of different minority groups; and provide positive peer support. Because they entail positive peer support, cooperative learning groups seem to be a natural education reform to promote feelings of connectedness among students at risk of dropping out or those who have other social and emotional problems. The potential to increase social capital and pro-social peer influence are especially important in cooperative peer learning groups.

Peer Support Networks

In earlier chapters, we cautioned against the potential negative influence of peer groups (see Chapters 4 and 13). Peer clusters can be for better or for worse. Grouping students together because they share a problem may increase interaction, mutual support, and camaraderie, but it can also have other unwanted effects: Positive peer models and influences on academic performance and behavior may be drastically reduced; negative peer modeling may escalate; the entire group may perform according to anti-adult and anti-social norms. Nevertheless, to be successful, classroom interactions must foster caring communities in which students feel they belong and where they believe they are supported by teachers and peers.

To increase their positive impact and to minimize their potential negative influence, we propose that cooperative learning groups be formed deliberately to increase the socioemotional supports for students. In this regard, we are following the suggestion of Meyer and her colleagues (Meyer & Henry, 1993; Meyer, Williams, Harootunian, & Steinberg, 1995) with which we have had independent success. By purposefully and deliberately designing peer support networks, high-risk students are provided with positive peer support, which promotes feelings of connectedness among them and other students and with the school. High-risk students are not identified in any formal or obvious way, but they are put in situations where they can maintain relationships with peers who provide positive models of academic performance and behavior. In this way, peer support networks are accessible to students regarded as being at risk. They also form a natural structure for psychoeducational support groups recommended by Morganett (1990, 1995) and O'Rourke and Worzbyt (1996).

In developing peer support networks, several steps are useful. Various predictor variables are utilized to identify students at risk. The checklist in Chapter 6 for identifying dropouts, especially the success issues category, can be useful here. Also, the five Cs of competency (see Chapter 5) can be used to help identify students with pro-social attributes.

After students have been identified, the teacher, counselor, or psychologist deliberately structures around each of these students a cooperative learning group that can also function as a peer support network. Figure 15.1 shows a classroom grouping form that can be used to structure peer support networks. Students with the greatest support needs are targeted, and their names are put in one of the five slots in each cluster. If at all possible, only one high-risk student is included in any single group. Attempts should be made to avoid putting together individuals who form friendship bonds that are a negative influence on academic motivation, school achievement, and behavior. The other four students in each peer support network cluster should be chosen with the intent of making the group as heterogeneous as possible with regard to gender, race, ability, and achievement (for example, European American, Hispanic, and African American; female and male; one low, one high, and three average achievers).

For each cooperative learning peer support group, include at least one student who is generally on-task in group activities and, if possible, one student who is a peace-keeper diplomat. Also, include at least one group member who might be a potential friend to the student at risk. Ideally, students in the peer support cooperative groups would be very much like the student at risk with an important exception—the potential friends are positive influences. Try to avoid individual personalities that may create negative group combinations. For example, two physically aggressive, volatile students may create a potentially explosive group; or timid or quiet students may be manipulated or intimidated by "macho" boys.

These peer support cooperative learning groups should stay together for their class cooperative learning activities for at least a 9- or 12-week grading period. Although modifications may need to be made when group combinations are not working, the intent is to put together high-risk students with less risky students to provide a peer support network.

Group 1			Group 2		

Group 3			Group 4		

Group 5			Group 6		

FIGURE 15.1   Peer support network form: Classroom grouping

After formation of the groups, it is important that the students engage in cooperative learning activities to help the interaction and mutual interdependent collaboration. In a recent study (Bassett, McWhirter, & Kitzmiller, 1997), we found that teachers who reported a commitment to cooperative learning groups were not really using the method. Many teachers believed that they were implementing cooperative learning when in fact they were missing its essence. Structured cooperative learning among students is more than just putting students into groups to learn. Students sitting together at the same table and talking with each other is not cooperative learning. Having one student do all the work on a group report and others in the group putting their name on it is not cooperative learning. Students who finish a task early and help slower students complete it is not cooperative learning.

Johnson, Johnson, and Holubec (1990) have identified five basic elements that are essential to cooperative learning groups: positive interdependence, individual accountability, face-to-face promotive interaction, social skills, and group process. Slavin's elements are very similar, although structured somewhat differently. Slavin (1991) also adds a sixth element: group's accountability/rewards. He argues that awards accruing to the whole group are useful and powerful in building the prestige and power of the cooperative learning group.

Positive interdependence. Students are linked with others in such a way that one cannot succeed unless the other members of the group succeed and vice versa. Goal interdependence, role interdependence, shared rewards, dependence on each other's resources, and a distributed division of labor help ensure positive interdependence.

Individual accountability. The performance of each individual student in the group is assessed and the results are reported back to the student and to the group. Randomly selecting one student's work to represent the entire group or randomly asking one group member to explain a problem, solution, or concept are ways to accomplish this element. Students need to know that they can't "ride" on the backs of others.

Face-to-face promotive interaction. This element exists when students assist, help, support, and encourage one another's efforts to learn. Discussion of strategies and concepts, explanations of how to solve problems, teaching knowledge, and making connections between past and present information fulfill this requirement.

Social skills. Working cooperatively requires specific social and interactional skills. Leadership, communication, trust building, decision making, and conflict management skills are necessary components of effective cooperative learning groups. As we have made clear elsewhere in this book, these skills have to be taught just as purposefully and precisely as academic skills. Many students have never had an opportunity to work cooperatively in a group before, and they need the social skills to do so.

Group process. Monitoring and discussing the interactional process of the groups is necessary. Students need to become aware and be encouraged to maintain effective working relationships in their groups and to consider whether they are achieving their goals. Group maintenance, feedback about participation, and other process issues need to be developed.

To develop and increase group cohesion, productivity, and interaction, ask the cooperative learning group members to respond to these two questions after each session: What was something that each member did that helped the group today? What can each person do at the next meeting to make the group better? The ten minutes that this processing takes provides feedback for members on their collaborative skills, allows the group to focus on group maintenance, and reminds students to use their collaborative skills consistently.

Cooperative learning groups that are deliberately structured to provide a social support network can change the way young people experience school. The social support network provides high-risk students with systematic opportunities to develop positive interaction patterns and to form friendships with peers who have been carefully selected as potential supports and friends based on personal, cultural, and social characteristics. Teaching social skills, critical thinking, and academic content is integrated in the context of group support.

CONCLUSION

Schools can intervene effectively in the lives of at-risk students in many ways. Programs can be implemented at all levels of the educational structure—elementary, middle, and secondary. Intervention can be organized within a single classroom, a whole school, or an entire district. Discussion in classrooms allows for practice in language skills and in making decisions, as well as for tolerance of others' ideas and refining students' individual views and decisions. When children are allowed to work cooperatively in small groups, such discussions are likely to take place. When the language spoken in a student's home is recognized, valued, and used to build further learning, the student is more likely to succeed academically. When students are provided with a classroom community that encourages them to discuss their work with others, accept one another's viewpoint, weigh their options, and make decisions on the basis of reasoning, the educational setting is meeting the needs of students who are at risk of failure.

FURTHER READINGS

In addition to those books and articles cited in the reference section, the following books may be useful to readers wishing to know more about educational interventions for high-risk students.

Adams, D., & Hamm, M. (1994). *New designs for teaching and learning: Promoting active learning in tomorrow's schools.* San Francisco: Jossey-Bass.

Comer, J. P. (Ed.). (1996). *Rallying the whole village: The Comer Process for reforming education.* New York: Teachers College Press.

Evans, I. M., Cicchelli, T., Cohen, M., & Shapiro, N. P. (1995). *Staying in school: Partnerships for educational change.* Baltimore: Paul H. Brooks.

Koplow, L. (Ed.). (1996). *Unsmiling faces: How preschools can heal.* New York: Teachers College Press.

Mohrman, S. A., Wohlstetter, P., et al. (1994). *School-based management: Organizing for high performance.* San Francisco: Jossey-Bass.

Sharan, S. (Ed.). (1994). *Handbook of cooperative learning methods.* Westport, CT: Greenwood Press.

Williams, J. A. (1994). *Classroom in conflict: Teaching controversial subjects in a diverse society.* Albany, NY: State University of New York Press.

CHAPTER 16

LEGAL ISSUES

Robert J. McWhirter

Attorney at Law, Assistant Federal Public Defender, District of Arizona

> *Federal law, state statutes, court rulings, civil codes, administrative procedures, ethical codes. . . . When two or more stretch out like railroad rails or telephone lines reaching perfectly parallel to an infinity point in the distance, the choice and the decision are easy. But sometimes two or more are like a pair of scissors—so joined they seem not to be separated, yet seemingly moving in opposite directions— punishing anyone who comes between.*

J. J. McWHIRTER

Chapter Outline

To work with at-risk youth is to be at the cutting edge of society's problems. The cutting edge of society's problems is also the cutting edge of the law. In this chapter we review legal issues of concern to teachers, counselors, and other human service professionals (whom we refer to as *practitioners*) as they work with at-risk children, adolescents, and their families. Because this book has a variety of audiences—teachers, counselors, psychologists, social workers—each with its own code of ethics, we do not focus directly on ethical issues unless they have legal ramifications.

We deal first with general issues of criminal and civil liability that relate to work with at-risk youth. Then we focus on specific legal considerations related to the at-risk categories of substance use, sexuality, delinquency, and suicide. We also consider legal aspects of work with families because they present particular complications. Finally, we list do's and don'ts for avoiding both criminal and civil liability.

The Legal System

Although a complete discussion of the American legal system is beyond the scope of this chapter, examining the rudiments of the law may help to clarify some issues. Generally, the law is divided into two broad categories: criminal and civil.

Criminal Law

Criminal cases are the ones most often seen on television and in the movies. Although the issues can be interesting, their relevance to most of us is often exaggerated. However, practitioners and teachers are beginning to be held criminally liable for failure to report suspected child abuse to authorities. We will discuss this in detail at the end of this section.

General criminal law.   Criminal law is rarely a major concern to practitioners, as their work seldom confronts them with criminal liability. However, it is illegal to contribute to the delinquency of a minor, and it is possible for a practitioner with good intentions to run afoul of someone's idea of what constitutes a contribution to a minor's delinquency (Hopkins, 1989; Hopkins & Anderson, 1985). Prosecution of a teacher or mental health professional for such "contributions," however, is not likely.

Practitioners could face criminal charges for contributing to the delinquency of a minor if they provide drugs to a youngster. Suppose an adolescent such as Jason Carter (of Chapter 3) was using a drug as a form of self-medication and the practitioner, hoping to build a better relationship, facilitated his access to the drug. In the past, pharmacists and osteopaths who prescribed dangerous drugs for minors have been convicted of contributing to their delinquency (*People v. Brac*, 1946; *State v. Tritt*, 1970). The best legal advice is obvious: Do not provide illegal drugs to anyone.

Perhaps the most obvious situation in which a practitioner could be accused of contributing to the delinquency of a minor is in the sexual realm. Moral and ethical considerations aside, states across the country are increasing the legal penalties for sexual liaisons with underage persons.

The child abuse quagmire.   Every state has mandatory child abuse reporting laws (Walker, 1990). Indeed, the U.S. Congress has passed its version of a child abuse reporting law for those practitioners who work on federal land or in a federally operated or contracted facility (Crime Control Act of 1990). In general, these laws require health care and educational professionals to report suspected child abuse; the federal law even requires commercial film and photo processors to report evidence of child abuse.

The extent of a practitioner's duty to report suspected child abuse varies from state to state. Some states require abuse to be reported no matter how long ago it may have occurred. Others have time limitations. The Andrews family (of Chapter 1) might represent a reporting issue of this kind. If Allie Andrews confided that her natural father, John Meadows, had sexually abused her, in some states this admission might create a duty to report the abuse, even though it occurred years earlier. Practitioners must consult the laws of their own state to find the precise definition and their legal responsibilities. State and local professional associations may well have this information prepared.

Most state laws require reporting child abuse of which a teacher or practitioner has "reasonable suspicion." What constitutes reasonable suspicion is often left to the individual state court, legislature, or practitioner to decide (Walker, 1990). The best advice in an unclear legal situation is to trust your own professional training and ethical standards. Consultation with a team of colleagues, and documentation of that consultation, may be particularly beneficial. In other words, write it down or tape it so you can corroborate what you did and why.

Knowing the definition of "child abuse" and what constitutes "reasonable suspicion," however, is not enough. In a survey of psychologists, nearly one-third of the respondents stated that they had seen children whom they suspected were abused but did not report their suspicions to child protection agencies. Only 15% believed that a subjective state of suspicion alone was sufficient to report (Kalichmant & Brosig, 1993). One possible reason for such inaction is that practitioners are concerned about destroying the counseling relationship they have established with the young person.

■ ■ ■ Box 16.1
When the Abused Is the Abuser

Janey, age 8, was sexually abused by the son of her mother's best friend when she was 4 years old. Her mother, Tanya, at first attributed the change in Janey's behavior to the fact that she herself was absent for long hours. In addition to working full time, Tanya was taking care of her dying father and her newborn daughter, Tracey. When Janey finally described the abuse to her mother, Tanya informed the authorities and sought counseling for herself and Janey. She responded quickly and appropriately and did everything she could to help Janey recover from the trauma she had experienced.

Two years later, however, she discovered that Janey was sexually abusing her little sister, Tracey. Janey was deeply ashamed and begged her mother not to tell anyone. Somehow Tanya found the courage to go to the appropriate authorities once again and entered both girls in a play therapy group for child survivors of sexual abuse.

This is not an isolated case; many child survivors of sexual abuse replay the abuse on other children. In this case, the mother's painful decision to report her older daughter's actions resulted in the provision of effective and appropriate support services for both children.

Ambiguity in the statutes and a lack of understanding of the practitioner's legal responsibility also make practitioners hesitate to report suspicions that may, after all, be unfounded. Perhaps the biggest factor in the failure to report, however, is the practitioner's concern regarding the negative consequences to the child and the family.

To appreciate the problem of a practitioner in such a situation, suppose a practitioner suspects that a child is being abused by her mother. Perhaps the practitioner knows that the mother was recently laid off and lost her own mother to cancer, and that the abuse, if it occurred, was an isolated incident. The law views the matter in black and white, but to the practioner the situation looks gray. Indeed, most practitioners train for work in gray areas. Or suppose a practitioner suspects that a child in therapy is abusing a younger sibling (see Box 16.1). In this case, most child abuse statutes mandate that authorities be notified. But if the practitioner believes the potentially abusing child is very near a major breakthrough, reporting may appear to be the more harmful alternative. Some practitioners in this situation would attempt to gather more information first; others would report at once.

Despite the universality of reporting laws, prosecution of practitioners under their provisions is rare. In fact, we have been unable to find one case of a psychologist or school practitioner who was actually prosecuted for failure to report suspected abuse. This is not to say that none ever will be, but in an area of such ambiguities the professional judgment of the practitioner ends up being the controlling factor.

Civil Law

Civil law is more likely than criminal law to affect teachers, counselors, and other mental health professionals. Before discussing the legal issues related to the at-risk categories, we treat general concepts of civil law, the duty to warn, and confidentiality.

General civil law.   Under civil law, unlike criminal law, nobody is in danger of going to jail. However, to establish a practitioner's civil liability, the plaintiff must prove four things: (a) that the practitioner owed the plaintiff a duty; (b) that the practitioner was negligent in the performance of that duty; (c) that the practitioner's negligence caused a harmful result; and (d) that the result damaged the plaintiff (Hopkins & Anderson, 1990). For example, mental health practitioners assume several duties when they accept a client. One of these duties is to conform to the ethical standards of the profession, including those of confidentiality. The professional has a duty not to disclose communications negligently. If the practitioner violates this duty and commits an act of negligence, perhaps by telling someone else of a confidential communication, the practitioner could be found liable for damages—but only if the practitioner's conduct actually caused a harmful result and the plaintiff was the one damaged.

Suppose a psychiatrist fails to provide necessary medication to a young person, say, to Jason Carter of Chapter 3. If Jason commits suicide, his parents, Doug and Lois, could certainly sue the practitioner for negligence in not preventing Jason's death, and they might win a jury award of money. Again, this is because the practitioner assumed a *duty*, performed it *negligently*, and *caused* the *harm* to Jason's family.

The legal system encourages professional associations to establish a standard of ethical conduct to guide the behavior of professionals. A mental health practitioner who works with at-risk youth should always try to conform to those ethical standards.

Duty to warn.   A practitioner may have a special duty to warn third persons of danger. In *Tarasoff v. Regents of the University of California* (1976), the California Supreme Court held that psychologists, and potentially all mental health practitioners, have a duty to take reasonable steps to warn a specific third person or persons to whom the patient poses a danger. In most states the patient or client must pose a serious risk to a specific third person before the professional has a duty to warn.

The *Tarasoff* case concerned a patient at a University of California psychiatric center who had stated during therapy that he intended to kill his former girlfriend, named Tarasoff. The therapist did not warn the Tarasoff family of the threat, and when the patient did in fact kill Ms. Tarasoff, her family sued the university. The Supreme Court of California held that the family had the right to sue.

Not all states have a *Tarasoff*-like rule that includes a duty to warn. Practitioners must consult the laws of their own state. In states that have a *Tarasoff* rule, teachers and practitioners who work with at-risk youth must consider whether any of their clients pose a possible danger to a specific third person. If the youth is dangerous, then the practitioner may have a duty to warn the third party or to take other measures to prevent imminent harm (Costa & Altekruse, 1994). Of course, as the American Psychological Association argued in *Tarasoff*, the problem is that this procedure may well destroy the therapeutic relationship.

Also, there is the question of how the privilege of confidentiality can affect the legal duty to warn. As discussed above with the duty to report child abuse, a given state or federal court rule or statute may prevent divulging such information as privileged (*Jaffe v. Redmond*, 1996). Some states may have written the answer to this question in statutes, and a practitioner should check this. When in doubt as to the law or the gravity of the threat to the third person, the best advice is to consult with colleagues. Also, it is wise to inform clients about the limits of confidentiality in the first session. Such a procedure clarifies the practitioner's responsibility and helps to avoid a situation in which a client could feel betrayed. We will return to the duty to warn when we address sexuality issues.

Confidentiality considerations in general.   The law has long protected certain communications between people. This protection probably had its genesis in the relationship between priest and penitent, with all its sacramental overtones. A natural outgrowth of this relationship is the attorney-client privilege. Doctors and patients enjoy a similar privilege, and in most states so do psychologists, counselors, and practitioners. However, the extent of the privilege varies from state to state. Indeed, confidentiality regulations have been described as a "patchwork quilt of standards" (*Jaffe v. Redmond*, 1996).

What further complicates this problem is that in a given state the level or degree of privilege accorded a psychologist may differ from that accorded to another mental health practitioner, such as a school counselor. Again, the best advice is to consult specific state law. This information is generally not too difficult to obtain; most states have an office that publishes a brochure or pamphlet on the issues, and state and local professional associations often compile this information.

Despite the patchwork quilt of obligations and duties that confront the practitioner, certain themes stand out. First, when we speak of confidentiality, we are usually referring to the ethical obligation of the professional not to disclose confidential information obtained in the course of the counselor-client relationship. When we speak of a privileged communication, we are dealing more with a legal right that relieves certain professionals (lawyers, doctors, psychologists, and possibly counselors) of an obligation to provide information to a party in a lawsuit or to testify in court regarding information they receive from their clients. The rules of confidentiality, in the narrow confines of legal privilege, exist for the benefit and protection of the client, not the practitioner (cf. McGuire, Parnell, Blau, & Abbott, 1994).

In states where practitioners have this privilege, they can discuss clients' communications with their colleagues, but those colleagues have the same duty to guard that communication. This is a critical point because practitioners must discuss cases; indeed, one way to avoid civil liability is to consult with colleagues on ambiguous matters.

Confidentiality issues also arise in the school setting. Some state courts hold that parents of public schoolchildren are entitled to inspect their children's records because they are public records (*In re Thibadeau*, 1960). The reasoning behind this ruling is that because the youth is a minor, the parents have the privilege of confidentiality and are therefore entitled to know their children's statements (Hopkins, 1989). Other states, however, hold that a young person's confidential communications should have the same protection as any other communication (Hopkins, 1989).

In certain situations, however, the law requires practitioners to reveal a confidence. As we have seen, in cases of child abuse or imminent danger to a third party, the law may require the information to be shared with the appropriate party (McGowan, 1991). In some situations, such as a group counseling session, a client can waive confidentiality. Practitioners should discuss the limits of confidentiality in the relationship at the outset, especially when the therapy group includes the youth's family. And, of course, practitioners can reveal the confidences of clients who raise the issue of their mental health in a lawsuit.

Otherwise, a practitioner should not divulge any communication given in confidence, regardless of the client's age. Unless a clear therapeutic benefit is possible, it simply is not appropriate to divulge confidential communications. Indeed, even when a court orders a professional to reveal confidential information, practitioners may find themselves ethically and even morally bound not to do so. Refusal would truly put the practitioner at the cutting edge of the law and could lead to a jail sentence for contempt of court. Sometimes, however, this is the only way to effect positive change.

SPECIFIC LEGAL CONCERNS

The behaviors that put young people at serious risk—the use of illegal substances, irresponsible sexual activity, delinquency, and behavior that can lead to suicide—all present unique legal complications.

Substance Use Problems

In state-funded drug programs, state laws and regulations control the practitioner's activities. Programs that receive federal funds, however, follow guidelines found in the Code of Federal Regulations (CFR) (Office for Substance Abuse Prevention, 1990). Technical reports from the U.S. Department of Health and Human Services periodically explain these guidelines.

The general requirement for federally funded substance use programs is that confidentiality must be maintained in nearly all aspects of treatment (42 CFR 2.12[e]). This regulation applies to any program that specializes in providing treatment, counseling, assessment, or referral services for youth with alcohol and other drug problems. In general, these regulations do not apply to teachers or practitioners in a traditional school setting who may deal with substance problems of at-risk youth.

Mental health practitioners in a federally funded program are not free to share any confidences obtained during treatment of at-risk youth, even with their client's parents, even when a therapeutic benefit is possible. Counselors do, however, have the option of obtaining a youth's consent to release information. Under this standard of confidentiality, it is hard to conceive of a situation in which a practitioner could be found negligent for failing to disclose substance use. Indeed, federal regulations require the exact opposite. That is, in most cases, confidentiality must be maintained unless a youngster has a specific self-destructive or suicidal intent in using substances. (We will deal with issues related to suicide shortly.)

Youth Sexuality

Confidentiality issues are key considerations when a practitioner deals with youth sexuality. Irresponsible sexual behavior may also raise the question of a practitioner's duty to warn third persons of a sexually active teenager's sexually transmitted disease.

Divulging confidences to parents.   As the number of sexually active teenagers in the country continues to be substantial (Brown & Eisenberg, 1995), sexuality issues are common topics in therapeutic settings. Current law is ambiguous on whether the practitioner must tell parents of a child's sexual activity.

On the one hand, it would be very difficult for parents to prevail in a lawsuit against a practitioner for failure to report sexual activity among teenage clients. This type of communication ordinarily must stay private to maintain the therapeutic alliance between counselor and client. Thus, when an irate parent calls a mental health practitioner and demands to know if his child is sexually active, as Burt Andrews of Chapter 1 might well do in his rage about Allie's behavior, the law is almost certain to support the practitioner's professional judgment not to reveal the information.

On the other hand, this is the age of a fatal and incurable sexually transmitted disease. If Burt sought information from the practitioner as to whether Allie was sexually active and the practitioner refused to divulge the confidence, conceivably Burt could sue the counselor if Allie later contracted AIDS. In this situation, Burt could come into court and say that if he had known that Allie was sexually active, he would have discussed "safe sex" with her, but because the practitioner refused him the information he sought, he was denied the chance to protect her. Although the potential for this type of lawsuit exists, the practitioner certainly has defenses. Burt obviously suspected that Allie was sexually active, or he would not have asked. What was to prevent Burt from discussing safe sex with Allie even if his suspicions were not confirmed? A practitioner cannot be held liable for a parent's failure to communicate with his child. Consequently, although legal risks exist, professionals cannot afford to exaggerate them or let them get in the way of their work.

Contraception and abortion.   The laws relating to a practitioner's duties in regard to contraception and abortion are very inconsistent. If the counseling facility is not a family planning program, some state laws may require that parents be notified of any contraception or abortion counseling provided to minors. However, because of the U.S. Supreme Court's decision on abortion in *Roe v. Wade* (1973) and the extensions of that ruling to minors (*Bellotti v. Baird,* 1979; *Carey v. Population Services International,* 1977), a practitioner who works with minors in a family planning program may not be bound by parental notification laws. Basically, minors share in the constitutionally protected right of privacy in regard to contraception and abortion decisions. Communications that practitioners in a family planning program receive from minors are confidential. Parents simply do not have the right to know of those communications, despite any state law to the contrary. However, the law is in a state of flux on this question. Every new appointment to the U.S. Supreme Court as well as to a federal circuit court of appeal may increase the probability that a minor's right to privacy will be curtailed.

The practitioner in a family planning program can provide access to birth control pills or other contraceptives. In general the courts have held that the minor's right to privacy outweighs the parent's right to be informed. Consequently, even if Burt Andrews demands to know whether Allie is receiving contraceptives, the practitioner should not divulge the information to him if the practitioner works in a family planning program. If not, however, state law may require the notification.

Of course, on the question of actually prescribing a contraceptive for a minor, the mental health practitioner must not act beyond his or her qualifications. Despite the right of privacy, a mental health practitioner who is not medically trained may be successfully sued for an improper prescription that causes harm.

The inconsistency of rulings on the confidentiality of contraception counseling extends to abortion counseling. The mental health practitioner who does not work in a family planning situation may have a duty under state law to inform the parents of a minor's decision to have an abortion. Conversely, the mental health practitioner who does work in a family planning situation is exempt from the requirements that state law may impose. However, in *H. L. v. Matheson* (1981) the U.S. Supreme Court held that a Utah law requiring a physician to notify a parent of an unemancipated minor's plans for an abortion was not unconstitutional. If a given state law requires notification to parents but allows for a mature or emancipated minor to go independently to a judge for permission to have an abortion, apparently the statute is constitutional. By extension, a mental health practitioner can provide a minor with abortion counseling and the opportunity to obtain judicial consent for an abortion without parental notification.

Most of the U.S. Supreme Court case law in this respect involves medical doctors. Mental health practitioners, however, need to stay abreast of the duties set forth for physicians and draw parallels with their own practice. In the right set of circumstances, the applications could as easily be extended to teachers and practitioners.

STDs/AIDS.   The danger of which a practitioner has a duty to warn a third party under *Tarasoff* can include a sexually transmitted disease. A patient with AIDS can pose an "explicit threat" to a specific foreseeable victim. If Allie Andrews became infected with AIDS, for example, and was sleeping with a specific noninfected person whom the practitioner knew of or could easily find, the law might require the practitioner to warn that person. To date, however, no courts have addressed a practitioner's duty to warn sexual partners in a case involving HIV (Hardin, Gray, & Neal, 1993).

Physicians have resolved this ethical problem by requiring that all "reportable" or "communicable" diseases be reported to the state or county department of health. These departments then take action to protect the public from the disease, which may include a warning to a third party who is at high risk. Further, these departments must protect confidentiality by not disclosing the source of the information.

It is good practice for a teacher, counselor, or other practitioner to notify the state public health agency of possible communicable or reportable diseases, including STDs and AIDS. Before reporting, the practitioner should determine exactly what measures will be taken to protect confidentiality. This protects both the third person and the client's confidence.

In addition, notifying a department of health of an at-risk youth's STD may protect the practitioner from civil liability. If a client transmits a disease to a third person, that person may sue the practitioner if the practitioner knew the situation and took no action. By confidentially reporting to a public health agency, the practitioner may be able to demonstrate that he or she took measures to prevent harm to the specific third person. Although this measure is not a perfect solution to the problem, it provides at least a partial solution.

Delinquency

In general criminal law does not require that practitioners report criminal activity, with the exception of child abuse. Even if you see a crime committed, you are unlikely to be prosecuted if you fail to report it. If you benefit from the crime or in any way facilitate it, however, you may be charged as an accessory (La Fave, 1996). A practitioner who learns of a youth's crimes through confidential communications is not likely to face criminal charges for failure to report them. Indeed, in federally funded programs for drug abuse treatment, a mental health practitioner cannot even request a court order to permit the reporting of any crime less serious than a felony—homicide, rape, kidnapping, and the like (42 CFR 2.65[d][1]). Even in these circumstances, the practitioner must refer to a particular client by a fictitious name.

Under civil law, however, the practitioner may have a duty to warn in certain circumstances. Under *Tarasoff*, a mental health worker who knows of a danger to specific third persons may have a civil duty to warn them. For example, if a practitioner hears in a therapy session with a gang member that the gang is planning a drive-by shooting of a specific person at a specific time and place, the practitioner may have a duty to warn that person. If the person is killed, the surviving relatives could conceivably sue the practitioner and the institution for failure to warn the victim.

Youth Suicide

Suicide. Contrary to popular belief, suicide is no longer a crime in this country, although aiding a suicide is still illegal—despite the movement in support of assisted suicide for the terminally ill (see Box 16.2). Teachers, counselors, social workers, and psychologists need not fear criminal sanctions if a client commits suicide unless they have aided the client in the act.

This is not to say, however, that a practitioner will not be sued. After the death of a youth, surviving family members often need an outlet for grief. That outlet sometimes takes the form of blame cast elsewhere. After a young person commits suicide, the practitioner or some other individual who has worked with the victim may become the target. Numerous suits for malpractice reported by practitioners involve suicide or attempted suicide (Bongar, 1992). These lawsuits not only relieve guilt-ridden family members but also protect the image of the victim. Given the psychological makeup of Doug Carter (of Chapter 3), no one would be surprised if he sued someone if Jason committed suicide.

Only recently have the courts held second parties responsible for deaths by suicide. Traditionally the law viewed suicide as an intentional, willful act by one individual, with no blame attaching to any other party. Thus, courts allowed the victim's relatives and heirs compensation only in exceptional circumstances (Jobes & Berman, 1993). In fact, even though courts are more willing today to hear a relative's claim against a second party, such cases are statistically rare.

The few suits that have been filed against practitioners have a different legal footing than most civil lawsuits. The issue is not causation. Families of suicide victims do not claim that the hospital, psychiatrist, or practitioner "caused" the death of their loved one. Rather, they claim that the practitioner or institution had a duty to prevent the suicide and failed to meet that duty. Because it is difficult to prove that anyone has a duty to prevent suicide, practitioners are protected against most charges of malpractice in such instances.

The setting where the practitioner works may also offer protection against lawsuits (J. J. McWhirter & R. J. McWhirter, 1988). The courts have reasoned that the primary responsibility of schools and their personnel is to educate students, not to treat their

■ ■ ■   Box 16.2

When Suicide Was a Crime

The legal system has never known what to do with suicide. Suicide was long a crime under English law. Punishments included refusal of burial in consecrated ground, mutilation of the body, burial at a crossroad, and a stake driven through the victim's heart (Drukteinis, 1985). Although these sanctions were not transported to America, suicide was once a crime in most parts of this country too (Marzen et al., 1985). This legal prohibition created obvious problems. How does one punish a suicide? The victim, of course, is immune to punishment, at least in this life. Sanctions, therefore, tended to be imposed on the surviving family of the person who had committed the crime. Partly in response to this inherent injustice and inconsistency, state legislatures abolished their suicide laws. Today it is no longer a crime to commit suicide (Litman, 1967; Marzen et al., 1985). In all states, however, active assistance in another person's suicide is treated as homicide (Model Penal Code 210.5[2]). This is still the law, despite Dr. Jack Kevorkian.

emotional problems. In other words, schools do not have a duty to care for the psychological health of students, so they do not have a duty to prevent suicide (*Bogust v. Iverson*, 1960). Although a school is not now liable for the suicide of a student, it is possible that under a particular set of circumstances a court could hold school personnel liable.

A practitioner who works at a hospital has a greater chance of being sued if a patient commits suicide (J. J. McWhirter & R. J. McWhirter, 1988). Because the insurance industry recognizes that one need not be a psychiatrist to be a valid health care provider (*Blue Shield of Virginia v. McCready*, 1982), the courts may begin to hold nonmedical health-care practitioners liable for suicide deaths. This acknowledgment, in combination with the fact that many practitioners and psychologists now have malpractice insurance, increases the likelihood that lawsuits will be initiated against practitioners and psychologists.

When the practitioner has acted with reasonable professional judgment, the chance of being sued successfully is minimal. What, though, constitutes reasonable professional judgment? This is obviously not an objective standard (Berman & Cohen-Sandler, 1983). A practitioner may not believe, for example, that a patient's history of assaults and homicidal tendencies necessarily signifies suicidal tendencies. Another therapist may think otherwise. The standard is undefined, and the practitioner is left with no clear guideline. The courts usually will hold a practitioner to the "generally accepted view of the profession" on a given point (*Fernandez v. Baruch*, 1968). Codes of professional ethics and discussions with colleagues are the best means to acquire information about the accepted professional standard of care (Jobes & Berman, 1993).

Attempted suicide. Persons who have attempted suicide can conceivably sue their therapists for the injuries caused by the attempts. Other legal considerations, too, enter the picture when a youth makes suicidal gestures. In certain circumstances, the courts may intervene after an adolescent attempts suicide.

Although the courts today generally do not punish people for attempting suicide, they may commit them to a psychiatric hospital (Wright, 1975). Most states have statutes that empower the courts to commit persons judged to pose a danger to themselves to the state psychiatric hospital. This power is especially likely to be exercised when the person who has attempted suicide is an adolescent who is a ward of the court.

When an adolescent's suicide attempt is serious enough to require hospitalization, an agency or hospital staff member should evaluate the patient. The evaluators may recommend a hearing to determine whether the adolescent should be committed to the state hospital. Practitioners must be aware of the possibility that their client may be committed.

State hospital systems are often too underfunded to handle all mental health problems, especially those of children and adolescents. In view of their financial stability, the Carter family could probably overcome this problem by finding a private mental health facility for Jason. When the family lacks these resources, however, the counseling professional must diligently try to locate resources available in the state mental health system through state agencies and mental hospitals. In some situations, the only way to help a suicidal youngster is to petition a court to order the client's commitment.

Practitioners should inject themselves into the state or county evaluation process. If no one contacts the practitioner after the attempted suicide of an adolescent client, the practitioner should contact the appropriate evaluating team or agency. His or her comments and recommendations to them may be invaluable; and the evaluation team may decide that it would be best for the practitioner to maintain a therapeutic alliance with the client.

Similarly, the practitioner should be familiar with legal resources in the community. If hospitalization is necessary, the therapist may be responsible for finding a suitable facility for a youth at risk for another suicide attempt. Contact with administrative agencies and the state court system can often yield helpful information on how to make appropriate resources available to the client.

LEGAL DO'S AND DON'TS IN WORK WITH AT-RISK YOUTH

Practitioners who act responsibly and professionally are not likely to be held liable for their client's problems, but they can minimize the risk of lawsuits by taking certain precautions (Jobes & Berman, 1993). We offer the following suggestions:

1. In an emergency situation, avoid a display of anger or sarcasm toward the client. With a client who has recently attempted suicide, for example, a statement on the order of "Next time cut vertically instead of horizontally and you'll get the main artery" would not impress a jury should the client later follow your advice.
2. Document your actions fully and professionally. Documentation should include your assessment of the risks involved in a particular course of treatment and your reasons for following it. The "reasonable professional judgment" standard will protect you against liability if you have clearly used reasonable professional

judgment. A client's records can be offered in evidence at a trial and can show that you did the best that could be done in the situation.

3. Consult frequently with your colleagues on therapeutic and legal questions. Common sense tells a juror that "two heads are better than one." If your colleagues supported your decision at the time, negligence will be hard to prove. Consultation with colleagues impresses juries. Again, document your consultations.

4. Good staff communication must be maintained. Bad communication between the "professionals" on a case will impress a juror negatively. To a juror, poor communication may be a clear indication of negligence.

5. Do not forget to deal with the family, particularly during treatment of a potential suicide victim and after a completed suicide. This approach has a dual purpose. First, it facilitates the family's resolution of grief and is offered as a matter of humane and responsible treatment. Second, the family's contact with you helps deter a hasty, emotion-driven decision to file a malpractice suit.

6. Know the code of ethics developed by the professional association in your field (such as the American Psychological Association, the American Counseling Association, or the National Education Association). All such codes specify a course of conduct that the profession accepts as reasonable and necessary. They define standard practice. Remember that the codes of ethical conduct are often produced with legal considerations in mind in the hope of helping professionals avoid legal problems.

7. Continue to update your professional training and keep a record of the seminars and classes you attend. Such a documented course of action will indicate to a jury or a judge that you are a conscientious practitioner who works to provide the best for your clients. These practices not only help practitioners defend themselves against lawsuits but enhance the professional practice of counseling and help-giving.

CONCLUSION

It is possible for practitioners to prevent many of the legal problems that may arise when they work with at-risk children and youth. An understanding of the legal system, the ethical guidelines of one's profession, and some of the legal restrictions and quagmires entailed in such work can be both helpful to the practitioner and therapeutically and educationally beneficial to the young client or student. Perhaps of greatest importance is the need to recognize the rights and restrictions of confidentiality in the practitioner-client relationship. As each state has its own guidelines for action, practitioners must have clear knowledge of their own rights and responsibilities, especially in regard to the duty to warn, divulging information to parents, and reporting the many forms of child abuse. Counselors, teachers, and other human service professionals need to be particularly aware of the legal issues related to young people's substance use, irresponsible sexual activity, delinquency and violence, and suicide. The seven suggestions offered at the end of this chapter can help practitioners protect themselves and at the same time work more effectively with children and youngsters who seek their help.

FURTHER READINGS

American Counseling Association Legal Series. A 12-volume series edited by Theodore P. Remley, Jr. Alexandria, VA: American Counseling Association.

Remley, T. P. (1991). *Preparing for court appearances* (Vol. 1).

Mitchell, R. W. (1991). *Documentation in counseling records* (Vol. 2).

Bullis, R. K. (1992). *Law and management of a counseling agency or private practice* (Vol. 3).

Salo, M. M., & Shumate, S. G. (1993). *Counseling minor clients* (Vol. 4).

Weikel, W. J., & Hughes, P. R. (1993). *The counselor as expert witness* (Vol. 5).

Arthur, G. L., & Swanson, C. D. (1993). *Confidentiality and privileged communication* (Vol. 6).

Stevens-Smith, P., & Hughes, M. M. (1993). *Legal issues in marriage and family counseling* (Vol. 7).

Ahia, C. E., & Martin, D. (1993). *The danger-to-self-or-others exceptions to confidentiality* (Vol. 8).

Strosnider, J. S., & Grad, J. D. (1993). *Third-party payments* (Vol. 9).

Disney, M. J., & Stephens, A. M. (1994). *Legal issues in clinical supervision* (Vol. 10).

Anderson, D., & Swanson, C. (1994). *Legal issues in licensure* (Vol. 11).

Crawford, R. L. (1994). *Avoiding counselor malpractice* (Vol. 12).

Anderson, B. S. (1996). *The counselor and the law* (4th ed.). Alexandria, VA: American Counseling Association.

Herlihy, B., & Corey, G. (1996). *ACA ethical standards casebook*. Alexandria VA: American Counseling Association Press.

Meyers, J. E. B. (1992). *Legal issues in child abuse and neglect*. Newbury Park, CA: Sage.

CHILD AND YOUTH DEVELOPMENT RESOURCES

The following agencies, clearinghouses, and organizations are useful resources for psychologists, counselors, teachers, social workers, and other professionals who are interested in developing prevention, intervention, and treatment programs for children and adolescents. Also, many state, county, city, and other local organizations that focus on children and adolescents provide information, support, training, and technical assistance.

These organizations provide a national network of resources for individuals working in child and youth development. Many have a state contact office that can provide direction to state programs, resources, and personnel.

Al-Anon/Alateen Family Group Headquarters
1600 Corporate Landing Parkway
Virginia Beach, VA 23454-5617
757-563-1600
800-344-2666

Alcohol Research Group
2000 Hearst Ave., Suite 300
Berkeley, CA 94709
510-642-5208

Alcoholics Anonymous
World Service Office
475 Riverside Drive
New York, NY 10163
212-870-3400

American Association for Marriage and Family Therapy
1133 15th Street, NW, Suite 300
Washington, DC 20005
202-452-0109

American Association for Protecting Children
c/o American Human Association
63 Inverness Drive East
Englewood, CO 80112
303-792-9900

American Association of Family and Consumer Sciences
1555 King Street
Alexandria VA 22314
703-706-4600

American Association of Suicidology
4201 Connecticut Avenue, NW, Suite 310
Washington, DC 20008
202-237-2280

American Bar Association Special Committee on Dispute Resolution
740 15th St. NW
Washington, DC 20005
202-662-1000

American Council for Drug Education
164 West 74th Street
New York, NY 10023
800-488-DRUG

American Counseling Association
5999 Stevenson Avenue
Alexandria, VA 22304-3300
703-823-9800

American Justice Institute
100 Capital Mall, Suite 700
Sacramento, CA 95814
916-442-0707

American Library Association
Young Adult Services Division
50 East Huron St.
Chicago, IL 60611
800-545-2433, ext. 4390

American Values: The Community Action Network
600 Madison Ave., 17th Floor
New York, NY 10022
212-702-0944

American Youth Policy Forum
1001 Connecticut Ave. NW, Suite 719
Washington, DC 20036-5541
202-775-9731

Association for Children and Adults with Learning Disabilities
4156 Library Road
Pittsburgh, PA 15234
412-341-1515

Association of Community Organizations for Reform Now
1024 Elysian Fields Avenue
New Orleans, LA 70117
504-943-0044

Association of Medical Education and Research in Substance Abuse
c/o David C. Lewis, M.D.
Center for Alcohol and Addiction Studies
Brown University
Providence, RI 02912
401-444-1817

Association of Science-Technology Centers (ASTC)
1025 Vermont Ave., NW, Suite 500
Washington, DC 20005-3516
202-783-7200

Association of Halfway House Alcoholism Programs of North America
912 Kinderkamack Rd.
River Edge, NJ 01661
201-986-7440

Better Boys Foundation
1512 South Pulaski
Chicago, IL 60623
312-277-9582

Big Brothers/Big Sisters of America
230 N. 13th Street
Philadelphia, PA 19107
215-567-7000

Boys and Girls Clubs of America
1230 W. Peachtree Street, NW
Atlanta, GA 30309
404-815-5700
800-815-5740

Boy Scouts of America
345 Hudson St.
New York, NY 10014
800-392-2677

Bureau of Justice Statistics Clearinghouse
Box 6000
Rockville, MD 20850
800-732-3277

Call for Action
5272 River Road, Suite 300
Bethesda, MD 20816
301-657-8260

Catholic Big Brothers
45 East 20th Street, 9th Floor
New York, NY 10003
212-477-2250

CDC National AIDS Clearinghouse
P.O. Box 6003
Rockville, MD 20849
800-458-5231

Center for Law and Social Policy (CLASP)
1616 P Street, NW, Suite 150
Washington, DC 20036
202-328-5140

Center for Organizational and Community Development
School of Education, Room 225
University of Massachusetts
Amherst, MA 01003
413-545-2038

Center for Research on Educational Diversity and Excellence (CREDE)
1156 High St.
Santa Cruz, CA 95064
408-459-3500
408-459-3502

Center for Research on Effective Schooling for Disadvantaged Students
The Johns Hopkins University
3505 North Charles Street
Baltimore, MD 21218
410-516-0370

Center for Substance Abuse Treatment—Drug Abuse Information and Treatment Referral Hotline
800-662-HELP

Center for the Improvement of Child Caring
11331 Ventura Boulevard, Suite 103
Studio City, CA 91604
818-980-0903

Center for Youth Development and Policy Research
Academy for Educational Development
1875 Connecticut Ave. NW, Suite 900
Washington, DC 20009-1202
202-884-8267

Center on Families, Communities, Schools and Children's Learning
Johns Hopkins University
3505 N. Charles St.
Baltimore, MD 21218
410-516-8808

Center on Human Policy
805 S. Crouse Avenue
Syracuse, NY 13244-2280
315-443-3851

Center to Prevent Handgun Violence
1225 I Street, NW, Suite 1100
Washington, DC 20005
202-289-7319

Centers for Disease Control and Prevention

- **National AIDS Clearinghouse**
  P.O. Box 6003
  Rockville, MD 20849-6003
  800-458-5231
- **National HIV/AIDS Hotline**
  c/o American Social Health Network
  P.O. Box 13827
  Research Triangle Park, NC 27709
  800-342-AIDS

The Chapin Hall Center for Children
University of Chicago
1313 E. 60th St.
Chicago, IL 60637
773-753-5900

Child and Family Policy Center
1021 Fleming Bldg.
2186 6th Ave.
Des Moines, IA 50309
515-280-9027

Child Welfare League of America, Inc.
Institute for the Advancement of Child Welfare Practice
440 First Street, NW, Suite 310
Washington, DC 20001-2085
202-638-2952

Childhelp USA., Inc.
P.O. Box 630
Los Angeles, CA 90028
800-422-4453

Children of Alcoholics Foundation, Inc.
P.O. Box 4185, Dept. N.A.
Grand Central Station
New York, NY 10163-4185
212-754-0656; 212-351-2680
800-359-COAF

Children of the Night
P.O. Box 4343
Hollywood, CA 90078
800-551-1300

Children's Aid Society
105 E. 22nd St.
New York, NY 10010
212-949-4917

Children's Defense Fund
25 E St., NW
Washington, DC 20001
202-628-8787

Clearinghouse for Drug-Exposed Children
Division of Behavioral and Developmental Pediatrics
University of California
San Francisco Medical Center
13350 7th Ave.
P.O. Box 1311
San Francisco, CA 94143-0314
415-476-9691

Clearinghouse on Child Abuse and Neglect Information
P.O. Box 1182
Washington, DC 20013
703-385-7565

Cocanon Family Groups
P.O. Box 64742-66
Los Angeles, CA 90064
310-859-2206

Committee for Children
2203 Airport Way, Suite 500
Seattle, WA 98134
206-343-1223

Community Board Program
Conflict Resolution Resources for Schools and Youth
Peer Mediation Training
1540 Market St., Suite 490
San Francisco, CA 94102
415-552-1250

The Congress of National Black Churches, Inc.
1225 Eye St., NW, Suite 750
Washington, DC 20005-3914
202-371-1091

Congress on Chemical Dependency and Disability (CCDD)
15519 Crenshaw Boulevard
Gardena, CA 90249
310-679-9126

Contact Center
P.O. Box 81826
Lincoln, NE 68501
402-464-0602

Cooperative Learning Center
60 Peik Hall
University of Minnesota
Minneapolis, MN 55455
612-624-7031

Cottage Program International
57 West South Temple, Suite 420
Salt Lake City, UT 84101
800-752-6100

Council for Exceptional Children
1920 Association Drive
Reston, VA 22091
703-620-3660
800-845-6232

Council for Learning Disabilities
P.O. Box 40303
Overland Park, KS 66204
913-492-8755

Council of the Great City Schools
1301 Pennsylvania Avenue, NW, Suite 702
Washington, DC 20004
202-393-2427

Crisis Intervention & Suicide Prevention Center (CISPC)
1860 El Camino, Suite 400
Burlingame, CA 94010
415-368-6655

DARE America
P.O. Box 2090
Los Angeles, CA 90051
800-223-DARE

Department of Education
400 Maryland Avenue
Washington, DC 20202
202-401-2000

Drug Policy Information Clearinghouse
Box 6000
Rockville, MD 20849-6000
800-666-3332

Educators for Social Responsibility
National Office
23 Garden Street
Cambridge, MA 02138
617-492-1764

Employee Assistance Professional Association
(formerly ALMACA)
2101 Wilson Blvd., Suite 500
Arlington, VA 22201
703-522-6272

Families Anonymous
P.O. Box 3475
Culver City, CA 90231
310-313-5800
800-736-9805

Families in Action
National Drug Information Center
2296 Henderson Mill Road, Suite 204
Atlanta, GA 30345
770-934-6364

Family Resource Coalition
200 South Michigan Avenue, Suite 1600
Chicago, IL 60604
312-341-0900

Family Service America
11700 West Lake Park Drive
Milwaukee, WI 53224
414-359-1040

Fetal Alcohol and Drug Unit
University of Washington School of Nursing
Department of Psychiatry and Behavioral Sciences
180 Nickerson St.
Seattle, WA 98109
206-543-7155

First American Prevention Center
P.O. Box 529
Bayfield, WI 54814
715-779-3755

Foster Grandparent's Program
c/o Corporation for National Service
1201 New York Avenue, NW
Washington, DC 20525
202-606-5000

Girl Scouts of the USA
420 5th Avenue
New York, NY 10018-2702
212-852-8000
800-223-0624

Hazelden Publishing and Education
15245 Pleasant Valley Road, Box 176
Center City, MN 55012-0176
800-262-5010
800-328-7800

The Health Connection
55 West Oak Ridge Drive
Hagerstown, MD 21740
301-790-9735
800-548-8700

Healthy Mothers, Healthy Babies Coalition
409 12th Street, SW
Washington, DC 20024-2188
202-863-2458

Hispanic Community Mobilization for Dropout Prevention
ASPIRA Association, Inc.
1444 I St. NW, Suite 800
Washington, DC 20005
202-835-3600

Hispanic Policy Development Project
36 East 22nd St., Ninth Floor
New York, NY 10010
212-529-9323

Impaired Physician Program
5448 Yorktown Drive
College Park, GA 30349
770-994-0185

Indian Health Service
Parker Indian Hospital
Route 1, Box 12
Parker, AZ 85344
520-669-2137

Institute for Social Justice
1024 Elysian Fields
New Orleans, LA 70117
504-943-5954

Institute for the Prevention of Addiction
Andrews University
Berrien Springs, MI 49104
616-471-3558

Institute on Black Chemical Abuse Resource Center
2616 Nicollet Avenue, South
Minneapolis, MN 55408
612-871-7878

International Commission for the Prevention of Alcoholism and Drug Dependency
12501 Old Columbia Pike
Silver Spring, MD 20904
301-680-6719

International Society for Prevention of Child Abuse and Neglect
332 South Michigan Avenue, Suite 1600
Chicago, IL 60604
312-644-6610, ext. 3273

Interreligious Foundation for Community Organization
402 W. 145th Street, 3rd Floor
New York, NY 10031
212-926-5757

Johnson Institute
7205 Ohms Lane, Suite 200
Minneapolis, MN 55439-2159
800-231-5165

Just Say No International
2000 Franklin St., Suite 400
Oakland, CA 94612
800-258-2766

Juvenile Justice Clearinghouse
P.O. Box 6000
Rockville, MD 20849-6000
800-638-8736

The Kaiser Family Foundation
Quadras
2400 Sand Hill Road
Menlo Park, CA 94025
415-854-9400

March of Dimes Birth Defects Foundations
1275 Mamaroneck Avenue
White Plains, NY 10605
914-428-7100

Marin Institute for the Prevention of Alcohol and
Other Drug Problems
24 Belvedere Street
San Rafael, CA 94901
415-456-5692

Minnesota Chemical Dependency Program for Deaf
and Hard of Hearing Individuals
2450 Riverside Avenue
Minneapolis, MN 55454
612-337-4402
TDD 612-337-4114
800-282-DEAF, Voice and TDD

Mothers Against Drunk Driving

- 511 East John Carpenter Freeway, Suite 700
  Irving, TX 75062
  214-744-6233; 1-800-GET-MADD
- P.O. Box 541688
  Dallas, TX 75354-1666

Nar-Anon Family Group Headquarters
World Service Office
P.O. Box 2562
Palos Verdes Peninsula, CA 90274
310-547-5800

Narcotics Anonymous World Service Office
P.O. Box 9999
Van Nuys, CA 91409
818-773-9999

National Alliance for the Prevention and Treatment
of Child Abuse
c/o New York Foundling Hospital
590 6th Avenue
New York, NY 10011
212-633-9300

National Assembly of National Voluntary Health
and Social Welfare Organizations
1319 F Street, NW, Suite 601
Washington, DC 20004
202-347-2080

National Association for Children of Alcoholics
(NACOA)
11426 Rockville Pike, Suite 100
Rockville, MD 20852
301-468-0985

National Association for Human Development
1424 16th Street, NW, Suite 102
P.O. Box 100
Washington, DC 20036
202-328-2191

National Association for Native American Children
of Alcoholics

- 1402 3rd Ave., Suite 110
  Seattle, WA 98101
  206-467-7686
- c/o Seattle Indian Health Board
  P.O. Box 3364
  Seattle, WA 98114-3364
  206-324-9360

National Association for the Education of Young
Children (NAEYC)
1509 16th Street, NW
Washington, DC 20036
202-232-8777
800-424-2460

National Association of Addiction Treatment
Providers
501 Randolph Dr.
Lititz, PA 17543-9049
717-581-1901

National Association of Alcoholism and Drug Abuse
Counselors, Inc.
1911 Fort Myer Drive, Suite 900
Arlington, VA 22209
703-741-7686

National Association of Community Health Centers (NACHC)
1330 New Hampshire Avenue, NW
Washington, DC 20036
202-659-8008

National Association of Lesbian/Gay Alcoholism Professionals
1855 Lucretia Ave.
Los Angeles, CA 90026
213-664-8146

National Association of Mediation in Education (NAME)
Institute for Dispute Resolution
1726 M St. NW, Suite 500
Washington, DC 20036
202-466-4764

National Association of Neighborhoods
1651 Fuller St. NW
Washington, DC 20009
202-332-7766

National Association of Perinatal Addiction Research Education (NAPARE)
200 North Michigan Avenue, Suite 300
Chicago, IL 60601
312-541-1272 (Publications)

National Association of Public Child Welfare Administration
c/o American Public Welfare
810 1st Street, NE, Suite 500
Washington, DC 20002-4205
202-682-0100

National Association of Secondary School Principals
1904 Association Drive
Reston, VA 22091
703-860-0200

National Association of Social Workers
750 First Street, NE, Suite 700
Washington, DC 20002-4241
202-408-8600
800-227-3590

National Association of the Physically Handicapped
1151 N. Niagra
Saginaw, MI 48602
513-961-8040

National Association of Town Watch
7 Wynnewood Road, Suite 215
Wynnewood, PA 19096
610-649-7055

National Black Alcoholism Council, Inc.
1101 14th St. NW, Suite 630
Washington, DC 20005
202-296-2696

National Black Child Development Institute
1023 15th Street, NW, Suite 600
Washington, DC 20005
202-387-1281

National Center for Children in Poverty (NCCP)
Columbia University School of Public Health
154 Haven Avenue
New York, NY 10032
212-304-7100

National Center for Education in Maternal and Child Health
2000 15th Street North, Suite 701
Arlington, VA 22201-2617
703-524-7802

National Center for Learning Disabilities (NCLD)
381 Park Avenue, Suite 1420
New York, NY 10016
212-545-7510

National Center for Urban Ethnic Affairs
c/o Catholic University of America
Room 300 Marist Hall
Washington, DC 20064
202-319-5129

National Center for Youth with Disabilities
University of Minnesota
Box 721
420 Delaware Street, SE
Minneapolis, MN 55455
612-626-2825
TDD 612-624-3939

National Center on Adult Literacy
Graduate School of Education
University of Pennsylvania
3910 Chestnut St.
Philadelphia, PA 19104
215-898-2100

National Center on the Educational Quality of the Workforce
Institute for Research on Higher Education
University of Pennsylvania
4200 Pine Street
Philadelphia, PA 19104-4090
215-898-4585

National Clearinghouse for Alcohol and Drug Information
P.O. Box 2345
Rockville, MD 20847-2345
301-468-2600
800-729-6686
TDD 800-487-4889

National Catholic Council on Alcoholism and Related Drug Problems
1550 Henrickson Street
Brooklyn, NY 11234-3514
718-951-7177

National Coalition of Hispanic Health and Human Services Organizations
1501 16th Street, NW
Washington, DC 20036
202-797-4342

National Cocaine Hotline
164 W. 74th St.
New York, NY 10023
800-COCAINE

National Committee to Prevent Child Abuse
332 S. Michigan Avenue, Suite 1600
Chicago, IL 60604
800-244-5373

National Community Action Foundation
2100 M Street, NW, Suite 604A
Washington, DC 20037
202-775-0223

National Council of La Raza (NCLR)
1111 19th St. NW, Suite 1000
Washington, DC 20036
202-785-1670

National Council on Alcoholism and Drug Dependence, Inc.
12 West 21st Street, 8th Floor
New York, NY 10010
212-206-6770
800-NCA-CALL

National Council on Crime and Delinquency
685 Market Street, Suite 620
San Francisco, CA 94105
415-896-6223

National Council on Family Relations
3989 Central Avenue, NE, Suite 550
Minneapolis, MN 55421
612-781-9331
888-781-9331

National Crime Prevention Council
1700 K Street, NW, Second Floor
Washington, DC 20006
202-466-6272

National Easter Seal Society
230 West Monroe St., Suite 1800
Chicago, IL 60606-4802
312-726-6200

National Episcopal Coalition on Alcohol and Drugs
876 Market Way
Clarkston, GA 30021
516-997-0476

National Exchange Club Foundation for the Prevention of Child Abuse
3050 Central Avenue
Toledo, OH 43606
419-535-3232

National Families in Action
2296 Henderson Mill Road, Suite 300
Atlanta, GA 30345
770-934-6364

National Family Partnership
11159B South Towne Square
St. Louis, MO 63123
314-845-1933

National Governors' Association
Hall of States
444 N. Capitol, Suite 267
Washington, DC 20001
202-624-5300

National Head Start Association (NHSA)
1651 Prince St.
Alexandria, VA 22314
703-739-0875

National Information Center for Children and Youth with Disabilities
P.O. Box 1492
1875 Connecticut Ave.
Washington, DC 20013
202-884-8200

National Institute for Citizen Education in the Law
711 G Street, SE
Washington, DC 20003
202-546-6644
202-546-6649 Fax
TDD 202-546-7591

National Institute on Drug Abuse Drug-Referral Helpline
5600 Fishers Lane
Rockville, MD 20857
800-662-HELP

National Maternal and Child Health Clearinghouse
2070 Chain Bridge Road, Suite 450
Vienna, VA 22182-2536
703-821-8955, ext. 5

National Mental Health Association
1021 Prince Street
Alexandria, VA 22314
703-684-7722

National Network of Runaway and Youth Services, Inc.
1319 F St. NW, Suite 401
Washington, DC 20004
202-783-7949

National Organization of Adolescent Pregnancy and Parenting and Prevention (NOAPPP)
1319 S St. NW, Suite 400
Washington, DC 20004
202-783-5770

National Organization on Fetal Alcohol Syndrome
1819 H Street, NW
Washington, DC 20006
202-785-4585

National Parents' Resource Institute for Drug Education
3610 Dekalb Technology Parkway,
Suite 105
Atlanta, GA 30340
404-761-6700

National PTA (Drug and Alcohol Prevention Project)
330 N. Wabash Avenue, Suite 2100
Chicago, IL 60611-3690
312-670-6782

National Research Center on Education in the Inner Cities
Temple University
933 Ritter Hall Annex
13th Street and Cecil B. Moore Avenue
Philadelphia, PA 19122
215-204-3001

National Youth Employment Coalition
1001 Connecticut Avenue, NW, Suite 719
Washington, DC 20009
202-659-1064

North American Council on Adoptable Children
970 Raymond Avenue, Suite 106
St. Paul, MN 55114
612-644-3036

Odyssey Institute Corporation
5 Hedley Farms
Westport, CT 06880
203-255-4198

Office for Substance Abuse Prevention
U.S. Department of Health and Human Services
5600 Fishers Lane
Rockville, MD 20857
301-443-0369

Office of Early Childhood Development
717 14th St. NW, Suite 73
Washington, DC 20005
202-727-1839

Office of Minority Health Resource Center
U.S. Department of Health and Human Services
Public Health Service
P.O. Box 37337
Washington, DC 20013-7337
800-444-6472

Office on Smoking and Health
3005 Rhodes Building (Koger Center), Suite 1415
14 Executive Park Drive
Atlanta, GA 30329
770-488-5705
800-CDC-1311

Office on Smoking and Health Technical Information Center
5600 Fishers Lane
Park Building, Room 116
Rockville, MD 20857
301-443-1690
800-232-1311

Orphan Foundation of America
380 Maple Ave. West, Suite LL5
Vienna, VA 22180
703-281-4226
800-950-4673

Pacific Research and Training Alliance
2165 Bunker Hill Drive
San Mateo, CA 94402
415-578-8047 Voice and TDD

Parent Resource Institute for Drug Education (PRIDE)
3610 Dekalb Technology Parkway, Suite 105
Atlanta, GA 30340
800-853-5867

Parents Anonymous
675 West Foothill Boulevard, Suite 220
Claremont, CA 91711-3475
909-621-6184

Parents Without Partners
401 North Michigan Avenue
Chicago, IL 60611
312-644-6610

Philadelphia Parent-Child Learning
National Center on Adult Literacy
911 W. Boston Ave.
Philadelphia, PA 19133
215-763-4333

Planned Parenthood Federation of America
810 Seventh Avenue
New York, NY 10019
212-541-7800

Program for Community Problem Solving
915 15th St., Suite 601
Washington, DC 20005
202-783-2961

Project Oz
502 South Morris Ave.
Bloomington, IL 61701
309-827-0377

Quality Education for Minorities Network
1818 N Street, NW, Suite 350
Washington, DC 20036
202-659-1818

Quest International
P.O. Box 4850
Newark, OH 43058-4850
614-522-6400

Rational Recovery Systems
P.O. Box 800
Lotus, CA 95651
916-621-4374

Research Society on Alcoholism, Inc.
4314 Medical Parkway, Suite 300
Austin, TX 78756
512-454-0022

Resource Center on Substance Abuse Prevention and Disability
1331 F Street, NW, Suite 800
Washington, DC 20004
202-783-2900
TDD 202-737-0645

RID USA (Remove Intoxicated Drivers)
P.O. Box 520
Schenectady, NY 12301
518-372-0034

Safe and Drug-Free Schools Program
Office of Elementary and Secondary Education
U.S. Department of Education
600 Independence Avenue, SW
Portals Building, Suite 604
Washington, DC 20202-6123
202-260-3954

Save the Children Federation
54 Wilton Road
Westport, CT 06880
203-221-4000

School-Age Child Care Project
Center for Research on Women
Wellesley College
106 Central St.
Wellesley, MA 02181-8259
617-283-2547

Secular Organizations for Sobriety (SOS)
P.O. Box 5
Buffalo, NY 14215
310-821-8430

SIDS Alliance
1314 Bedford Avenue, Suite 210
Baltimore, MD 21208
800-221-SIDS

Southern Early Childhood Association (SECA)
7107 West 12th St., Suite 102
Little Rock, AR 72204
501-663-0353
800-305-7322

Southern Mutual Help Association
3602 Old Jeanerette Road
New Iberia, LA 70560
318-367-3277

SPARK Program
Washington Irving High School
40 Irving Place, Room 94
New York, NY 10003
212-477-5442

Students Against Driving Drunk (SADD)
200 Pleasant Street
Marlboro, MA 01752
508-481-3568

Substance Abuse Resources and Disability Issues (SARDI)
Wright State University School of Medicine
P.O. Box 927
Dayton, OH 45401-0927
513-259-1384

The Other Victims of Alcoholism
P.O. Box 1528, Radio City Station
New York, NY 10101
212-247-8087

Therapeutic Communities of America
1611 Connecticut Ave. NW, Suite 4-B
Washington, DC 20009
202-296-3503

TOUGHLOVE International
P.O. Box 1069
Doylestown, PA 18901
215-348-7090
800-333-1069

The Urban Institute
2100 M Street, NW, 5th Floor
Washington, DC 20037
202-833-7200

U.S. Conference of Mayors
1620 I Street, NW
Washington, DC 20006
202-293-7330

Women for Sobriety
P.O. Box 618
Quakertown, PA 18951
215-536-8026

Youth Law Center
114 Sansome Street, Suite 950
San Francisco, CA 94104
415-543-3307

Youth Suicide Prevention
11 Parkman Way
Needham, MA 02192-2863
617-738-0700

Zero To Three: National Center for Infants, Toddlers, and Families
734 15th St. NW, Tenth Floor
Washington, DC 20005-2101
202-638-1144
800-899-4301

READING LIST FOR AT-RISK YOUTH

The references in this appendix are practical and applied resources that have been helpful to at-risk children, adolescents, families, and the professionals who work with them. Although all are written toward helping professionals, many are designed to be used directly with students, parents, or clients. Some are a bit old, but they focus on solidly based theory and can still be extremely helpful. The reader is asked to overlook the sometimes "quaint" language and dated examples and focus on the essential concepts.

GROUP WORK

Brigman, G., & Earley, B. (1991). *Group counseling for school counselors: A practical guide*. Portland, ME: J. Weston Walch.

Carrrell, S. (1993). *Group exercises for adolescents: A manual for therapists*. Thousand Oaks, CA: Sage.

Ferrara, M. L. (1991). *Group counseling with juvenile delinquents: The limit and lead approach*. Thousand Oaks, CA: Sage.

Fleming, M. (1990). *Conducting support groups for students affected by chemical dependence: A guide for educators and other professionals*. Minneapolis, MN: Johnson Institute.

Haasl, B., & Marnocha, J. (1990). *Bereavement support group program for children*. Bristol, PA: Accelerated Development.

Hansen, M., & Peterson, D. (1993). *How to conduct a school recovery support group*. Portland, ME: J. Weston Walch.

Johnson, D. W. (1981). *Reaching out: Interpersonal effectiveness and self-actualization* (2nd ed.). Englewood Cliffs, NJ: Prentice Hall.

Johnson, D. W., & Johnson, F. P. (1994). *Joining together: Group theory and group skills* (5th ed.). Boston: Allyn & Bacon.

Karns, M. (1995). *How to create positive relationships with students: A handbook of group activities and teaching strategies*. Champaign, IL: Research Press.

Lee, S. A. (1995). *The survivor's guide for teenage girls surviving sexual abuse*. Thousand Oaks, CA: Sage.

Morganett, R. S. (1990). *Skills for living: Group counseling activities for young adolescents*. Champaign, IL: Research Press.

Morganett, R. S. (1995). *Skills for living: Group counseling activities for elementary students* (2nd ed.). Champaign, IL: Research Press.

Peled, E., & Davis, D. (1995). *Groupwork with children of battered women: A practitioner's manual*. Thousand Oaks, CA: Sage.

Pfeiffer, J. W., & Jones, J. E. (Eds.). (1970). *A handbook of structured experiences for human relations training, 1–7*, (3rd ed.). Iowa City, IA: University Associates.

Wolfe, D. A. (1996). *The youth relationships manual: A group approach with adolescents for the prevention of woman abuse and the promotion of healthy relationships*. Thousand Oaks, CA: Sage.

SUBSTANCE ABUSE

Ackerman, R. (1987). *Children of alcoholics: A guidebook for educators, therapists and parents*. New York: Simon & Schuster.

Anderson, G. L. (1987). *When chemicals come to school: The student assistance program model*. Milwaukee, WI: DePaul Training Institute.

Fleming, M. (1990). *Conducting support groups: For students affected by chemical dependence.* Minneapolis, MN: Johnson Institute.

Gerne, T. A., & Gerne, P. J. (1986). *Substance abuse prevention activities for elementary children.* Englewood Cliffs, NJ: Prentice Hall.

Hanson, M., & Peterson, D. S. (1993). *How to conduct a school recovery support group.* Portland, ME: J. Weston Walch.

Hyppo, M. H., & Hastings, J. M. (1984). *An elephant in the living room.* Minneapolis, MN: Compcare Publishers.

Office of Substance Abuse Prevention (1988). *Children of alcoholics kits.* Rockville, MD: National Clearinghouse for Alcohol and Drug Information.

Office of Substance Abuse Prevention (1992). *The discovery kit.* Rockville, MD: OSAP's National Clearinghouse for Alcohol and Drug Information. Also *The connection kit* (1993).

Ryder, L. (1990). *Being free: Prevention curriculum for American Indian youth.* St. Paul, MN: Children Are People, Inc.

PROBLEM SOLVING AND PRO-SOCIAL SKILLS

Camp, B. W., & Bash, M. S. (1985). *Think aloud: Increasing social and cognitive skills—a problem solving program for children.* Champaign, IL: Research Press.

Goldstein, A., Sprafkin, R., Gershaw, N., & Klein, P. (1980). *Skill-streaming the adolescent: A structured learning approach to teaching prosocial skills.* Champaign, IL: Research Press.

Kendall, P., & Braswell, L. (1985). *Cognitive-behavioral therapy for impulsive children.* New York: Guilford.

McGinnis, E., & Goldstein, A. (1984). *Skill-streaming the elementary school child: A guide for teaching prosocial skills.* Champaign, Il: Research Press.

Santostefano, S. (1985). *Cognitive control therapy with children and adolescents.* New York: Pergamon.

Shure, M. B. (1992). *I can problem solve: An interpersonal cognitive problem-solving program for children: Intermediate elementary grades.* Champaign, IL: Research Press.

Shure, M. B. (1992). *I can problem solve: An interpersonal cognitive problem-solving program for children: Kindergarten and primary grades.* Champaign, IL: Research Press.

Shure, M. B. (1992). *I can problem solve: An interpersonal cognitive problem-solving program for children: Preschool.* Champaign, IL: Research Press.

COOPERATIVE LEARNING

Johnson, D. W., Johnson, R. T., & Holubec, E. J. (1990). *Cooperation in the classroom.* Edina, MN: Interaction Book Company.

Kagan, S. (1992). *Cooperative learning.* San Juan Capistrano, CA: Resources for Teachers.

Sharan, Y., & Sharan, S. (1992). *Expanding cooperative learning through group investigation.* Colchester, VT: Teachers College Press.

Slavin, R. E. (1986). *Using student team learning* (3rd ed.). Baltimore, MD: Center for Research on Elementary and Middle Schools, The John Hopkins University.

Slavin, R. E. (1990). *Cooperative learning: Theory, research, and practice.* Englewood Cliffs, NJ: Prentice Hall.

Stahl, R. J. (1994). *Cooperative learning in social studies: A handbook for teachers.* Menlo Park, CA: Addison-Wesley.

Stahl, R. J., & VanSickle, R. L. (Eds.), (1992). *Cooperative learning in the social studies classroom: An invitation to social study.* Washington, DC: National Council for the Social Studies.

PEER MEDIATION AND CONFLICT RESOLUTION

Copeland, N. D. (1989). *Managing conflict: A curriculum for adolescents* (Grades 7–12). Albuquerque, NM: New Mexico Center for Dispute Resolution.

Cray, E. (1994). *Kids can cooperate* (Grades K–8). King of Prussia, PA: Childswork/Childsplay.

Drew, N. (1994). *Learning the skills of peacemaking* (Grades K–8). King of Prussia, PA: Childswork/Childsplay.

Henriques, M., Holmberg, M., & Sadalla, G. (1987). *Conflict resolution: A secondary school curriculum* (Grades 7–12). San Francisco, CA: Community Board Program, Inc.

Johnson, D., & Johnson, R. (1991). *Teaching students to be peacemakers* (Grades K–6). Edina, MN: Interaction Book Co.

Lane, P. (1995). *Conflict resolution for kids: A group facilitator's guide* (Grades K–6). Muncie, IN: Accelerated Development.

McGinnis, K. (1993). *Educating for a just society* (Grades 7–12). Wilmington, OH: Institute for Peace and Justice, Wilmington College Peace Resource Center.

Sadalla, G., Holmberg, M., & Halligan, J. (1990). *Conflict resolution: An elementary school curriculum*

(Grades K–6). San Francisco, CA: Community Board Program, Inc.

Schrumpf, F., Crawford, D., & Chu, U. H. (1991). *Peer mediation: Conflict resolution in the school* (Grades 7–12). Champaign, IL: Research Press.

PEER FACILITATION AND COUNSELING

Myrick, R. D., & Bowman, R. P. (1991). *Children helping children: Teaching students to become friendly helpers: A leadership training program for young students.* Minneapolis, MN: Educational Media Corporation.

Myrick, R. D., & Sorenson, D. L. (1988). *Peer helping: A practical guide.* Minneapolis: Educational Media Corporation.

Samuels, M. (1975). *The complete handbook of peer counseling.* Miami, FL: Fiesta Publishing, Educational Books Division.

Scott, S. (1985). *Peer pressure reversal: An adult guide to developing a responsible child.* Amherst, MA: Human Resouce Development Press.

Scott, S. (1988). *Positive peer groups.* Amherst, MA: Human Resource Development Press.

Tindall, J. A. (1986, 1989). *Peer power, Book I and II, Peer counseling, In depth look at peer helping.* Muncie, IN: Accelerated Development.

Tindall, J. A., & Salmon-White, S. J. (1990). *Peers helping peers: Program for the preadolescent.* Muncie, IN: Accelerated Development.

SELF-ESTEEM

Amundson, K. (1991). *Building self-esteem: A guide for parents, schools, and communities.* Arlington, VA: American Association of School Administrators.

Pope, A. W., McHale, S. M., & Craighead, W. E. (1988). *Self-esteem enhancement with children and adolescents.* Boston, MA: Allyn & Bacon.

Reasoner, R. W. (1992). *Teacher's manual: Building self-esteem in the elementary schools* (2nd ed.). Palo Alto, CA: Consulting Psychologists Press, Inc.

Seligman, M. E. P. (1995). *The optimistic child: A revolutionary program that safeguards children against depression and builds lifelong resilience.* New York: Houghton Mills.

ANGER REDUCTION

Burns, D. (1990). *The feeling good handbook.* New York: Penguin Books.

Davis, M., Eshelman, E. R., & McKay, M. (1992). *The relaxation & stress reduction workbook* (2nd ed.). Oakland: New Harbinger Publications.

Ellis, A. (1977). *How to live with—and without—anger.* New York: Reader's Digest Press.

Hankins, G. (1988). *Prescription for anger: Coping with angry feelings and angry people.* Beaverton, OR: Princess Publishing.

McKay, M., Rogers, P. D., & McKay, J. (1989). *When anger hurts: Quieting the storm within.* Oakland, CA: New Harbinger Publications.

Tavris, C. (1982). *Anger: The misunderstood emotion.* New York: Simon & Schuster.

PARENT TRAINING AND EDUCATION

Becker, W. C. (1971). *Parents are teachers: A child management program.* Champaign, IL: Research Press.

Canter, L., & Canter, M. (1982). *Assertive discipline for parents.* Santa Monica, CA: Canter & Associates.

Dinkmeyer, D., & Lasoncy, L. (1980). *The encouragement book.* Englewood Cliffs, NJ: Prentice Hall.

Dinkmeyer, D., & McKay, G. (1986). *Systematic training for effective parenting* (STEP). Circle Pines, MN: American Guidance Service, Inc.

Dreikurs, R. (1964). *Children: The challenge.* New York: Hawthorne.

Dreikurs, R., & Grey, L. (1970). *A parents' guide to child discipline.* New York: Hawthorne.

Ginott, H. G. (1965). *Between parent and child.* New York: Avon Books.

Gordon, T. (1970). *P.E.T.: Parent effectiveness training.* New York: Peter H. Wyden.

Patterson, G. R. (1976). *Living with children.* Champaign, IL: Research Press.

Popkin, M. (1987). *Active parenting* (video-based program). Atlanta, GA: Active Parenting, Inc.

Satir, V. (1972). *Peoplemaking.* Palo Alto, CA: Science & Behavior Books, Inc.

Smith, J. M., & Smith, D. E. P. (1976). *Child management.* Champaign, IL: Research Press.

Wagonseller, B. R., & McDowell, R. L. (1979). *You and your child: A common sense approach to successful parenting.* Champaign, IL: Research Press.

Walton, F. (1980). *Winning children over.* Chicago, IL: Practical Psychology Associates.

Walton, F. (1980). *Winning teenagers over.* Chicago, IL: The Alfred Adler Institute.

CLASSROOM AND SCHOOL ISSUES

Canfield, J., & Wells, H.C. (1976). *100 ways to enhance self-concept in the classroom: A handbook for teachers and parents.* Englewood Cliffs, NJ: Prentice Hall.

Dreikurs, R. (1957). *Psychology in the classroom.* New York: Harper & Row.

Dreikurs, R., Grunwald, B. B., & Pepper, F. C. (1971). *Maintaining sanity in the classroom.* New York: Harper & Row.

Felker, D. W. (1974). *Building positive self-concepts.* Minneapolis: Burgess.

Mandel, H. P., Marcus, S. I., & Dean, L. (1995). *Could do better: Why children underachieve and what to do about it.* Somerset, NJ: Wiley.

Ross, D. M. (1996). *Childhood bullying and teasing: What school personnel, other professionals, and parents can do.* Alexandria, VA: American Counseling Association.

Schrumpf, F., Freiburg, S., & Skadden, D. (1993). *Life lessons for young adolescents: An advisory guide for teachers.* Champaign, IL: Research Press.

REFERENCES

Adams, D., & Hamm, M. (1994). *New designs for teaching and learning: Promoting active learning in tomorrow's schools.* San Francisco: Jossey-Bass.

Adler, A. (1930). *The education of children.* South Bend, IN: Gateway.

Adler, A. (1964). *Social interest: A challenge to mankind.* New York: Capricorn.

Aksamit, D. (1990). Mildly handicapped and at-risk students: The graying of the line. *Academic Therapy, 25,* 277–289.

Alan Guttmacher Institute. (1994). *Sex and America's teenagers.* New York: Author.

Alessi, N. E., McManus, M., Brickman, A., & Grapentine, L. (1984). Suicidal behavior among serious juvenile offenders. *American Journal of Psychiatry, 141,* 286–287.

Allen, M. L., Brown, P., & Finlay, B. (1992). *Helping children by strengthening families: A look at family support programs.* Washington, DC: Children's Defense Fund.

Alvy, K. T. (1994). *Parent training today: A social necessity.* Sudio City, CA: Center for the Improvement of Child Caring.

American College of Obstetricians and Gynecologists. (1993). Special needs of pregnant teens. *ACOG patient education pamphlet no. AP103.* Washington, DC: Author.

American Medical Association. (1990). *Healthy youth 2000: National health promotion and disease prevention objectives for adolescents.* Chicago: Author.

American Psychiatric Association. (1994). *Diagnostic and Statistical Manual of Mental Disorders* (4th ed.). Washington, DC: Author.

American Psychological Association Presidential Task Force on Violence and the Family. (1996). *Violence and the family.* Washington, DC: Author.

Amundson, K. (1991). *Building self-esteem: A guide for parents, schools, and communities.* Arlington, VA: American Association of School Administrators.

Anderson, G. L. (1987). *When chemicals come to school: The student assistance program model.* Milwaukee, WI: DePaul Training Institute.

Anderson, J. D. (1994, March-April). Breaking the silence: Creating safe schools for gay youth. *Student Assistance Journal,* 21–23.

Andrews, J. A., & Lewinsohn, P. M. (1992). Suicidal attempts among older adolescents: Prevalence and co-occurrence with psychiatric disorders. *Journal of the American Academy of Child and Adolescent Psychiatry, 31,* 655–662.

Angelou, M. (1969). *I know why the caged bird sings.* New York: Random House.

Annie E. Casey Foundation. (1994). *Kids count data book: State profiles of child well-being.* Washington, DC: Author.

Annie E. Casey Foundation. (1995). *Kids count data book: State profiles of child well-being.* Washington, DC: Author.

Apter, T. (1990). *Altered loves: Mothers and daughters during adolescence.* New York: St. Martin's Press.

Araki, D., Takeshita, C., & Kadomoto, L. (1989). *Research results and final report for the Dispute Management in the Schools project.* Honolulu. Program on Conflict Resolution, University of Hawaii at Manoa.

Arendell, T. (1995). *Fathers and divorce.* Thousand Oaks, CA: Sage.

Arnold, D. S., O'Leary, S. G., Wolff, L. S., & Acker, M. M. (1993). The parenting scale: A measure of dysfunctional parenting in discipline situations. *Psychological Assessment, 5*(2), 137–144.

Arnold, M. S. (1995). Exploding the myths: African-American families at promise. In B. B. Swadener & S. Lubeck (Eds.), *Children and families "at promise"* (pp. 143–162). Albany, NY: State University of New York Press.

Astone, N., & McLanahan, S. (1991). Family structure, parental practices, and high school completion. *American Sociological Review, 56,* 309–320.

Aubrey, R. F. (1988). Excellence, school reform, and counselors. In J. Carlson & J. Lewis (Eds.), *Counseling the adolescent* (pp. 189–204). Denver: Love.

Bagley, C. (1992). Development of an adolescent stress scale for use by school counselors. *School Psychology International, 13,* 31–49.

Baker, L. (1990, August 16). After school: Some programs help latchkey kids find something to do. *Southeast Community: Arizona Republic,* pp. 1, 3.

Bandura, A. (1977). *Social learning theory.* Englewood Cliffs, NJ: Prentice Hall.

Banks, J. A. (1997). *Teaching strategies for ethnic studies.* (6th ed.). Needham Heights, MA: Allyn & Bacon.

Barnett, W. S. (1992). Benefits of compensatory preschool education. *Journal of Human Resources, 27,* 279–312.

Barr, R. (1992). Teachers, materials, and group composition in literacy instruction. In M. J. Dreher & W. H. Slater (Eds.), *Elementary school literacy: Critical issues.* Norwood, MA: Christopher-Gordon.

Barron, A., & Foot, H. (1991). Peer tutoring and tutor training. *Educational Research, 33*(3), 174–184.

Barry, D. (1990, April). *Music and the at-risk child.* Paper presented at the Music Educators National Conference, Washington, DC.

Bassett, C., McWhirter, J. J., & Kitzmiller, K. (1997). *Teacher implementation of cooperative learning groups.* Unpublished manuscript. Arizona State University, Tempe, AZ.

Battin, M. P. (1995). *Ethical issues in suicide.* Englewood Cliffs, NJ: Prentice Hall.

Baumrind, D. (1990). Rearing competent children. In W. Damon (Ed.), *New directions for child development: Child development today and tomorrow.* (pp. 349–374). San Francisco: Jossey-Bass.

Baumrind, D. (1993). The average expectable environment is not good enough: A response to Scarr. *Child Development, 64,* 1299–1317.

Baumrind, D. (1995). *Child maltreatment and optimal caregiving in social contexts.* New York: Garland.

Beardslee, W., & Schwoeri, L. (1994). Preventive intervention with children of depressed parents. In G. P. Sholevar (Ed.), *The transmission of depression in families and children: Assessment and intervention.* Northvale, NJ: Aronson.

Beauvais, F., Chavez, E. L., Oetting, E. R., Deffenbacher, J. L., & Cornell, G. R. (1996). Drug use, violence, and victimization among white American, Mexican American, and American Indian dropouts, students with academic problems, and students in good academic standing. *Journal of Counseling Psychology, 43*(3) 292–299.

Beck, A. T. (1976). *Cognitive therapy and emotional disorders.* New York: International Universities Press.

Beck, A. T. (1991). Cognitive therapy: A 30-year retrospective. *American Psychologist, 46,* 382–389.

Beck, A. T., Kovacs, M., & Weissman, A. (1979). Assessment of suicidal intention: The Scale for Suicidal Ideation. *Journal of Clinical and Consulting Psychology, 47,* 343–352.

Beck, A. T., Ward, S. H., Mendelson, M., Mock, J., & Erbaugh, J. (1961). An inventory for measuring depression. *Archives of General Psychiatry, 4,* 561–571.

Beck, A. T., Weissman, A., Lester, D., & Trexler, L. (1974). The measurement of pessimism: The Hopelessness Scale. *Journal of Consulting and Clinical Psychology, 42,* 861–865.

Becker, E. (1981). *The denial of death.* New York: Free Press.

Becker, W. C. (1964). Consequences of different kinds of parental discipline. In J. L. Hoffman & L. W. Hoffman (Eds.), *Review of child development research* (Vol. 1, pp. 169–208). New York: Russell Sage Foundation.

Becker-Lansen, E., & Rickel, A. U. (1995). Integration of teen pregnancy and child abuse research: Identifying mediator variables for pregnancy outcome. *Journal of Primary Prevention, 16*(8), 39–53.

Bell, N. J., & Bell, R. W. (Eds.). (1993). *Adolescent risk taking.* Newbury Park, CA: Sage.

Belle, D. (1990). Poverty and women's mental health. *American Psychologist, 45,* 385–389.

Bellotti v. Baird, 428 U.S. 132 (1979).

Benard, B. (1991). *Fostering resiliency in kids: Protective factors in the family, school, and community.* Portland, OR: Western Center for Drug-Free Schools and Communities.

Benn, W. (Ed.) (1981). *STAR: Social thinking and reasoning.* Irvine, CA: Irvine Unified School District.

Benn, W. (Ed.) (1982). *PLUS: Promoting learning and understanding of self.* Irvine, CA: Irvine Unified School District.

Benson, H. (1992). *The relaxation response* (2nd ed.). New York: Random House.

Berg, C. A., & Clough, M. (1990–1991). Hunter lesson design: The wrong one for science teaching. *Educational Leadership, 48*(4), 73–78.

Berliner, D. C., & Biddle, B. J. (1995). *The manufactured crisis: Myths, fraud, and the attack on America's public schools.* Reading, MA: Addison-Wesley.

Berman, A. L., & Cohen-Sandler, R. (1983). Suicide and malpractice: Expert testimony and the standard of care. *Professional Psychology: Research and Practice, 14*(1), 6–19.

Berman, A. L., & Jobes, D. A. (1991). *Adolescent suicide: Assessment and intervention.* Washington, DC: American Psychological Association.

Bernhardt, G. R., & Praeger, S. G. (1985). Preventing child suicide: The elementary school death education puppet show. *Journal of Counseling and Development, 63,* 311–312.

Besner, H. F., & Spungin, C. I. (1995). *Gay and lesbian students: Understanding their needs.* Washington, DC: Taylor & Francis.

Bettencourt, H., & Blair, I. (1992). A cognition (attribution) emotion model of violence in conflict situations. *Personality and Social Psychology Bulletin, 18*(3), 342–350.

Beymer, L. (1995). *Meeting the guidance and counseling needs of boys.* Alexandria, VA: American Counseling Association.

Beyth-Marom, R., Fischhoff, B., Jacobs, M., & Furby, L. (1989). *Teaching decision making to adolescents: A critical review.* Washington, DC: Carnegie Council on Adolescent Development.

Bickel, A., & Ertle, V. (1991). *Parenting skills curricula: A descriptive guide.* Portland, OR: Northwest Regional Educational Laboratory.

Bissex, G. L. (1980). *GYNS AT WRK: A child learns to read and write.* Cambridge, MA: Harvard University Press.

Bjerregaard, B., & Smith, C. (1993). Gender differences in gang participation, delinquency, and substance abuse. *Journal of Quantitative Criminology, 9*(4), 329–355.

Blechman, E. A., Prinz, R. J., & Dumas, J. E. (1995). Coping, competence, and aggression prevention: Part 1. Development model. *Applied and Preventive Psychology, 4,* 211–232.

Blue Shield of Virginia v. McCready, 457 U.S. 465 (1982).

Blumenthal, S. J. (1990). Youth suicide: Risk factors, assessment, and treatment of adolescent and young adult suicidal patients. *Psychiatric Clinics of North America, 13*(3), 511–556.

Blumstein, A., Cohen, J., & Farrington, D. P. (1988). Criminal career research: Its value for criminology. *Criminology, 26,* 1–35.

Bogust v. Iverson, 10 Wis. 2d 129, 102 N.W. 2d 228 (1960).

Bongar, B. (1992). Effective risk management and the suicidal patient. *Register Report, 18*(6), 22–27.

Boozer, A. E. (1989). Tough enough: Gang membership. In D. Capuzzi & D. Gross (Eds.), *Youth at risk: A resource for counselors, teachers and parents* (pp. 305–324). Alexandria, VA: American Association for Counseling and Development.

Bortner, M. A. (Ed.). (1993). *Confronting violent crime in Arizona.* Phoenix, AZ: Arizona Town Hall.

Botvin, G. J., Baker, E., Dusenbury, L., Botvin, E. M., & Diaz, T. (1995). Long-term follow-up results of a randomized drug abuse prevention trial in a white middle-class population. *Journal of the American Medical Association, 273,* 1106–1112.

Botvin, G. J., Schinke, S., & Orlandi, M. S. (Eds.). (1995). *Drug abuse prevention with multiethnic youth.* Thousand Oaks, CA: Sage.

Bowen, M. (1978). *Family therapy in clinical practice.* New York: Jason Aronson.

Boxer, A. M., Cook, J. A., & Herdt, G. (1991). Double jeopardy: Identity transitions and parent-child relations among gay and lesbian youth. In K. Pillemer & K. McCartney (Eds.), *Parent-child relations throughout life.* (pp. 59–92). Hillsdale, NJ: Erlbaum.

Boyer, D., & Fine, D. (1992). Sexual abuse as a factor in adolescent pregnancy and child maltreatment. *Family Planning Perspectives, 24*(1), 4–11.

Bracken, B. A. (1992). *Multidimensional Self-Concept Scale.* Austin, TX: Pro-Ed, Inc.

Bransford, J. D., & Stein, B. S. (1984). *The IDEAL problem solver.* New York: W.H. Freeman.

Brennan, T. R. (1984). The reduction of disruptive classroom behavior of emotionally disturbed adolescents through the use of a relaxation procedure. (Doctoral dissertation, Columbia University Teachers College, 1983). *Dissertation Abstracts International, 44,* 3347A.

Brenner, A. (1984). *Helping children cope with stress.* Lexington, MA: D. C. Heath.

Brindis, C. D. (1991). *Adolescent pregnancy prevention: A guidebook for communities.* Palo Alto, CA: Health Promotion Resource Center.

Brindis, C. (1992). Adolescent pregnancy prevention for Hispanic youth: The role of schools, families, and communities. *Journal of School Health, 62,* 345–351.

Brook, J. S., Cohen, P., Whiteman, M., & Gordon, A. S. (1992). Psychosocial risk factors in the transition from moderate to heavy use or abuse of drugs. In M. Glantz & R. Pickens (Eds.), *Vulnerability to Drug Abuse* (pp. 359–388). Washington, DC: American Psychological Association.

Brooks, V., & Coll, K. (1994, April). *Troubled youth: Identification and intervention strategies.* Paper presented at the National Convention of the American Alliance for Health, Physical Education, Recreation, and Dance, Denver, CO.

Brown, S. A., Myers, M. G., Mott, M. A., & Vik, P. W. (1994). Correlates of success following treatment for adolescent substance abuse. *Applied and Preventive Psychology, 3,* 61–73.

Brown, S. S., & Eisenberg, L. (Eds.). (1995). *The best intentions: Unintended pregnancy and the well-being of children and families.* Washington, DC: National Academy Press.

Brownsworth, V. A. (1992). America's worst-kept secret. AIDS is devastating the nation's teenagers, and gay kids are dying by the thousands. *The Advocate,* 38–46.

Bruton, S. (Ed.) (1994). *On alert! Gang prevention.* Sacramento, CA: Department of Education.

Bumpass, L. L. (1984). Children in marital disruption: A replication and update. *Demography, 21,* 71–82.

Bureau of Labor Statistics (1995). *Report on the American Workforce,* Washington, DC: U.S. Department of Labor.

Burns, L. E. (1981). Relaxation in the management of stress. In J. Marshall & C. L. Cooper (Eds.), *Coping with stress.* London: Gower.

Burrell, N., & Vogel, S. (1990). Turfside conflict mediation. *Mediation Quarterly, 7*(3), 237–251.

Burt, M., & Cohen, B. (1993). *America's homeless.* Washington, DC: Urban Institute Report.

Bushweller, K. (1995, May). The resilient child. *The American School Board Journal,* 18–23.

Byrne, D., Kelley, K., & Fisher, W. A. (1993). Unwanted teenage pregnancies: Incidence, interpretation, and intervention. *Applied and Preventive Psychology, 2,* 101–113.

Cahape, P., & Howley, C. B. (Eds.). (1992). *Indian nations at risk: Listening to the people* (Summaries of papers commissioned by the Indian Nations at Risk Task Force). Charleston, WV: ERIC Clearinghouse on Rural Education and Small Schools.

Cahoon, P. (1988). Mediator magic. *Education Leadership, 45*(4), 92–95.

Calfee, B. E. (1992). *Lawsuit prevention techniques: For mental health professionals, chemical dependency specialists, and clergy.* Sarasota, FL: Professional Resource Press.

Cambone, J., Weiss, C. H., & Wyeth, A. (1992). *We're not programmed for this: An exploration of the variance between the ways teachers think and the concept of shared decision making in high schools.* Cambridge, MA: Harvard University, National Center for Educational Leadership.

Camp, B. W., & Bash, M. S. (1985a). *Think aloud: Increasing social and cognitive skills—A problem-solving program for children, Classroom program grades 1–2.* Champaign, IL: Research Press.

Camp, B. W., & Bash, M. S. (1985b). *Think aloud: Increasing social and cognitive skills—A problem-solving program for children, Classroom program grades 3–4.* Champaign, IL: Research Press.

Camp, B. W., & Bash, M. S. (1985c). *Think aloud: Increasing social and cognitive skills—A problem-solving program for children, Classroom program grades 5–6.* Champaign, IL: Research Press.

Canetto, S. S., & Lester, D. (1995). Gender and the primary prevention of suicide mortality. *Suicide and Life-Threatening Behavior, 25*(1), 58–69.

Canino, I. A., & Spurlock, J. (1994). *Culturally diverse children and adolescents: Assessment, diagnosis, and treatment.* New York: Guilford.

Caplan, G. (1964). *Principles of preventive psychiatry.* New York: Basic Books.

Capuzzi, D. (1994). *Suicide prevention in the schools: Guidelines for middle and high school settings.* Alexandria, VA: American Counseling Association.

Capuzzi, D., & Golden, L. (1988). Adolescent suicide: An introduction to issues and interventions. In. D. Capuzzi & L. Golden (Eds.), *Preventing adolescent suicide* (pp. 3–28). Muncie, IN: Accelerated Development.

Capuzzi, D., & Gross, D. R. (1996). "I don't want to live": The adolescent at risk for suicidal behavior. In D. Capuzzi & D. R. Gross (Eds.), *Youth at risk: A prevention resource for counselors, teachers, and parents* (2nd ed.) (pp. 253–282). Alexandria, VA: American Counseling Association.

Carey v. Population Services International, 431 U.S. 678 (1977).

Carkhuff, R. R. (1969). *Helping and human relations, Vol. 1.* New York: Holt, Rinehart & Winston.

Carlson, L., Grossbart, S., & Stuenkel, J. K. (1992). The role of parental socialization types on differential family communication patterns regarding consumption. *Journal of Consumer Psychology, 1*(1), 31–52.

Carnegie Corporation of New York. Carnegie Task Force on Meeting the Needs of Young Children. (1994). *Starting points: Meeting the needs of our youngest children.* New York: Carnegie Corporation of New York.

Carnegie Corporation of New York. Carnegie Council on Adolescent Development. (1995). *Great transitions: Preparing adolescents for a new century.* New York: Carnegie Corporation of New York.

Carnine, D., Silbert, J., & Kameenui, E. J. (1990). *Direct instruction reading* (2nd ed.). Columbus, OH: Merrill.

Carter, D. J., & Wilson, R. (1991). *Ninth annual status report: Minorities in higher education.* Washington, DC: American Council on Education.

Carter, E., & McGoldrick, M. (Eds.). (1989). *The changing family life cycle: A framework for family therapy* (2nd ed.). Needham Heights, MA: Allyn & Bacon.

Carter, J. L., & Russell, H. (1980). Biofeedback and academic attainment of LD children. *Academic Therapy, 15,* 483–486.

Cartledge, G., & Milburn, J. F. (Eds.) (1986). *Teaching social skills to children: Innovative approaches* (2nd ed.). New York: Pergamon Press.

Carville, J. (1996). *We're right, they're wrong: A handbook for spirited progressives.* New York: Random House.

Catalano, R. F., & Hawkins, J. D. (1996). The social development model: A theory of antisocial behavior. In J. D. Hawkins (Ed.), *Delinquency and crime: Current theories* (pp. 149–197). New York: Cambridge University Press.

Center, Y., Wheldall, K., Freeman, L., & Outhred, L. (1995). An evaluation of "reading recovery." *Reading Research Quarterly, 30*(2), 240–263.

Center for Substance Abuse Prevention. (1993). *Signs of effectiveness in preventing alcohol and other drug problems.* Washington, DC: U.S. Government Printing Office.

Centers for Disease Control. (1992). *Selected behaviors that increase risk for HIV infection, other sexually transmitted diseases, and unintentional pregnancy among high school students—United States, 1991.* Atlanta, GA: Author.

Centers for Disease Control and Prevention. (1993). *Mortality trends, causes of death, and related risk behaviors among U.S. adolescents.* Atlanta: Author.

Centers for Disease Control and Prevention. (1994). HIV/AIDS. *Surveillance Report, 6*(2), 1–39.

Charney, R. S., & Clayton, M. K. (1994). The first 6 weeks of school. *The Responsive Classroom, 6*(2), 1–3.

Chavers, D. (1991). Indian education: Dealing with a disaster. *Principal, 70,* 28–29.

Cheng, W. D. (1996). Pacific perspective. *Together, 24*(3).

Children's Defense Fund. (1991). *The state of America's children yearbook.* Washington, DC: Author.

Children's Defense Fund. (1994). *The state of America's children yearbook.* Washington, DC: Author.

Children's Defense Fund. (1995). *The state of America's children yearbook.* Washington, DC: Author.

Cicchetti, D., Rogosch, F. A., Lynch, M., & Holt, K. D. (1993). Resilience in maltreated children: Processes leading to adaptive outcome. *Development and Psychopathology, 5,* 629–647.

Clark, A. J. (1994). Conflict resolution and individual psychology in the schools. *Individual Psychology: Journal of Adlerian Theory, Research, and Practice, 50*(3), 329–340.

Clark, D. B., & Sayette, M. A. (1993). Anxiety and the development of alcoholism. *The American Journal on Addictions, 2*(1), 59–76.

Clarke-Stewart, A. (1989). Infant day care: Malignant or maligned? *American Psychologist, 44,* 266–273.

Clarke-Stewart, K. A., Gruber, C. P., & Fitzgerald, L. M. (1994). *Children at home and in day care.* Hillsdale, NJ: Erlbaum.

Clausen, J. A. (1993). *American lives: Looking back at the children of the great depression.* New York: Free Press.

Clay, M. M. (1985). *The early detection of reading difficulties.* Exeter, NH: Heinemann.

Cobb, P. (1994). Constructivism in mathematics and science education. *Educational Researcher, 23*(7), 4.

Cochran, D. (1994). *Young adolescent batterers: A profile of restraining order defendants in Massachusetts.* Boston: Massachusetts Trial Court Research Report, Office of Commissioner of Probation.

Cohen, D. K., McLaughlin, M. W., & Talbert, J. E. (1993). *Teaching for Understanding: Challenges for policy and practice.* San Francisco, CA: Jossey-Bass.

Cohen, S. B., & de Bettencourt, L. V. (1991). Dropout: Intervening with the reluctant learner. *Intervention in School and Clinic, 26,* 263–271.

Coie, J. D., Dodge, K. A., Terry, R., & Wright, V. (1991). The role of aggression in peer relations: An analysis of aggression episodes in boys' play groups. *Child Development, 62,* 812–826.

Coie, J. D., Watt, N. F., West, S. G., Hawkins, J. D., Asarnow, J. R., Markman, H. J., Ramey, S. L., Shure, M. B., & Long, B. (1993). The science of prevention: A conceptual framework and some directions for a national research program. *American Psychologist, 48*(10), 1013–1022.

Cole, J. D. (1990). Toward a theory of peer rejection. In S. R. Asher & J. D. Coie (Eds.), *Peer rejection in childhood* (pp. 365–401). New York: Cambridge University.

Coleman, J. (1991). *Parental involvement in education.* Washington, DC: U.S. Department of Education.

Coleman, J. S., & Hoffer, T. (1987). *Public and private high schools: The impact of communities.* New York: Basic Books.

Comiskey, P. E. (1993). Using reality therapy group training with at-risk high school freshman. *Journal of Reality Therapy, 12*(2), 59–64.

Comer, J. P. (Ed.). (1996). *Rallying the whole village: The Comer Process for reforming education.* New York: Teachers College Press.

Compas, B. E., Banez, G. A., Malcarne, V., & Worsham, N. (1991). Perceived control and coping with stress: A developmental perspective. *Journal of Social Issues, 47,* 23–34.

Conger, J. J. (1988). Hostages to fortune: Youth, values, and the public interest. *American Psychologist, 43*(4), 291–300.

Conger, R. D., & Elder, G. H., Jr. (Eds.). (1994). *Families in troubled times: Adapting to change in rural America.* New York: Aldine de Gruyter.

Cooper, M. L. (1994). Motivations for alcohol use among adolescents: Development and validation of a four-factor model. *Psychological Assessment, 6*(2), 117–128.

Corbin, S. K. T., Jones, R. T., & Schulman, R. S. (1993). Drug refusal behavior: The relative efficacy of skills-based and information-based treatment. *Journal of Pediatric Psychology, 18*(6), 769–784.

Costa, A. L. (Ed.). (1991). *Developing minds: A resource book for teaching thinking.* Alexandria, VA: Association of Supervision and Curriculum Development.

Costa, L., & Altekruse, M. (1994). Duty-to-warn guidelines for mental health counselors. *Journal of Counseling & Development, 72*(4), 346–350.

Cranston, K. (1991). HIV education for gay, lesbian and bisexual youth: Personal risk, personal power, and the community of conscience. *Journal of Homosexuality, 22,* 247–259.

Craven, R. G., March, H. W., & Debus, R. L. (1991). Effects of internally focused feedback and attributional feedback on enhancement of academic self-concept. *Journal of Educational Psychology, 83,* 17–27.

Cuban, L. (1989). At-risk students: What teachers and principals can do. *Educational Leadership, 45*(5), 29–33.

Culhane, D., Dejowski, E. F., Ibanez, J., et al. (1993). *Public shelter admission rates in Philadelphia and New York City: Working paper.* Washington, DC: Fannie Mae Office of Housing Research.

Cunningham, C. E., Bremner, R., & Boyle, M. (1995). Large group community-based parenting programs for families of preschoolers at risk for disruptive behaviour disorders: Utilization, cost effectiveness, and outcome. *Journal of Child Psychology and Psychiatry, 36*(7), 1141–1159.

D'Augelli, A. R. (1991). Gay men in college: Identity processes and adaptations. *Journal of College Student Development, 32,* 140–146.

D'Augelli, A. R., & Dark, L. J. (1994). Lesbian, gay and bisexual youths. In L. D. Eroh, J. H. Gentry, & P. Schlegel (Eds.). *Reason to hope: A psychosocial perspective on violence and youth* (pp. 177–196). Washington, DC: APA.

DaVanzo, J., & Rahman, M. O. (1993). *American families: Trends and policy issues.* Santa Monica, CA: RAND.

Davidson, N. (Ed.). (1990). *Cooperative learning in mathematics: A handbook for teachers.* Reading, MA: Addison-Wesley.

Davidson, N., & Worsham, T. (Eds.). (1992). *Enhancing thinking through cooperative learning.* New York: Teachers College Press.

Davis, M., Eshelman, E., & McKay, M. (1988). *The relaxation and stress reduction workbook* (3rd ed.). Oakland, CA: New Harbinger Publications.

Davis, S. (1989). Evening classes for at-risk kids cost only a little, but they help a lot. *American School Board Journal, 126,* 33.

DeBaryshe, B. D., Patterson, G. R., & Capaldi, D. M. (1993). A performance model for academic achievement in early adolescent boys. *Developmental Psychology, 29,* 295–804.

DeConcini, D. (1988). America's little red school house: How is it holding up? *American Psychologist, 43,* 115–117.

Devine, C., & Braithwaite, V. (1993). The survival role of children of alcoholics: Their measurement and validity. *Addiction, 88,* 69–78.

Devries, D., & Slavin, R. (1978). Teams-Games-Tournaments (TGT): Review of ten classroom experiments. *Journal of Research and Development in Education, 12,* 28–38.

Dewey, J. (1944). *Democracy and education.* New York: Free Press. (Original work published 1916)

Dickerson, B. J. (1995). *African American single mothers: Understanding their lives and families.* Thousand Oaks, CA: Sage.

Dielman, T. E. (1994). School-based research on the prevention of adolescent alcohol use and misuse: Methodological issues and advances. *Journal of Research on Adolescence, 4,* 271–293.

Dielman, T. E., Butchart, A. T., Shope, J. T., & Miller, M. (1990–1991). *The International Journal of the Addictions, 25*(7A & 8A), 855–880.

Diem, R., & Katims, D. S. (1991). Handicaps and at risk: Preparing teachers for a growing populace. *Intervention in School and Clinic, 26,* 272–275.

Diener, E., & Diener, C. (1996). Most people are happy. *Psychological Science, 7*(3), 181–189.

DiGangi, S. A., Maag, J. W., & Rutherford, R. B., Jr. (1991). Self-graphing of on-task behavior: Enhancing the reactive effects of self-monitoring on on-task behavior and academic performance. *Learning Disabilities Quarterly, 14,* 221–230.

Dodge, K. A. (1992, October 9–13). Youth violence: Who? what? where? when? how? WHY? *Tennessee Teacher.*

Dodge, K. A., & Price, J. M. (1994). On the relation between social information processing and socially competent behavior in early school-aged children. *Child Development, 65,* 1385–1397.

Dodge, K. A., Price, J. M., Bachorowski, J., & Newman, J. P. (1990). Hostile attributional biases in severely aggressive adolescents. *Journal of Abnormal Psychology, 99,* 385–392.

Dodge, K. A., & Somberg, D. R. (1987). Hostile attributional biases among aggressive boys are exacerbated under conditions of threats to self. *Child Development, 58,* 213–224.

Dolbeare, C. N. (1991). *Out of reach: Why everyday people can't find affordable housing.* Washington, DC: Low Income Housing Information Service.

Donmoyer, R., & Kos, R. (1993). *At-risk students: Portraits, policies, programs, and practices.* Albany, NY: State University of New York Press.

Donovan, P. (1993). *Testing positive: Sexually transmitted disease and the public health response.* New York: The Alan Guttmacher Institute.

Drazen, S. M. (1994, August). *Factors influencing student achievement from early to mid-adolescence.* Paper presented at the meeting of the American Psychological Association, Los Angeles.

Dreikurs, R. (1964). *Children: The challenge.* New York: Hawthorne.

Dreikurs, R. (1967). *Psychology in the classroom.* New York: Harper & Row.

Driver, R., Asoko, H., Leach, J., Mortimer, E., & Scott, P. (1994). Constructing scientific knowledge in the classroom. *Education Researcher, 23*(7), 5–12.

The dropout's perspective on leaving school (1988). *CAPS Capsule, 2,* 3.

Drukteinis, A. M. (1985). Psychiatric perspectives on civil liability for suicide. *Bulletin of the American Academy of Psychiatry and Law, 13*(1), 71–83.

Dryfoos, J. G. (1990). *Adolescents at risk: Prevalence and prevention.* New York: Oxford University Press.

Dryfoos, J. G. (1994). *Full-service schools: A revolution in health and social services for children, youth, and families.* San Francisco: Jossey-Bass.

Duany, L., & Pitmann, K. (1990). *Latino youths at a crossroads: Adolescent pregnancy prevention clearinghouse report.* Washington, DC: Children's Defense Fund.

Duffy, G., Roehler, L., & Herrmann, B. A. (1988). Modeling mental processes helps poor readers become strategic readers. *Reading Teacher, 41,* 762–767.

Dunford, F. W., & Elliott, D. S. (1984). Identifying career criminals using self-reported data. *Journal of Research in Crime and Delinquency, 21,* 57–86.

Durlak, J. A. (1995). *School-based prevention programs for children and adolescents.* Thousand Oaks, CA: Sage.

Durlak, J. A., Fuhrman, T., & Lampman, C. (1991). Effectiveness of cognitive-behavior therapy for maladapting children: A meta-analysis. *Psychological Bulletin, 110,* 204–214.

Duvall, E. M., & Miller, B. C. (1985). *Marriage and family development* (6th ed.). New York: Harper & Row.

Dyk, P. H. (1993). Anatomy, physiology, and gender issues in adolescence. In T. P. Gullotta, G. R. Adams, & R. Montemayor (Eds.), *Adolescent sexuality: Advances in adolescent development: Volume 5* (pp. 35–56). Newbury Park, CA: Sage.

D'Zurilla, J. (1986). *Problem-solving therapy: A social competence approach to clinical intervention.* New York: Springer.

Ebb, N. (1994). *Child care tradeoffs: States make painful choices.* Washington, DC: Children's Defense Fund.

Edelman, M. W. (1987). *Families in peril: An agenda for social change.* Cambridge, MA: Harvard University Press.

Edelsky, C. (1991). Authentic reading/writing versus reading/writing exercises. In K. S. Goodman, L. B. Bird, & Y. M. Goodman (Eds.), *The whole language catalog* (p. 72). Santa Rosa, CA: American School Publishers.

Edelsky, C., Altwerger, B., & Flores, B. (1991). *Whole language: What's the difference?* Portsmouth, NH: Heinemann.

Ehly, S. (1986). *Peer tutoring: A guide for school psychologists.* Washington, DC: National Association of School Psychologists.

Eisenberg, N., Fabes, R. A., Nyman, M., Bernzweig, J., & Pinuelas, A. (1994). The relations of emotionality and regulation to children's anger-related reactions. *Child Development, 65*(1), 109–128.

Ekstrom, R. B., Goertz, M. E., Pollack, J. M., & Rock, D. A. (1986). Who drops out of high school and why? Findings from a national study. *Teacher's College Record, 87,* 356–373.

Elder, G. H., Jr., Conger, R. D., Foster, E. M., & Ardelt, M. K. (1992). Families under economic pressure. *Journal of Family Issues, 13,* 5–37.

Elder, J. P., Wildey, M., de Moor, C., Sallis, J., Eckhardt, L., Edwards, C., Erickson, A., Golbeck, A., Hovell, M., Johnston, D., Levitz, M., Molgaard, C., Young, R., Vito, D., & Woodruff, S. (1993). The long-term prevention of tobacco use among junior high school students: Classroom and telephone interviews. *American Journal of Public Health, 83*(9), 1230–1244.

Ellickson, P. L., Bell, R. M., & McGuigan, K. (1993). Preventing adolescent drug use: Long-term results of a junior high program. *American Journal of Public Health, 83,* 856–861.

Ellis, A. (1962). *Reason and emotion in psychotherapy.* New York: Stuart.

Ellis, A. (1985). *Overcoming resistance: Rational-emotive therapy with difficult clients.* New York: Springer.

Ellis, A. (1996). *Better, deeper, and more enduring brief therapy: The rational emotive behavior therapy approach.* New York: Brunner/Mazel.

Elmore, R., Peterson, P. L., & McCarthey, S. J. (1996). *Restructuring in the classroom: Teaching, learning, and school organization.* San Francisco: Jossey-Bass.

Elmquist, D. L. (1991). School-based alcohol and other drug prevention programs: Guidelines for the special educator. *Intervention in School and Clinic, 27*(1), 10–19.

Entwisle, D., & Alexander, K. (1992). Summer setback: Race, poverty, school composition, and mathematics achievement in the first two years of school. *American Sociological Review,* 57, 72–84.

Eron, L. D., Gentry, J. H., & Schlegel, P. (1994). *Reason to hope: A psychosocial perspective of violence and youth.* Washington, DC: American Psychological Association.

Fad, K. S. (1990). The fast track to success: Social-behavioral skills. *Intervention in School and Clinic,* 26(1), 39–43.

Falco, K. (1991). *Psychotherapy with lesbian clients.* New York: Brunner/Mazel.

Falco, M. (1988, June). *Preventing abuse of drugs, alcohol, and tobacco by adolescents.* Working paper, Carnegie Council on Adolescent Development, New York.

Falco, M. (1992). *The making of a drug-free America: Programs that work.* New York: Times Books.

Felner, R. D., Brand, S., Adan, A. M., Mullhall, P. F., Flowers, N., Sartain, B., & DuBois, D. L. (1993). Restructuring the ecology of the school as an approach to prevention during school transitions: Longitudinal follow-ups and extensions of the School Transitional Environment Project (STEP). *Prevention and Human Services,* 10, 103–136.

Fenstermacher, G. (1986). Philosophy of research on teaching: Three aspects. In M. Wittrock (Ed.), *Handbook of research on teaching* (3rd ed.) (pp. 37–49). New York: Macmillan.

Ferguson, R. F. (1991). Paying for public education: New evidence on how and why money matters. *Harvard Journal on Legislation,* 28, 465–498.

Fergusson, D. M., & Lynskey, M. T. (1995). Childhood circumstances, adolescent adjustment, and suicide attempts in a New Zealand birth cohort. *Journal of American Child and Adolescent Psychiatry,* 34(5), 612–621.

Fernandez v. Baruch, 52 N.J. 127, 244 A2d 109 (1968).

Fincham, F. D. (1994). Understanding the association between marital conflict and child adjustment: Overview. *Journal of Family Psychology,* 8(2), 123–127.

Fincham, F. D., Grych, J. H., & Osborn, L. N. (1994). Does marital conflict cause child maladjustment? Directions and challenges for longitudinal research. *Journal of Family Psychology,* 8, 128–140.

Fincham, F. D., & Osborn, L. (1993). Marital conflict and children: Retrospect and prospect. *Clinical Psychology Review,* 13, 75–88.

Fleming, M. (1990). *Conducting support groups for students affected by chemical dependence: A guide for educators and other professionals.* Minneapolis, MN: Johnson Institute.

Forgatch, M. S. (1988, June). *The relation between child behaviors, client resistance, and parenting practices.* Paper presented at the Earlscourt Symposium on Childhood Aggression, Toronto.

Fraser, B. J. (1994). Research on classroom and school climate. In D. Gabel (Ed.), *Handbook of research on science teaching and learning* (pp. 493–541). New York: Macmillan.

Fraser, M. W. (1996). Aggressive behavior in childhood and early adolescence: An ecological-developmental perspective on youth violence. *Social Work,* 41(4), 347–356.

Freeman, B. (1995). Power motivation and youth: An analysis of troubled students and student leaders. *Journal of Counseling and Development,* 73, 661–671.

Frey, H. (1980). Improving the performance of poor readers through autogenic relaxation training. *Reading Teacher,* 33, 928–932.

Frey, J., Holley, H., & L'Abate, L. (1979). Intimacy is sharing hurt feelings: A comparison of three conflict resolution models. *Journal of Marital and Family Therapy,* 5(2), 35–41.

Fry, D. P. (1993). The intergenerational transmission of disciplinary practices and approaches to conflict. *Human Organization,* 52, 176–185.

Garbarino, J. (1994). *Raising children in a socially toxic environment.* San Francisco, CA: Jossey-Bass.

Garber, J., Deale, S., & Parke, C. (1986, November). *The Coping with Depression pamphlet revised for adolescents: Comprehensibility and acceptability.* Paper presented at the annual meeting of the Association for the Advancement of Behavior Therapy, Chicago.

Garcia-Vazquez, E., & Ehly, S. W. (1992). Peer tutoring effects on students who are perceived as not socially accepted. *Psychology in the Schools,* 29, 256–266.

Gardner, S. E., Green, P. F., & Marcus, C. (Eds.). (1994). *Signs of effectiveness II: Preventing alcohol, tobacco, and other drug use: A risk factor/resiliency-based approach.* Washington, DC: U.S. Government Printing Office.

Gardner, W., & Herman, J. (1991). Adolescents: AIDS risk taking: A rational choice perspective. In W. Gardner, S. Mielstein, & B. Wilcox (Eds.), *Adolescents in the AIDS epidemic.* San Francisco: Jossey-Bass.

Garland, A. F., & Zigler, E. (1993). Adolescent suicide prevention: Current research and social policy implications. *American Psychologist,* 43(2), 169–182.

Garrison, C., Addy, C., Jackson, K., et al. (1992). Major depressive disorder and dysthymia in young adolescents. *American Journal of Epidemiology,* 135, 792–802.

Gaustad, J. (1992). Tutoring for at-risk students. *Oregon School Study Council Bulletin,* 36(3), 1–74. (ERIC Document Reproduction Service No. ED 353 642)

Gazda, G. M. (1989). *Group counseling.* Boston: Allyn & Bacon.

Gersten, R., & Carnine, D. (1984). Direct instruction mathematics: A longitudinal evaluation of low-income elementary school students. *Elementary School Journal,* 84, 395–407.

Gersten, R., & Keating, T. (1987). Long-term benefits from direct instruction. *Educational Leadership,* 44(6), 28–31.

Gibbs, J. T., & Huang, L. N. (Eds.). (1991). *Children of color: Psychological interventions with minority youth.* San Francisco: Jossey-Bass.

Gibson, P. (1989). Gay male and lesbian youth suicide. *Report of the secretary's task force on youth suicide, Vol 3: Prevention and interventions in youth suicide.* Rockville, MD: U.S. Department of Health and Human Services.

Gillham, J. E., Reivich, K. J., Jaycox, L. H., & Seligman, M. E. P. (1995). Prevention of depressive symptoms in schoolchildren: Two-year follow-up. *Psychological Science,* 6, 343–351.

Gilligan, C. (1993). *In a different voice: Psychological theory and women's development.* Cambridge, MA: Harvard University Press.

Gingras, R. C., & Careaga, R. C. (1989). Limited English proficient students at risk: Issues and prevention strategies. *New Focus: National Clearinghouse for Bilingual Education, 10,* 1–11.

Giroux, H. A. (1989). Critical literacy and students' experience: Donald Graves' approach to literacy. *Language Arts, 64,* 175–181.

Glantz, K. (1983). The use of relaxation exercises in the treatment of reading disability. *Journal of Nervous and Mental Disease, 171*(12), 749–752.

Glasser, W. (1965). *Reality therapy: A new approach to psychiatry.* New York: Harper & Row.

Glasser, W. (1972). *The identity society.* New York: Harper & Row.

Glasser, W. (1976). *Positive addiction.* New York: Harper & Row.

Glasser, W. (1986). *Control theory in the classroom.* New York: Harper & Row.

Glasser, W. (1990). The quality school. *Phi Delta Kappan, 72,* 425–435.

Glynn, T., Bethune, N., Crooks, T., & Ballard, K. (1992). "Reading recovery" in context: Implementation and outcome. *Educational Psychology, 12*(3–4), 249–261.

Goetting, A. (1995). *Homicide in families and other special populations.* New York: Springer.

Goldstein, A. P. (1996). *The psychology of vandalism.* New York: Plenum Press.

Goldstein, A. P., Harootunian, B., & Conoley, J. C. (1994). *Student aggression: Prevention, management, and replacement training.* New York: Guilford.

Goldstein, A., Sprafkin, R., Gershaw, N. J., & Klein, P. (1980). *Skill streaming the adolescent: A structured learning approach to teaching prosocial behavior.* Champaign, IL: Research Press.

Good, T. L., & Brophy, J. E. (1994). *Looking into classrooms* (6th ed.). New York: HarperCollins.

Good, T. L., & Weinstein, R. S. (1986). Schools make a difference: Evidence, criticisms, and new directions. *American Psychologist, 41,* 1090–1097.

Goodlad, J. I. (1994). *Educational renewal: Better teachers, better schools.* San Francisco: Jossey-Bass.

Goodman, S. H., Adamson, L. B., Riniti, J., & Cole, S. (1994). Mothers' expressed attitudes: Associations with maternal depression and children's self-esteem and psychopathology. *Journal of the American Academy of Child and Adolescent Psychiatry, 33,* 1265–1274.

Gordon, T. (1970). *Parent effectiveness training.* New York: Wyden.

Gordon, T. (1974). *Teacher effectiveness training.* New York: Wyden.

Gordon, T. (1977). *Leader effectiveness training.* New York: Putnam.

Gordon, T. (1989). *Teaching children self-discipline . . . at home and at school: New ways for parents and teachers to build self-control, self-esteem, and self-reliance.* New York: Random House.

Gormley, W. T. (1995). *Everybody's children: Child care as a public problem.* Washington, DC: Brookings Institution.

Gould, M. S., & Shaffer, D. (1986). The impact of suicide in television movies. Evidence of imitation. *New England Journal of Medicine, 315*(11), 690–694.

Grant, G. (1982). The elements of a strong positive ethos. *National Association of Secondary School Principals Bulletin, 66*(452) 84–90.

Greenberg, B. S., Siemicki, M., Dorfman, S., et al. (1993). Sex content in R-rated films viewed by adolescents. In B. S. Greenberg, J. D. Brown, & N. L. Buerkel-Rothfuss (Eds.), *Media, sex and the adolescent.* Cresskill, NJ: Hampton Press.

Greenwood, C. R., Carta, J. J., & Maheady, L. (1991). Peer tutoring programs in the regular classroom. In G. Stoner, M. R. Shinn, & H. M. Walker (Eds.), *Interventions for achievement and behavior problems* (pp. 179–200). Washington, DC: National Association of School Psychologists.

Grossman, J., Hirsch, J., Goldenberg, D., & Libby, S. (1995). Strategies for school-based response to loss: Proactive training and postvention consultation. *Crisis, 16*(1), 18–26.

Gueron, J. M., & Pauly, E. (1991). *From welfare to work.* New York: Russell Sage Foundation.

Guetzloe, E. C. (1991). *Depression and the potential suicide: Special education students at risk.* Reston, VA: The Council for Exceptional Children.

Guy, S. M., Smith, G. M., & Bentler, P. M. (1993). Adolescent socialization and use of licit and illicit substances: Impact on adult health. *Psychology and Health, 8*(6), 463–487.

Guy, S. M., Smith, G. M., & Bentler, P. M. (1994). The influence of adolescent substance use and socialization on deviant behavior in young adulthood. *Criminal Justice and Behavior, 21*(2), 236–255.

Haberman, M. (1993). In M. J. O'Hair & S. Odell (Eds.), *Diversity and teaching: Teacher education yearbook I* (pp. 84–96). Orlando, FL: Harcourt Brace Jovanovich.

Hacker, A. (1992). *Two nations: Black, white, separate and unequal.* New York: Scribner.

Haffner, D. (1994). *Sexuality education and contraceptive instruction in U.S. schools.* Paper prepared for the Committee on Unintended Pregnancy. Washington, DC: Institute of Medicine.

Haggerty, R. J., Sherrod, L. R., Garmezy, N., & Rutter, M. (Eds.). (1994). *Stress, risk, resilience in children and adolescents: Processes, mechanisms, and interventions.* New York: Cambridge University Press.

Haley, J. (1976). *Problem-solving therapy.* San Francisco: Jossey-Bass.

Haley, J. (1984). *Ordeal therapy.* San Francisco: Jossey-Bass.

Hambright, J. E. (1988). *Effects of perceived life options on female adolescent sexual responsibility: A test of a conceptual model.* (Doctoral dissertation, Arizona State University, Tempe).

Hamburg, D. A. (1994). *Today's children: Creating a future for a generation in crisis.* New York: Time Books.

Hamburg, D. A. (1995). *A developmental strategy to prevent lifelong damage.* New York: Carnegie Corporation of New York.

Hammer, C. J. (1993) *Youth violence: Gangs on main street, USA.* Philadelphia: PEW Charitable Trust.

Hammond, W. R., & Yung, B. R. (1994). African Americans. In L. D. Eron, J. H. Gentry, & P. Schlegel, (Eds.), *Reason to hope: A psychosocial perspective on violence & youth* (pp. 105–118). Washington: APA.

Hanson, M., & Peterson, D. S. (1993). *How to conduct a school recovery support group.* Portland, ME: J. Weston Walch.

Harding, A. K., Gray, L. A., & Neal, M. (1993). Confidentiality limits with clients who have HIV: A review of ethical and legal guidelines and professional policies. *Journal of Counseling and Development, 71,* 297–305.

Harlow, L. L., Newcomb, M. D., & Bentler, P. M. (1986). Depression, self-derogation, substance use, and suicide ideation: Lack of purpose in life as a mediational factor. *Journal of Clinical Psychology, 42*(1), 5–21.

Harris, S. M. (1995). Psychosocial development and black male masculinity: Implications for counseling economically disadvantaged African American male adolescents. *Journal of Counseling and Development, 73,* 279–287.

Harris, S., & Harris, L. B. (Eds.) (1986). *The teacher's almanac.* New York: Facts on File.

Harter, S. (1985). *Manual for the Self-Perception Profile for Children (revision of the Perceived Competence Scale for Children).* Denver, CO: University of Denver.

Harter, S. (1990). Causes, correlates and the functional role of global self-worth: A life-span perspective. In R. Sternberg & J. Kolligian (Eds.), *Competence considered* (pp. 67–97). New Haven, CT: Yale University Press.

Haveman, R., & Wolfe, B. (1994). *Succeeding generations.* New York: Russell Sage Foundation.

Hawkins, J. D., Catalano, R. F., & Associates. (1992). *Communities that care: Action for drug abuse.* San Francisco: Jossey-Bass.

Hawkins, J. D., Catalano, R. F., & Miller, J. Y. (1992). Risk and protective factors for alcohol and other drug problems in adolescence and early adulthood: Implications for substance abuse prevention. *Psychological Bulletin, 112*(1), 64–105.

Hawryluk, M. K., & Smallwood, D. L. (1988). Using peers as instructional agents: Peer tutoring and cooperative learning. In J. L. Graden, J. E. Zins, & M. J. Curtis (Eds.), *Alternative educational delivery systems: Enhancing instructional options for all students* (pp. 371–389). Washington, DC: National Association of School Psychologists.

Hechinger, F. (1992). *Fateful choices: Healthy youth for the 21st century.* New York: Carnegie Corporation of New York.

Henshaw, S. K. (1992). Abortion trends in 1987 and 1988: Age and race. *Family Planning Perspectives, 24,* 85–86.

Herring, R. D. (1994, July/August). Substance use among Native American Indian youth: A selected review of causality. *Journal of Counseling and Development, 72,* 578–584.

Herrmann, D. S., & McWhirter, J. J. (1997). Refusal and resistance skills for children and adolescents: A selected review. *Journal of Counseling and Development.*

Herrmann, D. S., McWhirter, J. J., & Sipsas-Herrmann, A. (1997). The relationship between dimensional self-concept and juvenile gang involvement: Implications for prevention, intervention, and court referred diversion programs. *Behavioral Sciences and the Law.*

Hewlett, S. A. (1991). *When the bough breaks: The cost of neglecting our children.* New York: HarperCollins.

H. L. v. Matheson, 450 U.S. 398 (1981).

Hofferth, S. L. (1987). Social and economic consequences of teenage childbearing. In S. L. Hofferth & C. D. Hayes (Eds.), *Risking the future: Adolescent sexuality, pregnancy, and childbearing, Vol. II* (pp. 123–144). Washington, DC: National Academy Press.

Hofferth, S. L. (1991). Programs for high-risk adolescents: What works? *Evaluation and Program Planning, 14,* 3–16.

Hoffman, E. (1994). *The drive for self: Alfred Adler and the founding of individual psychology.* Reading, MA: Addison-Wesley.

Holinger, P. C., Offer, D., Barter, J. T., & Bell, C. C. (1994). *Suicide and homicide among adolescents.* New York: Guilford.

Holloman, F. W. (1993). Estimates of the population of the United States by age, sex, and race. U.S. Bureau of the Census, *Current population reports,* Series P-25, No. 1095.

Holmes, G. R. (1995). *Helping teenagers into adulthood: A guide for the next generation.* Westport, CT: Praeger/Greenwood.

Hopkins, B. R. (1989, February). Counselors and the law. *Guidepost,* p. 13.

Hopkins, B. R., & Anderson, B. S. (1985). *The counselor and the law* (2nd ed.). Alexandria, VA: American Association for Counseling and Development.

Hudelson, S. (1989). *Write on: Children writing in ESL.* Englewood Cliffs, NJ: Prentice Hall.

Hudson, R. A. (1980). *Sociolinguistics.* Cambridge: Cambridge University Press.

Hunter, J., & Schaecher, R. (1990). Lesbian and gay youth. In M. J. Rotheram-Borus, J. Bradley, & N. Obolensky (Eds.), *Planning to live: Evaluating and treating suicidal teens in community settings* (pp. 297–316). Tulsa: University of Oklahoma Press.

Hunter, M. (1991). Hunter design helps achieve the goals of science instruction. *Educational Leadership, 48*(4), 79–81.

Hyson, M. C. (1994). *The emotional development of young children: Building an emotion-centered curriculum.* New York: Teachers College Press.

In re Gault, 387 U.S. 1 (1967).

Information please almanac, atlas, and yearbook (44th ed.) (1991). Boston: Houghton Mifflin.

Interagency Council on the Homeless. (1994). *Priority: Home! The federal plan to break the cycle of homelessness.* Washington, DC: Author.

Jackson, N., Jackson, D., & Monroe, C. (1983). *Getting along with others: Teaching social effectiveness to children.* Champaign, IL: Research Press.

Jacobson, E. (1938). *Progressive relaxation* (2nd ed.). Chicago: University of Chicago Press.

Jaffe v. Redmond, 116 S.Ct. 1923 (1996).

Jaycox, L. H., Reivich, K. J., Gillham, J. K., & Seligman, M. E. P. (1994). Preventing depressive symptoms in school children. *Behavior Research and Therapy, 32,* 801–816.

Jaycox, L. H., & Repetti, R. L. (1993). Conflict in families and the psychological adjustment of preadolescent children. *Journal of Family Psychology, 7,* 344–355.

Jemmott, J. B., Jemmott, L. S., & Fong, G. T. (1992). Reductions in HIV-risk-associated sexual behaviors among black male adolescents: Effects of an AIDS prevention intervention. *American Journal of Public Health, 82,* 372–377.

Jessor, L. D., & Jessor, S. L. (1977). *Problem behavior and psychosocial development: A longitudinal study of youth.* New York: Academic Press.

Jessor, R. (1991). Risk behavior in adolescence: A psychosocial framework for understanding and action. *Journal of Adolescent Health, 12,* 597–605.

Jessor, R. (1993). Successful adolescent development among youth in high-risk settings. *American Psychologist, 48,* 117–126.

Jessor, R., Donovan, J. E., & Costa, F. M. (1991). *Beyond adolescence: Problem behavior and young adult development.* New York: Cambridge University Press.

Jessor, R., Van Den Bos, J., Vanderryn, J., Costa, R. M., & Turbin, M. S. (1995). Protective factors in adolescent problem behavior: Moderator effects and developmental change. *Developmental Psychology, 31,* 923–933.

Jobes, D. A., & Berman, A. L. (1993). Suicide and malpractice liability: Assessing and revising policies, procedures, and practice in outpatient settings. *Professional Psychology: Research and Practice, 24,* 91–99.

Johnson, D. W., & Johnson, R. T. (1988). Critical thinking through structured controversy. *Educational Leadership, 45,* 58–64.

Johnson, D. W., & Johnson, R. T. (1989a). *Cooperation and competition: Theory and research.* Edina, MN: Interaction Book Company.

Johnson, D. W., & Johnson, R. T. (1989b). Toward a cooperative effort: A response to Slavin. *Educational Leadership, 46,* 80–81.

Johnson, D., & Johnson, R. (1993). What we know about cooperative learning at the college level. *Cooperative Learning, 13*(3), 17–19.

Johnson, D. W., Johnson, R., & Holubec, E. (1990). *Circles of learning: Cooperation in the classroom.* Edina, MN: Interaction Book Company.

Johnson, D. W., Johnson, R. T., & Taylor, B. (1993). Impact of cooperative and individualistic learning on high-ability students' achievement, self-esteem, and social acceptance. *The Journal of Social Psychology, 133*(6), 839–844.

Johnson, S. (1977). *Cross-age tutoring handbook.* Corcoran Unified School District, CA. (ERIC Document Reproduction Service No. ED 238 826)

Johnson, S. M., & Boles, K. C. (1994). The role of teachers in school reform. In S. A. Mohrman & P. Wohlstetter (Eds.), *School-based management: Organizing for high performance* (pp. 109–137). San Francisco: Jossey-Bass.

Johnston, L. D., Bachman, J. G., & O'Malley, P. M. (1992). *Smoking, drinking, and illicit drug use among American secondary school students, college students, and young adults, 1975–1991.* Rockville, MD: National Institute on Drug Abuse.

Johnston, L. D., O'Malley, P. M., & Bachman, J. G. (1995). *National survey results on drug use from the monitoring the future study, 1975–1994.* Rockville, MD: National Institute on Drug Abuse.

Jones, L. K. (1996). A harsh and challenging world of work: Implications for counselors. *Journal of Counseling and Development, 74,* 453–459.

Jorgensen, J. A., & Newlon, B. J. (1988). Life-style themes of unwed, pregnant adolescents who choose to keep their babies. *Individual Psychology, 44*(4), 466, 471.

Kadel, S., & Follman, J. (1993, March). Reducing school violence. *SouthEastern Regional Vision for Education.*

Kagan, S. L., & Weissbourd, B. (Eds.). (1994). *Putting families first: America's family support movement and the challenge of change.* San Francisco: Jossey-Bass.

Kahn, J. S., Kehle, T. J., Jenson, W. R., & Clarke, E. (1990). Comparison of cognitive-behavioral, relaxation, and self-modeling intervention for depression among middle-school students. *School Psychology Review, 19,* 195–210.

Kalafat, J. (1994). On initiating school-based suicide response programs. *Special Services in the Schools, 8*(2), 21–31.

Kalichman, S. C., & Brosig, C. L. (1993). Practicing psychologists' interpretations of compliance with child abuse reporting law. *Law and Human Behavior, 17,* 83–93.

Kaminer, Y. (1994). *Adolescent substance abuse: A comprehensive guide to theory and practice.* New York: Plenum Medical/Plenum.

Kandel, D. B., & Davies, M. (1996). High school students who use crack and other drugs. *Archives of General Psychiatry, 53,* 71–80.

Kaplan, J. S. (1991). *Beyond behavior modification: A cognitive-behavioral approach to behavior management in the school.* Austin, TX: Pro-Ed.

Kashani, J. H., Daniel, A. E., Dandoy, A. C., & Holcomb, W. R. (1992). Family violence: Impact on children. *Journal of the American Academy of Child and Adolescent Psychiatry, 31*(2), 181–189.

Kazdin, A. E. (1994). Interventions for aggressive and antisocial children. In L. D. Eron, J. H. Gentry, & P. Schlegel (Eds.), *Reason to hope: A psychosocial perspective on violence and youth* (pp. 341–382). Washington: APA.

Kazdin A. E. (1994b). *Treatment of antisocial behavior in children and adolescents: Alternative interventions and their effectiveness.* Pacific Grove, CA: Brooks/Cole.

Keane, S. P., & Conger, J. C. (1981). The implications of communication development for social skills training. *Journal of Pediatric Psychology, 6,* 369–381.

Keefe, C. H., & Keefe, D. R. (1993). Instruction for students with LD: A whole language model. *Intervention in School and Clinic, 28*(3), 172–177.

Kelly, J. (1982). *Social skill training.* New York: Springer.

Kempton, T., & Forehand, R. L. (1992). Suicide attempts among juvenile delinquents: The contribution of mental health factors. *Behavior Research and Therapy, 30*(5), 537–541.

Kerr, M. E., & Bowen, M. (1988). *Family evaluation: An approach based on Bowen theory.* New York: W.W. Norton.

Kiernan, K. (1992). The impact of family disruption in childhood on transitions made in young adult life. *Population Studies, 46,* 213–234.

King, S. M. (1991). Benign sabotage and Dreikurs' second goal of misbehavior. *Family Therapy, 18*(3), 265–268.

Kinnier, R. T., & Krumboltz, J. D. (1984). Procedures for successful career counseling. In N. Gysbers (Ed.), *Designing careers: Counseling to enhance education, work and leisure.* San Francisco: Jossey-Bass.

Kirby, D. (1985). *School-based health clinics: An emerging approach to improving adolescent health and addressing teenage pregnancy.* Washington, DC: Center for Population Options.

Kirby, D., Short, L., Collins, J., et al. (1994). School-based programs to reduce sexual risk behaviors: A review of effectiveness. *Public Health Report, 109,* 339–360.

Kiselica, M. S. (1995). *Multicultural counseling with teenage fathers.* Thousand Oaks, CA: Sage.

Knitzer, J., Steinberg, Z., & Fleisch, B. (1990). *At the schoolhouse door: An examination of programs and policies for children with behavioral and emotional problems.* New York: Bank Street College of Education.

Koch, M. (1988). Resolving disputes: Students can do it better. *NASSP Bulletin, 72*(504), 16–18.

Koeppen, A. S. (1974). Relaxation training for children. *Elementary School Guidance and Counseling, 9*(1), 14–21.

Kohlberg, L. (1981). *The philosophy of moral development.* San Francisco: Harper & Row.

Koplow, L. (Ed.). (1996). *Unsmiling faces: How preschools can heal.* New York: Teachers College Press.

Koss, M. P., Goodman, L. A., Browne, A., Fitzgerald, L. F., Keita, G. P., & Russo, N. F. (1994). *Male violence against women at home, at work, and in the community.* Washington, DC: American Psychological Association.

Kovacs, M. (1981). Rating scales to assess depression in school-aged children. *Acta Paedopsychiatrica, 46,* 305–315.

Kovacs, M., & Beck, A. T. (1977). An empirical-clinical approach toward a definition of childhood depression. In J. G. Schulterbrandt & A. Raskin (Eds.), *Depression in childhood: Diagnosis, treatment, and conceptual models* (pp. 1–25). New York: Raven.

Kozal, J. (1991) *Savage inequalities: Children in America's schools.* New York: Crown.

Kumpfer, K. L., & Alvarado, R. (1995). Strengthening families to prevent drug use in multiethnic youth. In G. J. Botvin, S. Schinke, & M. A. Orlandi (Eds.), *Drug abuse prevention with multiethnic youth* (pp. 255–294). Thousand Oaks, CA: Sage.

LaFave, W. R. (1996). *Search and seizure: A treatise on the fourth amendment* (3rd ed.). St. Paul, MN: West.

La Fromboise, T. D. (1988). American Indian mental health policy. *American Psychologist, 43*(5), 388–397.

Lal, S. R. (1991). *A study of strategies employed by junior high school administrators to overcome disruptive gang-related activities.* Unpublished doctoral dissertation, University of California, Los Angeles.

Lal, S. R., Lal, D., & Achilles, C. M. (1993). *Handbook on gangs in schools: Strategies to reduce gang-related activities.* Thousand Oaks, CA: Corwin Press, Inc.

LaMorte, M. W. (1993). *School law: Cases and concepts* (4th ed.). Needham Heights, MA: Allyn & Bacon.

Landers, S. (1989). Homelessness hinders academic performance. *APA Monitor, 20*(11), 5.

Lane, P. S., & McWhirter, J. J. (1992). A peer mediation model: Conflict resolution for elementary and middle school children. *Elementary School Guidance and Counseling, 27*(1), 15–24.

Lane, P. S., & McWhirter, J. J. (1996). Creating a peaceful school community: Reconciliation operationalized. *Catholic School Studies, 69*(2), 31–34.

Lane-Garon, P. S. (1997). *Social-cognitive perspective taking in student mediators.* Ph.D. dissertation, Arizona State University, Tempe, AZ.

Lazarus, A. A. (1971). *Behavior therapy and beyond.* New York: McGraw-Hill.

Lebow, M. A. (1994). Contraceptive advertising in the United States. *Women's Health Issues, 4,* 196–208.

Lenz, R. K. (1992). Self-managed learning strategy systems for children and youth. *School Psychology Review, 21,* 211–228.

Levin, H. M., Glass, G. V., & Meister, G. R. (1984). *Cost-effectiveness of four educational interventions.* Stanford, CA: Institute for Research on Educational Finance and Governance Project Report No. 84-A11.

Levine, M. (1996). *Viewing violence: How media violence affects your child's and adolescent's development.* New York: Doubleday.

Levy, S. R., Jurkovic, G. L., & Spirito, A. (1995). A multisystems analysis of adolescent suicide attempters. *Journal of Abnormal Child Psychology, 23,* 221–234.

Lewinsohn, P. M., Hops, H., Roberts, R., Seeley, J. R., & Andrew, J. (1993). Adolescent psychopathology: I. Prevalence and incidence of depression and other DSM-III-R disorders in high school students. *Journal of Abnormal Psychology, 102*(4), 183–204.

Lewinsohn, P. M., Rohde, P., & Seeley, J. R. (1994). Psychosocial risk factors for future adolescent suicide attempts. *Journal of Consulting and Clinical Psychology 62*(2), 297–305.

Lewinsohn, P., Rohde, P., Seeley, J., & Fischer, S. (1993). Age-cohort changes in the lifetime occurrence of depression and other mental disorders. *Journal of Abnormal Psychology, 102,* 110–120.

Lickona, T. (1991). *Educating for character.* New York: Bantam.

Lieberman, C. (1994, May) *Television and violence.* Paper presented at the Council of State Governments Conference on School Violence, Westlake Village, CA.

Lindblom, E. (1991). Towards a comprehensive homeless prevention policy. *Housing Policy Debate, 2*(3), 957–1025.

Linney, J. A., & Seidman, E. (1989). The future of schooling. *American Psychologist, 44,* 336, 340.

Lipschitz, A. (1995). Suicide prevention in young adults. *Suicide and Life-Threatening Behavior, 25*(1), 155–169.

Litman, R. E. (1967). Medical-legal aspects of suicide. *Washburn Law Journal, 6,* 395–401.

Lochman, J. E. (1987). Self and peer perceptions and attributional biases of aggressive and nonaggressive boys in dyadic interactions. *Journal of Consulting and Clinical Psychology, 55,* 404–410.

Long, L. (1988). Providing assistance to latchkey families. *Pointer, 33*(1), 37–40.

Lord, S. E., Eccles, J. S., & McCarthy, K. A. (1994). Surviving the junior high school transition: Family processes and self-perceptions as protective and risk factors. *Journal of Early Adolescence, 14*(2), 162–199.

Lowe, G., Foxcroft, D. R., & Sibley, D. (1993). *Adolescent drinking and family life.* Langhorne, PA: Harwood Academic/Gordon & Breach Science.

Lowenthal, B. (1996). Integrated school services for children at risk: Rationale, models, barriers, and recommendations for implementation. *Intervention in School and Clinic, 31*(3), 154–157.

Lowry, D. T., & Shidler, J. A. (1993). Prime time TV portrayals of sex, safe sex and AIDS: A longitudinal analysis. *Journalism Quarterly, 70,* 628–637.

Lysynchuk, L. M., Pressley, M., & Vye, N. J. (1990). Reciprocal teaching improves standardized reading-comprehension performance in poor comprehenders. *Elementary School Journal, 90,* 469–484.

Maltbia, G. (1991). Cultural diversity as a labor management issue. *Employee Assistance Program Exchange, 21*(5), 26.

Manaster, G. J. (1990). Unique people drop out: To educate all or each. *TACD Journal, 18*(1), 7–14.

Marcus, G. F. (1996). Children's overregularization and its implications for cognition. In P. Broeder & J. M. J. Murre (Eds.), *Models of language acquisition: Inductive and deductive approaches.* Cambridge, MA: MIT Press.

Marston, D. B. (1989). A curriculum-based measurement approach to assessing academic performance: What it is and why do it. In M. R. Shinn (Ed.), *Curriculum-based measurement: Assessing special children* (pp. 18–78). New York: Guilford.

Marttunen, M. J., Aro, H. M., & Lonnquist, J. K. (1993). Precipitant stressors in adolescent suicide. *Journal of the American Academy of Child and Adolescent Psychiatry, 32*(6), 1178–1183.

Marzen, J. T., O'Dowd, M. K., Crone, D., & Balch, T. J. (1985). Suicide: A constitutional right? *Duquesne Law Review, 24*(1), 1.

Mash, J. M. (1989). *Adolescents' future orientation and goal-setting skills: Implications for conventional and problem behavior.* Master's thesis, Virginia Commonwealth University.

Massey, D. S., & Denton, N. A. (1993). *American apartheid: Segregation and the making of the underclass.* Cambridge, MA: Harvard University Press.

Maxwell, J. (1989). Mediation in the schools. *Mediation Quarterly, 7,* 149–154.

Mayer, S. E. (1990). How much does a school's racial and economic mix affect graduation rates and teenage fertility rates? In C. Jencks & P. Peterson (Eds.), *The urban underclass* (pp. 321–341). Washington, DC: Brookings Institution.

McCormick, M. (1988). *Mediation in the schools: An evalution of the Wakefield Pilot Peer Mediation Program in Tucson, Arizona.* Washington, DC: American Bar Association.

McCubbin, H. I., & McCubbin, M. A. (1988). Typologies of resilient families: Emerging roles of social class and ethnicity. *Family Relations, 37,* 247–254.

McDowell, E. E., & Stillion, J. M. (1994). Suicide across the phases of life. In G.G. Noam & S. Borst (Eds.), *Children, youth, and suicide: Developmental perspectives* (pp. 7–22). San Francisco: Jossey-Bass.

McGinnis, E., & Goldstein, A. P. (1984). *Skillstreaming the elementary school child: A guide for teaching prosocial skills.* Champaign, IL: Research Press.

McGinnis, E., & Goldstein, A. P. (1990). *Skillstreaming in early childhood: Teaching prosocial skills to the preschool and kindergarten child.* Champaign, IL: Research Press.

McGinnis, J. M., & Foege, W. H. (1993). Actual causes of death in the United States. *Journal of the American Medical Association, 270*(18), 2207–2212.

McGowan, S. (1991, October). Confidentiality: Breaking a sacred trust. *Guidepost,* pp. 14–15.

McGuire, J. M., Parnell, T. F., Blau, B. I., & Abbott, D. W. (1994). Demands for privacy among adolescents in multimodal alcohol and other drug abuse treatment. *Journal of Counseling & Development, 73*(1), 74–78.

McKee, P. W. (1993). *Suicide and the school: A practical guide to suicide prevention. Crisis intervention series.* Horsham, PA: LRP Publications.

McLanahan, S., & Sandefur, G. (1994). *Growing up with a single parent.* Cambridge, MA: Harvard University Press.

McLaughlin, T. F., & Vacha, E. F. (1992). School programs for at-risk children and youth: A review. *Education and Treatment of Children, 15*(3), 255–267.

McLean, P., & Taylor, S. (1994). Family therapy for suicidal people. *Death Studies, 18*(4), 409–426.

McLloyd, V. C. (1989). Socialization and development in a changing economy: The effects of paternal job and income loss on children. *American Psychologist, 44*(2), 293–302.

McMillen, M. M., Kaufman, P., Whitener, S. D. (1996). *Dropout rates in the United States: 1995.* Washington, DC: National Center for Education Statistics.

McReynolds, R. A., Morris, R. J., & Kratochwill, T. R. (1989). Cognitive-behavioral treatment of school-related fears and anxieties. In J. N. Hughes & Robert J. Hall (Eds.), *Cognitive-behavioral psychology in the schools* (pp. 434–465). New York: Guilford.

McWhirter, A. M. (1990). Whole language in the middle school. *Reading Teacher, 43,* 562–565.

McWhirter, B. T. (1990). Loneliness: A review of current literature, with implications for counseling and research. *Journal of Counseling and Development, 68*(4), 417–422.

McWhirter, B. T., & Horan, J. J. (1996). Construct validity of cognitive-behavioral treatments for intimate and social loneliness. *Current Psychology: Developmental, Learning, Personality, Social, 15*(1), 42–52.

McWhirter, B. T., McWhirter, E. H., & McWhirter, J. J. (1988). Groups in Latin America: Comunidades eclesial de base as mutual support groups. *Journal for Specialists in Group Work, 13*(2), 70–76.

McWhirter, B. T., & McWhirter, J. J. (1990). University survival strategies and the learning disabled student. *Academic Therapy, 25*(3), 345–351.

McWhirter, B. T., & McWhirter, J. J. (1995). Youth at risk for violence and delinquency: A metaphor and a definition. *Monograph on Youth in the 1990s, 4,* 17–28.

McWhirter, B. T., McWhirter, J. J., & Gat, I. (1996). Depression in childhood and adolescence: Working to prevent despair. In D. Capuzzie & D. Gross (Eds.), *Youth at risk: Prevention resources for counselors, teachers, and parents* (2nd ed.) (pp. 105–128). Alexandria, VA: American Counseling Association Press.

McWhirter, B. T., McWhirter, J. J., McWhirter, A. M., & McWhirter, E. H. (1993). Prevention of adolescent pregnancy: Self-understanding from an Adlerian perspective. *The Family Journal: Counseling and Therapy for Couples and Families, 1*(4), 324–330.

McWhirter, E. H. (1991). Empowerment in counseling. *Journal of Counseling and Development, 69*(3), 222–227.

McWhirter, E. H. (1994). *Counseling for Empowerment.* Alexandria, VA: American Counseling Association.

McWhirter, E. H., McWhirter, J. J., McWhirter, B. T., & McWhirter, A. M. (1993). Family counseling interventions: Understanding family systems and the referral process. *Intervention in School and Clinic, 28*(4), 231–237.

McWhirter, J. J. (1966). Family group consultation and the secondary schools. *The Family Life Coordinator, 15*(4), 183–184.

McWhirter, J. J. (1988). *The learning disabled child: A school and family concern* (2nd ed.). Lanham, MD: University Press of America.

McWhirter, J. J. (1995). Emotional education for university students. *Journal of College Student Psychotherapy, 10*(2), 27–38.

McWhirter, J. J. (1998). Will he choose life? In L. Golden & M. L. Norwood (Eds.), *Case studies in child counseling* (2nd ed.). New York: Merrill/Prentice Hall.

McWhirter, J. J., & Golden, L. (1975). Practicum experience in family group consultation. *Arizona Personnel and Guidance Journal, 1*(1), 44–46.

McWhirter, J. J., Herrmann, D. S., Jefferys, K., & Quinn, M. M. (1997). Anger reduction programs. *Catholic School Studies, 70*(1).

McWhirter, J. J., & Kahn, S. E. (1974). A parent communication group. *Elementary School Guidance and Counseling, 9*(2).

McWhirter, J. J., & Kigin, T. J. (1988). Depression. In D. Capuzzi & L. Golden (Eds.), *Preventing adolescent suicide* (pp. 149–186). Muncie, IN: Accelerated Development.

McWhirter, J. J., & Kincaid, M. (1974). Family group consultation: Adjunct to a parent program. *Journal of Family Counseling, 2*(1), 45–48.

McWhirter, J. J., & McWhirter, A. M. (1987). Family enrichment programs: Puppets as a pedagogical tool. *Guidance and Counseling, 2*(5), 77–84.

McWhirter, J. J., McWhirter, B. T., McWhirter, A. M., & McWhirter, E. H. (1994). Who is at-risk? A continuum and a metaphor. *Kappa Delta Pi Record, 30*(3), 116–120.

McWhirter, J. J., McWhirter, B. T., McWhirter, A. M., & McWhirter, E. H. (1995). Youth at-risk: Another point of view. *Journal of Counseling and Development, 73,* 567–569.

McWhirter, J. J., & McWhirter, E. H. (1989). Adolescents-at-risk: Poor soil yields damaged fruit. In D. Capuzzi & D. Gross (Eds.), *Working with at-risk youth: Issues and interventions.* Alexandria, VA: American Association for Counseling and Development.

McWhirter, J. J., & McWhirter, M. C. (1983). Increasing human potential: Relaxation and imagery training (RIT) with athletic and performing art teams. *Personnel and Guidance Journal, 62*(3), 135–138.

McWhirter, J. J., & McWhirter, R. J. (1988). Legal considerations for the practitioner. In D. Capuzzi & L. B. Golden (Eds.), *Preventing adolescent suicide.* Muncie, IN: Accelerated Development.

McWhirter, J. J., & Santos de Barona, M. (1995). *The CAP program: Final Report (#S184B 30225). Cross-age peers: Reducing alcohol/tobacco through prevention.* Washington, DC: Drug Free Schools and Communities.

McWhirter, P. T., & McWhirter, J. J. (1996). Transition-to-Work Group: University students with learning disabilities. *Journal for Specialists in Group Work, 21*(2), 144–148.

Meggert, S. S. (1996). Who cares what I think: Problems of low self-esteem. In D. Capuzzi & D. R. Gross (Eds.), *Youth at risk: A preventive resource for counselors, teachers, and parents* (2nd. ed.) (pp. 81–103). Alexandria, VA: American Counseling Association.

Meisels, S. J., & Liaw, F. R. (1993). Failure in grade: Do retained students catch up? *Journal of Educational Research, 87,* 69–77.

Melchert, T., & Burnett, K. F. (1990). Attitudes, knowledge, and sexual behavior of high-risk adolescents: Implications for counseling and sexuality education. *Journal of Counseling and Development, 68*(3), 293–298.

Metalsky, G. I., & Joiner, T. E. (1992). Vulnerability to depressive symptomatology: A prospective test of the diathesis-stress and causal mediation components of the hopelessness theory of depression. *Journal of Personality and Social Psychology, 63*(4), 667–675.

Metalsky, G. I., Joiner, T. E., Hardin, T. S., & Abramson, L. Y. (1993). Depressive reactions to failure in a naturalistic setting: A test of the hopelessness and self-esteem theories of depression. *Journal of Abnormal Psychology, 102*(1), 101–109.

Metha, A., & Dunham, H. (1988). Behavioral indicators. In D. Capuzzi & L. Golden (Eds.), *Preventing adolescent suicide* (pp. 49–86). Muncie, IN: Accelerated Development.

Meyer, L. H., & Henry, L. A. (1993). Cooperative classroom management: Student needs and fairness in the regular classroom. In J. W. Putnam (Ed.). *Cooperative learning and strategies for inclusion: Celebrating diversity in the classroom* (p. 116). Baltimore: Paul H. Brookes.

Meyer, L. H., Williams, D. R., Harootunian, B., & Steinberg, A. (1995). An inclusion model to reduce at-risk status among middle school students: The Syracuse experience. In I. M. Evans, T. Cicchelli, M. Cohen, & N. P. Shapiro (Eds.), *Staying in school: Partnerships for educational change* (pp. 83–110). Baltimore: Paul H. Brookes.

Michaelis, K. L. (1993). *Reporting child abuse: A guide to mandatory requirements for school personnel.* Thousand Oaks, CA: Corwin Press.

Milburn, N., & D'Ercole, A. (1991). Homeless women: Moving toward a comprehensive model. *American Psychologist, 46,* 1161–1169.

Miller, T. R., & Blincoe, L. J. (1994). Incidence and cost of alcohol-involved crashes in the United States. *Accident Analysis and Prevention, 26*(5), 583–591.

Minuchin, S. (1974). *Families and family therapy.* Cambridge, MA.: Harvard University Press.

Minuchin, S., & Nichols, M. (1993). *Family healing: Tales of hope and renewal from family therapy.* New York: The Free Press.

Mishel, L., & Bernstein, J. (1995). *State of working America, 1994–95.* Economic Policy Institute Series. Armonk, NY: M. E. Sharpe.

Mitchell, J. J. (1996). *Adolescent vulnerability: A sympathetic look at the frailties and limitations of youth.* Calgary, Alberta: Detselig Enterprises Ltd.

Moffitt, T. E. (1993). "Life-course-persistent" and "adolescent-limited" antisocial behavior: A developmental taxonomy. *Psychological Review, 100,* 674–701.

Monaco, V. C. (1982). Training manual for RIT groups. In V. C. Monaco, *Effects of relaxation/imagery training on children's anxiety, locus of control, and perception of classroom environment* (pp. 156–183). Doctoral dissertation, Arizona State University, Tempe.

Montagne, M., & Scott, D. M. (1993). Prevention of substance use problems: Models, factors, and processes. *International Journal of the Addictions, 28,* 1177–1208.

Moore, D. D., & Forster, J. R. (1993). Student assistance programs: New approaches for reducing adolescent substance abuse. *Journal of Counseling and Development, 71,* 326–329.

Moore, K. A. (1992). *Facts at a glance.* Washington, DC: Child Trends, Inc.

Moore, K. A. (1994). *Facts at a glance.* Washington, DC: Child Trends, Inc.

Moore, K. A. (1995). *Facts at a glance.* Washington, DC: Child Trends, Inc.

Moore, K. A., Myers, D. E., Morrison, D. R., Nord, C. W., Brown, B., & Edmonston, B. (1993). Age at first childbirth and later poverty. *Journal of Research on Adolescents, 3,* 393–422.

Morgan, D. P., & Jensen, W. R. (1988). *Teaching behavioral disordered students.* Columbus, OH: Merrill.

Morganett, R. S. (1990). *Skills for living: Group counseling activities for elementary students.* Champaign, IL: Research Press.

Morganett, R. S. (1995). *Skills for living: Group counseling activities for elementary students* (2nd ed.). Champaign, IL: Research Press.

Morris, L., Warren, C. W., & Aral, S. O. (1993). Measuring adolescent sexual behaviors and related health outcomes. *Public Health Report, 108*(suppl. 1), 31–36.

Mruk, C. (1995). *Self-esteem: Research, theory, and practice.* New York: Springer.

Mulroy, E. A. (1995). *The new uprooted: Single mothers in urban life.* Westport, CT: Auburn House/Greenwood.

Musick, J. S. (1993). *Young, poor, and pregnant.* New Haven, CT: Yale University Press.

Myrick, R. D., & Sorenson, D. L. (1985). *Peer pressure reversal: An adult guide to developing a responsible child.* Minneapolis: Educational Media Corporation.

National Center for Health Statistics. (1992). *Vital statistics of the United States: 1992, Volume I—Natality.* Washington, DC: U.S. Department of Health and Human Services.

National Commission on Children. (1991). *Speaking of kids: A national survey of children and parents.* Washington, DC: Author.

National Commission on Excellence in Education. (1983). *A nation at risk: The imperative for educational reform.* Washington, DC: Author.

National Gay and Lesbian Task Force Policy Institute (1994). *Anti-gay/lesbian/bisexual violence fact sheet: April 1994 update.* Washington, DC: Author.

National Institute on Drug Abuse. (1987). *National household survey of drug abuse: Population estimates, 1985.* Rockville, MD: Author.

National Institute on Drug Abuse. (1995a). *Drug use among racial/ethnic minorities.* Washington, D.C.: CSR, Inc.

National Institute on Drug Abuse. (1995b). *National household survey of drug abuse: Population estimates, 1994.* Rockville, MD: U.S. Dept. of Health and Human Services.

National Research Council. (1990). *Who cares for America's children?* Washington, DC: National Academy Press.

National School Safety Center. (1988). *Gangs in schools: Breaking up is hard to do.* Malibu, CA: National School Safety Center, Pepperdine University.

Newcomb, M. D., & Bentler, P. M. (1988). *Consequences of adolescent drug use: Impact on the lives of young adults.* Newbury Park, CA: Sage.

Newcomb, M. D., & Bentler, P. M. (1989). Substance use and abuse among children and teenagers. *American Psychologist, 44*(2), 242–248.

Newcomb, M. D., McGee, L. (1991). Influence of sensation seeking on general deviance and specific problem behaviors from adolescence to young adulthood. *Journal of Personality and Social Psychology, 61*(4), 614–628.

Nock, S. L., & Kingston, P. W. (1991). Time with children: The impact of couples' work-time commitments. *Social Forces, 67,* 59–85.

Nolen-Hoeksema, S., Girgus, J. S., & Seligman, M. E. P. (1992). Predictors and consequences of childhood depressive symptoms: A 5-year longitudinal study. *Journal of Abnormal Psychology, 101,* 405–422.

Norton, A. J., & Glick, B. C. (1986). One-parent families: A social and economic profile. *Family Relations, 35,* 9–17.

Norton, D. G. (1994). Education for professionals in family support. In S. L. K. Kagan, & B. Weissbourd (Eds.), *Putting families first: America's family support movement and the challenge of change* (pp. 401–440). San Francisco: Jossey-Bass.

Oetting, E. R., & Beauvais, F. (1986). Peer cluster theory: Drugs and the adolescent. *Journal of Counseling and Development, 65,* 17, 22.

Oetting, E. R., & Beauvais, F. (1987). Peer cluster theory, socialization characteristics, and adolescent drug use: A path analysis. *Journal of Counseling Psychology, 34*(2), 205–213.

Oetting, E. R., & Beauvais, F. (1990). Adolescent drug use: Findings of national and local surveys. *Journal of Consulting and Clinical Psychology, 58,* 385–394.

Office of Technology Assessment, U.S. Congress. (1991). *Adolescent health.* (Ota-H-468.) Washington, DC: U.S. Government Printing Office.

Office for Substance Abuse Prevention. (1990). *Legal issues for alcohol and other drug use and prevention and treatment programs serving high-risk youth.* Technical Report 2. U.S. Department of Health and Human Services, Public Health Service, Alcohol, Drug Abuse, and Mental Health Administration. Washington, DC: U.S. Government Printing Office.

O'Hearn, T. C., & Gatz, M. (1996). The educational pyramid: A model for community intervention. *Applied and Preventive Psychology, 5,* 127–134.

Oldridge, O. A. (1982). Positive suggestion: It helps LD students learn. *Academic Therapy, 17,* 279–287.

Olrich, F. (1983). A whole person spelling class. *Academic Therapy, 19,* 73–78.

O'Rourke, K., & Worzbyt, J. C. (1996). *Support groups for children.* Bristol, PA: Accelerated Development.

Oyserman, D., & Markus, H. R. (1990). Possible selves and delinquency. *Journal of Personality and Social Psychology, 59,* 112–125.

Pagliaro, A. M., & Pagliaro, L. (1996). *Substance use among children and adolescents: Its nature, extent, and effects from conception to adulthood.* Somerset, NJ: Wiley.

Palincsar, A. S., Ransom, K., & Derber, S. (1989). Collaborative research and development of reciprocal teaching. *Educational Leadership, 46*(4), 37–40.

Parham, T. (1991, April). *Effective counseling interventions for promoting wellness among African American males.* Paper presented at the American Association for Counseling and Development National Convention, Reno, NV.

Patterson, G. R., Crosby, L., & Vuchinich, S. (1992a). Predicting risk for early police arrest. *Journal of Quantitative Criminology, 8*(4), 335–355.

Patterson, G. R., DeBaryshe, B. D., & Ramsey, E. (1989). A developmental perspective on antisocial behavior. *American Psychologist, 44*(2), 329–335.

Patterson, G. R., Reid, J. B., & Dishion, T. J. (1992b). *Antisocial boys.* Eugene, OR: Castalia.

Peck, P. (1989). The child at risk: Closing in on success. *Instructor, 98*(6), 30–32.

People v. Brac, 167 P.2d 535 (1946).

Perry, N. J. (1988, November). Saving the schools: How business can help. *Fortune,* pp. 42–56.

Peterson, A. C., & Mortimer, J. T. (Eds.). *Youth unemployment and society.* New York: Cambridge University Press.

Peterson, C., Maier, S., & Seligman, M. (1993). *Learned helplessness.* New York: Oxford.

Pfeffer, C. R., Hurt, S. W., Kakuma, T., Peskin, J. R., Siefker, C. A., & Nagabhairava, S. (1994). Suicidal children grow up: Suicidal episodes and effects of treatment during follow-up. *Journal of the American Academy of Child and Adolescent Psychiatry, 33,* 225–230.

Pfeffer, C. R., Normandin, L., & Kakuma, T. (1994). Suicidal children grow up: Suicidal behavior and psychiatric disorders among relatives. *Journal of the American Academy of Child and Adolescent Psychiatry, 33,* 1087–1097.

Phillips, K. (1990). *The politics of rich and poor: Wealth and the American electorate in the Regan aftermath.* New York: Random House.

Phillips, V., McCullough, L., Nelson, C. M., & Walker, H. M. (1992). Teamwork among teachers: Promoting a statewide agenda for students at risk for school failure. *Special Services in the Schools, 6*(3/4), 27–49.

Pierce, M. M., Stahlbrand, K., & Armstrong, S. B. (1984). *Increasing student productivity through peer tutoring programs.* Austin, TX: Pro-Ed.

Piers, E. V. (1984). *Piers-Harris Children's Self-Concept Scale—Revised Edition.* Nashville, TN: Counselor Recordings and Tests.

Pines, D. (1991). *Parent training is prevention: Preventing alcohol and other drug problems among youth in the family.* Rockville, MD: Office for Substance Abuse Prevention.

Pinker, S. (1991). Rules of language. *Science, 253,* 530–555.

Pinnell, G. S., Lyons, C. A., DeFord, D. E., & Bryk, A. S. (1994). Comparing instructional models for the literacy education of high-risk first graders. *Reading Research Quarterly, 29*(1), 8–39.

Plunkett, K., & Marchman, V. (1993). From rote learning to system building: Acquiring verb morphology in children and connectionist nets. *Cognitive, 48,* 21–69.

Powers, D. (1994). Transitions into idleness among white, black, and Hispanic youth: Some determinants and policy implications. *Sociological Perspectives, 37,* 183–210.

Premack, D. (1965). Reinforcement theory. In D. Levin (Ed.), *Nebraska Symposium on Motivation: 1965.* Lincoln: University of Nebraska Press.

Price, J. H., & Telljohann, S. K. (1991). School counselors' perceptions of adolescent homosexuals. *Journal of School Health, 61*, 433–438.

Proeger, C., & Myrick, R. (1980). Teaching children to relax. *Florida Educational Research and Development Council Research Bulletin, 14*, 51.

Prothrow-Stith, D., & Weissman, M. (1991). *Deadly consequences: How violence is destroying our teenage population and a plan to begin solving the problem.* New York: Harper Perennial.

Queralt, M. (1993). Risk factors associated with completed suicide in Latino adolescents. *Adolescence, 28*(112), 831–850.

Quint, S. (1994). *Schooling homeless children.* New York: Teachers College Press.

Radke-Yarrow, M., Nottelmann, E., Belmont, B., & Welsh, J. D. (1993). Affective interactions of depressed and nondepressed mothers and their children. *Journal of Abnormal Child Psychology, 21*, 683–695.

Rafferty, Y., & Shinn, M. (1991). The impact of homelessness on children. *American Psychologist, 46*, 1170, 1179.

Rak, C. F., & Patterson, L. E. (1996). Promoting resilience in at-risk children. *Journal of Counseling and Development, 74*, 368–373.

Randolph, S. M. (1995). African American children in single-mother families. In B. J. Dickerson (Ed.), *African American single mothers: Understanding their lives and families* (pp. 117–145). Thousand Oaks, CA: Sage.

Ray, O., & Ksir, C. (1987). *Drugs, society, and human behavior.* St. Louis, MO: Times Mirror/Mosby.

Reasoner, R. W. (1992). *Teacher's manual: Building self-esteem in the elementary schools* (2nd ed.). Palo Alto: Consulting Psychologists Press.

Remafedi, G., Farrow, J. A., & Deisher, R. W. (1991). Risk factors for attempted suicide in gay and bisexual youth. *Pediatrics, 87*, 869–875.

Reminger, K., Hidi, S., & Krapp, A. (Eds.). (1992). *The role of interest in learning and development.* Hillsdale, NJ: Erlbaum.

Rexroat, C., & Shehan, C. (1987). The family life cycle and spouses' time in housework. *Journal of Marriage and the Family, 49*, 737–750.

Reyes, O., & Hedeker, D. (1993). Identifying high-risk students during school transition. *Prevention in Human Services, 10*(2), 137–150.

Richardson, D., Hammock, G., Smith, S., Gardner, W., & Signo, M. (1994). Empathy as a cognitive inhibitor of interpersonal aggression. *Aggressive Behavior, 20*, 275–289.

Rigg, P. (1990). Whole language in adult ESL programs. *ERIC/CLL News Bulletin, 13* (2), 1–7.

Riley, R. W. (1986). Can we reduce the risk of failure? *Phi Delta Kappan, 68*, 214–219.

Rivera, E., & Omizo, M. M. (1980). The effects of relaxation and biofeedback on attention to task and impulsivity among male hyperactive children. *Exceptional Child, 27*(1), 41–51.

Roberts, S. (1994, December 24). Gap between rich and poor widens in New York. *New York Times.*

Robertson, D., & Mathews, B. (1989). Preventing adolescent suicide with group counseling. *Journal for Specialists in Group Work, 14*(1), 34–39.

Robinson, R. B., & Frank, D. I. (1994). The relation between self-esteem, sexual activity, and pregnancy. *Adolescence, 29*(113), 27–35.

Robinson, W. L., Watkins-Ferrell, P., Davis-Scott, P., & Ruch-Ross, H. S. (1993). Preventing teenage pregnancy. In D. S. Glenwick & L. A. Jason (Eds.), *Promoting health and mental health in children, youth, and families* (pp. 99–124). New York: Springer.

Roderick, M. (1994). Grade retention and school dropout: Investigating the association. *American Educational Research Journal, 31*(4), 729–759.

Roderick, T. (1988). Johnny can learn to negotiate. *Educational Leadership, 45*(4), 86–90.

Roe v. Wade, 410 U.S. 113 (1973).

Rogers, J. R. (1990). Female suicide: The trend toward increasing lethality in method of choice and its implications. *Journal of Counseling and Development, 69*(1), 37–38.

Rosenshine, B. V. (1986). Synthesis of research on explicit teaching. *Educational Leadership, 43*(7), 60–69.

Rosenshine, B., & Meister, C. (1991, April). *Reciprocal teaching: A review of nineteen experimental studies.* Paper presented at the annual meeting of the American Educational Research Association, Chicago.

Ross, J., Quinn, T., Gardner, S. E., & Bass, R. D. (1993). *Signs of effectiveness.* Washington, DC: Department of Health and Human Services.

Ross, J. G., Saavedra, P. J., Shur, G. H., Winters, F., & Felner, R. D. (1992). The effectiveness of an after-school program for primary grade latchkey students on precursors of substance abuse. *Journal of Community Psychology, OSAP Special Issue,* 22–38.

Rotheram-Borus, M. J., Bradley, J., & Obolensky, N. (Eds.) (1990). *Planning to live: Evaluating and treating suicidal teens in community settings.* Tulsa: University of Oklahoma Press.

Rotheram-Borus, M. J., Rosario, M., & Koopman, C. (1991). Minority youths at high risk: Gay males and runaways. In M.E. Colten & S. Gore (Eds.), *Adolescent stress: Causes and consequences* (pp. 181–200). New York: Aldine de Gruyter.

Rothstein, R. (1993, Spring). The myth of public school failure. *The American Prospect, 13*, 20–34.

Roy, A. (1983). Family history of suicide. *Archives of General Psychiatry, 40*, 971–974.

Rumberger, R. W. (1987). High school dropouts: A review of issues and evidence. *Review of Educational Research, 57*, 101–121.

Rumberger, R. W. (1990). Second chance for high school dropouts: The costs and benefits of dropout recovery programs in the United States. In D. Inbar (Ed.), *Second chance in education: An interdisciplinary and international perspective* (pp. 227–250). Basingstoke, England: Falmer Press.

Rumberger, R. (1991). Chicano dropouts: A review of research and policy issues. In R. Valencia (Ed.), *Chicano school failure and success: Research and policy agendas for the 1990's* (pp. 64–89). New York: Falmer Press.

Sadker, M. P., & Sadker, D. M. (1987). *Teachers, schools, and society.* New York: Random House.

Sandau-Beckler, P. A., Salcido, R., & Ronnau, J. (1993). Culturally competent family preservation services: An approach for first-generation Hispanic families in an international border community. *The Family Journal: Counseling and Therapy for Couples and Families, 1*(4), 313–323.

San Francisco Community Board Program, Inc. (1982). *School initiatives* [video]. San Francisco: Author.

Satir, V. (1967). *Conjoint family therapy: A guide to theory and technique* (rev. ed.) Palo Alto, CA: Science & Behavior.

Satir, V., & Baldwin, M. (1983). *Satir step by step.* Palo Alto, CA: Science & Behavior.

Sautter, R. C. (1994). Standing up to violence. *Phi Delta Kappan, 76*(5), K1–K12.

Savin-Williams, R. C. (1994). Verbal and physical abuse as stressors in the lives of lesbian, gay male, and bisexual youths: Associations with school problems, running away, substance abuse, prostitution, and suicide. *Journal of Consulting and Clinical Psychology, 62*(2), 261–269.

Savin-Williams, R. C. (1995). Lesbian, gay male, and bisexual adolescents. In A. R. D'Augelli & C. J. Patterson (Eds.), *Lesbian, gay, and bisexual identities over the lifespan* (pp. 165–189). New York: Oxford University Press.

Savin-Williams, R. C., & Cohen, K. M. (Eds.). (1996). *Developmental and clinical issues among lesbians, gay males, and bisexuals.* Fort Worth: Harcourt Brace.

Savin-Williams, R. C., & Rodriguez, R. G. (1993). A developmental, clinical perspective on lesbian, gay male, and bisexual youths. In T. P. Gullotta, G. R. Adams, & R. Montemayor (Eds.) *Adolescent sexuality: Advances in adolescent development, 5,* 77–101. Newbury Park, CA: Sage.

Sayger, T. V. (1996). Creating resilient children and empowering families using a multifamily group process. *The Journal for Specialists in Group Work, 21*(2), 81–89.

Scarr, S., Phillips, D., & McCartney, K. (1990). Facts, fantasies, and the future of child care in the United States. *Psychological Science, 1*(1), 26–35.

Schliebner, C. T., & Peregoy, J. J. (1994). Unemployment effects on the family and the child: Interventions for counselors. *Journal of Counseling & Development 72*(4), 368–372.

Schorr, L. B. (1988). *Within our reach: Breaking the cycle of disadvantage.* New York: Doubleday.

Schweinhart, L. J., Weikart, B. P., & Larner, W. B. (1986). Consequences of three preschool curriculum models through age 15. *Early Childhood Research Quarterly, 1*(1), 15–45.

Scott, S. (1985). *Peer pressure reversal: An adult guide to developing a responsive child.* Amherst, MA: Human Resource Development Press.

Scott, S. (1988). *Positive peer groups.* Amherst, MA: Human Resource Development Press.

Seidel, J. F., & Vaughn, S. (1991). Social alienation and the learning disabled school dropout. *Learning Disabilities Research and Practice, 6*(3), 152–157.

Seligman, M. (1991). *Learned optimism.* New York: Knopf.

Seligman, M. (1993). *Helplessness: On depression, development, and death.* San Francisco: Freeman.

Seligman, M. (1994). *What you can change and what you can't.* New York: Knopf.

Seligman, M. (1995). *The optimistic child: A revolutionary program that safeguards children against depression and builds lifelong resilience.* New York: Houghton Mills.

Serna, I. A., & Hudelson, S. (1993). Emergent Spanish literacy in a whole language bilingual classroom. In R. Donmoyer & R. Kos (Eds.), *At-risk students: Portraits, policies, programs, and practices* (pp. 291–321). Albany, NY: State University of New York Press.

Shakeshaft, C., Barber, E., Hergenrother, M. A., Johnson, Y. M., Mandel L. S., & Sawyer, J. (1995). Peer harassment in schools. *Journal for a Just and Caring Education, 1*(1), 30–44.

Shannon, P. (1989). The struggle for control of literacy lessons. *Language Arts, 66,* 625–633.

Shapiro, E. S., & Cole, C. L. (1992). Self-monitoring. In T. H. Ollendick & M. Hersen (Eds.), *Handbook of child and adolescent assessment* (pp. 124–139). New York: Pergamon.

Shapiro, E. S., & Cole, C. L. (1994). *Behavior change in the classroom: Self-management interventions.* New York: Guilford.

Sharan, S. (Ed.). (1994). *Handbook of cooperative learning methods.* Westport, CT: Greenwood Press.

Shearer, C. (1990, January 17). Bankrupt: Education reforms costly. *State Press* (Tempe, AZ), p. 3.

Shedler, J., & Block, J. (1990). Adolescent drug use and psychological health: A longitudinal inquiry. *American Psychologist, 45,* 612–630.

Sheley, J., McGee, A., & Wright, J. (1992). Gun-related violence in and around inner-city schools. *AJDC, 146,* 677–682.

Shepard, L. A., & Smith, M. L. (1987). Effects of kindergarten retention at the end of first grade. *Psychology in the Schools, 24,* 346–357.

Sherman, A. (1992). *Falling by the wayside: Children in rural America.* Washington, DC: Children's Defense Fund.

Sherraden, M. W. (1986). School dropouts in perspective. *Educational Forum, 51,* 15–31.

Shifrin, F., & Solis, M. (1992). Chemical dependency in gay and lesbian youth. *Journal of Chemical Dependency Treatment, 5*(1), 67–76.

Shinn, M., Knickman, J. R., & Weitzman, B. C. (1991). Social relationships and vulnerability to becoming homeless among poor families. *American Psychologist, 46,* 1180–1187.

Shure, M. B. (1990). *Problem solving techniques in childrearing: Training script for parents of young children.* Philadelphia, PA: Hahnemann University.

Shure, M. B. (1992a). *I can problem solve (ICPS): An interpersonal cognitive problem solving program (preschool)*. Champaign, IL: Research Press.

Shure, M. B. (1992b) *I can problem solve (ICPS): An interpersonal cognitive problem solving program (kindergarten/ primary grades)*. Champaign, IL: Research Press.

Shure, M. B. (1992c). *I can problem solve (ICPS): An interpersonal cognitive problem solving program (intermediate elementary grades)*. Champaign, IL: Research Press.

Shure, M. B. (1993). I can problem solve (ICPS): Interpersonal cognitive problem solving for younger children. *Early Child Development and Care, 96*, 49–64.

Shure, M. B., & Spivack, G. (1978). *Problem-solving techniques in child rearing*. San Francisco: Jossey-Bass.

Shure, M. B., & Spivack, G. (1988). Interpersonal cognitive problem solving. In R. H. Price, E. L. Cowen, R. P. Lorion, & J. Ramos-McKay (Eds.). *14 ounces of prevention: A casebook for practitioners* (pp. 69–82). Washington, DC: American Psychological Association.

Silbert, J., Carnine, D., & Stein, M. (1990). *Direct instruction mathematics* (2nd ed.). Columbus, OH: Merrill.

Simons, R. L., Whitbeck, L. B., Conger, R. D., & Melby, J. N. (1991). The effect of social skills, values, peers, and depression on adolescent substance use. *Journal of Early Adolescence, 11*(4), 466–481.

Sitlington, P. L., & Frank, A. R. (1993). Dropouts with learning disabilities: What happens to them as young adults? *Learning Disabilities Research and Practice, 8*(4), 244–252.

Sklar, H. (1995). *Chaos or community? Seeking solutions, not scapegoats for bad economics*. Boston: South End Press.

Skolnick, A. (1991). *Embattled paradise: The American family in an age of uncertainty*. New York: Basic Books.

Slavin, R. E. (1983). *Cooperative learning*. New York: Longman.

Slavin, R. E. (1991). Cooperative learning and group contingencies. *Journal of Behavioral Education, 1*(1), 105–115.

Slavin, R. E. (1993). Ability grouping in the middle grades: Achievement effects and alternatives. *The Elementary School Journal, 93*(5), 535–552.

Slavin, R. E. (1994). Preventing early school failure: The challenge and the opportunity. In R. E. Slavin, N. L. Karweit, & B. A. Wasik (Eds.), *Preventing early school failure: Research, policy and practice* (pp. 1–12). Boston: Allyn & Bacon.

Slavin, R. E., Karweit, N. L., & Wasik, B. A. (Eds.). (1994). *Preventing early school failure: Research, policy, and practice*. Boston: Allyn & Bacon.

Slavin, R., & Madden, N. (1989). What works for students at risk: A research synthesis. *Educational Leadership, 46*(5), 4–13.

Smith, D. J., Young, K. R., Nelson, J. R., & West, R. P. (1992). The effect of a self-management procedure on the classroom academic behavior of students with mild handicaps. *School Psychology Review, 21*, 59–72.

Smith, F. (1988). *Understanding reading: A psycholinguistic analysis of reading and learning to read* (Vol. 4). Hillsdale, NJ: Erlbaum.

Smith, G. T. (1994). Psychological expectancy as mediator of vulnerability to alcoholism. *Annals of the New York Academy of Sciences, 70*(8), 165–171.

Smith, J. C., Mercer, J. A., & Rosenberg, M. L. (1989). Hispanic students in the Southwest, 1980–82. In *Alcohol, drug abuse, and mental health administration. Report of the secretary's task force on youth suicide, Volume 3: Prevention and interventions in youth suicide* (pp. 196–205). DHHS Pub. No. (ADM) 89–1623. Washington, DC: U.S. Government Printing Office.

Smith, K. W., McGraw, S., Crawford, S. L., Costa, L. A., & McKinlay, J. B. (1993). HIV risk among Latino adolescents in two New England cities. *American Journal of Public Health, 83*, 1395–1399.

Smith, M. J. (1986). *Yes, I can say no*. New York: Arbor House.

Smith, R. C., & Lincoln, C. A. (1988). *America's shame, America's hope: Twelve million youth at risk*. Chapel Hill, NC: MDC.

Smolowe, J. (1995). The downward spiral. *Time* [Online Serial]. Available: America Online, Education.

Smylie, M. A., & Tuermer, U. (1992). *Hammond, Indiana: The politics of involvement v. the politics of confrontation*. Claremont, CA: Claremont Graduate School, Claremont Project VISION.

Solow, R. M. (1994). *Wasting America's future: The Children's Defense Fund report on the costs of child poverty*. Washington, DC: Children's Defense Fund.

Spergel, I. A. (1995). *The youth gang problem*. New York: Oxford University Press.

Spivack, G., Platt, J. J., & Shure, M. B. (1976). *The problem solving approach to adjustment*. San Francisco: Jossey-Bass.

Spivack, G., & Shure, M. B. (1974). *Social adjustment of young children*. San Francisco: Jossey-Bass.

State v. Tritt, 23 Utah 365, 463 P.2d 806 (1970).

Steel, E. (1995). AIDS, drugs, and the adolescent. *National Institute on Drug Abuse Research Monograph, 156*, 130–145.

Stephens, T. M. (1992). *Social skills in the classroom* (2nd ed.). Odessa, FL: Psychological Assessment Resources.

Stevens, P., & Smith, R. (1996). *Substance abuse prevention and intervention: Theory and practice*. New York: Macmillan.

Stevens, R. J., & Slavin, R. E. (1995). The cooperative elementary school: Effects on students' achievement, attitudes, and social relations. *American Educational Research Journal, 32*(2), 321–351.

Stevens, R. J., Slavin, R. E., & Farnish, A. M. (1991). The effects of cooperative learning and direct instruction in reading comprehension strategies on main idea identification. *Journal of Educational Psychology, 83*(1), 8–16.

Stevens-Simon, C., & White, M. M. (1991). Adolescent pregnancy. *Pediatric Annals, 20*, 322–331.

Stivers, C. (1990). Promotion of self-esteem in the prevention of suicide. *Death Studies, 14*, 303–327.

Straus, M. A. (1964). Power and support structure of the family in relation to socialization. *Journal of Marriage and Family, 26*, 318–326.

Straus, M. B. (1994). *Violence in the lives of adolescents*. New York: Norton.

Suarez, E. M., Mills, R. C., & Steward, D. (1987). *Sanity, insanity, and common sense: The missing link in understanding mental health* (2nd ed.). New York: Ballantine.

Summerville, M. B., Kaslow, N. J., & Doepke, K. J. (1996). Psychopathology and cognitive and family functioning in suicidal African-American adolescents. *Current Directions in Psychological Science*, 5(1), 7–11.

Sussman, S., Dent, C. W., Burton, D., Stacy, A. W., & Flay, B. R. (1995). *Developing school-based tobacco use prevention and cessation programs*. Thousand Oaks, CA: Sage.

Swadener, B. B., & Lubeck, S. (Eds.). (1995). *Children and families "at promise": Deconstructing the discourse of risk*. Albany, NY: State University of New York Press.

Swaim, R. C., Oetting, E. R., Edwards, R. W., & Beauvais, F. (1989). Links from emotional distress to adolescent drug use: A path model. *Journal of Consulting and Clinical Psychology*, 57, 227–231.

Swanson, M. C. (1989). Advancement via individual determination: Project AVID. *Educational Leadership*, 46(5), 63–64.

Szapocznik, J., Santisteban, D., Kurtines, W. M., Perez-Vidal, A., & Hervis, O. (1984). Bicultural effectiveness training: A treatment intervention for enhancing intercultural adjustment in Cuban-American families. *Hispanic Journal of Behavioral Sciences*, 6, 317–344.

Szapocznik, J., Santisteban, D., Rio, A., Perez-Vidal, A., & Kurtines, W. M. (1986a). Family effectiveness training (FET) for Hispanic families. In H. P. Lefley & P. B. Pedersen (Eds.), *Cross-cultural training for mental health professionals* (pp. 245–261). Springfield, IL: Charles C Thomas.

Szapocznik, J., Santisteban, D., Rio, A., Perez-Vidal, A., & Kurtines, W. M. (1986b). Bicultural effectiveness training (BET): An experimental test of an intervention modality for families experiencing intergenerational/intercultural conflict. *Hispanic Journal of Behavioral Sciences*, 8(4), 303–330.

Szapocznik, J., Santisteban, D., Rio, A., Perez-Vidal, A., & Kurtines, W. M. (1989). Family effectiveness training: An intervention to prevent drug abuse and problem behaviors in Hispanic adolescents. *Hispanic Journal of Behavioral Sciences*, 11(1), 4–27.

Tansy, M., Santos de Barona, M., McWhirter, J. J., & Herrmann, D. S. (1996). Peer and cross-age tutoring programs: Counsellor contribution to student achievement. *Guidance and Counselling*, 12(1), 21–24.

Tarasoff v. Regents of the University of California et al., 17 Cal. 3d 425, 551 P.2d 334 (1976).

Tarter, R. E., Blackson, T., Martin, C., Loeber, R., & Moss, H. B. (1993). Characteristics and correlates of child discipline practices in substance abuse and normal families. *American Journal on Addictions*, 2, 18–25.

Tate, D. C., Reppucci, N. D., & Mulvey, E. P. (1995). Violent juvenile delinquents: Treatment effectiveness and implications for future action. *American Psychologist* 50(9), 777–781.

Telljohann, S. K., & Price, J. H. (1993). A qualitative examination of adolescent homosexuals' life experiences: Ramifications for secondary school personnel. *Journal of Homosexuality*, 26, 41–56.

Terros, Inc. (1988). *School mediation project training manual*. Phoenix: Community Mediation Publications.

Thomas, D. L., Gecas, V., Weigert, A., & Rooney, E. (1967). *Family socialization and the adolescent*. Lexington, MA: D. Heath.

Thomson, E., Hanson, T., & McLanahan, S. (1994). Family structure and child well-being: Economic resources vs. parental behaviors. *Sociological Forces*, 73, 221–242.

Thornton, A. (1991). Influence of the marital history of parents on the marital and cohabitational experiences of children. *American Journal of Sociology*, 96, 868–894.

Tidwell, R. (1993). Quality education for minority children: The concept of "at risk" re-examined. *People and Education*, 1, 249–255.

Tidwell, R., & Corona Garrett, S. (1994). Youth at risk: In search of a definition. *Journal of Counseling and Development*, 72, 444–446.

Tolan, P. H., & Guerra, N. G. (1994). Prevention of delinquency: Current status and issues. *Applied & Preventive Psychology*, 3, 251–273.

Tomlinson-Keasey, C., & Keasey, C. B. (1988). "Signatures" of suicide. In D. Capuzzi & L. Golden (Eds.), *Preventing adolescent suicide* (pp. 213, 245). Muncie, IN: Accelerated Development.

Torres, A., & Forest, J. D. (1988). Why do women have abortions? *Family Planning Perspectives*, 20, 169–176.

Towberman, D. B., & McDonald, R. M. (1993). Dimensions of adolescent self-concept associated with substance use. *The Journal of Drug Issues*, 23(3), 525–533.

Trimble, J. E., Bolek, C. S., & Niemcryk, S. J. (Eds.) (1992). *Ethnic and multicultural drug abuse: Perspectives on current research*. Binghamton, NY: Harrington Park Press.

Upchurch, D. M., & McCarthy, J. (1990). The timing of first birth and high school completion. *American Sociological Review*, 55, 224–234.

U.S. Bureau of the Census. (1992). *National data book and guide to sources. Statistical abstracts of the United States, 1988*. Washington, DC: Government Printing Office.

U.S. Conference of Mayors (1995). *The state of America's cities*. Washington, DC: National League of Cities.

U.S. Department of Commerce, Bureau of the Census. (1993). *Income, poverty, and valuation of noncash benefits: 1993*. Washington, DC: U.S. Government Printing Office.

Ventura, S. J., Martin, J. A., Taffel, S. M., Matthews, T. J., & Clarke, S. C. (1992). Advance report of final natality statistics. *Monthly Vital Statistics Report*, 43 (5 Suppl).

Vernon, A. (1983). Rational-emotive education. In A. Ellis & M. Bernards (Eds.), *Rational-emotive approaches to the problems of childhood*. New York: Plenum Press.

Vickers, H. S. (1994). Young children at risk: Differences in family functioning. *Journal of Educational Research*, 87(5), 262–270.

Vidal, J. A. (1989). *Student suicide: A guide for intervention.* Washington, DC: National Education Association.

Wagner, E. F. (1993). Delay of gratification, coping with stress, and substance use in adolescence. *Experimental and Clinical Psychopharmacology, 1*(1–4), 27–43.

Wagner, W. G. (1996). Optimal development in adolescence: What is it and how can it be encouraged? *The Counseling Psychologist, 24*(3), 360–399.

Walker, H. M., Colvin, G., & Ramsey, E. (1995). *Antisocial behavior in school: Strategies and best practices.* Pacific Grove, CA: Brooks/Cole.

Walker, L. E. A. (1990). Psychological assessment of sexually abused children for legal evaluation and expert witness testimony. *Professional Psychology: Research and Practice, 21*(5), 344–353.

Walker, L. E. A. (1996). *Abused women and survivor therapy: A practical guide for the psychotherapist.* Washington, DC: American Psychological Association.

Wallace, J. M., Jr., Bachman, J. G., O'Malley, P. M., & Johnston, L. D. (1995). Racial/ethnic differences in adolescent drug use. In G. J. Botvin, S. Schinke, & M. A. Orlandi, (Eds.), *Drug abuse prevention with multiethnic youth* (pp. 59–80). Thousand Oaks, CA: Sage.

Walsh-Bowers, R. T. (1992). A creative drama prevention program for easing early adolescents' adjustment to school transitions. *Journal of Primary Prevention, 13*(2), 131–147.

Watkins, K. P., & Durant, L. (1996). *Working with children and families affected by substance abuse: A guide for early childhood education and human service staff.* West Nyack, NY: The Center for Applied Research Education.

Watt, D., & Roessingh, H. (1994). ESL dropout: The myth of educational equity. *Alberta Journal of Educational Research, 40*(3), 283–296.

Wehlage, G. G. (1991). School reform of at-risk students. *Equity and Excellence, 23*(1), 15–24.

Wehlage, G. G., & White, J. A. (1995). Citizens, clients, and consumers [microform]: Building social capital. Washington, DC: Office of Educational Research and Improvement.

Weinberg, N. Z., Dielman, T. E., Mandell, W., & Shope, J. T. (1994). Parental drinking and gender factors in the prediction of early adolescent alcohol use. *International Journal of the Addictions, 29*(1), 89–104.

Weissman, M., Leaf, P., & Bruce, M. (1987). Single-parent women: A community study. *Social Psychiatry, 22,* 29–36.

Weisz, J. R., Sweeney, L., Proffitt, V., & Carr, T. (1993). Control-related beliefs and self-reported depressive symptoms in late childhood. *Journal of Abnormal Psychology, 102,* 411–418.

Wenz, K., & McWhirter, J. J. (1990). Enhancing the group experience: Creative writing exercise. *Journal for Specialists in Group Work, 15*(1), 37–42.

Werner, E. E. (1995). Resilience in development. *Current Directions in Psychological Science, 4*(3), 81–82.

Werner, E. E., & Smith, R. S. (1992). *Overcoming the odds: High risk children from birth to adulthood.* Ithica, NY: Cornell University Press.

West, P. (1992). Indians go on offensive to fight alcohol's effects. *Education Week, 11*(1), 12–13.

Whisman, M. A., & Kwon, P. (1993). Life stress and dysphoria: The role of self-esteem and hopelessness. *Journal of Personality and Social Psychology, 65*(5), 1054–1060.

White, P. D. (1989). Reaching at-risk students: One principal's solution. *Thrust, 19*(1), 45–46.

Wiig, E. H. (1983). *Let's talk: Developing prosocial communication skills.* Columbus, OH: Merrill.

Wilkinson, J., & Canter, S. (1982). *Social skills training manual: Assessment, program design, and management of training.* New York: Wiley.

Williams, B. F. (1992). Changing demographics: Challenges for educators. *Intervention in School and Clinic, 27*(3), 157–163.

Williams, J. G., & Smith, J. P. (1993). Alcohol and other drug use among adolescents: Family and peer influences. *Journal of Substance Abuse, 5,* 289–294.

Williams, J. M., Bachman, J. G., O'Malley, P. M., & Johnston, L. D. (1995). Racial/ethnic differences in adolescent drug use. In G. J. Botvin, S. Schinke, & M. A. Orlandi (Eds.), *Drug abuse prevention with multiethnic youth* (pp. 59–80). Thousand Oaks, CA: Sage.

Williams, S. M. (1994). *Environment and mental health.* Chichester, England: John Wiley & Sons.

Wilson, J. Q. (1993). *The moral sense.* New York: Macmillan.

Winbush, R. A. (1988). Growing pains: explaining adolescent violence with developmental theory. In J. Carlson & J. Lewis (Eds.), *Counseling the adolescent: Individual, family and school interventions* (pp. 57–71). Denver: Love.

Winfield, L., & Millsap, M. A. (1994). Characteristics of programs and strategies. In S. Stringfield, L. Winfield, M. A. Millsap, M. J. Puma, B. Gamse, & B. Randall (Eds.), *Urban and suburban/rural special strategies for educating disadvantaged children: First year report* (Chapter 2). Washington, DC: U.S. Government Printing Office.

Wohlstetter, P. (1994). Education by charter. In S. A. Mohrman & P. Wohlstetter (Eds.), *School-based management: Organizing for high performance* (pp. 139–164). San Francisco: Jossey-Bass.

Wohlstetter, P., & Smyer, R. (1994). Models of high-performance schools. In S. A. Mohrman & P. Wohlstetter (Eds.), *School-based management: Organizing for high performance* (pp. 81–107). San Francisco: Jossey-Bass.

Wolin, S., & Wolin, S. (1993). *The resilient self: How survivors of troubled families rise above adversity.* New York: Random House.

Workman, E. (1982). *Teaching behavioral self-control to students.* Austin, TX: Pro-Ed.

The world almanac and book of facts. (1991). New York: World Almanac/Pharos.

Wright, D. M. (1975). Criminal aspects of suicide in the United States. *North Carolina Central Law Journal, 7,* 156–163.

Wright-Strawderman, C., Lindsey, P., Navarette, L., & Flippo, J. R. (1996). Depression in students with disabilities: Recognition and intervention strategies. *Intervention in School and Clinic, 31*(5), 261–275.

Wu, L., & Martinson, B. (1993). Family structure and the risk of a premature birth. *American Sociological Review, 58,* 210–232.

Yondorf, B. A. (1992). *Adolescents and AIDS: Stopping the time bomb.* Denver, CO: State Legislative Report.

Younge, S. L., Oetting, E. R., & Deffenbacher, J. L. (In press). Correlations between maternal rejection, school dropout, and drug use. *Journal of Clinical Psychology.*

Zenker, E. (1984). In the dark about teaching spelling? Just relax! *Academic Therapy, 20*(2), 231–234.

Zenker, E., & Frey, D. (1985). Relaxation helps less capable students. *Journal of Reading, 28*(4), 242–244.

Zigler, E. (1995). Reshaping early childhood intervention to be a more effective weapon against poverty. *American Journal of Community Psychology, 22*(1), 37–47.

Zigler, E. F., & Lang, M. E. (1991). *Child care choices: Balancing the needs of children, families, and society.* New York: Free Press.

Zigler, E. F., & Muenchow, S. (1992). *Head start: The inside story of America's most successful educational experiment.* New York: Basic Books.

Zigmond, N. (1990). Rethinking secondary school programs for students with learning disabilities. *Focus on Exceptional Children, 23*(1), 1–22.

Zill, N., Morrison, D., & Coiro, M. J. (1993). Long-term effects of parental divorce on parent-child relationships, adjustment, and achievement in young adulthood. *Journal of Family Psychology, 7,* 91–103.

SUBJECT INDEX

TO THE OWNER OF THIS BOOK:

We hope that you have found *At-Risk Youth: A Comprehensive Response*, Second Edition, useful. So that this book can be improved in a future edition, would you take the time to complete this sheet and return it? Thank you.

School and address: _____

Department: _____

Instructor's name: _____

1. What I like most about this book is: _____

_____

_____

2. What I like least about this book is: _____

_____

_____

3. My general reaction to this book is: _____

_____

4. The name of the course in which I used this book is: _____

_____

5. Were all of the chapters of the book assigned for you to read? _____

    If not, which ones weren't? _____

6. In the space below, or on a separate sheet of paper, please write specific suggestions for improving this book and anything else you'd care to share about your experience in using the book.

_____

_____

_____

_____

_____

Optional:

Your name: _____ Date: _____

May Brooks/Cole quote you, either in promotion for *At-Risk Youth: A Comprehensive Response,* Second Edition, or in future publishing ventures?

Yes: _____ No: _____

Sincerely,

The McWhirters

FOLD HERE

‐ ‐

NO POSTAGE
NECESSARY
IF MAILED
IN THE
UNITED STATES

BUSINESS REPLY MAIL
FIRST CLASS   PERMIT NO. 358   PACIFIC GROVE, CA

POSTAGE WILL BE PAID BY ADDRESSEE

ATT: *The McWhirters* _____

**Brooks/Cole Publishing Company
511 Forest Lodge Road
Pacific Grove, California 93950-9968**

FOLD HERE